CROMWELL'S CAPTAINS

C. E. Lucas Phillips

CROMWELL'S
CAPTAINS

TABLE OF CONTENTS

Les grands esprits sont ceux qui luttent.

— DE VIGNY

PRESENTATION

BIOGRAPHERS of the period dealt with in this book have been so preoccupied with the outstanding presence of Cromwell, or with the romantic effigies of a Stuart, a Montrose or a Rupert, that too little attention has been given to other characters who were almost equally remarkable. On the Puritan side, especially, there was a group of men who played parts of the greatest importance and who exercised a penetrating influence on affairs. But, overshadowed by Cromwell, many of them have missed the personal scrutiny that they deserve.

This book is therefore intended to fill that gap, to introduce to the general reader some of the more notable of these Cromwellian soldiers, and to emphasise the importance of the parts that they played in the most dramatic pageant of our historical stage; thereby, moreover, enabling the story of the civil wars to be told in a new way through the eyes of some of its chief participants. It owes its origin to a conversation I had with Lord Tweedsmuir, whose kind help I gladly acknowledge and whose encouragement has given me heart.

The group of "Napoleon-marshals," as Carlyle called them, that clustered round the Cromwellian sun formed a strange and diversified galaxy. The hero and the bully, the martyr and the mountebank, the high-principled servant of the state and the shameless profiteer — all had their motions in one sphere. They shared, however, at least two qualities in common — an indomitable high courage and a conscientiousness in steady day labour that made them the finest fighting men in the world and the most able administrators in our history. The New Model was the envy of Europe — "an army," in the words of John

Lambert, "fit for God Almighty to do miracles withal." The administration of the Commonwealth navy has never been equalled by any modern board of admiralty. In a nation that has forgotten how to pray and does not want to fight, in a system of administration in which the clerks of admiralty, of army, of education, of trade, of colonial government seek to hamper, rather than to help the men who have an active duty to perform, we have something to learn from these men who, for all their high-pitched stridulations and for all their straining after precise focussings of the unsearchable, were nevertheless united by a singleness of purpose and inspired with a lively zeal for the ungrudging service of God's People.

From this gallery it was intended that several should have been chosen, but I have to admit that I have not found it possible, for the time, to take more than the four presented here. They have been selected as representative of different types — Hampden the high-souled political patriot, Skippon the plain and simple soldier, Blake the indomitable seaman, Lambert the most brilliant of Cromwell's captains and the man who was personally responsible for making Oliver Protector. It is my hope that I may later be able to do similar studies of others in that remarkable gallery, particularly Ireton, who was a greater man than many have supposed, and whose keen speculative brain was the first to conceive the modern constitutional structures of the British and American peoples. Thomas Morgan, the fiery little Welshman who carried the renown of English arms to the walls of Ypres and Dunkirk, Venables and Penn, who voyaged with mixed fortunes to the West Indies, Pride, who purged the House and slew the bears in their pit, Harrison, the fiery horseman, Deane, the seaman-soldier, Hugh Peters, the prancing warrior-priest from New England — all these deserve a place.

Of those now included Hampden was not properly speaking one of Cromwell's captains, but he serves to introduce the scene, without which the drama cannot be understood. Much has already been written of him, but the material available about his life does not really warrant a whole book, and I make no excuse for presenting this shorter sketch of him with the purposes of showing him in proper perspective and of upsetting the notion that he was a meek and gentle student. On the contrary, once the fires had been lit, he was the flame of the revolutionary cause. I have sought, as well, to give more emphasis than has commonly been given to the fact that the revolt against absolute monarchy, in England if not in Scotland, was due only partly to religious factors and that the growing idea of the rule of law, so dominant in Hampden and so rudely offended by those whose duty it was to administer the law, was a large incentive. To-day, when even in this country the rule of law begins to be encroached upon by the rule of government, we would do well to brood upon the example of a man who would put all to the test for the sake of twenty shillings.

Skippon, of whom no biography has yet been written, represents the best type of the God-fearing Puritan soldier; he had no political gifts and he could not move multitudes, but he was brave and simple and generous and was one of the prime creators of the New Model. He played a much larger part than most historians have given him credit for, and thoroughly deserves a closer acquaintance. Perhaps the most interesting part of his story is the Battle of Lostwithiel, an action which (Cromwell not having been there) has been much neglected, though it was quite as important as Marston Moor, was Charles's only considerable victory and was fought in one of the most romantic places in England, where Tristram and

Iseult pursued their tragic love. The plan here given is, so far as I am aware, the first of its kind.

Robert Blake is still a man little known to the general reader. His defeat at Dungeness and a popular song about Tromp's broom are the sum of many people's knowledge. Yet he is second only to Nelson in our maritime story, and was the true founder of the navy — turning a congregation of ships into a Service with a corporate spirit and breathing into it not only the fire of his own indomitable will, but also his own sense of duty to the State and his own precepts of unselfish devotion. Such things were new among a breed of men whose tradition had been built on plunder and prize money, and those who lightly speak of Charles's part in maintaining the navy should read their Blake again. Preoccupied so much with Cromwell, most writers on the Commonwealth and the Protectorate have given too little thought to the burly little admiral, but no story of those times can be complete without a study of his heroic feats. Apart from short sketches and longer studies mostly occupied with tactical operations, no really satisfactory study of Blake has been made, and I have here endeavoured, so far as the evidence permits, to re-create something of the man — a fierce, remarkable little man — instead of reproducing the lay figure that occupies most histories.

Of Lambert, likewise, no adequate historical study has yet been made; and this is perhaps a little remarkable, for he was the man who made Cromwell Protector and he was the chief architect of one of the most important constitutional documents of this country, the influence of which may be seen also in the constitution of the United States. Lambert has indeed been much misjudged by most writers, and the memoir here presented will, I hope, correct the notion that he was an unscrupulous adventurer. Unlike many of these godly warriors, he came of a good family, and to his superb courage he added rare qualities of charm, of culture and of tolerance. His constant generosity to defeated enemies, and to their wives and families, commended him even to the most uncompromising royalists, who, indeed, sought again and again to win him to the King's side and to induce him to take a lead in the restoration of the monarchy. It is greatly to his credit, and it is an answer to the charge that he sought personal aggrandisement, that, even in the days of darkest despair, he rejected all such offers and remained true to his republicanism, preferring to risk poverty and the gallows rather than accept the glittering prizes that would have been the reward of desertion, and that adorned instead the broad breast of one who twice changed sides. That Lambert was ambitious is true; but that he sought to usurp Cromwell, or that subsequently he sought by intrigue to become Protector himself — though his was the outstanding claim — is shown on a close analysis to be a charge without good foundation.

Even as a soldier, in which his brilliance is accepted, Lambert's reputation will, I hope, be further advanced by this study, for in the Preston campaign and in the Battle of Dunbar he manifested a military genius hardly less than Cromwell's own, and in his own devastating action of Inverkeithing, of which a plan is here for the first time produced, he won a victory which, though so neglected by historians, was strategically far more important than Dunbar itself. Even Dunbar, as I have shown, must now be regarded in a special sense as Lambert's battle, and it is clear that he is entitled to a very large share in the credit for that brilliant action.

In the memoir on Hampden I have made few annotations, as it is based on evidences already sufficiently well known, and I have gone to no new sources. In the other biographies, however, I have thought it desirable to give fairly full annotations, particularly in the case of Lambert, since the material is less well known and since some of it is requisite of support. For the general reader's convenience, I have as a rule grouped the references to authorities together at the end of each phase or episode.

I have already acknowledged my indebtedness to Lord Tweedsmuir, and I readily express thanks to all those others who have kindly helped me — particularly to the Rev. J. R. Powell and to Mr. Brian Tunstall, for their assistance and appreciation in the study of Blake; to the Revd. William Stephen for assistance in the topography and history of Inverkeithing; to Mr. Hugh Ross Williamson and Colonel R. Beadon for permission to draw upon their books on Hampden and Blake; to Major A. Carey Curtis, Archivist of the Royal Court of Guernsey; to Mr. P. K. Lucas Phillips, who drew the maps, and to the librarians of the British Museum, the London Library, the Bodleian and the Record Office.

C. E. LUCAS PHILLIPS.

I: JOHN HAMPDEN

In pride of his calling good warriorship
welcometh the challenge of death.
       — BRIDGES, *The Testament of Beauty*.

I. THE GATEWAY OF ENDEAVOUR

FULLY 600 years before Cromwell a Hampden already possessed great estates in and about Buckinghamshire. How deep down in the soil of time the roots extend cannot be told exactly, but it seems likely that the family that, through the female line, still to-day holds Great Hampden in fee was seated there nearly a thousand years ago. In those wooded vales, where for hundreds of years the flying deer was still to be hunted by the arrow, and the falcon and noble greyhound pursued the heron and the hare, Baldwyn de Hampden was acknowledged occupier by the Domesday surveyors of William the Conqueror in 1086.

Afterwards the Hampdens spread their roots still wider. They acquired lands in Oxfordshire, in Berkshire, and in Essex. They were lords of Great and Little Hampden, Stoke Mandeville, Kimble, and many another parish where the towered churches lie half-revealed within their enfolding oaks. They prospered considerably; and though under the rude imperious surge of the Plantagenets the winds of war and fortune stripped them of much of their possessions, under the Tudors they grew again great and wealthy. Sir John Hampden commanded the *Saviour* in Henry VIII's great new fleet, and attended the Queen at the Field of the Cloth of Gold; and his daughter, Sybil, who was ancestress to William Penn, was charged with the nurture of Edward VI. At length a new spring in history was tapped when William Hampden, who sat in Elizabeth's Parliament of 1593, married Elizabeth Cromwell, daughter of Sir Henry Cromwell of Hinchinbroke, in Huntingdonshire, and aunt of the great Oliver. To William and Elizabeth was born, in 1594, John Hampden.

Thus was John Hampden born to great traditions and great estates and in a glorious age. Behind him was a long record of honourable service to the State. Around him a new terrestrial world was opening to invite the imagination of a high-spirited mankind, a new religious world illumined by the golden light of the Protestant Gospel, a new intellectual world revealed by Erasmus and More and many others, and, actuated by all these, a new national life in which Englishmen had found wealth, glory, and adventure in all the known and unknown seas of the world. Only six years before they had humbled the ensign of the proudest nation on earth, and they had earned for their race a new respect among all peoples. It was in truth a brave new world, a glamorous world, in which for every lad who had eyes to see the gates were open to every kind of high endeavour. John was altogether English. The springs of history were in his blood. No Celtic mountains gave him fire or vision, but he succeeded to the heritage of essential worth that is native to the shires, and he was to have a consciousness of the virtues of steady day-labour. The idea of rights was inherent in him, as well from his own long tradition as from the development of constitutional notions in men's minds. The ideas of self-respect and self-reliance were his also.

This child of destiny, the cousin and the friend of Oliver Cromwell, appears to have been born in London, six years after the Armada, and five years before Cromwell.[1] His birthday may have been June 18th, on the anniversary of which he was to shed his blood. He came very early into possession of the great estates to which he was born heir, for three years afterwards his father died.

---

[1] Anthony à Wood, *Athena Oxoniensis*, ed. Bliss, iii, 59.

Young Hampden's early education was received, it is fairly certain, at the Grammar School of Thame, near-by in Oxfordshire, under the care of Richard Bourchier.[2] His attic bedroom and the low, broad-panelled bed in which he is reputed to have slept may still be seen. According to the habit of the day, the curriculum was almost entirely classical and religious, beginning early in the morning with the Testament in Greek, and continuing through the day mainly with Greek, Latin, Hebrew, and divinity. Thame was a school of very good standing, and there Hampden, who throughout life was to be fortunate in his friendships, began that intimate and precious comradeship with Arthur Goodwin that ceased not until, there in that same town of Thame, Goodwin was to be beside his friend in a soldier's death. There, too, he probably met William Lenthall, who was afterwards to be Speaker of the House of Commons.

In 1610, at the age of fifteen, he entered Magdalen College, Oxford, where he clearly made good progress and earned some reputation. Here one of the odd ironies of history was manifested. In 1613 he and a certain William Laud, the austere and unpopular Master of St. John's, were chosen to write Oxford's classical congratulations upon the marriage of the Elector Palatine to the Princess Elizabeth, Jonson's "queen and huntress chaste and fair," and "Queen of Hearts" to every Englishman. From that marriage was to proceed Prince Rupert, from whose foraying horsemen Hampden was to receive his death blow; and from that same marriage was to proceed also our present Royal House.

Without having attained any recorded achievement of outstanding merit, Hampden was therefore clearly a conscientious student. The scraps of evidence that there are

---

[2] Lee, *History of the Church of Thame*, 483.

show that he was already bending his mind to constitutional studies, and Sir Philip Warwick says that "he had a great knowledge, both in scholarship and the law," that he was very well read in history, and in particular was a close student of Davila's history of the French civil wars.[3] This close interest in history and in constitutional practice remained with him throughout life and was one of the factors that contributed to his development as a great Parliamentarian.

But Hampden was not a student merely. He was acknowledged by all to be of great personal charm and of handsome appearance. He was a great favourite, and throughout life was both admired and respected by every sort of person, for he was of a flawless sincerity. But Hampden was a complete man, and in their due season enjoyed his May of youth and bloom of lustihood. Clarendon, the accomplished historian of the Great Rebellion, first his friend, afterwards his enemy, but always his admirer, whose silver pen has given us the liveliest of all sketches of Hampden's character, says that in his early life "he indulged to himself all that licence in sports, and exercise, and company, which was used by men of the most jolly conversation."[4] He took his full part in manly exercises, and, like all others of his tradition and his time, he was born to a horse. They were hard riders in those days, and with their long stirrup-leathers would spend days in the saddle as a matter of course. Charles I rode from Berwick to London, a distance of 339 miles, in four days, and in later years Hampden himself habitually rode from the army in the field to

---

[3] *Memoirs*, 240.

[4] This and most of the subsequent quotations from Clarendon are in the famous passage, Sec. vii, pars. 82-84, of his *Great Rebellion*, and accordingly will not be further annotated.

a Parliamentary debate at Westminster and back again the same evening.

The portraits of Hampden that have come down to us vary a good deal, and not all may be authentic, but it is possible by a study of them to see certain characteristics with some clarity. It is a face alive, open and full of character, very different from the long-faced gravity or the meekness with which tradition has invested him. In the fashion of the time the fair hair falls in full flowing waves well on to the beautiful lace collar that yokes the shoulders, but the pointed beard and the brushed-up moustaches of that day are absent, and instead the face is clean-shaven save perhaps for a faint pencilling on the upper lip. There is thus revealed a strong and resolute jaw with rounded chin, and a firmly-moulded mouth, with a glint of humour lurking in the corners. The strong nose is faintly arched, the eyes "very vigilant"[5] and the brows calm. The whole face is keen with intelligence and the bearing is of one having at once the habit of authority and the felicity of culture.

Still pursuing the normal course for young men of his quality, John, after leaving Oxford in the summer of 1613, proceeded in November of the same year to the Inner Temple. There he had all the opportunities both for learning and for "jolly conversation" which the Inns of Court have always afforded. Within their ancient halls the tides of ale and argument flowed with inspirational vigour, and at night there were the masques, then in their hey-day and produced by the greatest poet-dramatists, of whom the rotund Ben Jonson was the genial laureate. Shakespeare had but just retired from the stage, and in the same year he bought his house hard by in Blackfriars.

---

[5] Carlyle, *Cromwell's Letters and Speeches*, iii, 65.

It was a vivid common life on which Hampden now entered, genial and industrious, but often boisterous and sometimes turbulent. At eight in the morning he would walk through the famous gardens down to the marshy banks of the Thames, upon which the fat geese and ducks of the citizens kept fretful company with the pirate gulls. There he would take boat for Westminster, and in the great hall of William Rufus would study a Selden and many a lesser lawyer in their pleadings before the courts, or hear the judgments of Coke himself in the King's Bench. At noon the students returned to dinner in the great hall of the Inner Temple, which had been the refectory of the Knights Templars four hundred years before, but which is now no more. Afterwards they attended the Reader's lectures, and after supper practised their own powers of advocacy at the moots, which were then held in the gardens or in the covered walks about the mediaeval church of the Crusaders. Hampden's special study is said by Anthony à Wood to have been municipal law.

Among those grey stones and ancient books, tradition and precedent further set their seal on the impressionable mind of Hampden, but encouraged, too, the instinct for enquiry, for reform, for amelioration, which has always been strong in English law, however subservient and pedantic the leading practising lawyers may at that time have been. There were at the Inner Temple at the time of Hampden's studentship two of the greatest English lawyers of that or of any other age — Sir Edward Coke, the fiery prosecutor of Walter Raleigh, and John Selden. Coke, whom he must often have seen at the Benchers' table in Hall, was then Lord Chief Justice, and his famous "Reports" were being published. Selden had been called to the Bar only the year before Hampden's arrival, and both were afterwards to be closely associated with him in Parliament.

During these years at the Temple, despite the judges' servile dependence upon the King, and despite the contempt and hatred into which the Courts had sunk under James's encroachments, Hampden must no doubt have sensed the tendency of men everywhere to reach forward to the idea of the rule of law. Bacon, whose *Advancement of Learning* had been published in 1605 and who was presently to be appointed Lord Chancellor, had sought for law in material nature. Hooker asserted the rule of law over the spiritual world. The temper of the advanced Protestants was noticeably based on an element of law. This growing sense of law was in 1616, during Hampden's studentship, to be outraged amongst all decent citizens when in a case affecting the royal prerogative King James had enforced compliance with his wishes upon a grovelling bench of judges, who, timid though they were, had for once decided against him. In that lamentable incident, when the judges in the royal closet had fallen on their knees, Coke alone stood out, for his reverence of the law overrode every other instinct. For that resistance he was dismissed, and his dismissal is described by Gardiner as the turning point in the relations between King and people. On the other hand, the first signs had already appeared that from the House of Commons at least a like subservience was no longer to be expected.

These were the influences of Hampden's early manhood. Our next news of him is his marriage, which took place on June 24th, 1619, at the church of Pyrton, in Oxfordshire, Hampden being then 25. The lady of his choice, Elizabeth Simeon, came from the borders of his own country, being the daughter of Edmund Simeon, lord of the manor of Pyrton. To this lady, who bore him nine children, he was tenderly attached to the day of her death. For a year after their marriage they remained at Great Hampden.

About this time a change seems to have come over John Hampden, as it did over his cousin Oliver Cromwell at about the same point in his life. The gaiety of blossom fell from the tree of life, and the solid fruit within waxed and took form. His way of life became more reserved and more conscious of responsibility, as indeed it well should in one now married and having the administration of a great estate, and in one who was now beginning to hear, more and more clearly, two calls — the spiritual call and the call to political effort. It was no "conversion" of the profligate into the Puritan. John was never a riotous youth; nor on the other hand was he ever a mere sobersides. But, as a man who was always sensitive to the spirit and movement of the time, a man progressive and inquiring, his essential sincerity responded naturally to the rising tones of Puritanism and to the new demand for upright and godly living. Nevertheless, he continued to preserve, now and always, "his own natural cheerfulness and vivacity, and, above all, a flowing courtesy to all men." A natural dignity combined with a personal charm made him the type of man who was naturally looked up to, and Clarendon also says that "he was very temperate in diet, and a supreme governor over all his passions and affections."

II. THE DAWN OF DISCONTENT

It is common to describe the struggle that was about to dawn as having been fought on two fronts — the political and the religious. But in truth the real issue was emphatically politics. The religious problem was resolved, through the actions of King and ecclesiastic, into an aspect of the political scene, and if the ancient constitutional pieties had been observed by the King and his ministers, if they had understood the new aspirations of a people no longer content with paternal feudalism, and if the public administration had at least not been corrupt, the extremer Puritans would have had no following in Parliament.

Protestantism was now the dominant faith of the nation — a fluid Protestantism, allowing, after the English manner of compromise, much latitude both in dogma and in ceremony. But there was arising in the new Church, by law established, a new body of clergy, exemplified by such men as Laud and Manwaring, who preached an interpretation of the Protestant faith deeply influenced by the anti-Calvinist doctrines of Jacobus Arminius, the great Dutch theologian who had been teaching at Leiden when Hampden was a boy. These new High Churchmen, as they were deemed in that day, still young in their creed, discountenanced by Archbishop Abbot and having not the sacerdotal independence of the Church of Rome, turned to the Crown, when they saw the trend of opportunity, as a new fount of compelling authority. Dependent upon the Crown for all favours, and anxious to gain its blessing, they took to their bosom James's notion of the divinity of kingship, of the "mystical reverence that belongs unto them that sit on the throne of God," as James himself taught them, and nourished it to its logical development that all the acts of the Sovereign had the sanction of God, and therefore opposition to them by the subject would bring upon him the terrible swift sword of God's anger. Tyranny was given divine licence, and the infallibility of the monarch became a religious dogma. In fact, the new Churchmen (and even more so the Catholics) made themselves hostile to the growing idea of the rule of law, because they became associated with those who desired to silence the voice of law. It was natural that men whose palates could not relish the political savour of these religious meats should turn to others less highly seasoned.

What was more serious from the political point of view was that it was likewise natural for men to think that the forms and ceremonies of High Churchmen savoured strongly of Rome, though they were in fact a good deal farther away from Rome than the High Churchmen of to-day. Among a people predominantly "Protestant" and newly reawakened to a proud nationalism, the idea was held that Catholicism was the enemy of the nation. James's blundering flirtations with Catholic Spain, the arch-enemy of victorious Elizabethanism, and his encroachments in ecclesiastical government made even moderate men to fear that national freedom and individual freedom were alike at stake, and from the same cause — the lurking devildoms of "Popery." The attempted ordering of men's consciences served only to drive earnest men farther to the Left. Prolonged resistance to moderate claims drove high spirited men to claim more again.

To the extremer Protestants, indeed, the matter went farther than a consideration of politics or nationalism, for to them the struggle with "papacy," which existed in their own fevered minds rather than at Whitehall or Lambeth, was a struggle between darkness and light, between death and eternal life. "I will make them conform," said James of the Puritan remonstrance at the Hampton Court Conference, "or I will harry them out of the land." He did indeed. In 1620, the year of Hampden's appearance on the active political scene, and a twelvemonth after his marriage, he learnt that the *Mayflower* had sailed from Plymouth to the New England beyond the seas.

Hampden was returned to Parliament for the Cornish borough of Grampound in the elections of 1620 and took his seat in 1621. With him came his friend Arthur Goodwin, elected by Chipping Wycombe. The House of Commons sat at that time, as it was to sit for still another two hundred years, in the ancient chapel of St. Stephen's built by Edward III. It stood at right angles and immediately adjacent to Westminster Hall, and in that part of the Houses of Parliament known to-day as St. Stephen's Hall, through which the ordinary visitor must pass. Its exterior was of pure and simple beauty, but within it was severely plain, for its rich mural paintings had been boarded up when it had become secularised as the "Parliament House" in Edward VI's time. The Chamber was also extremely small, the members not only sitting in close ranks facing inwards choir-wise as to-day, but also crowding together in the space behind the Speaker's chair. Its tall chapel windows, plain-glazed, were sited high in the walls, and at the east end a big window filled all the wall behind the Speaker's chair. The chair itself stood high and throne-like, and before it, its stretcher-boards scarred by spurs, was the low table at which the clerks of the House squatted and on which rested the mace.

Hampden attached himself at once to the popular party, the party of opposition, though certain of his friends were anxious that he should seek advancement rather by means of attachment to the Court. His mother, in particular, was anxious that he should obtain a peerage, which could easily have been his as the head of an honourable and well-dowered family. In a letter still preserved in the British Museum, Mrs. Hampden wrote:[6]

> If ever my son will seek for his honour, tell him now to come; for here is multitudes of lords a-making… I am ambitious of my son's honour, which I wish were now conferred upon him, that he might not come after so many new creations.

But John never had social ambitions, nor personal vanity. He was, says Clarendon, of a "rare temper and modesty," and his own ancient family was more honourable by far than those of the "multitudes of lords," whose coronets were merely King James's merchandise for filling his depleted treasury.

The politics of James and of the Parliament of 1621 must not detain us long, for Hampden was for a time little more than a spectator. The newcomer in Parliament, like the new boy at school, must watch and listen, but in this his first term he had an excellent schooling. In particular he saw soon enough how the destinies of the State could be misdirected by an obtuse King and the gilded favourite whom he had raised from plain George Villiers to Duke of Buckingham. "Christ," said the King, "had his John, and I have my George." The swift urge of Buckingham's ambition, his vanity and his greed carried him to dominance in the affairs of state and to immense riches, but he was completely without any natural ability or qualifications for the administration of the multiple offices of state he rapaciously assumed. The beetle of corruption ate deep into the nation's timbers, and misdirection crept into every office.

---

[6] Nugent, i, 36.

But this Parliament was one of a spirited temper, in no mood for subservience. Hampden as he watched saw their attack on corruption and commercial monopolies, the significant impeachment of Bacon, the King's contempt for the Commons' representations on foreign affairs, which he judged them too ignorant to understand, and their outraged feelings when, instead of sending men and guns to help the cause of his daughter Elizabeth, the lovely "Queen of Hearts," who had been driven out of the Palatinate by the Catholic armies of Spain and the Empire, he proposed that Prince Charles should be married to the Catholic Infanta of hated Spain. Parliament answered with the famous "Protestation," claiming a new right to participation in foreign affairs, but the King, in an access of rage, with his own hand tore out the record of it from the Journal of the House, and sent Parliament about its business by dissolving it.

Throughout these momentous proceedings Hampden had pursued his political apprenticeship conscientiously and with system. He made careful notes on Parliamentary practice and procedure, and the assiduity of his studies, which were later to be so useful to him, is shown in the manuscript volume of Parliamentary cases compiled from his notes which is still preserved. He had already begun to show that spirit of high seriousness which was to distinguish him among men all his life. Clarendon records that "he was of an industry and vigilance not to be tired out or wearied by the most laborious, and of parts not to be imposed upon by the most subtle and sharp." Measured speech and ordered action became to him a rule of life in an age when hysteria and the distempers of religious fervour would dissolve a Parliament into passionate tears or quicken the pulse-beat of an excited sword-arm.[7]

---

[7] Nugent, i, 121.

Moreover, he had made a new friendship of the greatest importance. He had met John Pym, and the two had been drawn together. On November 28th, 1621, John Pym had made his first big speech. He made an abiding impression. The burly man, with his genial face and shaggy mane, brought a new dynamic force into the old Chamber of St. Stephens, and he and Hampden remained the closest friends and collaborators until their deaths within a few months of each other — Pym the convincing speaker, Hampden the thinker, the planner, the authority on practice and precedent. Pym's volubility in debate gave him the greater prominence, but it was Hampden, as Clarendon shows, who before long was often the directing brain.

Hampden rode back after the dissolution in January of 1622 to the enjoyment of home and family, and for two years he was free to attend to his own affairs and to fulfil the many public duties expected of the landed gentry — the administration of justice and the poor law, the provision of employment, the adjustment of wages and prices of the chief commodities. In the autumn of 1622 was born to him his daughter Elizabeth, for whom he was always to have a particular affection.

So two years passed before he was again called to the public scene. In 1623 Buckingham and "Baby Charles," fretting under the delays of James's long-range diplomacy, resolved to bring the love action with the Spanish court to close quarters. In spite of the tearful protests of "dear Dad and Gossip" they sailed to Spain, incogniti, to woo the Infanta point-blank. But the assault failed ignominiously, for the lady was well guarded. The adventurers returned to England with rage in their hearts, and to their own surprise suddenly became popular heroes by supporting the demand for war against Spain. Hampden was accordingly summoned to Parliament again early in 1624 and, patriotic fervour for once uniting all parties, the Houses voted £300,000 for the war. Buckingham prepared a military expedition to help the Protestant cause in Holland, but under his incredible incompetence it flickered out in hunger, in disease, and in shame.

On March 27th, 1625, James I died.

The new King, Charles, came to the throne at the age of twenty-four with every opportunity for making a success of his kingship. His personal charm and grace, his dignity, his cultured taste, his exemplary private life, were an agreeable contrast to his father's indecorum. James's lax court was reformed into a strict etiquette. Charles was at one with the popular demand for a war of revenge against Spain. "We can hope everything from the King who now governs us," cried Sir Benjamin Rudyerd in the Commons, and for a moment it seemed that the spirited days of Elizabeth were to return.

But the first act of the new King, after a breach with one Catholic lady, was to marry another. Henrietta Maria, that high-spirited princess who was afterwards to cause so much trouble, was the daughter of Henry IV of France, the first of the Bourbons, and she was to exercise a vital influence upon Charles. "Her She-Majesty," Queen Mary, as she came to be called, was of a compelling vivacity, a high courage, a mettlesome spirit, and was by much the dominant partner in that fateful alliance; but her passion for intrigue and her rash impetuosity were the worst qualities in a political helpmate for a man such as Charles. Her refusal, as an ardent Catholic, to take part in Charles's coronation and the swarm of priests, friars and foreign "papists" whom she brought in her train created from the first a strong prejudice against this "daughter of Heth." Her Catholic propaganda and some small concessions that Charles made to her faith stirred the hackles of the watching Puritans, for never was suspicion more stuck full with eyes. A Catholic was an enemy within the ranks, not only of the soldiers of God, but also in the fortress of England's national spirit, and even a Protestant with High Church leanings was deemed to be traitorous. Not to be a Protestant was not to be a patriot. It was as bad as to have been a pacifist in 1914 and the years thereafter. Much of the peevishness of Charles's Parliaments was due to his impolitic favouring of High Churchmen, and, with a Catholic queen beneath his roof, his passion for strict and orderly government, springing from a pragmatical instinct to push rather than to guide, seemed to justify their belief that Catholicism in religion was synonymous with tyranny in government. Men had indeed only to turn their eyes across the Channel to feel convinced in this fear.

In these circumstances it was that Hampden attended Charles's first Parliament in June, 1625, a year when there was a visitation of the plague in London. He sat now for Wendover, for which he had after a considerable struggle secured the right of representation in the last Parliament.[8] There was soon a quarrel about the supplies necessary for the war. Charles was not frank as to his intentions, and Parliament was niggardly. That early mistrust so unhappily generated was never to be allayed. Nettled by their refusal of his full demands and by the withholding of the usual life grant of tonnage and poundage, Charles soon dissolved them and plunged into a mad expedition against Cadiz.

But again Buckingham's work ended in ignominy, for, victualled with putrid meat and tainted beer, led by incompetent officers, the ships jostling each other in helpless confusion, it returned broken with mutiny and disease. This

---

[8] Nugent, i, 93; Official Return of M.P.s, 1878, 450, 462, 464, 474.

gallant exploit had to be paid for, and, after trying unsuccessfully to raise a loan under Privy Seal, Charles was obliged to recall Parliament in 1626. Hampden sat again for Wendover and was soon to become active in politics.

Now arose in the Commons the gallant spirit of Sir John Eliot, a man too much impetuous but possessed of a mind "exquisitely cultivated and familiar with the poetry and learning of the day, a nature singularly lofty and devout," and with him there began also a new and precious friendship for Hampden. Eliot, scion of an old Cornish family and ancestor of the Earls of St. Germans who still live at Port Eliot, resolved upon the audacious step of impeaching the King's favourite himself. He took careful soundings from his Parliamentary friends and in particular from Hampden, who, young though he was, had already become known for his knowledge of Parliamentary practice. It was to Hampden that there was now entrusted the task of drawing up the main heads, or "The Causes," of the indictment against Buckingham, and, having before him the precedent of Bacon and the more recent one of Middlesex, he proceeded to outline charges of four kinds — increased countenancing of the Papists, the decay of the national defences, the maladministration of revenue, and the corruption of public office.[9]

Charles was exceedingly angry. Haughtily he forbade the Commons to attack his chosen ministers, and reminded them "that Parliaments are altogether in my power for their calling, sitting and dissolution." Eliot and his friends were not to be frightened, however, and the impeachment went forward till at last Charles, having thrown Eliot into prison but failed to find any grounds upon which to indict him, dissolved Parliament to

---

[9] Forster, *Life of Eliot*, i, 490.

save his favourite without having wrung from the House the funds he needed.

III. GATHERING CLOUDS

At war with Spain, and threatened with war in France, Charles was now heavily in debt, and in 1626 he had recourse to the idea of appealing to the nation for a "free gift." There was a wholesale refusal, and Charles grimly proceeded to levy a forced loan. The aid of the pulpit was called in, and the Laudian clergy became the King's chief propaganda agents. To resist the King was to resist God, and eternal damnation would ensue, said Dr. Manwaring. Poor men who refused to pay were "pressed" into the army or navy. Tradesmen were bundled into prison. The judges had the temerity to declare the loan illegal, and Chief Justice Crew was accordingly dismissed. But the judges' verdict fortified the doubting as well as the determined, and resistance to the loan became general.

It was now that John Hampden made his first stand. He had reluctantly subscribed to the loan of the previous year, but now he was summoned to appear before the Privy Council, and he rode up to London from Buckinghamshire one cold winter's day in January, 1627. There he stood face to face with Buckingham. Reminding him, it is said, of the curse of Magna Carta, he refused to give way, and for his contumacy was committed to prison in the Gate House, a gloomy and insanitary jail hard by Westminster Abbey. Here also was his cousin, Sir Edmund Hampden, and here also he was soon to be joined by Sir John Eliot, both incarcerated for the like offence. The privations of a cold winter within those iron bars soon struck at John Hampden's health. He was brought up again before the Council, but in spite of the sufferings of his body and his spirit his resolution held. He was sent back to detention, but was moved to a less rigorous custody somewhere in Hampshire.[10]

His detention lasted several months, and it was to leave its mark on him for life. "He never after did look like the same man he was before." The summer of the vine receded in his veins, and he took on some relish of the saltness of time. But it was a change of spirit more than of physique. To a man of his wealth the money was nothing, and to one of his position prison was no easy penance. He saw his cousin Edmund die a lingering death. He could, if he liked, have abandoned the strife of politics and settled down to the enjoyment of his great heritage. Instead, he became a more determined Parliamentarian. His soul, in those months of confinement, had been through its first ordeal, for he had had to resolve the problem of conflicting loyalties, perhaps the hardest trial for any man of integrity. There was no question of his loyalty to the King. That remained steadfast until almost the last. The King's Majesty was still sacred to all men. He was God's lieutenant. The resentment of the Commons was only against Buckingham and his minions, and it is important to remember that almost to the very end the attacks of the Parliamentary leaders were not against the King's Majesty, but against his ministers, and that their prayer was ever that he would be freed of his evil counsellors.

During his confinement the administration of Charles and Buckingham had gone from bad to worse. The country was now at war with France as well as Spain, and Buckingham had achieved another ignoble military failure against La Rochelle. At a loss for money, Charles with a wry face was obliged once

______

[10] *Verney Papers*, 120, 126, 283; Rushworth, i, 428, 473; Cal. S. P. Dom. 1627-9, 31; Nugent, i, 107; Forster, 312. The quotation of Magna Carta is of doubtful authenticity.

more to call a Parliament together, and, as a measure of conciliation, he set free Hampden, Wentworth, Eliot and others who had been imprisoned for non-payment of the loan.

His third Parliament met on March 17th, 1628, a turbulent, hysterical yet memorable Parliament. Not often, as Mr. Buchan observes, has destiny brought under one roof so many of her children. She brought indeed one of the greatest of all in Hampden's cousin, Oliver Cromwell, the rugged Fenland squire, who now made his first appearance in the Chapel of St. Stephen's. It was an unimpressive appearance, but when one member asked Hampden who was this uncouth man, John replied with prophetic insight:

> That sloven whom you see before you hath no ornament in his speech; that sloven, I say, if it should ever come to a breach with the King (which God forbid), in such a case, I say, that sloven will be the greatest man in England.

Hampden himself was one of the leading members of the Lower House, and was appointed to nearly all important committees. As the result of a private meeting of the leaders of the Commons, it was agreed, instead of resuming the impeachment of Buckingham, which the headstrong Eliot desired, to support the more conciliatory and constructive course urged by Wentworth for a new bill making clear precisely what the liberties of the subject were. If the King would accept this bill the Commons were prepared to be exceptionally generous in the way of money. Unhappily, Charles immediately made it clear that the only purpose for which he considered the Houses existed was for voting him money, without asking what the money was for. This "great, warm and ruffling Parliament" embarked with the winds fairly set for a great and useful voyage, but it was shipwrecked on the attitude of the King, for he deemed himself not only captain of the ship of state but also proprietor.

Charles utterly denied Wentworth's bill, and the result was the far more formidable Petition of Right. That historic document was chiefly the work of that old storm cock of the Temple, Edward Coke. Turbulent scenes, tears and the wringing of hands accompanied its debates. Charles through peremptory orders to the Speaker, had endeavoured to stop discussion of it, but finally it was through Buckingham himself and the Lords that he was persuaded to sign — having been privately assured by the judges that he could still do as he liked, since the interpretation of laws was for them. The Petition, which was to rank as a second Magna Carta, laid down that henceforth no man should be compelled to pay taxes or other impositions without consent of Parliament, that no man should be imprisoned without a stated charge, that soldiers should not be billeted on the people, and that commissions for executing martial law should be annulled "lest by colour of them any of your Majesty's subjects be destroyed and put to death."

The Petition of Right was passed on Saturday, June 7th, 1628. It was acclaimed with ringing bells, flaming beacons, and shouts of applause. Shouts of applause, too, greeted a different kind of deliverance, for on August 23rd the gilded Buckingham was struck to the heart by the dagger of Lieutenant John Felton.

He was succeeded by the colourless and harassed Richard Weston, later Earl of Portland, a man of big looks and abject spirit, and the wheel of the ship was now altogether in Charles's hands. He had no sooner signed the Petition of Right than he proceeded to break it, for he again levied forces and again billeted soldiers. Parliament re-assembled after the prorogation in January, 1629, in a truculent mood, and under the inflamed leadership of Eliot pressed with too great a fervour their attacks upon the King's methods of collecting taxes. Charles therefore determined to arrest the Parliamentary inquiries by commanding an adjournment of the House. The Commons obtained wind of his intention, and there followed one of the most disgraceful scenes in the history of St. Stephen's. Early on the morning of March 2nd, after prayers, the Speaker (Sir John Finch) announced that he had received his Majesty's command to adjourn until March 10th, and he made to leave the House, and thus to render any discussion out of order. Denzil Holles and Benjamin Valentine leapt forward and held him down in his chair, Holles crying:

God's wounds! You shall sit till we please to rise.

Another member locked the door of the Chamber against the armed servants of the King who were threatening an entry by force, and put the key in his pocket. In tumult the House passed a declaration drawn by Eliot against popish innovations in religion and illegal taxation, the doors were unlocked and Hampden and his fellow members streamed out to find the King's soldiers drawn up outside. Charles, justifiably incensed, had done with Parliaments, and for eleven long years he ruled by his own hand alone, with results that were not to be forgotten.

Hampden took no part in that stormy scene — that "most gloomy, sad and dismal day for England," as Sir Simonds d'Ewes called it. But his friends Eliot, Valentine, and Holles were arrested the next day and clapped into prison. Eliot's lot was the Tower, and from that time he committed his two sons to Hampden's care.

Hampden now retired to his estates and the next few years must have been the happiest of his life. To the biographer an outstanding feature of it was the long correspondence that took place between him and gallant Eliot. These famous letters reveal much that is delightful in the character of Hampden — his gentle feeling, his generosity, his conscientiousness in the care of the young Eliots, his culture and his love for all good and gracious things. They show him also as a man of good sense, well informed, well versed in literature, and following the courses of military events abroad and politics at home. He watched over the education of his friend's children as though they were his own and wrote long letters to their father on the advisability of sending Bess to boarding-school, John to travel on the Continent, and Richard to serve in the wars of religion. The two boys went to Oxford, but spent most of their vacations in Hampden's own home. At Oxford they led something of a riotous life, especially Dick, the younger, for whom in spite of his naughty spirit Hampden had a special affection. If only he would "adorn that lively spirit with flowers of contemplation," Dick would, he wrote, raise great expectations.[11]

Hampden paid two or three visits to Eliot in prison, and on at least one occasion sent him "a buck out of my paddock." But these visits grew rarer. The King, who of deliberate intent designed to bring about his death, ordered Eliot to receive fewer visitors, and he fell into a decline; presently he was removed to gloomier quarters "where candlelight may be suffered but scarce fire." The Lieutenant of the Tower was severely reprimanded because air from an open window had

---

[11] The Hampden-Eliot correspondence is given mainly in Nugent's *Memorials*, in Forster's *Life of Eliot*, and in Mr. Williamson's *Life of Hampden*.

been allowed to reach him, and yet again he was moved to a room still darker and smokier. Consumption set in.

Eliot's friends appealed to Charles that he might be allowed the benefit of some fresh air, and later, when the consumption was further advanced, they prevailed upon Eliot to write personally and ask for temporary liberty until his health and should recover:

> I am fallen into a dangerous disease. I humbly beseech Your Majesty you will command your judges to set me at liberty, that for the recovery of my health, I may take some fresh air.

He was quite willing to go back to prison again afterwards, but Charles remained flinty-hearted. Even when, after Eliot had sunk at last to a painful death in the winter of 1632, the first martyr for Parliamentary liberty, his son petitioned the King that the body might be taken to Cornwall for burial with his ancestors, Charles, capable of so much generosity to those he loved, coldly wrote: "Let Sir John Eliot's body be buried in the Church of that parish where he died." The death of this friend, for whom he had so much admiration and such a dear respect, seems to have had a deep and enduring effect on John Hampden, and when the years of autocratic rule were over, he and his friends did not forget to demand redress.

During these years Hampden became actively interested in the colonisation of the New England beyond the Atlantic by men and women in search of religious freedom, and in 1629 Eliot had sent him a paper entitled "The Grounds for Settling a Plantation in New England" — a paper which is still preserved. Lord Saye and others of Hampden's friends were about that time engaged in the newly formed Massachusetts Bay Company, and he himself presently became concerned in the foundation of Connecticut. On March 19th, 1632, the Earl of Warwick made a grant of a large tract of land in what is now that territory to twelve people. Of these Hampden was one, and others were Lord Saye and the gallant young Lord Brooke. Each subscribed capital to the enterprise, and in 1635 a small band of colonists from Massachusetts founded in Connecticut a fort which was named Saybrook, in honour of the two peers. Hampden thus had a stake in the colonies and his thoughts were to turn thither in the dark days soon to come.[12]

But the greater part of John's time was taken up with his duties as landowner and justice of the peace and with his home life under the woody brows of his beautiful Chilterns. Little pictures are preserved of him taking measures to obtain improvements in the roads and bridges, to prevent excessive prices for wheat and to ensure the true weight of bread.[13] He followed always the course of public events and watched with lively satisfaction the victories of Gustavus Adolphus in the Protestant cause. At home he entertained a good deal, and saw much of Arthur Goodwin, his life-long friend, who lived at Winchendon. Sometimes John would ride over to Beaconsfield to see his cousin, the poet Edmund Waller. More notable were visits paid to meetings of the "Philosophers' Club," at Lord Falkland's mansion of Great Tew, twelve miles from Oxford. Falkland, then in his early twenties, was a young patrician of the noblest instincts and the loftiest principles of public service, and his fine house and valuable library were thrown open to all men of culture, who were free to come and go unbidden and to lodge as long as they liked under that hospitable roof. Here Hampden met many of the leading intellects of the day.

---

12 Trumbull, *History of Connecticut*, i, 495; Forster, *Eliot*, ii, 531.
13 Cal. S. P. Dom. 1629-31, 1; 1632, xxxviii; 1637, xl; Stowe MSS. 142, fols. 39 and 40 (given in Mr. Williamson's *Life*).

"Wisdom doth live with children about her knees." Before 1634 the Hampdens had nine children — three sons and six daughters. One of them, Richard, was destined to be Lord Chancellor. One daughter, Mary, by second marriage to Sir John Hobart, of Blickling, Norfolk, became ancestress of the Hobart-Hampdens, the house of the Earls of Buckinghamshire who still to-day hold Great Hampden; another daughter, Ruth, married Sir John Trevor and became ancestress of the Trevor-Hampdens; a third, Anne, married Robert Pye. They were a cultured and, we may suppose, a happy family. On Sundays and holy days they attended Great Hampden church (but not always, as we shall see), where the Rev. Egeon Askew seems to have been an able and a learned ministrant.

Half-way through this period of Parliamentary inaction, in 1634, Hampden suffered a great loss by the death of his wife. She lies buried in Great Hampden church, where an epitaph on plain black marble, composed by John, stands to her memory.

IV. BLACK TOM AND WILLIAM THE FOX

Meanwhile "the aspect of public affairs grew darker and darker." Charles had veritably taken the law into his own hands and had become the dictator-King. But he had raised up on either hand two inexorable lieutenants whose names had become by-words in men's mouths. Laud and Wentworth had come into their own.

Sir Thomas Wentworth we have already had occasion to mention. Swarthy, pallid, with defiance seated on his lofty brows and ruthlessness on his bearded lips, the resolute Yorkshireman was one of the most striking figures of the Stuart scene. He was a man of simple habits but strong affections, very fond of children, and, like many men of stricken health, he had unquenchable courage. He had exquisite hands, and his sullen eyes could leap in a moment to a radiant charm or a volcanic fury. Of considerable wealth, he had come to Parliament on the popular side after elections of questionable legality. With Eliot, Pym, and Coke he was one of the most redoubtable of the Parliamentary leaders in their opposition to the Court. Like Eliot and Hampden, he had suffered imprisonment for non-payment of taxes. He was in the forefront of the Petition of Right. Almost immediately afterwards, however, having been presented to the King by Lord Treasurer Weston, he had crossed to the King's side, and Charles was quick to put to his use his great abilities, his vigour, his capacity for practical action. He was created Viscount. There was in his blood a passion for efficient and strong administration, and he had come to the conclusion that such an administration could be better achieved through the machinery of the Crown than through the debates of Parliament. A policy of "Thorough" was the right medicine for the distemper of the age.

"Black Tom Tyrant," as he was later to be called, after having been President of the Council of the North, was now Lord-Deputy of Ireland, where with great success he had restored the King's authority, had achieved striking reforms, and had chastened the Irish Parliament to that proper mood of dutiful compliance which Charles had so lamentably failed to secure from the Westminster assembly. He had not yet come back to England and was still unknown by the multitude, but when he did, great administrator though he was, he failed in the first requisite of a statesman — the capacity to understand and assess the mind and heart of a people.

William Laud, a don at Oxford when Hampden was a student, had become Archbishop of Canterbury in 1633. He has been much "whitewashed" of late, but, though he had great qualities and a sincere faith, it is folly for religious sympathies to blind one to his political mischiefs. Small of stature, shrill of voice, petulant and excitable of nature. Beneath the great crescent-moons of his eyebrows his alert bird-like gaze looked upon a world that seemed for ever to startle him by its departure from his own strict code. The ferment of his mental energy caused him to bubble over with a passion for minute and meddlesome activities. No man in his religious observances must be allowed to wear any coat of informal cut. The rubrics of life must be infinitesimally observed. An aloof scholar, a precise ecclesiastic, he lacked the human qualities for securing the willing service of the hearts of men. Of great personal piety, and of outstanding honesty in an age when peculation and bribery were rife, the benefactor of

Oxford and perhaps the greatest intellectual of his day, "William the Fox" was nevertheless cold, intolerant, myopic, and amazingly superstitious. There was a special destiny in the fall of a leaf. Every dream was carefully recorded and had its special meaning, and according to such meaning it brought him either terror or joy.

In religion Laud would be accounted to-day no more than a moderate High Churchman. He was much behind the modern Anglo-Catholic. Like the King, he was opposed at once to the Church of Rome and to Puritanism. Catholics were as much subject to punishment for recusancy under his regimen as Puritans, but it was the Puritans who found the gaoler and the executioner most employment. The Catholic had but to pay his fines regularly, but for the Protestant who departed from the forms and ceremonies prescribed by the Archbishop there were the whip, the knife, the pillory and the prison. Laud, if he had had his way, would have been much more severe upon Catholics; he refused the offer from Rome of a Cardinal's hat, and on the scaffold he prayed that the clamour of *Venient Romani* would not be realised; but he found in Queen Mary the one influence in all the land that held a greater persuasion than his own in the mind and heart of Charles.

Laud's purpose, though he was notably tolerant and sober in matters of doctrine, was to enforce orthodoxy in the outward form of worship according to the Book of Common Prayer. His passion for propriety and orderliness was deeply offended by the laxity of behaviour which permitted men to bring their dogs into the House of God and to use the Communion table as a seat, a hat-stand or a desk. His zeal for orthodoxy and discipline was likewise offended by the variations in the practice of public worship which the liberalism of Elizabeth had designedly sanctioned to satisfy fluid and opposing views, and he set himself to abate these indecencies and to restrain this latitude by means of a disciplinary enforcement of the Church canons and of the forms and ceremonies of the Prayer Book. It was his initial and his typical error that he concerned himself with the outward forms and ceremonies without any corresponding interest in the manifestations of inner spiritual life. In an age when attendance at church was by law compulsory on all persons he sought to inculcate outward reverence in the hope that inward reverence would follow. He could not see, as Baxter did, that the proper remedy was to quicken souls to a higher life. He was concerned, not with the soul, but with behaviour. Like so many ecclesiastics, he served the Church rather than God, the institution rather than the spirit. He was indeed a great ecclesiastic, but it was never in him to be a crusader.

His second error — of course, only a political error — was that in pursuing this course in an age when Protestantism was the dominant vogue, he sought to impose upon all congregations an Arminian interpretation of Church forms and ceremonies — an interpretation in the direction of Rome rather than of Geneva. The son of Oxford fought the influence of Cambridge. The Communion table must be removed from the centre of the church and be placed at the east wall; it must be guarded from the congregation by a rail and men must do reverence to it. At the name of Jesus men must bow. The Prayer Book must be rigidly followed, without omissions or additions.

To a people not deeply religious these were at first matters of small moment, but to these two errors of principle and of policy Laud added a third, an error of method. When it was seen with what rigour, with what harshness, with what partiality towards the High Churchman the regulations were enforced, when it was seen that (by the nature of things) the lash and the knife fell most fiercely upon men of the purest lives and the highest consciences, then there grew up in the mass of moderate law-abiding men a sense of wrong, a conviction that that was being enforced as law which was not law, and that an effort was being made to bring England back under the Papal yoke. Even so, the religious exactions alone would have caused no revolution if they had not run concurrently with Charles's financial exactions, and if both had not been part of a religious dogma which, preached from many a pulpit, asserted the political notion that the King was endowed with God's licence to do as he liked, regardless of Acts of Parliament, of the constitution, and of his own pledges. The result was that, in revulsion, moderate Protestants were driven into the arms of the Puritans, and moderate conservatives into the tents of the radicals.

Immense indeed was that consequence, for it was during these years that there took place that steady stream of freedom-seeking emigrants to the new American colonies which set a lasting model that is reproduced throughout Canada and the United States to-day — the English Common Law, the English town council, and the Puritan moral code. Nor were they Protestants alone who sought the new pastures, for while the Puritan flocks were colonising Massachusetts, Connecticut, Rhode Island, Virginia and Newfoundland, Lord Baltimore, in 1634, founded a new colony for Catholics, and called it Maryland after Charles's Queen.

After the death of Portland (as a Catholic) in 1635, Laud became, below Charles, the dominant voice in State as well as Church, and his influence with the King was such that he secured the succession as Lord Treasurer of his nominee, Bishop Juxon — the first time, as Laud noted with pride in his diary, that the office had been filled by a cleric since the days of Henry VII. The corridors of Whitehall, said one courtier, became "choked with lawn sleeves." Laud established a rigid censorship of religious writings. He instituted a Metro-political Visitation in which his Vicar-General, Sir Nathaniel Brent, toured the country for three years, inquiring minutely into the religious practices and moral behaviour of the clergy and of the public in every parish. Hampden was himself a minor victim of this inquisition, for in '34 he was summoned before Brent for having attended a church other than his own and for having permitted a muster of the trained bands in the churchyard of Beaconsfield.[14] The ecclesiastical courts became a curse from their eternal processes against men and women for pettifogging offences. Writers and preachers of Puritan thought were persecuted without mercy. Men such as Prynne the lawyer, Burton the cleric and Bastwick the physician were fined enormous sums, flogged through the streets, their ears cut off, their flesh burned with the branding-iron to enforce conformity, and when Alexander Leighton was so sentenced Laud raised his hands to heaven and "gave thanks to God."

These were but the normal inhumanities of the time, to be practised by Puritans in their days as well as by the bishops. But the Laudian regimen went farther, for, though torture had some time before been declared illegal, John Archer, the London tradesman, was put to the rack and his limbs torn before he was executed. Even burning would have been revived for the benefit of a Dover dissenter had he not tactfully recanted.

Some of these incidents took place later in time than the period we have now reached, but they serve to show the kind of affection with which the nation regarded Laud. The little

---

[14] Cal. S. P. Dom. 1634-5, 250.

Archbishop's writings are filled with piety and much Christian feeling, but it was by his actions that men judged him.

Laud has received more than his due share of historical blame for the discontents of those days. Not so His Majesty's judges. An inherent fault of Charles's attempt at personal government of England was that, since he was his own law-giver, his judges, to use their own term, were virtually estopped from ruling against him. His father's bad system of dictating to the judges had brought the Bench, with honourable exceptions, to a condition of dependence and sometimes servitude upon the Crown. The judges, appointed by the King, had now to administer the laws that he promulgated, and if, in any constitutional issue, they were moved to find against the hand that fed them they were made sharply aware, poor humans, of the results that might follow to themselves. The faults of the system caused bishops and judges alike to conspire to magnify the King's authority. As we shall see, Charles used the judges very shrewdly. His encroachments on the rights of his subjects were made under the cloak of the law and under the sanction of those who should have been its guardians. The King found a perfect servant for this purpose in the Lord Chief Justice, the arrogant Sir John Finch, who, as Speaker in the Parliament of 1628-29, had been forcibly held down on that turbulent last day. Another such was Sir Robert Berkeley, who was presently to enunciate the convenient doctrine

> that there was a rule of law and a rule of government, and that many things which might not be done by the rule of law might be done by the rule of government.

In other words, since the King was the government, he could override the law.

Materially, these years were a time of peace and, in some directions, of prosperity; capitalism developed; there was a rise of manufactures in the West Riding. A drainage of the fens was undertaken; a regular post was established by which a letter could be sent eighty miles for twopence; hackney carriages made their first appearance in the streets of London — to the great discontent of the Thames watermen, who were till then the chief means of transport east and west. Joint-stock companies began to expand. Trade had acquired an increasing influence, accounting in a high degree for the growing demand of Parliament to have some voice in foreign affairs. Charles, however, continued to find himself hard pressed for the financial power to drive his machine. The shrinkage in value of the ordinary revenues of the Crown, which had obliged him to ask Parliament for subsidies, drove him, since he was out of patience with Parliaments, to dig up old workings and bore into virgin earth in the urgent search for gold. All sorts of devices were tried. Old and disused impositions were revived; new ones devised. Men were compelled to accept knighthood or pay a fine. The ancient forest laws were revived, and men whose distant ancestors had encroached on the forests had to pay sometimes enormous fines. An ancient and illegal proclamation of James's, prohibiting the extension of London, was similarly revived, and owners of new suburban houses were forced to pay three years' rental to avoid demolition. Juries were threatened and intimidated. The Court of Star Chamber expanded the administration of justice into an enterprise of profit to the Exchequer. Worst of all was the sale of monopolies. By an Act of 1624 monopolies could no longer be given to private persons; so Charles sold them to corporations. They spread to every department of life — to salt, soap, coal, starch, liquor, shipping, and many other things.

To the merchant they were a vexatious restraint of trade, and to the consumer they meant an enormous rise in prices. In the late thirties there came a serious economic depression.

Thus, though outwardly tranquil, "the country," Clarendon frankly admitted, "was full of pride and mutiny and discontent." The price of corn was very high, and the growing sense of insecurity in the country, sent people into the towns. Thousands were sailing away to America, and in the midst of all Hampden was suddenly to come to the forefront of national life.

V. SHIP MONEY

In 1634 the King, in the course of an antic foreign policy, in which he sought in vain to induce other monarchs to serve his own designs, was moved to consider afresh the uses of his navy as a bargaining weapon.

Charles had always shown a close and genuine interest in the navy, attending with great ceremony the launchings of new ships, laying down their specifications with his own hand and personally altering the technical details prescribed by the experts (with the inevitable results). But it was typical of him that he had no understanding how to employ a fleet effectively, that his chief concern was to enforce upon foreign ships, by the dipping of their colours, the recognition of the personal sovereignty of the seas that he claimed, and that the fleet was not to him an instrument for the protection of his subjects' interests, but merely a weapon with which to impress foreign powers in his bargainings for money or for the restoration of his nephew to the Palatinate. He was altogether unconcerned with the shameful treatment of the crews who manned his ships and whom he regarded as rebels to be "put down with shot." It was nothing to him if a commander had to sell his sails and anchors to pay his men, or if seamen fleeing from a diseased ship were refused admission to their own ports and were left to die on the open beach.

For under James I the glorious tradition of Elizabeth had been eaten away by corruption and lassitude and its vigorous enterprise had sunk into a slothful and hollow vainglory. That degeneracy continued throughout Charles's administration likewise and the humiliating expeditions against Spain and

France had demonstrated the almost unbelievable decadence into which English seamanship had sunk. "The whole breed of sailors had temporarily disappeared."[15] Putrid food, diseased and mutinous seamen cheated with the most heartless chicanery of their food, their money and their clothes, leaking ships with rotten cordage, under ignorant and gilded captains who knew neither how to command nor how to obey — these were the conditions prevailing in the fleet of a King who claimed in lofty periods the personal sovereignty of the sea and demanded that the ships of other states should dip their colours to the Standard of England. The Dutch treated English maritime interests with contempt. Dunkirk privateers (to whom Charles sold munitions) preyed upon English shipping even in its own harbours. Morocco pirates raided the shores of England and Ireland to carry off their inhabitants as lifelong slaves.

Accordingly, it was beyond doubt a good intention in Charles to give new thought to the navy, and, still faced with large financial deficits, he had recourse in 1634 to a new fiscal device. It had for long been customary in times of war for a tax known as ship money to be levied on coastal counties, the ports being required to provide, equip and man a ship of a determined size, or alternatively to furnish a sum of money in lieu. In October, 1634, though war had ended some years before, Charles levied ship money on the coastal counties on the plea of the prevalence of piracy. The tax was paid, reluctantly, and brought in £104,000.

Charles was then emboldened to try the unprecedented measure of extending the tax to the inland counties as well, on the theory that to the safety of all, all should contribute — but ignoring his constitutional obligation to secure the consent of

15 Callender, *The Naval Side of British History*, p. 83.

all. The writs were issued in August, 1635, demanding a payment of exactly twice the sum raised the previous year from the seaports. The plea of piracy was no longer maintained, and the new demand was made "to secure this realm against those dangers and extremities which have distressed other nations."

Under this decree the county of Buckinghamshire was required to provide a ship of war of 450 tons, together with 104 mariners, cannon, ammunition, muskets, pikes, and other arms — in default, the sum of £4,500.[16]

John Hampden was assessed separately in respect of each of his properties in different parishes — 31/6 in respect of his estate in Great Kimble, 20/- for Stoke Mandeville, etc., to a total of probably less than £20. The money was trifling, but John, like Lord Saye in Oxfordshire, Sir Marmaduke Langdale in Yorkshire, afterwards one of Charles's stoutest cavaliers, and many others elsewhere, declined to pay. In Oxfordshire the constables refused even to assess, and incumbents and overseers refused to produce their books, demanding to know by what law the tax was being levied.

Hampden's was no factious refusal. He had known already too well what were the consequences of resisting the King's levies, and he could have bought peace at a cheap price. But he was undeterred by that experience, for, watching the shifts and devices of Charles's government in the last few y ears, he saw that ship money was not only an illegal imposition, but that it was also a political challenge. If the King were right in his desire to strengthen the fleet, he was none the less wrong in extracting the funds for doing so without the consent of Parliament. A levy to meet a sudden danger was within the King's right, but the plea of emergency, which figured so much in the whole dispute, simply did not exist. It was a patent

---

[16] Rushworth, iii, App. 213.

infringement of the King's pledges under the Petition of Right. To Hampden it must have been clear that ship money was, in a word, a new device for ruling without Parliament, and if the King were allowed to succeed, gradually penetrating and overleaping indeterminate boundaries, then the whole Parliamentary constitution, which had slowly been developing for so many centuries, might well pass away. In short, the issue was freedom.

The opposition to the new demand was so widespread that in December Charles had recourse to the judges for a ruling. He required them to advise him whether he, "in his princely wisdom," had acted rightly. Finch and ten of his colleagues had no difficulty in finding a verdict that satisfied the King. In times of peril (and the King was the only judge of when peril existed) they declared that His Majesty was justified in extending this tax to the kingdom in general.

Fortified by this judgment, Charles ordered that the collection of ship money by the sheriffs should be enforced and expedited.

John was now apparently legally in the wrong, but politically he felt more than ever that the tax ought to be resisted, trivial though it was in amount. He therefore persisted in his refusal, but this time he was one of few. By the autumn of 1636 only £20,544 remained outstanding of the £208,000 demanded; even in Hampden's own county, where his example carried so much weight, all but £188 1s. 11d. had been paid out of the assessment of £4,500. Accordingly, in October of 1636, Charles issued a third writ for ship money.

There was immediate consternation. It was clear now that he intended to make the tax a regular annual one. The danger of the kingdom seemed more than ever a fiction. No new ships at all had been built in 1635. Men of the highest rank, and of the most loyal and devoted character, saw that the whole future constitution of England was at stake. The old Earl of Danby, a tried veteran in the public service, stepped from his retirement to warn the King of the universal discontent of his subjects.

Charles was deeply vexed, but he desired, at least, that his action should have the appearance of legality, and he therefore once again had recourse to the judges. This time he required them not only to advise on the main issue, but more particularly on whether or not he was the sole judge of when a state of national danger existed. The manner of his asking, however, was patently not for the purpose of enlightening or guiding him in the policy he was to pursue, but simply to hinder his subjects from bringing a case to be legally argued in the courts of Westminster Hall. In short, he wished the issue pre-judged, and again the obedient judges obliged him.

Yet Hampden, and Lord Saye with him, resolved to stand firm. They consulted Hampden's proud and taciturn cousin, Oliver St. John, who was one of the rising barristers of the day and who had himself suffered imprisonment on another matter. St. John thought he had a sound line of argument in spite of the prior rulings of the judges, and it was decided to fight as a test case the simple issue of Hampden's liability for the twenty shillings tax on Stoke Mandeville. On this trivial sum was fought one of the most famous of State trials. As Burke was to say a century and a half later in a speech on American taxation: "Would twenty shillings have ruined Mr. Hampden? No, but the payment of half that sum, on the principle it was demanded, would have made him a slave."[17]

Proceedings began in the Court of Exchequer in the spring of 1637, and Hampden was now a national figure. Clarendon pays him one of his most generous tributes at this moment.

---

[17] Works, ed. 1852, iii, 185.

Hampden, he says, "was rather of reputation in his own country, than of public discourse or fame in the kingdom, before the business of the ship money; but then he grew the argument of all tongues, every man enquiring who and what he was, that durst, at his own charge, support the liberty and property of the kingdom, and rescue his country, as he thought, from being made prey to the court. His carriage throughout this agitation was with that rare temper and modesty, that they who watched him most narrowly to find some advantage against his person, to make him less resolute in his cause, were compelled to give him a just testimony."

The case came to trial in November of 1637, a few weeks after Charles's shipbuilding policy had reached its peak in the launching of the grandiose and clumsy *Sovereign of the Seas*. St. John and Robert Holborne were for Hampden; Sir John Banks, Attorney-General, and Sir Edward Lyttelton, Solicitor-General, for the Crown. St. John's argument was that the power which the King possessed could properly be employed only through Parliament. The King was the fount of power, but the law had marked out careful channels in which the waters of authority must flow, guarded by banks against flooding indiscriminately over the countryside; otherwise there was no limit to the demands that the King might make upon a citizen's goods. Just as the courts of law were the channel by which justice was administered in the King's name, so was Parliament the proper channel for raising money. No previous Sovereign had attempted any such claim, and there was no excuse, on grounds of national safety or otherwise, for having avoided the proper course of a Parliamentary vote.

Holborne was even more emphatic, ridiculing the idea of national danger, and roundly declaring to the shocked judges that Parliament and not the King was the main representative of the nation's sovereignty. It was the direct constitutional issue.

Banks and Lyttelton based their case, in a word, on the assertion of the King's supreme jurisdiction: "He is an absolute monarch and holdeth the kingdom under none but God himself." They asserted, moreover, that a citizen's enjoyment of his goods could hardly be said to be jeopardised by measures which were taken by the Crown specifically for their protection. Likewise, how was it reasonable in a time of danger to suffer the delay of a summons of Parliament?

The hearing lasted six weeks, being concluded on December 18th. The findings of the twelve judges were given separately and at long intervals, and it was six months before all were declared. There was small expectation of a decision against the Crown, but to the surprise of all the majority against Hampden was the smallest possible. Five of the twelve judges were for Hampden; and of the seven against him, the verdict of Sir William Jones was a conditional one. The final pronouncement of judgment in favour of the Crown was given in the Exchequer Court on June 12th, 1638.

Hampden had lost his case in the Courts, but he had achieved his purpose with the nation. He had brought all men's eyes to see the constitutional issue. The King, unless restrained by Parliament, had unrestricted power to do whatever he liked with the whole of men's possessions — "and so no man was, in conclusion, worth anything." Chief Justice Finch had roundly declared that any Act of Parliament which restrained the King from commanding his subjects, their persons, their goods and their money, was void. "*No Acts of Parliament make any difference.*"[18]

---

[18] The ship money trial is given in the *State Trials*, in Rushworth, ii, 481 *et seq.*, and in *The Tryal of Mr. Hampden*, 1719.

The matter could not have been put more baldly than that, and of Hampden himself Clarendon said: "The judgment proved of more advantage and credit to the gentleman condemned than to the King's service." Ship money had been adjudged lawful "upon such grounds and reasons as every stander-by was able to swear was not law." The case "left no man anything he could call his own." There was one man, however, who was little pleased at the acclamation of Hampden. To Wentworth, Hampden had been actuated only by "the vain flatteries of an imaginary liberty," and he wrote home from Ireland to Laud that Hampden and his friends "were they rightly served, they should be whipped home into their wits." And again later, though paying tribute to Hampden's abilities: "I still wish (and take it to be a very charitable one) Mr. Hampden and others of his likeness were well whipped into their right senses; if the rod be so used that it smart not, I am the more sorry."[19]

Hampden's stand was justified as well on grounds other than principle, for seldom has public money been more misapplied. Seldom has a sovereign shown himself more ignorant of the uses to which a fleet should be put. The first ship money fleet put to sea in the summer of '35, well-equipped, but once again with ignorant commanders, carrion food, mutinous men "barefoot and scarcely rags to hide their skins," ravaged by typhus and deserting by hundreds. Though there was a successful minor expedition against Sallee in 1637, the pirates still swarmed in the Channel and descended upon the coasts of Devon and Cornwall. The fleet achieved nothing but the irritation of neighbour states. In '39, while the English fleet stood irresolutely by under Charles's ambiguous orders, Tromp did not hesitate to flout the sovereign of the sea even in his

---

[19] Strafford, *Letters*, ii, 138, 158, 176.

own anchorage when, in contempt of Charles's navy, he thundered down upon the Spaniards sheltering in the neutrality of English waters and dashed them to ruin beneath the white cliffs of Kent.

Moreover, during the ship money years there were fewer new ships actually built than in the corresponding number of years before,[20] and the climax of pecuniary misuse was reached when the grandiose *Sovereign of the Seas* was launched in 1637. She cost £40,833 8s. 1½d. — enough to build seven ordinary 40-guns ships. The biggest ship of her time, a great three-decker of 1,500 tons mounting 102 guns, she was built out of sheer vanity to impress Richelieu across the water. Charles himself prescribed her tonnage, and with his own pen increased the armament professionally calculated for her by more than ten per cent. The gilding and carving of her ornate hull alone cost enough for a single ship. In spite of all that his apologists have pleaded for his good intentions, the place of England as a sea power was in 1640 even lower than when he had ascended in 1625.[21]

Of the effects of the ship money verdict upon John himself we know nothing for certain. It appears that, three months before judgment was given, but when the result was already certain, he prepared to cross the Atlantic to America, and that his cousin Oliver Cromwell and Sir Arthur Hazelrig were among those who were to go with him. It is reported that they embarked together in the Thames, where eight ships lay bound for the colonies, but that on Charles's command the fleet was forbidden to sail. There is no proper historical corroboration

---

[20] Two new ships were built in each of the years 1632, 1633 and 1634; none in 1635; two in 1636; three in 1637; and then no more till 1640. On the other hand, there were many hired merchantmen.

[21] Oppenheim, *Administration of the Royal Navy*, 216-301: Callender, *The Naval Side of British History*, ch. vi.

of this report, but, *pace* Sir Charles Firth, it has an intrinsic likelihood. Hampden had for some years had an interest in Lord Warwick's Connecticut settlement, and, after the death of a wife to whom he was so much attached, and with the sun of liberty being ever more darkened by threatening clouds, there is every likelihood that he should at least wish to see the colonies if not to settle there. As for Cromwell, he was certainly by religion and temperament of the sort of men who were then emigrating. We know from later evidence that the idea had been in his mind at least once.[22]

Be that as it may, the cousins never crossed the Atlantic, but remained at home to play a greater part in the struggle for the constitutional progress of the Anglo-Saxon peoples, and one of them to give his life for it.

---

[22] Nugent, i, 254; Neal, *History of the Puritans*, ed. 1822, ii, 287.

VI. SCOTLAND SHOWS THE WAY

And now greater events were to begin. The tempo quickens. With a folly that is scarcely to be believed, Charles and Laud had attempted in the past few months to force an Anglican High Church liturgy upon the people of Scotland, most of whom were Calvinist, and all of whom were nationalist to the core. To all shades of Scottish thought (and there was a considerable body of mild Arminianism) the idea of an alien ritual, dictatorially imposed upon them without a by-your-leave, was as offensive as cow-flesh to a Hindu. Never had the feelings or the temper of a nation been more misjudged. The hackles of every Scotsman rose. Peer and peasant were at one. There were riots and meetings of protest, and the bishops were utterly cast out. Now, in 1638, was put forth that famous instrument called the National Covenant, destined to give its name to a body of thought which to this day is a power in Scottish life, and to a force of men who were to prove the hammer of the cavaliers and the flail of easeful living. The Covenanters swore to defend the Protestant religion and to resist all contrary errors and corruptions. They raised an army and appointed as its commander the veteran General Leslie, home from the service of Gustavus Adolphus, and prepared for action.

Wholly ignorant of the people from whom he had himself sprung, Charles resolved to put down their "impertinent and damnable" risings by force, and in 1639 at York scratched together an unwilling muster of troops (under a Catholic earl). They had not the slightest enthusiasm, however, for the cause of Laud and his bishops, for this war to prick English vestments upon the Scottish clergy with the point of the sword, and in face of the boldness and resolution of the Scots, Charles was obliged to conclude with them in the Treaty of Berwick, by which the Scots were to control their own souls and both sides were to disband their troops.

As usual, however, Charles had not the slightest intention of honouring the pact, and on his return to London he immediately set out to plan how he might cozen the Scots by appearing to yield everything, while secretly preparing to retake all. Wentworth was now returned from Ireland from a brilliant proconsulship, and to the shrill fury of Laud he added the cool and practical advice that his principle of "Thorough," which had been so successful in Ireland, should now be applied to the insurgent Scots. Wentworth cared nothing about the details of religion, but he had at heart the passion for firm and orderly government, of which the first necessity was obedience. His practical voice told Charles also that, if he was to subdue the Scots by force of arms, he must have money immediately. To do that he must summon Parliament. The idea was distasteful to Charles. But Wentworth pressed his point, won it, and was made Earl of Strafford.

So Valentine and Strode, co-sufferers with Eliot, were released into the light of day after eleven years' imprisonment.

Thus the voice of the people's representatives was to be heard again. Hampden, we may assume, received the news with the satisfaction of a war-horse snuffing the breeze of battle after long idleness. The opportunity for action had come, and he was ready for it, for the whole temper of the man had changed. The example of Scotland must have shown to a mind less perceptive than his the direction that the rising waters must take unless the springs of discontent that fed them were dammed. Henceforth he went forward actively with the current. He became a leader, if not yet of rebellion, at least of a new determined demand for popular action — not merely for the maintenance of old liberties, but for the acquisition of new ones. Hampden was not, as he has so often been represented, the grave, retiring gentleman of a passive melancholy. To Richard Baxter, indeed, he was a saint whom he looked forward to meeting in heaven and a man who had "the most universal praise of any gentleman that I remember of that age,"[23] but certainly he was not the meek martyr of Nugent's Memorials. He had all the qualities of resolute leadership, and the ardour that had long lain dormant in his soul now began to burn with a brighter light.

In the elections for the new assembly, to be famous in history as the Short Parliament, he and his friend Arthur Goodwin were returned as the members for Buckinghamshire. When he rode up to the gathering at St. Stephen's in April, 1640, he left his beloved Great Hampden never to return save for a few brief hours at rare intervals. Henceforth to the day of his death he gave himself up to public affairs. He took lodgings in Gray's Inn Lane, and he and Pym were constantly together. He was now "the most popular man in the House," and was looked up to by all parties as a great moral leader. If Pym was the party leader and director of operations for the opposition, yet he was "in private designings much governed by Mr. Hampden," as Clarendon testifies. The striking feature in Hampden as a Parliamentarian was that he was not a man of many words, seldom made "speeches" and rarely began a debate; instead, he would listen patiently to other speakers, observe how the House was inclined, and then with a few telling words bring the issue to the end he desired, or, if he found the inclinations of the House were against his own, he

---

[23] *Saint's Rest*, ch. vii; *Reliquia Baxteriance*, ed. 1696, iii, 177.

was never at a loss for means of diverting or adjourning the debate. When he did speak his language was "concise and significant." As in tactics he had abundant dexterity and resourcefulness, so in speech he had a singular persuasiveness. "He was," says Clarendon again, "a very wise man, and of great parts, possessed with the most absolute spirit of popularity — that is, the most absolute faculties to govern the people — of any man I ever knew."

Spite of the past eleven years it was a moderate House, "exceedingly disposed to please the King and to do him service." The sole purpose, however, for which the King had summoned it was so that it should provide him with money, and he had no intention of agreeing to its proposal that grievances should be discussed first. He nourished hopes that the rising of the Scots would awaken the national feeling of the English and unite Parliament and Crown in an access of patriotism, but Hampden, Pym, Cromwell and all their friends saw only too well that Scotland was fighting the battle of English liberty. They immediately began an inquiry into the matter of ship money, which Charles had continued to levy since the Hampden verdict.

In May, becoming short-tempered, the King made a final bargaining offer to the Commons that he would give up his claim to ship money for the price of a subsidy of £840,000. He offered, that is to say, to give up a claim to which, in fact, he had no right, and the Commons were thrown at once into a critical debate on May 4th, in which Hampden intervened with quick dexterity to oblige the House into facing without equivocation the great constitutional issues before them. Hyde and the younger members, not knowing their Charles, would have sought lawyer-like to tread daintily with plea and counter-plea, but when the King's secretary announced that Charles would accept nothing save on his stipulated terms they were taken aback and the House adjourned for the day in concern and uncertainty.

That there should be such a questioning of the wishes of a king was to Charles a deep affront. Soon after dawn next day (May 5th) he sent Parliament packing again, rating them like so many naughty schoolboys, after a session of only three weeks.

Even Clarendon says: "No man could imagine what offence the Commons had given," and the nation received news of the dissolution with disappointment and anger. But some of the old hands were undismayed. Indeed, the dark and gloomy features of Oliver St. John were alight with joy. Meeting young Edward Hyde, downcast, afterwards, he said cheerfully:

"All's well. Things must be worse before they can be better."

VII. "THE WORD OF A KING"

The day after the dissolution Hampden and some others were arrested. With the object of finding some evidence against him, not only his chambers but also his pockets were rifled. Nothing treasonable was to be found in his rooms, however, and on his person all that was found, as is shown on a list that still exists, was a letter from Bishop Williams and certain confused notes on Parliamentary business written in several paper books with black lead. John Williams, Bishop of Lincoln, in prison and in disgrace, was Hampden's cousin, and he had begged Hampden to exert his prestige to secure his liberty to sit in the House of Lords, but Hampden sent him only a reply that was a masterpiece of polite refusal.[24]

At the Court there was despair and rage. Strafford, who was fond of penal metaphor, was insistent that the Scots must be "whipped back." He offered, so it was credibly reported, to provide an army of 10,000 Irishmen for reducing them — 10,000 Popish savages to subjugate England to the King's obedience. The horror of the very notion, whether really intended or merely breathed, was sufficient to start in Englishmen the black hatred of Strafford which was not to be assuaged but by his blood. Moreover, the Queen, with a folly that on the most generous basis is to be explained only by her complete failure to understand English public opinion, took the mad step of appealing for money and troops to the Pope himself. Charles also, with scarcely less folly, made a move to appeal likewise to the most hated of enemies — Spain. No

---

[24] Cal. S. P. Dom. 1640, 152; Tanner MSS., lxxxviii, 116; the Williams correspondence is in Lipscomb, ii, 237.

wonder patriotic Englishmen and Scotsmen were but the more incensed.

In this year, at a date not exactly known, Hampden married again. The lady was Letitia, the young widow of Sir Thomas Vachell, of Cowley or Coley House, Reading, and daughter of Sir Francis Knollys.

Hampden now remained in London, to be at the heart of things. They were feverish days, full of comings and goings and of rumours of plots. The mob was out against Laud, the prisons were broken open, the Queen was insulted. There were hangings, whippings, imprisonments. Hampden was in frequent conference with Pym and the other Parliamentary leaders, whose eyes were all on the Scots. There is reason to suppose that it was Hampden who now proposed that the Scots should be invited to make common cause with them, and endeavour to secure the reassembly of Parliament, for the Scots were already beginning "to ask for more," and very soon England was to do likewise. A letter, of which Hampden was one of the authors, was addressed to them and signed by the leading opposition peers — Saye, Bedford, Brooke, Essex, Warwick, and Mandeville — in which they and their friends in the Commons pledged themselves to stand by the Scots in a Parliamentary way. A further letter to which the peers' signatures were forged by Lord Savile promised the Scots armed assistance if they would march, and on this they acted. Leslie and his Covenanters in determined mood took arms, donned the blue bonnets of their faith, raised the standard of St. Andrew, and crossed the border on August 20th, 25,000 strong, with the intention of obliging the King to summon Parliament.

The invasion was charged by royalist writers directly to Hampden's instigation, and the poet Sir John Denham makes him say:

> the plot
> Was Saye's and mine together.

There is no evidence, however, that he had yet counselled any resort to arms.[25]

With haste Charles again turned his face to the North, and Strafford went with him. But, with as pitiable an army as was ever press-ganged into unwilling service, he was again unable to face the well-found Scots, who, after a trivial skirmish at Newburn-on-the-Tyne, continued unimpeded their march into England. The news of their progress was received at Westminster with rejoicing. Pym and St. John prepared a petition, signed by twelve peers and presented by them to the King at York, urging him to call a Parliament and setting out grievances, and a similar petition was signed by 10,000 citizens of London. Charles was desperately at a loss. Once more he was able by treaty to stay the advance of the Scots, but it was to cost him £850 a day, and if that payment stopped the Scots would march on London. The only power that could find the money was the English Parliament. With wrath and shame in his heart, Charles ordered Parliament to meet again on November 3rd.

Hampden, who was now putting all his energies into the cause he had at heart, saw that in the new House that cause must be represented by the best possible men — men of resolution and integrity. He therefore, it is said, persuaded Pym

---

[25] Cal. S. P. Dom. 1640, 652; Nugent, i, 296; *Mr. Hampden's Speech Against Peace, The Rump*, i, 9; Gardner, *History of England*, ix, 231, x, 130.

to an unusual enterprise. He proposed that the two should undertake an intensive election campaign on horseback. Pym, now grown very fat and unused to much riding, gallantly agreed, and the two set out for a hard forty days. It was the first party election campaign in history. Throughout October they rode from county to county, past stubbled fields and gathered orchards, through beech woods bearing still their russet shrouds full leaved against autumnal frost, through pastures veiled with the chill low mists of dawn and dusk. They splashed through miry autumn roads and clattered across market-squares, addressing the electors, calling upon the leading gentry, exhorting them to send to Parliament the men who would defend the purity of the Gospel, the sanctity of their ancient liberties and the security of their possessions. Their work was not in vain.

The new Parliament, to be known to history as the Long Parliament, began its twenty years' life on November 3rd, 1640. It was the most fateful assembly in the history of English politics, "destined," in Macaulay's typical words, "to every extreme of fortune, to empire and to servitude, to glory and to contempt." It was a brilliant gathering. The Speaker was William Lenthall, who was to prove the first of the great Speakers in the modern tradition. Hampden's gloomy cousin St. John was there, and so was his fellow-Templar Selden. Among its younger members was the chivalrous Falkland and the boyish Edward Hyde, observant, pink-cheeked, fair-haired, afterwards to become famous as the historian Lord Clarendon. Pym, massive, shaggy, genial, autocratic, was the acknowledged captain-general of the popular forces. But even he had not the same renown and prestige as his chief-of-staff, John Hampden.

"When this Parliament began," says Clarendon in a glowing tribute, "the eyes of all men were fixed on him as their *patriae pater*, and the pilot that must steer the vessel through the tempests and the rocks which threatened it. And I am persuaded that his power and interest at that time was greater to do good or hurt than any man of his rank hath had in any time; for his reputation for honesty was universal, and his affections seemed so publicly guided that no corrupt or private ends could bias them." Like Pym, he was now filled with a determined singleness of purpose, and was moving, insensibly as yet, to the idea of a resort to arms. For the first year of this Parliament, says Clarendon, Hampden "seemed rather to moderate and soften the violent and distempered humours than to inflame them; but wise and dis-passioned men discerned plainly enough that the moderation proceeded from prudence, and observation that the time was not ripe, rather than that he approved of the moderation."

The leaders of the Parliamentary causes in the two Houses formed a sort of "shadow cabinet," a group of the leading men in their cause who met in secret, sometimes at Lord Saye's castle of Broughton in Oxfordshire; sometimes at the house of John's son-in-law, Richard Knightly, at Fawsley, in Northamptonshire, where there was a secret room and a private printing press, and where also John was able to see his much-loved daughter Elizabeth; sometimes at the younger Vane's country mansion at Hampstead. They had also a most efficient intelligence service, their agents being in every tavern and in the inner circles of the Court itself, as we shall presently see.

Under this determined leadership the new House, as soon as it met, launched an immediate assault with horse, foot and guns upon the strongholds that had so long frowned upon them. They were at last in power and the King was helpless to restrain them. They acted with a swiftness and an energy that must be the envy of all Parliaments. They went straight for one of the key bastions and within a week had commenced impeachment proceedings against Strafford himself. Laud also they impeached and lodged fast in the Tower, and they voted reparations to Burton, Prynne and the other mutilated victims of that regimen, who in their release were led in triumph through cheering streets. They abolished the historic Court of Star Chamber, the High Commission Court, and the Council of the North, which had become hateful to men as courts of religious and executive persecution rather than courts of justice. They swept away the scandal of monopolies. They passed a measure that Parliament must be summoned at least every three years, and another that this particular Parliament must not be dissolved without its own consent.

Ship money was one of the first matters that they tackled. On December 7th the Commons declared the judgment in Hampden's case to be "against the laws of the Realm, the right of property, the liberty of the subject, and contrary to former resolutions in Parliament and to the Petition of Right"; and early next year the Lords voted similarly. The judges who had concurred in the verdict were impeached and deprived of office. Finch himself was found guilty by impeachment for "soliciting, persuading and threatening the judges to deliver their opinion for the levying of ship money," together with other charges, but on the day sentence was to be passed he slipped down the Thames at dawn and escaped to Holland.

The Long Parliament was hardly a week old when Strafford advised the King to arrest Hampden, Pym and others on charges of treasonable correspondence with the Scots. Information of the purpose was brought to Pym by his intelligence service. He rose in the Commons, moved that the doors be locked, and by a stroke of tactical genius turned the tables by there and then retaliating with a resolution for the impeachment of Strafford himself. Hampden, who had drawn up the articles of impeachment of Buckingham, was on November 11th appointed with six others to do the like service for Strafford. It was quickly done, and John was also appointed one of the eight managers of the impeachment under the chairmanship of Bulstrode Whitelocke.

Much has been written of that famous trial, round which argument has raged for nearly 300 years. On grounds of law there were no charges on which Strafford could be condemned to suffer the last penalty of human life. But neither had there been any in the calculated death of Eliot, whose "blood still cries either for vengeance or repentance." Hampden's earlier biographers have sometimes tried to excuse his part in the affair, but to shirk it suggests a failure to appraise the situation. The failures of ministers are not commonly due to felony or treason, but the bludgeons of impeachment and attainder were the only weapons that Parliament then possessed for getting rid of a bad or unpopular minister. The action against Strafford was political, not merely legal. If Black Tom be not destroyed, Parliament would be itself by him destroyed. Not punishment, but fear. Not the law, but the cause. "Stone dead hath no fellow," said even the gentle Essex.

The trial began in William Rufus's venerable Hall of Westminster on March 22nd, 1641, and Strafford, racked with pain, dressed in deep black and wearing the George, faced his accusers with unflinching courage and put forward an able defence. The tide was running much in his favour, when news of a design to march the army upon London and seize the Tower — a plot betrayed by the odious George Goring — bent the Commons to a grimmer purpose. If the impeachment were to go awry, as well it might, there was yet the more deadly weapon of a Bill of Attainder.

Hampden and Pym strove against the desperate proposal, which came from the violent mind of the hot-tempered Hazelrig. They desired to stand by legal process and to avoid a quarrel with the House of Lords, with whom a serious difference arose over the attainder. Attainder was condemnation to death without trial, and Hampden urged that the prisoner must not be judged without a hearing of his defence. The House was clamant that the attainder should go forward, but Hampden, intervening once more with convincing effect in the debate of April 16th, was able to secure a compromise by pointing out that the two processes could well go on together. Let the impeachment proceed, and let Strafford's Counsel be heard.

"The Bill now depending," he said, "doth not tie us to go by bill. Our Counsel hath been heard; ergo, in justice we must hear his."

So it was agreed, and Strafford's Counsel was heard the next day, and a quarrel with the Lords averted. But the tide of the Commons' demand was too strong to be stemmed, and, largely under the hand of St. John, the Bill of Attainder went forward to its inevitable result by a majority of 204 to 59. It is noteworthy that Pym and Falkland both voted with St. John; Hampden abstained.[26]

There remained still the consents of the Lords and the King before the Bill could be an Act. The Lords needed for persuasion only the revelation of a new army plot, of another plot to land a French army, and of a third for the escape of

---

[26] Rushworth, *Trial of Strafford*, 3, 14, 20, 22, 33, 40, 45; Forster, *Grand Remonstrance*, ed. 1860, 133, 141; Sanford, 337; Gardiner, *History*, ix, 329, 337; Verney, *Notes on the Long Parliament*, 50.

Strafford; for even the most upright, the most just, and the most moderate of men, and the most devoted of the King's supporters were stirred to the deepest misgiving by Queen Mary's mischievous designs for the use of force or for foreign invasion.

But the King?

The King had more than once assured Strafford that he would never sign the death warrant of his friend and trusted minister. "I cannot satisfy myself in honour or conscience," he wrote to him, "without assuring you now, in the midst of your troubles, that, upon the word of a King, you shall not suffer in life, honour or fortune." But now the mobs were out, howling round Whitehall for Strafford's head. To his last appeal for mercy for his servant Parliament was as pitiless as he himself had been to Eliot, and, wrung with agony, distracted by the contrary advices given him by the bishops and by the judges, tortured by a vision of his loved queen, who more than anyone else had been responsible for this sorry day, being torn to pieces by the angry people, he bowed his head to the storm and the word of a King was drowned in the shouts of that frenzied wind. Strafford was beheaded on Tower Hill on May 12th, preserving to the last his fine courage and his pride.

VIII. THE FIVE MEMBERS

But if Parliament was virtually at one on many of these matters, there came a sharp cleavage over attempts to abolish the episcopacy and to exclude the bishops from the House of Lords. Hampden as a representative Puritan had become an opponent of the bishops' government of the Church. "They who conversed nearly with him," says Clarendon, "found him growing with a dislike of the ecclesiastical government of the Church, yet most believed it rather a dislike of some churchmen, and of some introducements of theirs, which he apprehended might disquiet the public peace." On most Church matters — the impeachment of several bishops, the abolition of Laud's innovations in ritual, the exclusion of the bishops from the House of Lords (rejected by the Lords themselves) — Hampden found support from all sides of the House; but when the Root and Branch petitions came forward in December, 1640, signed by 15,000 Londoners and calling for the abolition of episcopacy altogether, there began gradually a breach in the ranks of the Commons. Hampden strongly supported the petitions, as well as the resulting Bill, but Falkland, Hyde, Selden and others — not for religious reasons, but because they saw that it must lead to a democratic tearing down of immemorial secular things — began to draw away from their allies. Lord Digby, the exquisite and perfumed favourite of the Queen, had already gone.

"I am sorry," Hampden said of Falkland, "to find a noble Lord here has changed his opinion since the time the last Bill to this purpose passed the House, for he then thought it a good Bill, but now he thinks it an ill one."

"Truly," retorted Falkland, "I was persuaded at that time by the worthy gentleman who has spoken to believe many things which I have since found to be untrue, and therefore I have changed my opinion in many particulars, as well to things as to persons."

It marked the end of Hampden's friendship with the tragic young lord and the beginning of the formation of a constitutional royalist party, which found much support in the country. The Commons, if they executed some valuable work, were in a great hurry. After their long suppression they were in a high fever of reform, inflamed by the bad faith of Charles's plots to overthrow them by force or to undermine them by guile, and they struck down constitutional ninepins with such rapidity that a good deal of moderate opinion was taken aback. They were not without their moments of panic, and the creak of a board aroused memories of Guy Fawkes, sending members scuttling out of the House. The air was thick with rumours of plots.

The new resistance, however, served only to stiffen the attitude of Pym and Hampden, to drive them farther to the Left, and to hurry them to the idea that an appeal to arms was inevitable. Charles was alternately appearing to propitiate the Commons and endeavouring to stab them in the back by foolish intrigues for their overthrow. There was the first dim notion of a responsible ministry. He made St. John Solicitor-General. He appears to have considered appointing Pym Chancellor of the Exchequer, and Hampden perhaps Secretary of State; Hampden's own ambition for office, however, was to be governor of the Prince of Wales, so that he might imbue the Prince with "principles suitable to what should be established as laws."[27]

---

[27] Cal. S. P. Dom., 1641-3, 53, 63; Warwick, 242.

Pym and Hampden, however, knew their Charles too well. *Timeo Danaos…* Charles, continuing still to regard Parliament as an enemy to be overcome and having no scruples as to the means of doing so, persisting still in intrigues that he knew not how to conduct and in force that he knew not how to employ, was at that very time scheming to turn the Scots, who were still in arms, against the English. He visited Scotland in August, 1641, yielded to Edinburgh's every demand, attended kirk, and lavished titles and favours on the Earl of Argyll and other Scottish leaders. After all, he was a Scot himself.

Parliament was perturbed. It was the best scheme that Charles had yet employed, and it looked like succeeding. The two Houses therefore, acting for the first time independently of the Crown, appointed Hampden, Nathaniel Fiennes, and four others to act as a commission in Scotland, ostensibly to conclude a treaty with the Scots, but, equally important, to keep an eye on the King. Hampden and his colleagues arrived in Edinburgh two weeks after Charles, and although the King refused to recognise their attempt to usurp his functions as maker of treaties, they remained, and Hampden was able to despatch to the Commons early news of "The Incident." The first-hand knowledge he gained in Edinburgh of Charles's intrigues with the Scottish nobles led him to distrust the King more than ever.[28]

Then came news of new carnage in Ireland, the Irish Catholics murdering thousands of Protestants with a refinement of ferocity that revolted all parties in England. There was the greatest alarm, and Hampden, having urged the King to return to England, took leave of Fiennes and his fellow-commissioners and rode back alone through the sharp

---

[28] L. J., iv, 372, 401 and v, 398; Historical MSS. Commission, Fourth Report, 102.

November frosts and the gathering moorland mists on the long road to Westminster.

He arrived back in time for the Grand Remonstrance, and his presence was to be singularly effective. That wearisome document, important as the first conscious appeal to public opinion, received John's full support. He considered it wholly true in substance and a very necessary vindication of Parliament. It was a recital, in 206 paragraphs, of the misgovernment of the reign, but, although there was a general concurrence, portions of it relating to Church government excited the active opposition of a large group in the Commons, particularly the group, headed by Lord Falkland and Edward Hyde, that was now turning in favour of the King. On November 22nd, as the fog crept up out of the Thames, there took place a critical debate. The House sat for fourteen hours and the debate lasted far into the night. Candles were lit. The debate grew acrimonious. The Remonstrance was carried by only eleven votes, and when Hyde and Geoffrey Palmer demanded that a protest against its printing should be recorded on behalf of the minority, tumult arose. Hands went to swords. Then it was that John Hampden's quiet authority and his resourcefulness in a debating crisis averted what looked like certain bloodshed. Says Warwick:

> I thought that we had, all sat in the valley of the shadow of death; for we, like Joab's and Abner's men, had caught at each others locks and sheathed our swords in each other's bowels, had not the sagacity and great calmness of Mr. Hampden by a short speech prevented it.

Dryly reminding Palmer that he could not know other men's minds, he persuaded the House to postpone further discussion until their tempers had been calmed by sleep, and at four o'clock of that November morning the Commons streamed wearily out into the night, wrapping their cloaks about their necks against the clinging mist.[29] Cromwell, on the way out, remarked to Falkland:

> Had the Remonstrance been rejected I would have sold all I possess next morning and never seen England more, and I know that there were other honest men of the same resolution.

London was now in a state of the greatest excitement. The army plot and the plots for foreign invasion had men's nerves on edge. The mobs were out. With cries of "No bishops!" "No popish lords!" they taunted the officers outside Whitehall Palace, they swarmed around Westminster, invaded Westminster Hall and harried the bishops and others on their way to Parliament. The Houses asked Charles to provide a guard, which had recently been taken away, but he would do no more than "engage unto you solemnly the word of a King that the security of all and every one of you from violence, is, and shall ever be, as much our care as the preservation of us and our children." Those words were written on December 31st, 1641.

The Parliamentary leaders remained deeply suspicious of the Queen. The meddlesome folly by which she plotted violence or schemed for military intervention from abroad, and even from the Pope himself, did nothing but mischief to her husband's cause, and now Pym and Hampden dared that even she should be impeached. The Court was soon aware of the intention. The King, incensed at this audacity, and bearing in mind how Parliament had forestalled Strafford's intention of

---

[29] Warwick, 202; Verney, *Notes of the Long Parliament*, 124; Gardiner, *History of England*, x, 77 and note.

arresting their leaders by striking their own blow at him first, determined to imitate their example. Their leaders should be themselves impeached.

On January 3rd, 1642, the Attorney-General was despatched to the House of Lords, and there he preferred formal charges of high treason against Hampden, Pym, Denzil Holles, Hazelrig, William Strode, and Lord Mandeville.[30] The charges against them were of having aspersed the King and his government, encouraged the Scots to invade England, raised tumult, levied war against the King and subverted the government. The Sergeant-at-Arms was sent to arrest them, but the Commons refused to give up their members, ordering them instead to attend daily in their places to answer any legal charge brought against them. Officers were sent by the King to seal up the chambers of the members, but Lords and Commons alike voted this step to be a breach of privilege, and the unfortunate officers who had performed the duty were arrested.

Then, the next day, says Mr. John Buchan, "came folly on folly." There was some case against the accused, but Charles's wrath and impatience, spurred by the passion of the Queen and the intemperance of Digby, were such that he could not stay for the decencies of proper procedure. Forgetting his majesty, forgetting the promise he had given four days before "on the word of a King" that all and every one of the Members should be secure from violence, he assumed the office of a constable. He would himself "pull the rogues out by the ears." In the afternoon of the 4th he set out by coach from Whitehall for St. Stephen's with an armed force of about 400 men. He alighted in New Palace Yard. He walked up Westminster Hall.

---

[30] Edward Montague, Lord Kimbolton in his own right and afterwards Earl of Manchester.

At the southern end, outraging the constitutional privilege of the House (for a King may not pass within the door of the Commons), he strode into the Chamber, accompanied by the young Elector Palatine, the soldiers crowding round the door with threats and jeers at the Members, with pistols cocked and with cries of "Fall On!" As the King entered the Members rose, uncovered, but said not a word.

"By your leave, Mr. Speaker," he said, "I must for a time borrow your chair."

He shot a glance towards Pym's usual seat. Pym was not there. Neither were Hampden and the others. The King demanded to know where they were, but there was a dead silence.

"I must have them wheresoever I find them," he said, and paused, but the stillness was unbroken.

"Is Mr. Pym here?" There was still no answer.

"Is Mr. Holles here?" Silence.

Turning then to Speaker Lenthall, the King asked specifically of him where the five members were. Lenthall returned the famous answer:

"May it please your Majesty, I have neither eyes to see nor tongue to speak in this place, but as the House is pleased to direct me, whose servant I am."

"Well," replied Charles, his gaze again going carefully along the benches. "I see the birds are flown. I do expect from you that you shall send them unto me as soon as they return hither. If not, I will seek them myself, for their treason is most foul. But I assure you, on the word of a King, I never did intend any force."

With that he strode from the Chamber, angry, frustrated and fatally compromised. The Commons of England had but by a hair's-breadth escaped massacre, for the ruffianly soldiers, led by such scoundrels as Captain David Hide, were itching to do butcher's work. The orderly D'Ewes testified his state of mind by going at once to his lodgings and making his will.

Hampden and his four accused colleagues of the Commons had indeed escaped in the nick of time. The Queen, as soon as she had persuaded Charles to his mad purpose, had rashly revealed it to her confidante, Lady Carlisle, and that dangerous lady at once passed the information on to the Earl of Essex. The accused members had slipped out of the House even as Charles was on his way from Whitehall. They escaped by the river and took refuge in the friendly City, where they found safe hiding in a house in Coleman Street.

Charles sought them there next day, and in person demanded their surrender from the aldermen in the Guildhall. Not a finger was lifted to obey, and the crowd pressed round his carriage with shouts of resentment as he returned. To the Houses' cry for help the City made a ready response and appointed Phillip Skippon, the stalwart commander of the Honourable Artillery Company, to provide a Parliamentary guard from the trained bands of London.

Charles had made the worst of all tactical mistakes: he had attempted force and failed, and a few days later, hearing that the five members were to be returned in triumph to Westminster, the writ for their arrest unheeded, he quitted London, never to return until he was led back to face the scaffold.

Hampden and his friends made a triumphal return from the City to Westminster by the water, escorted by a great number of citizens and seamen in boats and barges, with guns and flags, "braying as they passed by Whitehall," and with Skippon's trained bands guarding the approaches to the House. Among his own people of Buckinghamshire the news of

John's attempted arrest and impeachment was received with anger, and Westminster now witnessed one of the most remarkable spontaneous demonstrations of loyalty and affection that has been accorded to a politician. Four thousand gentlemen and freeholders of the county mounted and marched to London to support him, each wearing in his hat a copy of the recent protestation of the Commons. They brought two petitions: the one to Parliament, offering their service and declaring they were resolved to live and die in the just defence of the privileges of the Commons, the other to the King himself, declaring that they had ever had good cause to confide in the loyalty of John Hampden, and attributing the charges made against him to the malice of his enemies.

On February 6th the impeachment proceedings were formally dropped.[31]

---

[31] Rushworth, iv, 473, 487; *Nicholas Papers*, 62; C. J., ii, 367.

IX. THE FIRST MUSTER

Hampden emerged from this new experience with purpose still firmer set. His nature and carriage, says Clarendon, now seemed much "fiercer" than before. He was remarkable for his "close, thin lips and his very vigilant eyes." He spoke "very snappishly" to Hyde, remarking tartly that at least he now knew who were his friends. It was the parting of the ways, and on January 20th, when the Commons were considering an answer to a conciliatory message from the King, it was Hampden who struck in to demand that the King should place the Tower of London and other forts, together with the militia, into the hands of such men as Parliament should approve. It was a thing unheard of, but Charles's inevitable dissent resulted in the far more hostile Militia Ordinance, by which, ignoring the King's passionate refusal, the Houses empowered the counties to levy troops for the Parliamentary cause, and Hampden at once threw himself into the enforcement of the Ordinance in his own county.[32]

Then came the first acts of war. Skippon was ordered to besiege the Tower, and Charles, with all London lost to him, rode north, to secure the important fortress of Hull, where was situated the greatest arsenal of the kingdom and where the Queen had planned to disembark foreign troops. He found it held by Sir John Hotham, newly appointed to its charge by Parliament. He attempted to enter with a force of horsemen, but the gates were shut in his face. Both sides then openly armed themselves for the fight. Hyde, Falkland, Sir John

---

[32] Carlyle, *Cromwell's Letters and Speeches*, iii, 65; C. J., ii, 389; Sanford, 475; Stowe MSS., 188, fols. 3 and 5.

Culpepper and some sixty other royalist sympathisers in the Commons quitted Westminster, and soon the first blood was shed at Manchester.

But at the very beginning of hostilities the King suffered one grievous and irrecoverable loss, for the whole of the navy, which had been so much the object of his care and the symbol of his pride, but which loathed the royal service with a profound loathing, declared for Parliament almost to a man. Without that significant turn of fortune the Parliamentary cause would probably have been doomed from the outset. In July, 1642, Hampden's friend, the jovial and adventurous Earl of Warwick, was appointed by Parliament to command the fleet, and throughout the wars the seas were held secure for that cause, save for the depredations of a few royalist privateers.

Hampden's first revolutionary duty came when Parliament appointed him its Deputy-Lieutenant for Buckinghamshire, and in June he attended a meeting of militia officers at Aylesbury. He was active in every direction, urging the Parliamentary cause by writing and by voice wherever he had influence, and winning nearly everywhere an enthusiastic response. He was nominated also to the Committee of Public Safety that Parliament appointed on July 4th. Since the militia was not enough, Parliament authorised the raising of an army of 10,000 and appointed the Earl of Essex Lord-General of the Parliamentary forces. Three other main armies were also presently raised — the Northern Army under old Lord Fairfax, the Army of the Eastern Counties Association under Lord Manchester, and the Army of the associated South-Eastern Counties under Sir William Waller, "William the Conqueror," as he was soon to be called. There were also numerous local forces. Hampden himself undertook to raise a regiment of

1,000 foot at his own charge from his native Buckinghamshire, while Arthur Goodwin undertook the like duty for the county cavalry, and both were appointed to the rank of colonel. Hampden also interested himself actively in the scheme for the plantation of Ireland, and subscribed £1,000 towards it.

By the irony of history he held the first muster of his men in that same place where so soon he was to receive his death-wound, Chalgrove Field, midway between Henley and Oxford, fourteen miles from his mansion of Great Hampden.[33] With him was his eldest son, John, whom he appointed a captain. Colonel Hampden was received with enthusiasm, and the parishes and hundreds, often with their clergy at their head, assembled at their market-places and marched forth to join the ensign that bore the ancient device of the Hampdens — *Vestigia nulla retrorsum.* Motley in appearance, their arms were yet more so, for each man brought such weapons as he had, even strange antique cross-bows and brown bills that had hung on their walls since the Wars of the Roses.

> 'Tis time to leave the books in dust,
> And oil the unused armour's rust,
> Removing from the wall
> The corselet of the hall.

Each colonel dressed his regiment in a colour of his own choosing, and Hampden's Greencoats were to become famous in the pleasant lanes and villages of England that were now to become battlefields. He set about equipping his men with the pikes and muskets, the corselets and helmets of the day, and drilling began at once.[34]

---

[33] Warwick, 239; Clarendon, vii, 82; à Wood, 61.

[34] It will be left to the memoir on Skippon to deal a little more fully with the equipment and battle formations of the day.

From Cromwell's famous conversation with Hampden at a later date it has generally been supposed that the great commander's criticism of the quality of the Parliamentary troops was directed, in part at least, against Hampden's own regiment; but this was not so.

"Your troopers," Cromwell said, "are mostly old decayed serving-men and tapsters, and such kind of fellows, and their troopers are gentleman's sons, younger sons and persons of quality. Do you think that the spirits of such base and mean fellows will ever be able to encounter gentlemen who have honour and courage and resolution in them? You must get men of spirit; and take it not ill what I say — I know you will not — of a spirit that is likely to go on as far as gentlemen will go. Or else you will be beaten still."[35]

Cromwell was thus comparing cavalry and cavalry. Hampden's men were infantry, and Sir Charles Firth describes Hampden's Buckinghamshires as "one of the best regiments in the Parliamentary service." As Gardiner says, it is a mistake to attribute to Cromwell alone the sole credit of an attempt to recruit the regiments from men of piety; what distinguished Cromwell was the measure in which he succeeded. Nevertheless, it is true that the best infantry in the Parliamentary service, until 1645, were Skippon's London trained bands.

Apart from Rupert's gentlemen-riders, however, there was little difference between the rival troops, but between their respective commanders there was all the world. Essex, the Parliamentary commander, was no man of war. Gentle and humane, "Old Robin" had but the slenderest military talent

---

[35] Carlyle, *Cromwell's Letters and Speeches*, iii, 64-66; the "your" is of course not personal to Hampden. The often-used "troops" should without doubt be "troopers."

and he desired nothing more of life than to smoke his pipe the day long. He owed his position as generalissimo more to prestige than to such military experience as he had had, for there were few men in the whole country who had had any military training, and there had been no standing army in England since the time of Henry VIII. Essex was competent enough in action and lacked nothing in personal courage, but his dilatoriness and his reluctance to strike a decisive stroke, springing from the persistent hope in his simple breast that the King might yet be persuaded rather than forced, was a main reason for the prolongation of the war.

Prince Rupert of the Palatinate, whom Charles, with his incurable instinct for choosing the wrong man, presently appointed the royalist commander, was a very different man. He was the son of the Elector Frederick and Elizabeth Stuart, and the brother of the then dispossessed Elector. Twenty-two years old, he was a splendid young animal — of tall and strapping stature, dark-haired, handsome and imperious of mien, a splendid horseman, fearless to the point of folly. Wherever he rode he was conspicuous by his scarlet cloak, his collar of silver lace, his black charger and his white dog "Boy." He had also a keen and enterprising intellect, and was a talented artist and an early voyager in the dawn of science. But it was not till time and the bitterness of experience had worn away the rude edges of his upbringing that he realised the promise of his better faculties, for in these early years his romantic presence carried all the blemishes of the blustering tradition of the Germanic wars in which he had been bred. He did great harm to his uncle's cause. He was overbearing and insolent, and he caused irreparable offence to the older men of honourable family and good breeding in Charles's camp whom he ruthlessly shouldered aside. Ignorant of English politics, he rode rough-shod over the best instincts of Englishmen, seeking to make war in the continental method as though he were in an enemy country, and in the rape of Bolton, the sack of Leicester and the slaughter of Brentford, he acquired among the peaceful inhabitants of the countryside an evil reputation for plunder and devastation.

In a resort to arms such ruthlessness might have been excused if Rupert had been a good general. But the truth is, in spite of his romantic tradition, that he was a thoroughly bad one. He never won a single major action, and he was quite incapable of controlling the combined operations of a whole army. He forgot all but his own mad cavalry charge. It is the truth that he was nothing more than a dashing young horseman.

Thus began a war that was soon to rend the kingdom, a war that divided father from son and brother from brother, that taxed the conscience of many an honourable man who knew not where his duty lay. The tradition of monarchy was deep-seated in the people. From the beginnings of history they had been bred to the idea of loyalty to the King's person and to believe that to raise arms against him was black treason. It was from tradition, heritage and instinct that thousands of Charles's subjects

> offered free from stain
> Courage and faith; vain faith and courage vain.

Even the Parliamentary forces at the beginning maintained the fiction that they were levying war not against the King's person but against his evil counsellors. The military objective of the Parliamentary forces was "to rescue" the person of the King "out of the hands of those desperate persons who were about him." The banner of the Earl of Stamford, for example, commander of one of the Parliamentary forces, bore the device: "For Religion, King and Country." Hampden himself to the end — even, it is said, on his death-bed — professed loyalty to him and prayed that God might send him good counsel. The *Weekly Intelligencer*, published just after John's death,[36] reports the following utterance of his:

> Perish may that man and his posterity that shall not deny himself in the greatest part of his fortune (rather than that the King shall want) to make him both potent and beloved at home, and terrible to his enemies abroad, if he will be pleased to leave those evil counsels about him, and take the wholesome advice of his great counsel the Parliament.

It was natural, then, that doubting folk at least should side with their liege lord, but so too did many who thought his cause bad. Sir Edmund Verney, Hampden's friend and near neighbour in Buckinghamshire, who in politics sided with Parliament, but who had held the office of Knight Marshal for many years and whom Charles appointed as his standard-bearer, said to Edward Hyde:

"For my part I do not like the quarrel, and do heartily wish that the King would yield and consent to what they desire." But he added with prophetic insight: "I have eaten his bread and served him near thirty years, and will not do so base a thing as to forsake him, and choose rather to lose my life — which I am sure I shall do — to preserve and defend those things which are against my conscience to preserve and defend."

He was indeed killed in the first battle.

So, too, Lord Robert Spencer wrote to his wife from the King's camp:

---

[36] June 27th to July 4th, 1643.

I am much unsatisfied with the proceedings here, nor is there wanting daily handsome occasion to retire, were it not for grinning honour… If there could be an expedient found to solve the punctilio of honour, I would not continue here an hour.

He, also, fell under the royal standard.

John Hampden had no such doubts, and the long summer days were thronged with work. It is not necessary here to deal at length with the several minor actions in which he was engaged, for they were unimportant and the facts are sometimes uncertain. Moreover it is not as a soldier that Hampden was important, for destiny denied him that opportunity. His physical courage we may take for granted, for it was amply attested by friend and foe alike.

What is more important is that from the first he was the flame of the Puritan cause. "Without question," says Clarendon, "when he first drew his sword he threw away the scabbard." He set his hand to his new work as a soldier with an ardour and an impatience that were something new in his character, and which might not have been expected of the patient Parliamentarian. In the dilatory movements which manifested on both sides the reluctance of Englishmen to make war upon Englishmen, Hampden's was from the first moment the spur that urged his own side to strike for a more swift and early victory. In Parliament, likewise, he resolutely opposed the peace proposals that continued all the time to be discussed, for both he and Pym were undeceived by the King's willingness to negotiate, knowing well that he had no intention of making any peace but the peace of victory and that he was merely playing for time while he gathered more strength. Both sides, indeed, put their demands too high.

Hampden's first act of hostility was on August 16th to seize the person of the Earl of Berkshire, who had come to Watlington to raise troops for the King, and when the Earl pleaded that he had done nothing, Hampden made the good reply that he "was therefore sent to prevent him." His baptism of fire came when he joined in the march to relieve Coventry, which had shut its gates against the King, and he bore himself well, as the King looked on, in the action on August 23rd, when the royalists were dispersed. He then marched his Greencoats to join the main body of the Parliamentary forces which were mustering about Northampton and Rugby, and waited there patiently during a long period of inaction while the reluctant Essex still lingered in London. He was much put out by the indiscipline of the Parliamentary infantry, who, he said, were making themselves as odious to the countryside as the cavaliers, and urged the Lord-General to lose no more time.[37]

At last on September 9th "Old Robin" reluctantly left London, taking with him not only his pipe but also his coffin and his winding sheet as emblems of a heart bowed down. Charles did not stay at Nottingham to be "rescued," moving westwards to gather reinforcements from Wales. Essex followed. At Powick Bridge Hampden's friend Nathaniel Fiennes was scattered in a narrow lane by the first of Rupert's furious charges, but the main armies made no attempt to meet, and Essex, loitering at Worcester, allowed Charles to gather his reinforcements at Shrewsbury and move upon London.

Then had Essex to put on all speed, and, his heavy guns impeding his progress in the miry roads, he went on without them and ordered Colonel Hampden with two regiments to

---

[37] Whitelocke, 62; Cal. S. P. Dom. 1641-3, 382; Sanford, 519; L. J., v, 321; Tanner MSS., lxii, 115, lxiii, 153.

escort them and make the best speed possible after the main body. The duty was fretful to Hampden, who thirsted for swift action. On October 18th he entered Stratford-on-Avon and drove off a royalist force that disputed possession of the bridge. On the 23rd, many hours behind the Lord-General, he heard the voice of guns break the afternoon silence beyond the village of Kineton ahead of him. Essex had overtaken Charles, and in the Vale of the Red Horse, between Banbury and Stratford, the battle of Edgehill had begun.

Impatiently, Hampden laboured forward. At length, when the afternoon was far gone, he saw scattered groups of horsemen flying towards him. They were Ramsay's cavalry, routed by the impetuous charge of Prince Rupert. Presently behind them came Rupert's cavaliers themselves, wasting their success by pursuing the flying Roundheads far beyond the scene of battle. Hampden brought his force into action, and by a few volleys checked the cavalier pursuit.

When Hampden arrived at last the battle was over, and the victory no man's. He found that, though the main bodies of the Roundhead cavalry had been routed on both wings, the infantry and the undefeated horsemen of Balfour and Stapleton had desperately engaged the King in front and flank and rear, so desperately that the King himself had been in personal danger, and there beside him his standard-bearer, the knightly Verney, had fulfilled his prophetic vision.

As night fell both sides had withdrawn apart exhausted, but next morning Hampden, who, says Mr. John Buchan, "was now the Rupert of the Parliamentary side," urged a renewal of the attack and condemned the retreat that was made upon Warwick. Thus Charles was enabled to secure Oxford, which he established as his headquarters, but his delay there enabled the Roundheads, marching by Northampton, to return to

London in time to protect it. For a time Hampden again attended Parliament, until the news came that Charles was now marching upon London and that Rupert, sweeping down the Thames valley, was plundering the countryside and striking terror into its pleasant townships. On November 12th Hampden heard that Rupert, bursting out of the dawn mist, had fallen upon Holles's London Redcoats and Brooke's Purplecoats in Brentford, and he called his own men to arms and hastened to their assistance. He saw in Brentford a bloody street battle, in which the Roundheads were fighting back even into the Thames and being there drowned. Hampden therefore counter-attacked with his Greencoats, and with pike and musket stood the charge of Rupert's horsemen to cover the retreat of Brooke and Holles. No more could be done, and Rupert, left in possession of the town, proceeded, royalist though it was, to sack it with his devastating thoroughness.

That night Hampden fell back towards London as, with all the capital roused, the trained bands streamed westward under Skippon to join the army of the Lord-General at Turnham Green. The next day he drew up his regiment among that great army of 24,000, and he watched the King, dressed all in white, with Rupert beside him in red, approach them and halt frustrated. London was saved, but Hampden was not content with that negative achievement and urged that the King's smaller army should now be attacked and defeated. Sir James Ramsay held Kingston bridge in the royalist rear with 3,000 horsemen, but the professional soldiers dissuaded Essex from allowing him to attack, and Hampden then urged that he should be allowed to assault the other wing by sweeping round through Acton. To this the Lord-General hesitatingly agreed, and Hampden advanced with some other troops. He had not gone far, however, when he saw Sir John Meyrick riding after him, his orange scarf flying. He brought an order for Hampden's recall, and Hampden turned back troubled and disappointed. Charles therefore retired safely to Oxford, and both sides settled down to a winter of organisation that was urgently necessary.[38]

It was a winter of intense activity for Hampden. His time was divided between the business of Parliament, the army, and his duties as Deputy-Lieutenant for his county. In Buckinghamshire money had to be raised as well as men; in Parliament the peace party had to be strenuously opposed; with the army training and equipping had to go on. He was constantly in the saddle, and the roads of Middlesex and Berkshire knew him as well as those of his own county. After the chill early morning debates at Westminster he would ride out to his own regiment at Windsor, and back again the same night for next morning's debate. In a squib directed against him, the royalist poet Denham puts these words into Hampden's mouth:

> Have I so often passed between
> Windsor and Westminster, unseen,
> And did myself divide
> To keep His Excellence in awe,
> And give the Parliament the law?
> For they knew none beside.

Hampden was indeed during these months the constant spur of the Parliamentary cause. Many spoke of him as the leader who should take the place of Essex, and it was believed in Oxford that this was actually to be done. The idea was not, however, seriously considered by the Parliamentary leaders themselves, for Brooke was a more likely name. Had it been so

---

[38] Whitelocke, 65, 66; *The Scots Design Discovered*, 1654, p. 66.

the war might have come to a swifter and happier conclusion. One is tempted to think, with Macaulay,[39] that "the military art is no very profound mystery, that its principles are the principles of plain common sense, and that a quick eye, a cool head and a stout heart will do more to make a general than all the diagrams of Jomini." His disapproval of the strategy and tactics of Essex, however, in no way diminished Hampden's loyalty to his commander, and at all times their relations were of the most friendly. It is clear that he was always very close to the Lord-General, and was often the mouthpiece by which Essex communicated orders, or by which reports were made of actions or undertakings, as shown, for example, in his letters to Arthur Goodwin on the expedition against Brill.[40]

These months also brought Hampden great personal sorrow. His eldest son, Captain John, died serving with his father's regiment. Died, too, his much-loved daughter Elizabeth Knightley. His friend and close comrade-in-arms, the gallant Lord Brooke, was killed by a chance shot from Lichfield Cathedral. His cousins Alexander Hampden and Edmund Waller brought shame to him by intriguing for the betrayal of his cause to the King. His cup was nearly full. The shadows of his life began to lengthen and he worked feverishly to accomplish his task before the day's light was gone.

The return of spring brought to Hampden fresh hopes of resolute action, and, deploring the waste of energy in minor actions, he "very earnestly insisted" that they should "strike at the root," which was Oxford. Essex, however, began the 1643 campaign with the siege of Reading, and at its capture Hampden led one of the advance forces, himself and Skippon making the first entry into the town.

---

[39] Essay on Nugent's Memorials.
[40] Carte MSS., ciii, 121, 123.

Sickness and mutiny then visited the army of Essex and crippled his movements, so that Queen Mary, "her she-majesty the generalissima," was allowed unhindered to enter Oxford with her treasure and munitions from the continent. Hampden returned to Parliament for a while, but was recalled to employ his unequalled prestige in pacifying the mutinous troops at Reading. He was also engrossed in the work of the counties' association, and on June 9th he wrote to his cousin Sir Thomas Barrington, the member for Colchester, exhorting him to stir up the county of Essex to provide men and money. It was his last recorded utterance.[41]

---

[41] Tanner MSS., lxii, 85; Egerton MSS., 2643, fol. 7

X. CHALGROVE FIELD

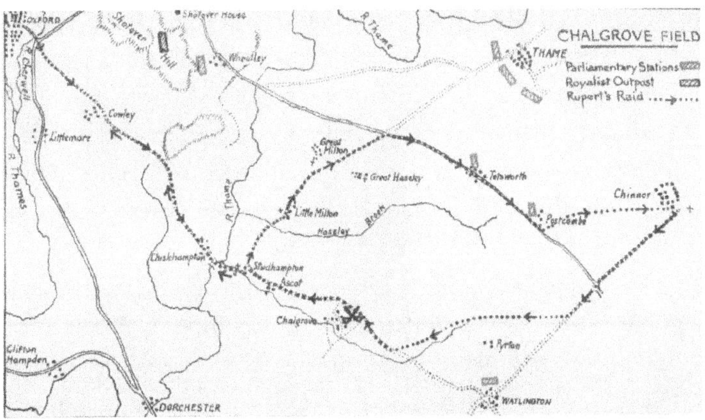

And now the last scene unfolds as Essex reached Thame, twelve miles from the King, on June 10th, 1643. It was Hampden's own country; every lane and every hamlet had been familiar to him since boyhood. From Thame the Lord-General put out detachments in the neighbouring villages against surprise — at Chinnor and Postcombe and Watlington and Wheatley. In the country round Watlington were Colonel Gunter's dragoons, with Captains Crosse and Sheffield. Wheatley, five miles from Oxford, gave command over the bridge on the direct line from the city to Thame, but, five miles to the south, there remained the bridge at Chislehampton, open to the swift sword of Rupert.

To John Hampden, as a child of that country and a hunter over its woods and meadows, it was plainer even than to others that a bold fox, raiding by the unguarded southern bridge, might create havoc among outlying coveys that were far too widely dispersed. He remonstrated to Essex, urging either that Chislehampton bridge should be held or that the scattered regiments should be drawn in. But neither thing was done, and so the army lay for some days.

On June 17th the fox stole out. Hearing, through Colonel John Urry, the odious triple-turncoat, that a convoy with £21,000 for Essex's troops was on the way from London to Thame, Rupert resolved to strike for the prize, and set out at four in the afternoon with a mixed force of nearly 2,000 to waylay it about Wycombe. In the summer evening he passed unimpeded over Chislehampton bridge. All through the night he rode, and at 2 a.m. he came upon a troop of Parliamentary horse asleep in their quarters at Postcombe. Half-naked and half-asleep, they were strung to his men's horses as captives. Then, still before dawn, he flew to the village of Chinnor and there fell upon the Bedfordshire dragoons. About fifty he shot or cut down and the remainder he captured.

The alarm that was thus given forced him to abandon his attempt on the convoy and, well satisfied with his raid, he turned for home.

Meanwhile, the hunter had lain that night in the Hare and Hounds Inn at Watlington, six miles away, and to him the news of the raid was brought in the early hours of the day. Hampden dressed hurriedly. This fox must not escape. The only way to its earth lay through Chislehampton, and well the hunter knew that road; if Rupert could be cut off at the bridge, or if he could be delayed till Essex's main army came up, he must be lost. Hampden resolved to pursue Rupert and to harry his retreat with such troops as it was possible to collect, and he accordingly despatched a horseman immediately to the Lord-General informing him of his purpose and requesting that a force might be sent out with all speed from Thame. His own

Greencoats were not with him, nor would infantry have been of much avail in a pursuit, but at Watlington lay Captain Sheffield's troop of Gunter's dragoons. He asked if they would go with him, and, receiving a ready assent, he made off, collecting also a few other troops. His friends tried to persuade him against the enterprise, but, "carried on by his fate," he paid no heed. The Roundheads, by the testimony of Rupert's own cavaliers, were to fight that day as Roundheads had never fought before.

At eight that Sunday morning, when the June sun was shining in a cloudless sky, he overtook Rupert outside the hamlet of Chalgrove, some three miles away. Already Rupert had been boldly engaged by Colonel Gunter's own troop of dragoons, but, with overwhelming numbers, he had thrown them off with their commander slain, and Hampden, as he came out upon Chalgrove Field, saw Gunter's horsemen retreating towards him. He immediately advanced to rally them, and, having now also been joined by Captain Crosse's troop, and other details, he assembled the whole mixed force and assumed command, for "he was of that universal authority that no officer paused in obeying him."

Rupert, greatly superior in numbers, stood to meet the new attack. Having ordered his infantry to hurry forward to Chislehampton and prepare an ambush, he drew up his cavalry behind the shelter of the hedges about Chalgrove Field, with pistols and carbines cocked against the coming charge. Colonel Hampden went straight for them. Putting himself at the head of Captain Crosse's troop, he charged.

Rupert held his fire. As the Roundheads swept up to the guarded hedgerows his horsemen flung a volley at them at short range, and then another. At the first discharge Hampden was struck. Two bullets lodged in his shoulder, shattering the bone and entering the body, and his arm fell useless to his side.

Then, says the chronicler, he was observed to turn about and "to ride off the field before the action was done, which he never used to do, with his head hanging down, and resting his hands upon the neck of his horse."

There remains an affecting tradition that as he rode faintly off the field he made first towards Edmund Simeon's house at Pyrton, whence Elizabeth had come as his bride twenty-four years before. It wanted but six days to the anniversary of that happy marriage in the little village church. Some of Rupert's cavalry being near, however, he turned his horse's head north-east towards Thame, where the main body of the army lay. The lark was mounting to the blue June heaven as he began his last ride. By the footpath across the stretched meadows of Great Hazeley he went, past knots of anxious country people, whose Sabbath sanctity had been so roughly shaken, and past farms where the milkmaids had but freshly filled their pails. At Hazeley Brook, he must either make a long detour by the road, or jump it. Summoning with set purpose his ebbing strength, Nugent tells us, he collected his horse, clapped spurs and cleared the leap.

He was not alone. Arthur Goodwin, they say, was with him now. So they rode on into Thame, passing for the last time the school where their life's friendship had begun. In great pain and almost fainting John was helped from his horse at the house of Ezekiel Browne[42] and taken within.

For six days he lingered in great pain. Besides the surgeons, he was attended by Dr. William Spurstowe, chaplain of his own Greencoats, and Arthur Goodwin was also beside him. Under the gathering clouds he still laboured for his cause. He

---

[42] Known, until recently, as the Greyhound Inn.

dictated advices to Parliament, urging yet a last time a more ardent enterprise in the conduct of the war, an advice with which Pym, angered by the hurt to his old friend, passionately agreed.

On June 24th, the anniversary of his wedding to Elizabeth Simeon, he said his last good-bye to Arthur, received the last sacrament, and sank into the last coma. Before he died he was visited by his old friend, Dr. Gyles, the rector of Chinnor, whom the King himself, learning of Hampden's wound from Sir Philip Warwick, had sent to offer the help of his own surgeons. But a few hours later John Hampden was dead.[43]

He was buried next day in his own church of Great Hampden, ten miles distant. His own regiment, with detachments of other troops, followed his coffin, on which his gilded helmet sat, with ensigns draped and all the ceremony of a soldier's last leave-taking. To the words of the 90th Psalm they lowered him into the good Buckingham earth, and to the hope of the 43rd they returned to the battlefield.

Arthur Goodwin stayed on at Great Hampden with little Richard Hampden, who at the age of twelve now succeeded his father and who was in due season to become William III's Chancellor of the Exchequer. On June 26th Goodwin wrote to his daughter, Lady Wharton, in words that again recall Hamlet.[44]

> Dear Jenny,
>
> I am now here at Hampden doing the last duty for the deceased owner of it, of whom every honest man hath a share in the loss, and therefore will likewise in the sorrow. All his thoughts and endeavours of his life was zealously in for this cause of God's, which he continued in all his sickness, even unto death. For all I can hear, the last words he spake was to

---

[43] Warwick, 240-1.
[44] J. Webb, *Civil War in Herefordshire*, i, 306.

me, though he lived six or seven hours after I came away as in a sleep. Truly, Jenny (and I know you may easily be persuaded to it), he was a gallant man, an honest man, an able man, and, take all, I know not to any man living second. God in mercy hath rewarded him…

AUTHORITIES FOR HAMPDEN

Various biographies have been written, but all the older ones are historically unreliable. Nugent's was for long the best known, but owed its fame mainly to Macaulay's great Essay. Macaulay's and Mr. Williamson's are the best works. The following are the principal authorities that have been consulted, besides the general authorities for the period and those quoted in the annotations:

The Stowe MSS.

"Memoirs," Sir Philip Warwick, 1701.

"Notes on Proceedings of the Long Parliament," Sir Ralph Verney (Camden Society), 1845.

"Letters and Papers of the Verney Family" (Camden Society), 1853:

"Memoirs of the Verney Family" (Camden Society), edition 1904.

"Athenae Oxoniensis," Anthony à Wood, ed. Bliss, 1813.

"History and Antiquities of Buckinghamshire," G. Lipscomb, 1847.

"John Hampden," H. Ross Williamson, 1933.

"Memorials of Hampden," Lord Nugent, 1831.

Macaulay's Essay, "Edinburgh Review," December, 1831.

"Sir John Eliot," John Forster, 1864.

Forster's Life of Hampden in "Eminent British Statesmen" series, 1837.

"Studies of the Great Rebellion," J. L. Sanford, 1858.

"Autobiography of Sir Symonds D'Ewes," ed. Halliwell, 1845.

"Speeches and Passages of this great and happy Parliament," W. Cook, 1641.

"History of the Long Parliament," Thomas May, edition 1853.
"John Hampden's England," John Drinkwater, 1933.

II: PHILLIP SKIPPON

A jewel in a ten times barred up chest
Is a bold spirit in a loyal breast.
— RICHARD II.

I. BIBLE AND SWORD

A MIGHTY fighter and a mighty gospeller before the Lord was Major-General Phillip Skippon, who now carries on our tale. He was of a type found in the best British armies throughout the centuries — not overendowed with brains, but stout of heart, loyal of spirit, direct of speech, generous to a fault, God-fearing, the first into action and the last out of it.

> th' investing of so many towns
> Scor'd on his breast, and character'd in wounds,

his shoulders bore the burden of other men's faults, and his capable hands grasped readily the unwelcome tasks that others thrust into them. He was the Sergeant-Major *in excelsis* and no man more fittingly carried the old title of Sergeant-Major General that was the origin of the modern style. "Pray and fight" was the device that he adopted, and the title of "Christian Centurion" that he took to himself never suited any man better.

Coming of good country stock, Skippon was one of the few who at the beginning of the Civil War had had military training, for he had spent many years in the Dutch wars. He was invaluable at such a time, and the merit of his patient and courageous service earned him in the fullness of time a seat on Cromwell's Council, and another in his House of Lords. But he was never a politician, being a man "too wise and grave for this mercurial quick age."[45] He was plain soldier. He was

---

[45] Lansdowne MSS., 822, fol. 132.

perhaps the best of that band of veterans whom Carlyle called Cromwell's "Napoleon-marshals," and his special value to Cromwell in later years was the immense respect in which he was held by all parties by reason of his reputation for integrity, above all in the City of London, at once the strength and the seat of danger to the Commonwealth cause. Skippon is one of those to whom history, overshadowed by the figure of Cromwell, has never done full justice. Yet, since he stormed no constitutional redoubts, nor led any great party, his special interest for us must remain that he personifies admirably the best type of soldier who fought those wars, with their merits and their faults.

Phillip Skippon came from a good family of West Lexham, Norfolk. The date of his birth has not been ascertained. He is generally supposed to have been an "old man" at the time of the English Civil Wars and is referred to by that style at the time of Naseby in 1645. But the evidence in Carthew's *Hundred of Launditch* shows that his father, Luke Skippon, was born only in 1574, and, for a variety of reasons, the probability is that Phillip was little older than the new century. The family had long been settled in Norfolk, having branches also elsewhere in the county. Luke Skippon owned lands about West Lexham and was to acquire more, such as those in Swaffham and Foulsham, either by his own efforts or by the testaments of his yeoman brothers.

Nothing is known of Phillip's first years, but at an early age he took military service against Spain and the Empire. How soon he started on that career is not certain. Walker, who is provably in error in such details, speaks disparagingly on two later occasions of Skippon's having been "waggoner to Sir Francis Vere," commander of the English contingent of Elizabethan time who fought for the Dutch against Spain; but this is scarcely likely, for Francis had already been succeeded by his brother Sir Horace before 1605. In that year Horace and his men had covered themselves with glory at the battle of Mulheim, and immediately afterwards a long truce was signed. It is not till a good deal later that Skippon appears upon the scene.

In 1613, as we have seen, Princess Elizabeth of England, James's daughter, the "Queen of Hearts" as all true Englishmen called her, "who in those days carried a great stream of affection towards her," had married Frederick, the Protestant Elector of the Palatinate. In that beautiful land of the Niebelungenlied she had spent five happy years with her Siegfried. But the dragon ambition had come out of Bohemia. Frederick was offered the crown of that land in 1619, and his acceptance brought upon him the fury of the Catholic Empire. The Emperor hurried forward plans to invade Bohemia, and the Spanish army of the Netherlands prepared to march upon the Palatinate.

Englishmen were eager for help to be sent to their Queen of Hearts, and in spite of the niggardliness of her father, the flower of the young nobility sprang up to serve in the little volunteer expedition organised under the command of Sir Horace Vere. In July, 1620, the expedition sailed from Gravesend and not the least of its members was the young gentleman of Norfolk, Phillip Skippon.

It seems probable that Skippon's motive in volunteering for such service was, not adventure or the need of a career, but a zeal for the Protestant cause. Throughout life that zeal was to colour all his conduct and all his thought. The tides of religious emotion that were sweeping men's minds caught him up, but carried him to waters calmer and kinder than they did many men of that day. Though in later years he was identified as a

Presbyterian, his was never the Covenanters' religion of gloom and reprobation, nor Cromwell's furrowed perplexity. No hatred of Catholics or any other sect is in his writings, nor are there the posturing, the mountebanking, and the strident ecstasies of "hot gospellers" such as John Lilburne and Hugh Peters. There is no marqueterie in the solid oak of his character. Yet, like all these, he drew his inspiration from the Testaments alone. His Bible — a "breeches" Bible of 1610 — was his constant companion, its pages heavily underlined in ink, and it is from the end leaves of this volume that we find the only known records of his family. These records are included in a privately printed volume of pedigrees in the Bodleian Library.[46]

Beyond this we know little for certain of Phillip Skippon as a young man. From later observations, however, we may take him to be a well-built and lusty fellow. As a son of the smaller gentry he had some private means, but not much. He complained while in Holland of long arrears of pay, obliging one to live on one's means. He did not go to the university, and had no scholarship beyond his intense poring over the Testaments, but, like many of that day, he had a disposition, if no talent, for writership and rhyming. A predominant quality was his physical courage, to which all men bore ready witness and he was always certainly of simple and homely ways. Yet he was far from the honest duffer, and he had his full share of native shrewdness. "Simplicity without circumspection," he wrote later, "is folly. Circumspection without simplicity is cunning."[47]

Such, as far as we can see him, was the young man who joined the colours of the fighting Veres as an infantry soldier.

---

[46] 218, d. 131.
[47] *The Christian Centurion.*

Clarendon says later that he had been a "common soldier," like many others of good stock in those campaigns, but if so he very soon won promotion. We can spare but little notice for those early campaigns, full of romantic interest though they were. Arrived in the Palatinate, Vere soon found himself almost deserted by his German allies, but his little force, garrisoning the towns of Heidelberg, Mannheim and Frankenthal, held out valiantly for long against some of the first soldiers of the age in Tilly and Cordova. In the Frankenthal garrison, commanded by Sergeant-Major General Burrough, was young Phillip Skippon, and there he underwent the rigours of two hard sieges. In the second of them, however, he enjoyed the solace of a wife, for, on May 4th, 1622, he married Maria Comes in the Netherlands church in Frankenthal. She was then twenty-one.

In 1623, with Frederick's cause lost, his lovely queen carried a fugitive from the Imperial armies on the pillion of Sir Ralph Hopton through the stubborn snows, the English volunteers quitted the Palatinate and proceeded to Holland. Skippon went with them, and he spent the next thirteen years in active campaigning under Sir Horace Vere in that grand war of Dutch redemption. He took his young wife to Holland with him and there they made their home. Their first child, Anna, was born in October, 1623, at Utrecht. The baby died before she was a year old, but in January, 1625, a second daughter was born at Montfort and was also named Anna.

The Dutch wars were a hard and searching school. Until Gustavus Adolphus the Spaniards were still the first soldiers in Europe, hard and insensitive as steel, capable of extraordinary endurance, valour and cruelty, and sometimes of chivalry. As in the Palatinate, many noble English families followed the "fighting Veres" for the cause of Holland, and nearly all the principal commanders in the Civil War that was to come in Britain learnt their knowledge of war in those hard campaigns — Sir Jacob Astley, Sir Ralph Hopton, Lord Byron and George Goring for the King; Sir Thomas Fairfax, Lord Essex and Lord Warwick for the Parliament. All these and others did Skippon serve with, to emerge with a reputation equal to the foremost. It was mainly a war of infantry, and mainly of sieges. The walled and moated towns, often made difficult of approach by the flooded lands and the innumerable rivers and canals, frequently held out with the tiniest garrisons against considerable armies. It was a war fought at close quarters at push of pike, of sudden sallies and midnight surprises, a war of trenches and saps, of mine and counter-mine, of the storming of ramparts and the hot defence of ravelin, in which the courage of the junior commander was a paramount factor.

In these battles Skippon's name occurs frequently. In the spring of 1625, by then a captain, he was wounded in the hazardous assault upon the Spanish redoubts before the fortress of Breda. In 1628 he served in the trenches at the investment of Bois-le-Duc, and here it was that Sir Thomas Fairfax, the future commander of the Parliamentary forces and Skippon's close associate in raising the New Model, received his first lesson in war as a stripling of sixteen. In 1632 Sergeant-Major[48] Skippon specially distinguished himself in the siege of Maastricht, personally leading the parties that repulsed the sorties of the Spaniards. He was again before Breda in 1637, when the town was captured from the Spaniards; on this occasion the English *tercio* was led by Sir Jacob Astley, who was afterwards to lead the royalist infantry as Skippon was to lead Parliament's, and here Skippon was also in more significant

---

[48] i.e., a senior captain or major.

company, for the boy princes, Rupert and Maurice, were with him.

In 1628, or perhaps earlier, Skippon and his wife and little Anna moved their home to Amersfoort, where they were to remain for five years or more, and where three more children were to be born. William, their first son, was born there in 1628; and in 1631 another daughter, Maria, arrived after a painful and dangerous delivery "when all was past hope." When she was nine weeks old, so the old family Bible tells us, the baby girl developed small-pox and was in grave extremity, but happily recovered. The last child to be born in the Netherlands was Phillip in 1633, but the Bible tells us in great distress of his present death at a date that is indecipherable.

In 1639, after nearly twenty years of soldiering, Skippon thought it was time to go home, for the simple captain had come into property and he was now something over forty years of age. His wife had perhaps already come home, for in May, 1635, she gave birth to another daughter, Susanna, in her father-in-law's home at West Lexham. In 1638 Luke Skippon died, leaving to Phillip the residue of his property in Foulsham. Phillip's uncle William, of Tavistock, Devonshire, had also recently left him property of about 150 acres in Foulsham, Woodnorth and Bintre. Foulsham Hall was a copyhold, and here Phillip had already taken up residence in 1638, his seventh child, named Luke after its grandfather, being born there in August of that year. There were several others of the family in Norfolk, his brother Luke being sometime rector of Whissingset and Vicar of South Lynn.

II. MAJOR-GENERAL

Skippon came home with a considerable reputation for soldierly valour. He had shown to men that he was one who could

> tell pale-hearted fear it lies,
> And sleep in spite of thunder.

As a regimental and a staff officer he was considered one of the best and most experienced organisers who had been brought up in the school of the fighting Veres. He was "stout Skippon," "honest Skippon," "magnanimous Skippon." From such portraits of him as have come down to us, those epithets seem well to describe him. He is dark visaged, even swarthy, and he has the little beard, abrupt moustaches and long curled hair of the time. He appears somewhat full in the face, with strong well-moulded features, rather thick in the nose, composed and yet aware in expression, with apparently a scar across the right cheek. It is a face of character, of a soldierly bearing, of one who is yet in the incontaminate vigour of manliness. The native lustiness has been refined by privation and by the pinch of

> The night's cold damp, wrapt in sheet of steel.

Yet, though his heart was deep in religion, his face bears no mark of the inward torture of soul that was Cromwell's, for his was a calmer faith, and composure is seated on his brow. He had a frank and hearty manner. Clarendon says of him at this moment that he "had served very long in Holland, and from a common soldier had raised himself to the degree of a captain and to the reputation of a good officer: he was a man of order and sobriety, and untainted with any of those vices which the officers of that army were exercised in."

Skippon had begun writing his little devotional works while serving in the Low Countries, and it is in those odd little books that we can see his heart and his mind, and much of the quality that made him what he was. Clarendon says that he was "altogether illiterate," but this is clearly incorrect. His first published work, *A Salve for Every Sore*, was intended for the intimate use of his wife and children, but in 1643 it was printed for the use of his soldiers, as were his subsequent writings.

They are entirely personal writings. They show a man of simple and sincere piety, who has found comfort for his afflictions in the Word of God and who is tenderly anxious that his fellow-men shall share with him that precious discovery. He has no use, he says, for a "sour countenance, harsh carriage, bitter language and distasteful dealing," nor is his God a God of Battles or a God of Punishment. The manner of his writings, peppered thickly with quotations, is of course wearisome to the modern mind, but his own touches reveal him. Most notably they reveal that emotion in him from which spring the habit of faithful duty, the sense of public service, and the readiness to forgo personal interest or inclination that seem to have guided so much of his life. At the height of his fame he was ready "to lay down all I am and have in this world" for the public service. By attachment to the Protestant cause, which he served all his life, abroad and at home, he never prospered in the material wealth of the world, until the last few years. That service, he says, "undid" him, but conscience forbade him to shirk it.

> Much have I lost, and still may lose,
> Farewell to all.

So wrote he in one of his queer but touching little rhymes. And he continues —

> I am not like (as 'tis) to gain
> Except my labour for my pain.[49]

We know, too, without being aware of the circumstances, that he suffered much from "distractedness of estate and family." Throughout his maturer life he was pursued by some secret unhappiness, which wrung his heart, but for which he found solace always in the "Promises" of heaven.

Consonant with these impulses was an outstanding characteristic of the man which endeared him greatly to his soldiers — his very real sense of comradeship with the meanest of them, and his constant watchfulness over their welfare, both spiritual and material. On the battlefield and the parade-ground he was always the commander, but if in action he had the courage of a lion, his heart was tender to all men, and he could pause in the heat of battle to comfort a wounded soldier and give him money to procure relief. It was his rule "to run the same fortunes and hazards" with his soldiers, and it was his practice to go among them urging them "to pray heartily and fight heartily." Had he possessed political driving power he might have commanded the nation in the quarrels that followed Naseby, but outside military matters he was a simpleton, as most men are who have spent their lives in tent and barrack. "I am no scholar," he said, "I desire to be a Christian." And again: "I desire to honour God, not to humour men."

It was only in accord with the temper of the times that the man of faith should march with a sword in his hand. If

---

[49] *A Salve for Every Sore.*

inclination urged him to prayer, destiny led him to fight, and his whole life is expressed in the device that he adopted: "*Ora et pugna. Juvat et juvabit, Jehovah.*" Conformably, his arms included a sword issuing from the clouds and a closed book.[50] "Pray and fight" were the commands he enjoined on his soldiers as well as on himself, but "Fight" meant more than the carriage of arms, for the Christian Centurion condemned the waging of war unless the cause required it.

> I say, God send them sorrow that love it; if it made them smart in their own persons, wives, children, friends, houses or goods, they would soon be weary of it; for doubtless none but fools or madmen can take delight in it.
>
> True, the calling is lawful, honourable and necessary, where the causes urging are just, and the ends good, and he that declines it is base in the extremity.[51]

That is Hamlet again:

> Rightly to be great
> Is not to stir without great argument,
> But greatly to find quarrel in a straw
> When honour's at the stake.

Such was the man who appears from his own thoughts and actions and from the testimony of others. At first Skippon's life at home was quiet enough, but he did not stay long to enjoy his Norfolk property, for, on the recommendation of the King, he was elected as leader of the Honourable Artillery Company on October 23rd, 1639. Accordingly he moved with his family to Hackney to be near London, and at this period there appears a letter which is the only manuscript letter

---

[50] Rawlinson MSS., 942, 2b and 3; Prestwich, *Respublica*, 38.
[51] *The Christian Centurion.*

dealing with Skippon's personal matters that has so far come to light. It is addressed to Lieut. John Cruso, who, now apparently Skippon's factor in Norfolk, had fought beside him in Holland and three years later was to dedicate to Skippon one of his military manuals. Skippon wrote:[52]

Good Lieutenant Cruso. Be pleased according to the times appointed by Mr. John Pepis, in this enclosed to me from him, to receive of him five and thirty pounds, being in full payment of all that I disbursed for reparations at West Lexham, and give Mr. John Pepis this acquittance from me. Tender my true regrets to Mr. John Pepis and entreat him to speak to Mr. Winneyue to pay me the rest that will still remain due to me from him, viz.:

For grass in the new close and two horse closes, with my ploughs and harrows behind: £10

For the muck: £2 5s

For ploughing 37 acres of Somerly: £3 1s 8d

For a coper: £1 10s

In all, after this £35 shall be paid, due to me £16 16s 8d.

This I entreat I may have the next week, for I must pay a great sum of money before this month be out. You may leave this note with Mr. Pepis, I entreat him to let Mr. Winneyue see it. I am not well, the Lord's will be done. Tell Mr. John Pepis I have taken order for the paying my half year's rent at the appointed time. My love to Mrs. Winneyue. Pay yourself the £12 I owe you and send the rest to me. Pardon my boldness. The Lord be with you.

Yours really,
Ph. Skippon.

Hackney, the 12th of October, 1640.

Just twelve months later his eighth and last child, who was also

---

[52] Egerton MSS., 2716, fol. 360. John Pepis very likely belonged to the Mileham family, near Lexham, who were related to the diarist.

named Phillip, and who was in due time to be knighted by Charles II, was born at Hackney. Later we hear of the family living at St. Bartholomew's and finally at Acton.

Skippon had a reputation for the training of troops,[53] and no doubt he found it congenial work putting the young men of the City through their military "postures" in the old Artillery Garden, with good fellowship to follow, for he had a hearty and genial manner. One of his colonels, commanding the First London Regiment, ancestor of The Buffs, was Marmaduke Rawdon, afterwards to become famous for his part in the siege of Basing House. On January 8th, 1642, Skippon received the freedom of the City of London, and in the same month he appeared at last actively upon the English political scene. Four days before Skippon had received the City's freedom, Charles had made his raid on the House of Commons in his attempt to arrest the five members, and the Commons, feeling themselves to be no longer safe, desired the Lord Mayor and Common Council of London to provide them with a guard. The City agreed, and on January 10th they appointed Skippon Sergeant-Major General to take command of all the City trained bands and to protect the Houses, voting him £300 a year as long as he should remain in the City's service.[54] His duty fell immediately on the morrow, for on that day the five members returned in triumph to Westminster by the river, and Skippon marched out his trained bands alongside by the Strand in scenes of frenzied excitement.

The strained peace at length broke down, and it was to Skippon that there fell the first overt act of war, for in the same month he was ordered by the Houses to blockade the

---

[53] Bariffe's well-known manual *Military Discipline* was also dedicated to Skippon.
[54] Sharpe, *London and the Kingdom*, ii, 161.

Tower, which Sir John Byron held for the King. When after a month Byron could no longer hold out, Charles agreed to the Commons' demand for the command of the fortress to be transferred to Sir John Conyers, and Skippon received the thanks of Parliament.

Presently Charles made his move to the North, and at York began to gather together the gentry and the trained bands of the county. Skippon's services were much sought for the royalist cause, and on May 13th Charles himself directed a letter to him, peremptorily commanding his personal attendance at York, "all excuses being set apart."[55] Skippon immediately acquainted Parliament, and the Houses by resolution declared the order illegal and prohibited him from going. Probably he needed no such direction from Parliament, for the Puritan code he had followed in Holland ranged him naturally and willingly on Parliament's side, and "the good old cause" was the only one to which his inclinations led him. As early as 1612 the English Baptists in Amsterdam had declared that the civil power had no right "to meddle with religion or matters of politics, nor compel men to this or that form of religion," and Clarendon says that, "having been bred always in Holland he brought disaffection enough with him from thence against the Church of England, and so was much caressed and trusted by that party."

As it was at present his duty simply to defend London, he did not march with Essex's army and was not present at Edgehill, though some contemporary accounts state that he was. But when, after that action, Charles turned south-east, occupied Oxford and advanced upon London, and when news came of Rupert's cutting-up of the regiments of Brooke and Holles and the sack of Brentford, then the population rose in

---

[55] Add. MSS., 34, 253, fol. 13.

defence of the capital. While the women and children laboured with the men to throw up earthworks at the City's approaches, Skippon mustered his trained bands and all through the evening of November 12th they streamed out upon the western road to face the King with the army of the Lord-General. We have a typical glimpse of him on that march from the memoirs of Whitelocke. "He made," said the diarist, "short and encouraging speeches to his soldiers, which were to this purpose:

> Come, my boys, my brave boys, let us pray heartily and fight heartily. I will run the same fortunes and hazards with you. Remember, the cause is for God, and for the defence of yourselves, your wives, and children. Come, my honest brave boys, pray heartily and fight heartily, and God will bless you.

Thus he went all along with the soldiers, talking to them, sometimes to one company, and sometimes to another; and the soldiers seemed to be more taken with it than with a set formal oration."[56]

Thus did Charles find himself checked the next morning with the great array of Turnham Green. Essex, who had trailed a pike with Skippon in the Palatinate, saw on this occasion that the services of so experienced and practical a soldier would be of the greatest value to the Parliamentary forces. He determined to secure him as his Sergeant-Major General, and although the City governors were loath to lose his services, they reluctantly agreed on November 17th.

Skippon accordingly joined the army in the field, becoming its second-in-command and president of the Lord-General's council of war in place of Sir John Meyrick, who was appointed to command the artillery. In the incompetence that

---

[56] Whitelocke, *Memorials*, 65.

the gentle Essex was to show in his command, there is a
natural inclination to inquire whether his second-in-command
was not also largely to blame, but it seems likely that Skippon
had little voice in matters which to Essex were of political
policy, such as whether the King's defeat should be sought or
not; nor is any blame laid at Skippon's door by the critics of
Essex, and when it came to fighting an action there was to be
found nothing amiss with the dispositions that were made.

Something has already been said in the sketch of Hampden
on the nature of those citizen soldiers, but to have a brighter
picture of the engagements that were to come more must be
seen of their appearance and their ways. The regiments were
still raised chiefly by individual commanders, and every
regiment, in both camps, was dressed as pleased its colonel
best, so that in battle there was nothing to distinguish friend
from foe save the favours that were picked from field or
hedgerow or other emblems. The arms and ammunition for
Essex's army, however, were supplied by Westminster and
were fairly uniform.

An infantry regiment at this time consisted of one-third
pikemen and two-thirds musketeers. The pikes were steel-
tipped poles of ash eighteen feet long, but were so heavy that
men often cut a foot or two off the butts of them, which was
against orders and "a damned thing to be suffered." To carry
this formidable weapon the biggest and strongest men were
selected, and they were armed also with swords, but the swords
were of inferior quality and their chief use was in cutting wood.
The pikeman wore an iron corslet, or "back and breast," and
an iron headpiece crowned with a ridge like a cock's comb.
Both pikemen and musketeers wore loose knee breeches, with
stockings and shoes.

The musketeer was only just beginning, with the slow improvements in firearms, to assume an importance at least equal to that of the puissant pikemen. He carried no armour, but wore a long coat and a big broad-brimmed felt hat. His musket, loaded from the muzzle, fired a heavy round bullet bigger than the modern shrapnel ball and weighing over an ounce, propelled by a charge of powder which was fired by a priming charge placed in a little pan at the breach of the musket-barrel. The extreme effective range seems to have been about 400 yards. The weapon in general use was the matchlock, that is to say, one for which the ignition of the charge was effected by a slow-burning match. The match was a thin cord of tow boiled in vinegar, and every musketeer carried a "link" two or three yards long. On service every man carried in his hand a piece of this match about two feet long constantly lighted at both ends, a necessity which often revealed the presence of an enemy at night, but which often enabled an army to cozen the enemy very prettily when a surreptitious retreat was desired.

Bullets were carried in a pouch, but in battle one or two were always held in the mouth. The charges of powder were made up in little cases of tin, leather or other material, and dangled from a bandolier worn over the shoulder. Thus accoutred, the musketeer was sometimes as dangerous to himself and his comrades as to the enemy, for contact between the glowing match and the dangling cartridges occasionally blew him to bits. Besides his fighting gear, the infantryman carried a "snapsack" for his rations, but no water-bottle.

In battle formation the pikemen were disposed in the centre of each regiment and the musketeers on the flanks. They were commonly drawn up six deep, each rank firing in turn by volleys and falling back to the rear to reload. The pikemen then, at the given moment, charged home.

The cavalryman, like the pikeman, wore an iron "back and breast," or light cuirass, with beneath it a buff, or jerkin, and on his head a light helmet called a "pot." Loose breeches and big jack-boots completed his attire, and for weapons he carried sword and pistols. In the earlier years of the war he carried also a harquebus or carbine, being a light musket, fired, not by a match, but by a flint and steel lock, but these were soon relinquished save by officers and by the dragoons. The pistol also was fired by a flint and steel mechanism, and a cavalry onset, whether against infantry or other cavalry, began, after the charge, with the discharge of pistols at point-blank, the pistol being then hurled at the faces of the enemy before falling on with the sword. Very soon, however, both Cromwell and Rupert adopted the tactics of charging straight home with the sword. The charge was made at a fast trot and in solid order, "every left-hand man's right knee close locked under his right-hand man's left ham." The royalist cavalry carried also a small pole-axe, and it is noteworthy that there were no lancers on either side, except among the Scots.

Midway between the cavalry and the infantry were the dragoons, or mounted infantry, who carried either harquebus, carbine or dragon, all of them flint-and-steel operated firearms. Their organisation was that of infantry (by companies and not by troops), and, like infantry, they answered to the call of the drum and not the trumpet.

Parliament's army was particularly well equipped with artillery, but in some of the battles it was little used. Exceedingly slow in their rate of fire, and very heavy in proportion to their calibre, the guns were often a serious impediment to the mobility of an army on the bad roads of that time. Of course, all guns were muzzle-loaders, and commonly fired a solid round shot, not explosive, though explosive "grenadoes" were often used in siege work. The heaviest piece, not often used in the field, was a culverin, firing a shot of from 16 lbs. to 20 lbs. to an extreme range of 2,000 yards, but the guns most frequently used, however, were the light field pieces called sakers, minions and drakes. The saker was a five- or six-pounder, the drake a three-pounder, and the minion something in between. They could fire only one round in four minutes, and required from three to five horses for their draught, though oxen were often used instead. The artillery column and the baggage, forming together the "train," were escorted by a regiment of infantry armed with flint-and-steel muskets instead of matchlocks, because of the danger of carrying burning match near the powder barrels; for the gunner's propelling charge was seldom made up into cartridges, but was simply scooped out of the powder barrel with a ladle and thrust straight into the gun.

Such was the equipment of the field army of Lord Essex which Skippon joined. It was the custom for each general officer to have his own regiment, according to the arm that he followed, administered in all routine matters by a lieutenant-colonel, but led into action always by the Colonel-in-chief himself. Skippon's own regiment of infantry was therefore very shortly formed. Following him wherever he went in the first Civil War, it was known throughout the army as "Major-General's" and was recognised by its red banner bearing his device of a sword issuing from a cloud to protect a clasped Bible. He now proceeded with Essex on his slow and hesitating march, braked by the abortive peace negotiations, towards Oxford in the spring of 1643. At the siege of Reading he was in charge of the approach works, and with Hampden was the first to enter the town after capitulation. Then came the tragedy of Chalgrove Field, and for some time Essex continued to loiter aimlessly outside Oxford, until at length the turn of events obliged him to return to London, for the Parliamentary cause was everywhere going amiss. In the North old Lord Fairfax and his great and gallant son, Sir Thomas, with a handful of Parliamentary troops, waging an unequal struggle against the superior forces of the Earl of Newcastle, had been defeated at Adwalton Moor and had taken refuge within the walls of Hull. In the West the royalists had defeated the rebels at Stratton, at Lansdowne and at Roundway Down, in a vivid campaign in which the yellow standard of Sir William Waller, commanding the army of the South-Eastern counties, had been raised for Parliament against his friend, Sir Ralph Hopton, and against that valiant scion of a famous Cornish house, Sir Bevil Grenville, who had testified by a soldier's death his consanguinity with the immortal hero of the *Revenge*.

III. FIRST NEWBURY

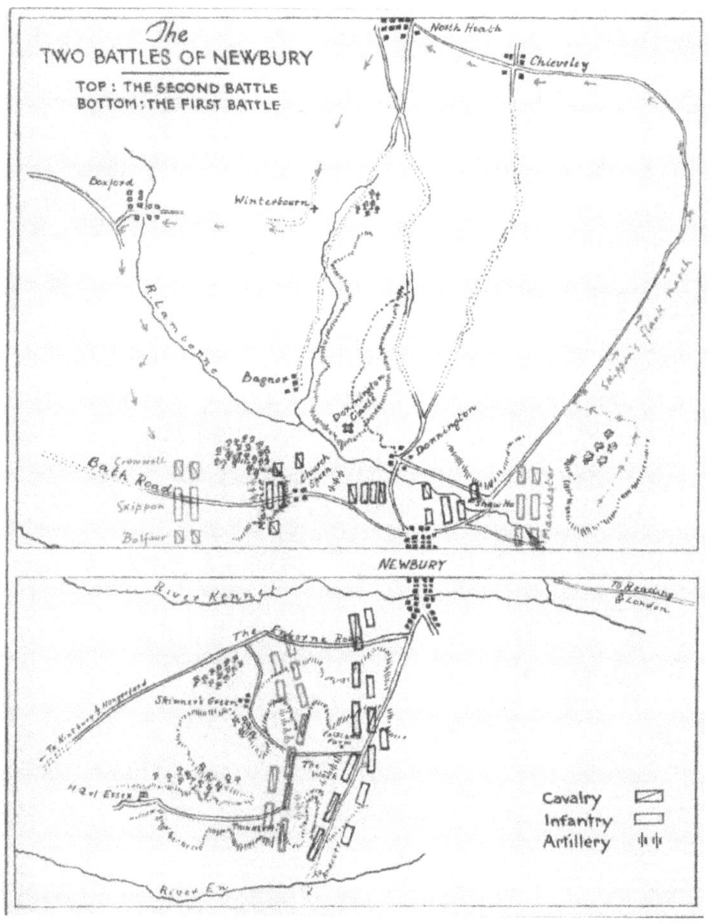

The cause of the two Houses, through their own feebleness
and through their divided counsels, was therefore in August,
1643, at its nadir. All the North save Hull and all the West save

Gloucester and a few coast towns were in the King's hands. A concerted advance on London by his three main armies would have given him the victory before the autumn leaves had fallen. For all these the roads were clear. But the same wind that brought the hope of victory laid bare his Achilles' heel. For his men would not march. With him, as with the Parliament, there was the greatest difficulty in persuading men who had been raised by their local leaders to fight outside their own counties, and so long as Hull, Plymouth and Gloucester were in Parliament's hands to threaten their homes, the men of Yorkshire, Cornwall and Wales would not budge beyond an easy recall. As things were, Charles decided that he must reduce Gloucester before he advanced on London, and that decision, or that necessity, cost him the war.

He sat down before Gloucester on August 10th, and the news of Edward Massey's gallant defence immediately roused London to fresh efforts for its relief. Six of the regiments of London trained bands that Skippon had been drilling were placed by the City at Essex's disposal. On August 22nd he drew up 8,000 men on Hounslow Heath for the Lord-General's inspection, and they moved off four days later on an arduous march, encased in the hot iron of their armour in the slumbrous heat of August and with food made scarce by Rupert's plunders. Reaching the Cotswolds, they found Rupert himself upon them, confident that in these open uplands his superior cavalry would discomfort them; but the rebels threw them off on each occasion. Near Stow-on-the-Wold, almost at the gates of Gloucester, Rupert drew up a strong force beyond a pass in the hills to bar their approach, but with only 200 musketeers, two guns and a few horse, Skippon attacked with determination and forced them to retire.[57] The resolution of

---

[57] Washbourne, *Bibliotheca Gloucestrensis*, 239.

the Londoners was unexpected, and, Charles refusing battle, Gloucester was relieved in early September when its stock of powder had dwindled to three barrels.

But now Essex had to make his way back again to London, with an unbeaten enemy standing in his path. After marches and counter-marches the King succeeded again in heading him off, and on the night of September 19th, 1643, he barred the rebels' path at Newbury, and the two forces faced each other for a vital battle.

Skippon, whose duty it was to prepare the order of battle, found that the enemy lay just to the south-west of the town between the En Brook and the River Kennet, which flow roughly parallel to one another west and east and about two miles apart. The road into Newbury from Kintbury, by which Essex had come, marched also roughly parallel with the Kennet and at a few hundred yards from it. Charles, facing west, had his right flank resting on this road, and his left, with Rupert and his horsemen, stretched down to the En Brook — a frontage of about a mile and a half. On this flank the ground north of the brook rose up to a long ridge running east and west, and all that slope, called Enborne Heath, was mainly open ground. In the centre, however, and towards the northern limit of the battle-line, the country was cut up into deep lanes or chequered with hedges. Against the strength of Rupert's cavalry Essex must avoid those southern slopes, nor could he take the northern road from Kintbury into Newbury. His way, therefore, lay straight through the centre of Charles's army, where, among the hedges and lanes, he might fight an infantry action. It was a hazardous prospect, but his army was short of food, and fight he must.

Early on the morning of September 20th, Skippon having ordered forward the artillery, the Parliamentary forces moved forward on their left to seize a line of hedges that the royalists had neglected to occupy, and battle was joined. From hedge to hedge and from bank to bank the action raged, spreading now from the left to the centre of the line, each meadow a cockpit, each lane a valley of death. From one such meadow the Roundheads forced back the royalist foot and occupied the farther hedge, pouring a rain of bullets through a trampled gap. Riding in Charles's ranks was the pure-hearted Falkland. Death called to his tortured spirit as the only mistress in whose arms he might find relief in the dark night of his country's pain. Alone he spurred his horse straight for the breach and in that driving rain of bullets gave his spirit release.

Crisis came now upon the southern wing. Rupert with itching heels could not endure to wait until the Roundhead infantry should have struggled through the lanes and hedges into the open country beyond. On Enborne Heath, the open ground on the extreme right of the Roundheads, he espied the Red and the Blue regiments of the London trained bands that Skippon had drilled, with some horse on either flank. Under his sky-blue standard he galloped forward at the head of a great flood of horsemen. He charged the Parliamentary horse and scattered them like autumn leaves.

Thus isolated, the two regiments of London trained bands, whose only knowledge of war thus far had been Skippon's teaching in the Artillery Garden, found themselves open to the onrush of Rupert's horsemen and the fury of his guns. They formed square, bristling pikes without, musketeers within. Though the solid shot of the gun-fire tore them fearfully, and "were somewhat dreadful when men's bowels and brains flew in our faces," yet they kept their ranks closed up, and stood "like stakes" as the horsemen, striving with pistol volleys at point-blank to open a way, dashed themselves in vain against the serried pikes. Nor did they falter when, the cavalry failing, Rupert brought up his infantry and set them on. Guile also shook them not, for a royalist regiment that rode up wearing in their hats the green sprays that distinguished the Roundheads that day and crying "Friends! Friends!" got for welcome a volley of musketry.

Skippon now rode into the van of the battle with his infantry in the centre. All day he was in the heat of this "soldiers' battle," encouraging his "brave boys," as his habit was, by example and by comradely exhortation. So for hours the conflict raged all along the line among the hedgerows and the narrow lanes. Sometimes a little field would be taken and retaken again and again; sometimes a sally of horsemen, pouring rashly down a sunken lane, would be caught by musketry on either side and shot down to a man. Skippon was over all the field — bringing up guns to attack a house from which the enemy were keeping up a damaging fire, moving a brigade to repel an attack on the left wing, sending his own regiment to answer Essex's call for help, rallying the trained bands, charging to recover the guns of his own regiment that had been lost.[58]

So until night fell they fought on, the Parliament gaining ground inch by inch, yet failing to break through a stubborn and resolute resistance. When at last darkness brought relief to weary arms that trembled with the weight of the long pikes and to limbs that hung limp in the saddle, the victory, as in the first major action at Edgehill, belonged to no one. When he had seen sentries set with extra care against surprise at such close quarters, Skippon, as he lay down to sleep, the matches of the musketeers glowing in the darkness, was certain that another hard struggle must have to be fought again next day.

---

[58] Washbourne, *Bibliotheca Gloucestrensis*, 245-7.

But with the morning light he found the enemy clean gone. There had been terrible slaughter among the flower of the King's gentry, and the valour of Skippon's London infantry had shaken them sorely. Moreover, if the Roundheads' food was nearly gone, so, it seemed, was Charles's powder. He had made his way that night back into Newbury, and so on next day to Oxford, leaving the road to London free at last to Essex. So, though neither side had gained a success in arms, the royalists had failed in their purpose, and for the merit of the Roundheads' performance first praise must go to Skippon, who had borne the brunt of the battle. He had shown that the London infantry of his training was the best in the rebel armies and a match for the King's horse and foot alike.

On September 28th Skippon marched into London with the army in triumphal procession, and his soldiers went back once more to their shops and their benches. He found that while the Gloucester expedition was in progress Parliament had struck a bargain with the Scots by which the Houses were to declare for the Presbyterian faith and to embrace the austerity of the Covenant, and in return General Leslie (now Lord Leven) was to march to Parliament's help with a Scottish army, the English Parliament paying the bill. This fateful bargain, the last accomplishment of John Pym, was indeed the most decisive step of the war, for, apart from imposing upon the English an unpopular religion, it made the breach with the King final. Skippon in due course took the Covenant, as required of all Parliament's officers.

More dangerous than the seizure of Reading for the King was the news that Rupert was plundering the midland shires and had left Sir Lewis Dyves to fortify Newport Pagnell, in the north of Buckinghamshire, which throughout the Civil Wars was an important strategic position. Essex and Waller, therefore, instead of relieving Reading, marched upon Newport Pagnell, and, Dyves giving way before their strength, occupied it on October 30th. Skippon was left to hold it with a strong garrison, and throughout the winter of 1643-44 he was engaged in a number of expeditions against royalists in the neighbouring counties. On Christmas Eve, '43, after an initial repulse, he stormed and captured Grafton House, a fortified house in Northamptonshire of great strength and the Queen's own jointure, and destroyed it by fire against its future use.[59] It was in his garrison at Newport that Cromwell suffered a grievous loss in the death from smallpox of his eldest son, Oliver, and it was here that later the youthful John Bunyan began his term as a stripling soldier.

On December 8th, 1643, the Parliamentary cause suffered a great loss in the death of John Pym. He had not long survived his great coadjutor, Hampden, and the Commons, left without any leader worth the name, were in the days to come to have need of so wise a head. He remains as one of the greatest figures in British constitutional development, for, though he knew not whither he was going, he stood like a rock for certain great principles, and it was due to him and Hampden that the breach with traditional despotism was made deliberately and firmly.

---

[59] *A True Relation of the Taking of Grafton House*; Vicars, 53: Whitelocke, 79.

IV. LOSTWITHIEL SURRENDER

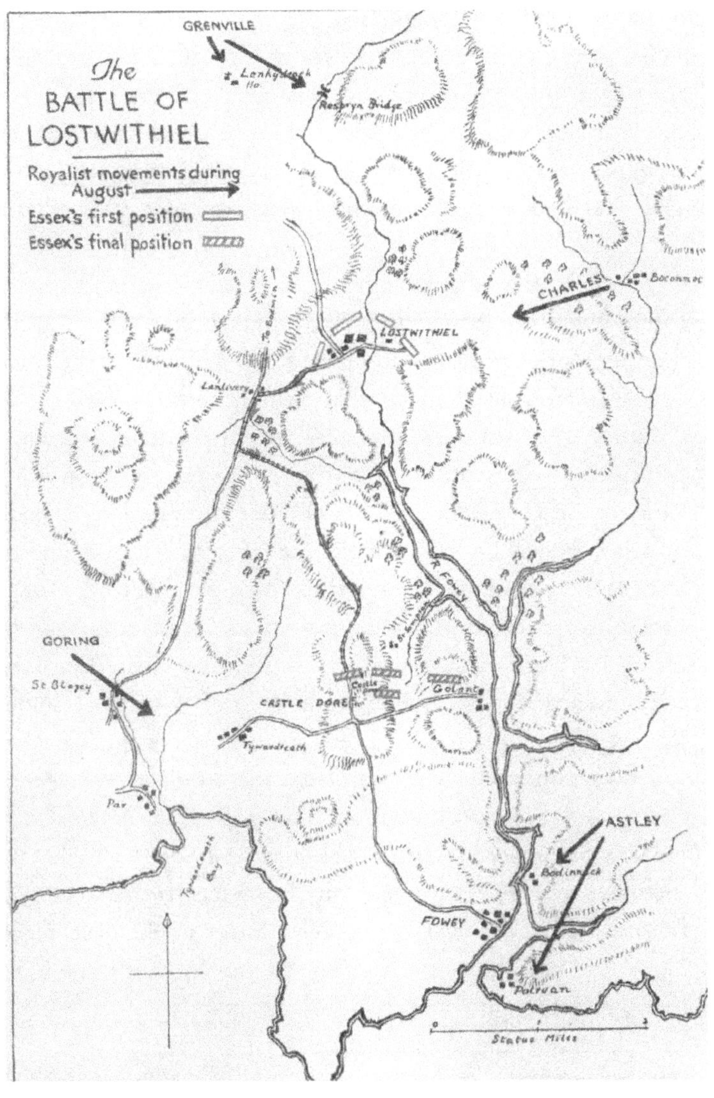

In February of the next year, 1644, the Houses at Westminster joined with their new Scottish allies in appointing a "Committee of Both Kingdoms" which should have charge over the military operations. It was far from being a satisfactory arrangement, but was a considerable advance on the previous system of directing a war by a debating society. In the scattered military campaigns the prospects of Parliament were now better. The Scots had crossed the border on January 19th and had immediately engaged all the attention of Lord Newcastle, thereby releasing the active arm of the Fairfaxes, who routed Byron at Nantwich, stormed Selby, and, joining forces with the Scots and Lord Manchester, shut up the Marquess of Newcastle within the walls of York. In the South Sir William Waller, that "able shifter and chooser of the ground," "William the Conqueror" to his friends and soldiers, had paid off old scores on his adversary-friend, Hopton, for at Cheriton, in Hampshire, on March 29th, in every circumstance of disadvantage, he had defeated the forces of Hopton and the Earl of Forth. In the West Prince Maurice, with 6,000 men, had set siege to Lyme (having not yet its royal suffix), but the sturdy townsmen, behind the flimsiest defences, but strengthened by the heroic leadership of a certain Colonel Robert Blake, repulsed his every assault. At Newport Pagnell, too, Skippon and Cromwell held the Midland royalists in check, and in March Skippon built a fort at Phyllis Court, Henley, to protect the approaches to London.[60] Charles was therefore almost everywhere on the defensive. An energetic prosecution of the war from Westminster might have placed him at the last throw, but such energy was still not to be found there, and Skippon was now to take part in a half-hearted

---

[60] Whitelocke, 83.

offensive movement against the King that was to flicker out in a melancholy humiliation.

The King himself prepared to take the field again in the spring, and Essex and Waller were charged with the campaign against him. The two commanders, Skippon being with Essex, met at Reading, which had been abandoned by the King, on May 19th. For some time Essex and Waller had been on the most strained terms, for Waller was a man quick to anger, and among the mixed qualities of Old Robin there lay a streak of jealousy. By a fools' bargain it was agreed that their armies were to operate separately. Here was Charles's chance. His numbers were too small to face the combined forces of his opponents, but once they separated he might defeat each separately. He therefore took the field, and for some time manoeuvred nervously around Oxford. On June 6th the Parliamentary generals held another council of war at Stow-on-the-Wold, and came to an astonishing decision — not that they should combine to destroy the King's army, but that Essex should sail away into the west to relieve Lyme while Waller remained to engage the King. It may be supposed that Skippon as a plain soldier would oppose such stupidity at the Council, but considerations of policy, sentiment and personality so overtopped the counsels of nearly all the leaders on both sides, save such men as Cromwell, Rupert and Fairfax, that problems either of strategy or even tactics were rarely at this stage seen in their simple military aspect.

The decision indeed angered the Committee of Both Kingdoms, who ordered the Lord-General to remain before Oxford, but the gentle Essex was adamantine on this occasion, and he set a westward course with good speed under a hot sun for that campaign of disastrous memory. Besides Skippon, he had with him Sir William Balfour in command of the horse,

Christopher Whichcote as Sergeant-Major General of the London Brigade, of which there were seven regiments, and Sir John Meyrick in command of the powerful artillery train. Lyme still held out stoutly after two months' siege, and on June 15th it was at last delivered, for on the approach of Essex Maurice had folded his tents.

Essex was not satisfied, however, with so small accomplishment, and, determined to subdue all the south-west, he marched with Skippon farther yet into the sunset. He occupied Weymouth, and though Waller had failed to defeat the King in the indecisive engagement of Cropredy Bridge, near Banbury, on June 29th, he still lingered in Devonshire. Waller's army now disintegrated and Charles seized upon the chance thus given him to pursue Essex and destroy him. He was all the more eager to do so as the Queen herself was in Exeter, and had there on June 16th given birth to the little Princess Henrietta. Queen Mary suffered much after her delivery, and she pleaded with Essex for a safe-conduct that she might take the healing waters of Bath. But to this kindly man, so humane and generous in his habitual ways, the Queen was a dangerous mischief-maker, and he would give her a safe-conduct to nowhere but to London, where not only the best doctors, but also the best prisons were available to her. She refused the Greek gift and escaped by Falmouth to France, only a few days after the news that, at the great battle of Marston Moor, the royalist cause in the North had been overwhelmed.

On July 26th, Charles himself, despite that news and despite the loss of York, arrived at Exeter. On that day the Lord-General was in Tavistock, within a few hours' march of the shelter of friendly Plymouth, which was now open to him by the abandonment of Grenville's siege. But a curse seems to have lain upon Essex during the whole of this expedition. His danger from Charles was clear, his opportunity for refuge or for picking his own battle-ground was ample, yet, deceived by his easy advance, he chose to creep yet farther into the lobster-trap of Cornwall. One may well imagine that his Major-General must have been deeply anxious throughout all this summer's expedition. It was clean against all the Dutch military tradition in which Skippon had been reared. But in Essex's force there were men, such as Lord Robartes, who swayed their commander to this western course merely for the recovery of their own estates that lay there. The impending action, however, was far from the feeble snuffing-out it has been represented to be. As an operation it has much more interest than other battles of the first Civil War, most of which were plain stand-up fights, and although it was Charles's only important victory, it has seldom been given in the history-books the importance it deserves.

From Tavistock, Essex and Skippon turned yet again west, and, driving Sir Richard Grenville before them, crossed the Tamar and came to Bodmin. Essex had been told that Parliament's army would find much support in Cornwall, but he should have known better, since Cornwall had stood fast for the King from the beginning, and the Cornishmen who in the earlier days had marched under Hopton and Grenville had been the bravest and the most victorious of the King's men. Accordingly the soldiers of Essex, though their conduct throughout this westward campaign had been marked by civility and good behaviour, marched hungry in a hostile land, and from Bodmin, hearing of the King's approach, they turned southwards to the sea over the arduous hills till they came, on August 3rd, to stony Lostwithiel, where, on the wooded heights that surround the town, they took up a posture of defence in the hope that relief would come from Waller or from Warwick's fleet.

On the previous day Charles, pursuing them, reached Liskeard, ten miles to the east. Yet the King thought first of peace rather than battle, and his officers, free from the presence of the hated Rupert, were of the same mind. Twice were proposals made to Essex from the royal camp for the discussion of peace proposals, but Essex, himself more anxious for peace than most men, could reply only that he had no authority from Parliament to treat for peace.

Upon failure of these approaches, therefore, the King pressed on with the action. His forces outnumbered those of Essex by 16,000 to 10,000, and he had with him that veteran Scottish soldier the Earl of Forth, now Lord Brentford, who, though old, deaf, and a hard drinker, was a shrewd tactician. With him also were the armies of Prince Maurice, Hopton and Grenville, the command of the horse being entrusted to that dissolute and drunken Lord, George Goring. The King now moved against the Roundheads with all his forces, and there was fighting every day, for the most part actions of cavalry, in which, said Essex, "we beat them every day." Skippon's own regiment lay on the east of Lostwithiel, over against the King at Boconnoc. Yet slowly but skilfully the King's forces drew their net about the unhappy Essex. Lingering at Lostwithiel for nearly a month, Essex made no attempt whatever to secure himself against encirclement in this hostile country, and contented himself with writing heart-cries to Westminster for help which there was little to send, and with calling for provisions that now could reach him only tardily from the sea.

Thus the King's forces first occupied Boconnoc, three miles east of Lostwithiel, on August 4th. On August 11th Grenville seized Respryn Bridge over the Fowey the same distance to the north, together with Lord Robartes's house at Lanhydrock. Having thus blocked Essex up on the land side, the royalists proceeded also to cut him off even from his retreat to the sea. Essex had indeed taken care to possess himself of Fowey, the birthplace of Hugh Peters, on the western side of the river-mouth, but he had neglected to secure any point in the eastern bank, and on the 14th Sir Jacob Astley, Skippon's old comrade-in-arms of the Dutch wars and fellow-countryman of Norfolk, secured command of Bodinnick Ferry, and even Polruan Fort, which faced the town of Fowey across the mouth of the river. Accordingly Essex could no more bring his supply vessels up the creek and had to be content with such provisions as could be landed by boat on the open beach of Tywardreath Bay. From all sides Charles's forces closed in. On the 21st he occupied the commanding hills north-east of Lostwithiel and Grenville took Restormel's ruined castle. From then onwards there was continual fighting at close range. The infantry became wearied out with watching and fighting in heavy rain on the steep hill-sides, where surprise might come at any moment from copse or spur. Essex's regiment had but sixty musketeers, who were never able to be relieved. Finally, on the 26th, Goring's horse occupied St. Blazey on the left rear, and the investment of the Roundheads was now almost complete. Their position was like that of a navy caught in a land-locked anchorage. Their horses could scarcely find forage, and their cheese and biscuit were still upon the seas.

To have remained any longer now at Lostwithiel was to have made certain a disaster which was already threatening enough, for the town lies within a hollow of encircling hills. Moreover, the men were being murdered in their quarters by the hostile Cornishmen, and their food was almost exhausted. Unless they were to risk a break-through into a country barren of food

supplies, there was only one move still possible for Essex —
back into Fowey to await transports. That was the step decided
upon on August 30th for the infantry and guns, but for the
cavalry a bolder move was possible. About 3 o'clock in the
morning of August 31st 2,000 Parliamentary horsemen, being
the whole of their sabres except for a regiment from Plymouth,
broke out from Lostwithiel under Sir William Balfour in wild
and stormy weather, and, riding through the royalist lines
almost unmolested, found safety at length in Plymouth.

The same day the unhappy infantry and the Plymouth Horse,
hungry and rain-soaked, climbed the steep hill out of
Lostwithiel on their retreat to Fowey over a road "extreme foul
with excessive rain." The royalists, warned of their enemy's
intentions by two deserters, did not let slip the infantry so
easily as they had the horsemen. They fell upon the retreating
force vigorously with all arms, charging again and again as the
Roundheads, burdened with guns and baggage, laboured over
the hills in the mud and rain. Yet the Roundheads, fighting
back step by step, from hedge to hedge, among the
honeysuckle and the fading foxgloves, not only held off all the
attacks of the royalists, but also took sixty prisoners, and
maintained their retreat in good order. Skippon himself fought
in the utmost rear all morning — "like a lion." His glove and
his sleeve were shot through, and two bullets passed through
his buff, yet he remained unhurt. Seeing some guns sunk deep
in the mud and the gunners helpless to move them, he at once
rode over and put thirty draught horses to each gun, but the
rotten harness would not stand the strain, and he was obliged
to order the guns to be abandoned.[61]

Fighting thus the most difficult of all actions, in pelting rain,
the soldiers so tired with standing the shock of many cavalry

---

[61] Whitelocke, 102. Rushworth, v, 702.

charges that they could hardly be kept to their colours, the expedition came at last to an eminence upon which stood the earthworks of an ancient British encampment, known as Castle Dore. Here it was that, more than 1,000 years before, Tristan and Iseult had loved, here had stood the great wooden hall that like enough was King Mark's own, and hard by at the church of St. Samson had Mark married the fair Iseult.[62] On that romantic and mysterious hill, with the sea already in clear view behind them, the scream of the gulls about the wild cliffs almost in their ears, and the desolate hills of Bodmin Moor stretching away in front, Essex and Skippon decided to make a stand, though they had covered but four miles in that long wet August morning. To cover the operation of assembling the guns and baggage within the little compass of the old entrenchments, the Plymouth Horse, Essex's regiment and other musketeers charged the enemy, driving them back for two or three fields and taking some colours.[63]

Then came the critical moment of the action. The guns, to the number of thirty-four, and the baggage having been dragged up the hill and brought within the shelter of the ancient earthworks, through breaches which can still be seen, Skippon ordered Colonels Butler, Wear and Bartle, with some guns, to occupy the mile or so, of country on their east flank falling sharply down from Castle Dore to the Fowey. Butler seemed unwilling for the duty. Skippon was astonished at this

---

[62] The recent work of the Excavations Committee of the Royal Institution of Cornwall has clearly revealed the plan of the old wooden settlement on Castle Dore. Its chief feature is a large wooden hall of the sort used by important chieftains, and from the fragments of evidence available this was quite likely the hall of King Mark himself. The bullets of Skippon's musketeers are still to be found in the earth.

[63] Essex to Sir Philip Stapleton.

unwillingness and again commanded him to the post, warning him to maintain it at all costs. Here, therefore, the Parliamentary army made its last stand, and from before noon till sunset beat off assault after assault. As night drew on, however, Wear came in, wounded, and told Skippon he could no longer maintain his post. Skippon angrily ordered him back, but it was too late, for, to Skippon's fury, Butler also came in and reported to him that he had drawn in his regiment, though Skippon knew he was not being seriously pressed. The Royalist horse poured in through the gap, and, wheeling right, immediately commanded the road to Fowey and surrounded their enemy.[64]

As he lay down to armoured sleep that night on the soaked ground in the old earth-fortress of the ancient Britons, Skippon must have known that, if the night did not bring an assault, the morrow must bring either a risky fight against heavy odds or a surrender. The troops were hungry, wet through, and wearied by the strain of the day's rearguard fighting. They had bread and ammunition only for one more day. When the morrow dawned he sought out his commander and reported that the soldiers could not be relied upon to endure another battle.

The immediate effect of this statement was one which must have shocked Skippon and did little for Essex's good report. Death on the battlefield Essex was always ready to face unafraid, but the scorn of Charles's courtiers if he surrendered as a prisoner was to his spirit, as he afterwards wrote, a greater terror than a thousand deaths. He shrank from sharing with his men that more bitter hazard of humiliation, and, in company

---

[64] This is Skippon's own account, given at the subsequent inquiry. Wear and Butler were tried and imprisoned. Rushworth, v, 710-11 and E. 21, 34.

with Lord Robartes and Sir John Meyrick, the commander of the artillery, he slipped away to the riverside and escaped in a small vessel to Plymouth, without telling Skippon.

Thus was the old "Sergeant-Major" left "to carry on" with an army that was surrounded and outnumbered by the enemy by two to one. Before Essex left he sent a message to Skippon bidding him make the best terms he could, and he added in a letter:

> Sir, if you live I shall take as great a care of you as of my father if alive; if God otherwise dispose of you, as long as I have a drop of blood I shall strive to revenge yours on the causers of it.

Left thus alone, Skippon called a council of war of his principal officers. "Gentlemen," he said, "you see our general and some chief officers have thought fit to leave us, and our horse are got away; we are left alone upon our defence. That which I propound to you is this, that we, having the same courage as our horse had, and the same God to assist us, may make the same trial of our fortunes, and endeavour to make our way through our enemies as they have done, and account it better to die with honour and faithfulness than to live dishonourable."[65]

Only a few of Skippon's council concurred in his resolution, however. They emphasised that the horse had advantages for a break-through which the foot had not; the men were weary, and dismayed at their commander's desertion; moreover, intimation had already been received from the King that he was ready to give merciful terms for a surrender. Fortunate it was for them that the King, though they knew it not, was in

----

[65] Rushworth, v, 704; Whitelocke, 102.

almost as great straits as they. He, too, had been sorely pressed to find food, and his soldiers had little stomach for another fight. "Had our success," he afterwards wrote to Rupert, "been either deferred, or of another kind, nothing but a direct miracle could have saved us."

Therefore, when Skippon was obliged to seek a parley with the enemy, the King was found to grant to him not only merciful but also magnanimous terms of surrender, and a treaty was signed on September 1st by Maurice and Brentford on the King's side and by Skippon and Whichcote on the other. By its terms the Parliamentary army was permitted to march out with colours, trumpets and drums, and officers above corporals were permitted to carry sword and pistol — terms which were a personal tribute to Skippon, whose courage in those days alone redeemed the sorry story. All other ranks were to lay down their arms, and Skippon was also to surrender all guns and ammunition. Since the country was hostile, Charles on his part went so far as to provide an escort of 100 royalist horse as far as Poole or Wareham to protect the rebels against his friends.[66]

Accordingly on September 2nd the rebels laid down their arms and marched away with their escort, under the command of Lieutenant-Colonel Adrian Scroop.[67] The rain fell in torrents, and the rebels, drenched, exhausted, coated with mud, were reduced to misery. As they passed unarmed through the jeering enemy ranks the royalists, contrary to the articles, fell upon them savagely, beating them and stripping them of their clothes and their possessions. Skippon at once rode up to the King, who stood to watch the army pass by, and protested to

---

[66] Sloane MSS., 1983, B. fol. 14.
[67] Son of Sir Gervase Scroop, not to be confused with the regicide of the same name, who was the son of Robert Scroop, of Oxfordshire.

him "it was against his honour and justice that his articles should not be observed."

Charles at once responded, himself riding up and down and commanding that there should be no plunder, while his officers furiously beat their own men with the flat of the sword, but the royalist soldiery were beyond control and the plunder continued.

Skippon's carriage and demeanour made a marked impression on the royalists. "He carried himself," said Sir Richard Bulstrode, "with a very good grace." The King himself urged him to change sides, but Skippon replied: "I am fully resolved of those principles to which I stand to be for God and His glory, in which by God's assistance I shall live and die."

But he was still to be sorely tried. As his men passed again through Lostwithiel, the inhabitants, men and women alike, fell upon them with savage cruelty, stripping them sheer to the skin, taking even their shoes and the last scanty vestige of their food. The women camp-followers fared worse still; stripped, beaten, knifed, many of them died on the road.

So, naked, without food or shelter, Skippon's men continued their march for three days in the unceasing rain, sleeping in the sodden fields and living on water. At Okehampton Skippon forced the town to sell them food, but he was made to pay half a crown for a penny loaf and still more for cheese. Out of a total of 6,000, who had marched with him from Castle Dore, 5,000 died by the way from starvation, from wounds and from exposure in this terrible retreat.

Yet he maintained order throughout, and when at length the remnants of the army came to friendly country and were about to enter Bridgwater, Skippon ordered that the royalist convoy, which had afforded them so ineffectual a protection, should be treated with every courtesy, and when he parted from Scroop they exchanged letters of testimony as to the good behaviour of each side, attested in cordial terms.

"In all this trouble," wrote one of Skippon's officers, "I observed Major-General Skippon in his carriage; but never did I see any man so patient, so humble, and so truly wise and valiant."[68]

Thus, through perversion of generalship by his enemy too deplorable for words, Charles cheaply gained a victory which was at least as valuable to his cause as Marston Moor had been to Parliament's. "By that miscarriage," wrote a Parliamentary newspaper when news of the Lostwithiel surrender had reached London, "we are brought a whole summer's travel back."

---

[68] The main authorities for the campaign of Lostwithiel are: Rushworth, 698-711; Walker, *Historical Discourses*, 48-80; Richard Symons Diary (Camden Soc.), 46,54-57,66-67,98; E. 254, 10, 12, 13, 19 and 27, E.6,16, E.9, 3, E, 10, 16, E. 21, 34; Goodwin Pamphlets (Bodleian), 2641, 16; Whitelocke, 98-103; C. S. P. Dom. for the whole period; Clarendon, viii, 169; Cotton, *Barnstaple in the Civil War*, 320. For a detailed account see Mary Coate, *Cornwall in the Great Civil War*, ch. 9.

V. SECOND NEWBURY

Late in September, 1644, Skippon's men straggled unarmed and weary into Portsmouth. Here they were met by Essex, who had been awaiting their arrival, and, though it may seem strange, there were no recriminations. Old Robin, indeed, was always personally popular. Immediate provision was made for rearming Skippon's infantry at Portsmouth, and the City again came forward to offer five new regiments on condition that pay was guaranteed. The Houses, like the King, were at their wits' end for money.

As soon as his army was re-equipped Essex was ordered by the Committee of Both Kingdoms to join forces with Waller and with Lord Manchester, commander of the army of the Eastern Counties Association, fresh from the victory of Marston Moor. The King, his purpose in the West accomplished, had moved back into the Thames Valley, intending to relieve the royalist garrisons beleaguered at Basing House, Donnington Castle and Banbury, while Rupert was making his way southwards from Marston Moor, and then to attack the army of Manchester and Cromwell in the eastern shires. Again the armies of Parliament had a golden chance of crushing the King's army if they had acted with only normal expedition. But the amiable Manchester was but another Essex, shrinking from any heart-blow against the King, and the quarrel between him and Cromwell, his Lieutenant-General of horse, was now developing, as the quarrel between Essex and Waller had already developed on different grounds.

Tardily Manchester moved southwards, but in due time he joined forces with Essex and Waller in Hampshire, thus forming a united army of 19,000 men. Westminster was faced with the delicate question of who was to command this combined force, and took the worst possible of all courses by deciding that it should be commanded by a committee. Essex, however, fell ill, leaving Manchester as the senior commander, while of Essex's own army Skippon took command of the infantry and Sir William Balfour of the cavalry.

Against such a force, the King, with but 10,000 men, was obliged to abandon his attempt to relieve Basing House, and he withdrew towards Newbury, which he entered on October 22nd. The Parliamentary Council of War resolved that he should be followed and brought to battle, and accordingly the armies, after a northward movement towards Reading, swung westwards along the valley of the Kennet towards Newbury.

There was some skirmishing between the two armies about Thatcham, and on the morning of October 26th the Parliamentary forces arrived at Clay Hill, north-east of Newbury beyond the Lambourne, and from that eminence Skippon and the other commanders observed the royalist army drawn up in a position of great strength. Facing eastward, it lay, behind hedges and earthworks, to the north and east of Newbury, athwart the angle made by the confluence of Lambourne and Kennet. Its right flank rested on the town, its left on the Lambourne, but immediately beyond this left extremity, on the north bank of the Lambourne, it held the mansion of Shaw House with some other entrenched buildings as an advanced strong-point. About a mile to the left rear of the royalists Donnington Castle stood on a commanding height of the Berkshire Downs, its guns protecting the King's left flank and rear and covering the road to Oxford. Farther yet in the rear the King had posted Prince Maurice with a reserve or rearguard force, and a battery of guns, occupying the village of Speen and the hill to its west.

As Skippon and the other Parliamentary commanders reconnoitred the position, it was clear that to attack such a position frontally was unwise. It was resolved accordingly to detail a force to effect a wide encircling movement and to take Prince Maurice in the rear at Speen. This task was assigned to Skippon and Waller, and to them were attached also Cromwell and Balfour with their cavalry. These four were the most enterprising and resolute of the army's leaders. As soon as the guns were heard in action at Speen Manchester was to attack Shaw House. It was to be Phillip's first association with Oliver, though he had perhaps already met him in the operations about Newport Pagnell, and it was to mark the begirding of a long friendship.

The force of manoeuvre assembled without delay and moved off northward, keeping out of range of the guns of Donnington Castle. The weather was very cold, and the trees, stripped of their golden autumn shrouds, were already in the skeletal nakedness of winter. Marching by Chieveley, the column slept the frosty night of October 26th in the open fields. The next morning they turned southward over the hills, waded the Lambourne at Boxford after a brisk skirmish, and, as the bells were ringing for worship on that Sunday morning, advanced up the slope of Wickham Heath.

There was, of course, no secrecy in the manoeuvre, royalist skirmishers having hung on Skippon's flank throughout his march, and the King was well prepared for the attack in his rear. He had sent orders to Maurice to face westwards, and the young prince had thrown up earthworks upon the hill and had posted several guns — guns that had been surrendered by Skippon at Castle Dore — in emplacements behind them.

As the attacking force came out up the heath, drum and trumpet called them to deploy. Skippon, with Waller, took the centre with the infantry, having Balfour's cavalry on the right and Cromwell's on the left. On these wings hedges and enclosures again hampered the cavalry, so that practically the whole action was fought by Skippon's and Waller's foot, and notably by Skippon's London regiments. For these, moving forward with singing of psalms, the terrain ahead was a long narrow up-hill stretch of open ground, raked by Maurice's battery of sakers, which began to play upon them as Skippon moved to the assault some time before 3 o'clock of that autumn afternoon, with the sun low behind him.

In the face of a plunging fire the foot advanced steadily, the cannon, said Skippon, making "our ground very hot." As they neared the earthworks a heavy fire of musketry struck them in the face, but a high spirit was in them that day and they did not falter. When almost at gun's mouth Skippon put his infantry to the assault. They leapt the ditch, swarmed up the defences and the gun emplacements, and there they fell upon the enemy with levelled pike and musket clubbed. In Waller's testimony, Skippon's "brave boys" fought that day "undauntedly." Breastwork and guns were taken, and the soldiers, recognising the guns, "clapped their hats on the touch-holes on them to claim them as their own." Others embraced them with joy, saying they would give them "a Cornish hug." On the Cornish soldiers whom they drove before them at the point of pike, the Londoners, remembering their treatment at Lostwithiel, took their revenge with full measure as they dashed down the hill and rolled the enemy into Speen village, where they captured four more guns, and pursued them flying yet beyond. They carried their attack almost to the main body of the King's army, and Charles himself was in danger. Balfour's cavalry, pushing on by the marshy ground beside the Kennet, was at the last barrier and threatening the King when an opportune charge by the royalist horse under Cansfield threw him back, but Skippon, observing the movement, allowed Cansfield's sabres to pursue their charge until within a few yards of his infantry, when he assailed them with massed pikes and volleyed musketry and threw them into retreat. Again his Londoners had shown the merit of his training.

All this time Manchester with his main army had made no move. Had he struck when he should have done, the enemy's resistance to Skippon must have been more quickly overcome, and indeed the force of manoeuvre came near to winning the whole action without that help. Cromwell waited only for Skippon's infantry to clear the last hedges before hurling his cavalry upon the enemy's in the open plain beyond. Slowly and doggedly the foot were accomplishing this task, but the early autumn dusk was now falling under a sky heavy with clouds, and all hope of pressing the attack was now lost.

Not until dusk did Manchester, goaded by his officers, deliver his attack upon Shaw House, and though it was assaulted with gallantry, the attack was repulsed. The action died away, and there was to die away, too, any immediate hope of beating the King. For in the night, seeing himself now at a disadvantage, Charles mustered his forces and marched silently away. He himself, with a body of horse, set off towards Bath to meet Rupert; his stores, ammunition and heavy guns were parked within the shelter of Donnington Castle; and the main body of his troops stole away towards Wallingford. Manchester's crass inefficiency of the day was followed by the equal inertia of the night, and the enemy was allowed to make good his escape unmolested. Thus did Skippon, who once more had borne the brunt of the battle, see his meritorious success thrown uselessly away.

The next few days were occupied by the Parliamentary forces in a half-hearted and dilatory pursuit, in a feeble attempt to besiege Donnington Castle, and in farcical councils of war which did nothing but reveal more clearly not only the timidity and "backwardness to all action" of Manchester, but also the discords of the commanders. "Thou art a bloody fellow," said Manchester to the fiery cavalryman Sir Arthur Hazelrig, "God send us peace." Cromwell, though himself in a strange lethargy, was furious with Manchester, and the quarrel between the two was now boiling up.

While thus at odds they learnt that the King, reunited with Rupert, was marching back to relieve Donnington Castle. It was to Skippon that Manchester now turned for advice, and both agreed that, the cavalry being then quartered at a distance, it was necessary to bring them in the next day before giving action. Manchester and Skippon thereupon wrote to Balfour to summon his squadrons, which he accordingly did, but when Manchester wrote also to Cromwell to the like effect, the Lieutenant-General came to him "in a discontented manner," asking him whether Manchester intended to flay his horses, for their condition was such that if they were again called upon the Earl might have "their skins, but no service from them."[69]

The next day (November 8th) Skippon and other commanders selected a site upon which to give battle to the King in his path to Donnington, but when, on November 9th, the King's army passed by, 11,000 strong, Cromwell's horse and part of Balfour's were still three miles away on Newbury Wash, where Rupert had been drawn up at the first battle. Accordingly, Parliament's main body, having only infantry and

---

[69] Manchester to House of Lords, Rushworth, v, 734.

guns, could not think of attacking, and had to take up a position of defence to the west of Shaw House. It was, in fact, the King who attacked, launching all arms against the Parliamentary foot; but they were "soundly pelted" by the musketeers of Skippon and Manchester, who stood their ground firmly. The royalists, thus repulsed, called off the action, and marched away in "leisurely and soldier-like" manner.

Manchester and Skippon then marched back into Newbury, and the Major-General, in a dispatch written the next night to Essex, complained that in that town the infantry were "miserably pestered" and begged him to do what he could to secure them better quarters, suggesting Reading as a suitable place for winter quarters. The Parliamentary army was, in truth, in low condition. It was a very cold, hard autumn, and Skippon's men were suffering a great deal not only from sickness, but also from the shortage of "firing, food and covering." Many were indeed almost starving, for Newbury was by now as a garden through which the locusts have passed, and Manchester could not even move to prevent the royalists' relief of Basing House.

Thus, in spite of Marston Moor, in spite of the surrender of Newcastle, of York, of Liverpool, of Lincoln and other important points, the year ended with the military aspect well charged with hope for the King. Moreover, he had had news from Scotland that the valiant spirit of Lord Montrose, scrambling over the wildness of the Highlands at the head of a tiny band of fierce Macdonalds, had defeated the Covenanters at Tippermuir and at Aberdeen; and he also had vivid hopes of a secret scheme by the Earl of Glamorgan for raising a great Catholic army from the Continent. But there were spirits at Westminster who had now resolved that the war should no longer be conducted with the old inefficiency, and that step was about to be taken which was to decide the fate of the nation.

VI. NEW MODEL

The immediate results of the Second Battle of Newbury were two — first Cromwell's arraignment of Manchester before Parliament, and more important, the organisation of the New Model.

In the earliest days of the war Cromwell and Hampden had discussed the need for recruiting men who "made some conscience of what they did," and Cromwell had shown to all men how that could be done in his matchless Ironsides. But Waller was the first who gave thought to the idea of a new army of professional soldiers rather than of the local levies whose hearts were in their shops and their pastures. Cromwell now urged the matter upon the Commons. "I hope," he said in a memorable speech, "that we have such true English hearts and zealous affection towards the general weal of our Mother Country as no member of either House will scruple to deny themselves and their private interest for the public good." At last resolved upon a vigorous prosecution of the war, the Houses after much wrangling passed the two complementary measures, the New Model Ordinance and the Self-Denying Ordinance.

The first provided at last for a standing army, free from the obligations of local county committees, available for general service wherever required, and paid regularly out of national funds instead of spasmodically out of local funds. The Self-Denying Ordinance required that all members of both Houses should surrender any military commands that they held within forty days, but that they should be eligible for re-appointment if required. This necessitated the resignations not only of Essex and Manchester, against whom it was chiefly aimed, but also of such valuable men as Lord Warwick, who as Lord High Admiral had successfully held the seas for Parliament during those anxious years, Sir William Waller, who was brave, loyal and resolute, and even Cromwell himself — but that was soon to be remedied.[70]

The New Model Ordinance was not passed in all its stages until February 15th, and the Self-Denying Ordinance until April 3rd, but already on January 21st the Commons had appointed Sir Thomas Fairfax as the new Captain-General of the Parliamentary forces, and Phillip Skippon as Major-General of the foot, the post of Lieutenant-General of the horse being significantly left open. For the fleet William Batten was appointed to succeed Warwick. Fairfax and Skippon were perhaps the best possible men for the posts. Skippon had borne the main burden in three important actions, had shown a great ability in the training of citizen soldiers, and was much valued for his skill in the science of fortifications. Fairfax, for his part, was one of the most sterling characters of the age. Young, tall, swarthy as Strafford, his dark face seamed with wounds and ravaged with constant illness, he was as brave as a lion and as honest as the light. He had no great gifts for strategy or tactics, but he had a thorough competence. In battle he was a flame, his lean, emaciated frame awakening into ecstasies of fearless energy and seeking always the red heart of the fight. His rapid blows in the fight for the Yorkshire clothing towns early in the war, with the brilliant young

----

[70] This is one of the points upon which Mr. Belloc is not fair to Oliver, whose subsequent reappointment to his command was not due to any scheming on his part, but to the urgent entreaty of Fairfax's officers. Moreover, Cromwell was not the only member of the House so reappointed, Sir William Brereton, Sir Thomas Middleton and Lord Warwick being others.

Colonel Lambert as his chief lieutenant, followed by his fierce thrust at Nantwich, marked him out as a general who would not shrink like Manchester or stray like Essex. He could suffer distress with fortitude and patience or spur to the first beckoning of opportunity. Though a stammer imposed upon him the habits of diffidence and silence, he had great personal charm and that quality of leadership by example which gives to a commander a devoted following. Moreover, he was clean of politics, and the warring sects of Westminster knew not whether he was Presbyterian or whether he was one of the new "tender consciences."

The New Model mustered about Windsor. It may be said to mark the birth of the British Army of to-day, with which it has an unbroken connection, and in particular it is to the New Model that British soldiers owe their traditional red tunics, for, as befitted a national army, the clothing now became for the first time a uniform, red, with drab breeches, throughout all regiments except the firelocks of the artillery, who wore coats of a tawny hue. Each regiment continued, however, to be distinguished by the facings selected by or for each commander. Those of Fairfax's regiments, horse and foot, were blue, and so it is that the "royal" colours of red and blue are still the colours of the Guards and of the Royal Regiment of Artillery and of the Royal Engineers.

The New Model Ordinance provided for an army of eleven regiments of cavalry, each of 600 sabres and divided into six troops; twelve regiments of infantry, each of 1,200 men divided into ten companies of varying strengths; a thousand dragoons and a train of artillery. In addition Parliament still had at its service the armies of Poyntz in the North, Massey in Wiltshire, Brown in the Midlands, besides several other forces — and the Scots. Skippon's old foot from the army of Essex formed the core of the New Model infantry, together with 600 from Waller and others from Manchester. A notable feature of the new army was the youth of the officers. Fairfax himself was but thirty-three, and some of his colonels were even younger.

To Skippon was specially entrusted the task of scrutinising the lists of officers and selecting those best fitted to be retained, and he did this regardless of social position or political influence. Nevertheless, contrary to a widely-held notion, the officers were at first nearly all men of good birth, though in Okey, the ship-chandler who commanded the dragoons, Pride, the drayman who was afterwards to become famous for his "Purge," and Ewer, the serving-man, there was evidence of those revolutionary ideas by which the first test of a man should be his fitness for his duties. The work of organising and training the New Model devolved chiefly upon Skippon, an achievement for which he has never received his full share of credit. He added, said Sprigge, "much life and expedition to the business" and performed "singular and extraordinary service."[71] Cromwell, it must be remembered, was not present. In particular Parliament ordered that Skippon's certificate of "good carriage" should be required of all officers who were no longer employed, before payment of their arrears, and he was very soon called upon to deal with some serious trouble at Reading, the reorganisation requiring that the six regiments there should be reduced into three regiments, and there was great dissatisfaction, the men showing signs of mutiny.

Skippon accordingly proceeded to Reading on April 4th to abate the discontent and to put the reorganisation into motion. He was welcomed by the officers, to whose necessitous and

---

[71] *Anglia Rediviva*, 10.

"tottering condition" he found that the discontents were chiefly due. He ordered all the regiments to muster the next morning, and when he appeared before them was greeted by the soldiers with a "general shout and acclamation."[72] "Being," as Whitelocke said, "more a soldier than an orator, he spake plainly to them to this purpose:

> Gentlemen and fellow-soldiers all, I am now to acquaint you with the commands of Parliament, to which in conscience to God, and love to our country, we are bound to give all cheerful and ready obedience. There is a necessity lies upon us (since three armies are to be reduced into one) that some commanders and officers must go out of their employments wherein they now are; it is not out of any personal disrespect to any of you that shall now go off, therefore I hope you will behave yourselves accordingly. I have received order from the House of Commons to take notice what the comportment shall be of those who must now go off, and to certify unto them: I know you will behave yourselves like men of honour and honesty (as indeed you are) and that I shall have no cause but to make a good report of you, which I shall do according to your carriage in this reducement, both to the Speaker of the honourable House of Commons, and the Committee of Both Kingdoms, and that particular Committee appointed to take you into consideration and to take in your accounts and pay you part of your arrears at present; and for the rest, you are to have a debenture upon the public faith of the kingdom.
>
> But if there shall be any among you, who out of any personal respect, or private discontent shall make any disturbance in this reducement, so as to obstruct or hinder a work of so public concernment, I shall not fail to give him his true character to the State, without personal respect to any: and therefore let no man deceive himself, for although he may

---

[72] *Several Letters* (Th.); Whitelocke, 141.

perhaps occasion some trouble in the present business, yet in the issue, the greatest mischief will fall upon him himself: but I hope I shall find none such here.[73]

He continued in the same strain to assure them that pay and new clothes would be immediately provided, and the whole of the rank and file consented willingly to the new terms of service, some of the sergeants and corporals even agreeing to re-enlist as privates. Later Skippon performed a similar service with the cavalry, and the inhabitants of Reading, who had been witnesses of the mutinous disposition, did very much wonder, said the army treasurers in their report to the Houses, at so great a change.[74]

In one respect at least the New Model was to prove more acceptable than the King's troops. The wholesale plunders by the King's armies in the West under such men as Colonel George Goring and Sir Richard Grenville, by which large areas had been stripped bare of food, animals and valuables, and the worse tradition of Rupert by which civilian populations, such as that in Bolton, had been butchered and raped in the full-blooded Spanish manner, had made their names hateful to the countryside, and if the Parliamentary armies also sometimes ate a county clean, yet their rare outbursts of slaughter fell only upon the hated Irish barbarians and the "harlots" who followed in their train. Their record under the decent influence of Fairfax and Skippon was to be further improved with the stimulus of regular pay and the rule of a regular discipline. "Those under the King's command," Clarendon admitted bitterly, "grew insensibly into all the licence, disorder and impiety with which they had reproached the rebels," while the

---

[73] Rushworth, vi, 17; *Several Letters* (Th.).
[74] *Several Letters* (Th.).

rebels on the other hand grew into "great discipline, diligence and sobriety."

While Parliament had been making these plans for its new army it had also been engaged in further fruitless peace discussions with the King, but the prospects of peace were not advanced when on January 10th, 1645, Archbishop Laud, after a dreary four years' trial, laid down his old grey head upon the executioner's block,

An old weak man for vengeance thrown aside,

praying that the grace of repentance might be given to all men of blood. Charles continued at Oxford, uncertain whether to join Goring in the West, or to march with Rupert to Scotland, where Montrose, with his tiny band, had crushed the power of the Campbells in another fierce Highland battle at Inverlochy. Cromwell, however, dispatched by the Houses while the new army awaited its artillery, immobilised the King by a brilliant raid in which he swept round Oxford and carried off all the heavy draft horses.

VII. NASEBY

Thus, when Fairfax was ready to move from Windsor, his brand new army was already at the King's gates. Against all common sense, however, the Committee of Both Kingdoms, who yet for a little while kept the control of strategy in their own infirm hands, ordered him to march far into the West, where the heroic Blake was holding the frail wooden fences of Taunton against all the assaults of Goring and Hopton. Taunton, certainly, was important to Parliament, but the Committee could never see with military eyes. Fairfax accordingly on April 30th, 1645, set off for the relief of Taunton at the head of 11,000 men in their new red coats, and was joined presently by Cromwell (who had not yet been appointed to the New Model). The Army, however, was still so unready and so much below strength that Skippon had to remain behind to hasten the supply of recruits, guns and stores, and a letter from him to Fairfax, one of the few that remains in manuscript, shows that he was still at Reading on May 17th.[75] In this letter he suggests that Fairfax should halt for a day before effecting a junction with Cromwell while the guns were being sent forward and he asks for an escort of cavalry for them.

Thus the King, reinforced by Rupert and Goring, who had tired of besieging Blake in Taunton, was able to march out from Oxford, free to strike where he liked, and Fairfax had travelled as far as Blandford before he was ordered to halt. His new orders, however, were as bad as his first, for he was now

---

[75] Sloane MSS., 1519, fol. 116.

required, after sending on a force for the relief of Taunton, to waste his time in laying siege to Oxford, though the King had escaped from it. The investment was begun on May 22nd, but Skippon, who had now joined Fairfax, was detached to lay siege to Borstall House, a few miles away, where Sir William Campion was holding out for the King.

Fortunately for Parliament, the royalists' strategy was on this occasion as bad as their own. Uncertain what to do in the face of conflicting counsels, Charles foolishly sent Goring back to the West against Blake, and himself marched north with diminished numbers. At the end of May he delighted Rupert's robber heart by throwing him at Leicester, where he sacked that city to the uttermost crevice of every shop, house and hovel, and rolled off to Newark with 140 carts of plunder.

Leicester, however, brought the Westminster Committee to its senses, for it threatened the eastern counties, "the holy land of their cause"; and from Scotland came news that at Auldearn the genius and valour of Montrose had again shattered the Covenanters, so that Lord Leven's Scottish army, instead of marching south against the King, had had to turn back in Yorkshire from its intent. Fairfax was therefore ordered to leave the siege of Oxford and march to the defence of the eastern counties, and he was at last released from the leading rein of the Committee and given full authority to ride as he thought fit. He broke up from before Oxford on June 5th, but before going forward turned aside in his march to join Skippon before Borstall House, which was still holding out. That night Skippon attempted to carry the house by storm, but, the moat being found to be much deeper than expected, he was repulsed with loss, and, Fairfax having no intention to be further delayed, the next day the siege was raised.

So they marched, to dig for Charles the grave of his hopes. On the 8th Fairfax learnt that the King was still at Daventry, and, a council of war having declared for the simple plan of seeking him at once and fighting him, Skippon was directed to draw up a plan of battle and assign to every regiment its place. Cromwell, whose name was on all men's lips, had now been obliged by the Self-Denying Ordinance to quit his command, but an urgent request was sent by the Army to the Houses that he might be appointed to the vacant post of Lieutenant-General of the horse, and on the very eve of the battle to come the great commander brought the magic of his presence on to that field of destiny.

On June 12th the King hunted in Fawsley Park, the house of Elizabeth Knightley, Hampden's daughter, where Hampden, Pym and Saye had, hatched so many of their schemes. So great a contempt had the King's officers for the "New Noddle," under its "brutish general," as Charles spoke of Fairfax, that they were unaware of its so near presence until, on that day, a body of Parliamentary horse appeared at Kislingbury, eight miles from the royal army at Daventry. The King was summoned from the chase, the scattered regiments called in, and on the 13th he moved on to Market Harborough, pursuing his march to the North. Fairfax, following hard, sent forward Ireton's horse to outmarch the enemy if possible and fall upon his flank. The same evening Ireton dashed into the little village of Naseby, so unexpectedly that he took prisoner some twenty of Rupert's horse who were playing quoits at their leisure and another party sitting easily at supper.

Battle was now certain, and in the moist dawn of June 14th Rupert drew up the King's army on a long hill a little south of Market Harborough, waiting for the enemy to bend their course over the rolling land that lies to the north of Naseby.

The hours sped by and no enemy appeared. Rupert sent forward his scoutmaster to discover them, but Ruce returned saying they were nowhere to be found. Rupert, in his scarlet cloak and silver lace, accordingly rode forward through the village of Clipston on a personal reconnaissance, and discovered the serried redcoats of Fairfax on the hills between that village and Naseby, apparently in full retreat. They were, however, merely retiring on Cromwell's advice to the higher ground of Mill Hill behind, and when Rupert brought forward his army to attack advantageously from Dust Hill, on the half flank, Fairfax moved to the left to conform. Had Rupert marshalled on the high steep spur near Clipston and stood for his enemies' up-hill attack, he would likely have won the day, but his sanguine spirit saw them already defeated, and his fighting heart could not abide to wait.

The rival armies were thus facing each other in parallel, Fairfax, with 14,000 men, outnumbering the King's 7,500 by nearly two to one. On all sides successive waves of little hills stretched to a distant horizon. The two long ridges upon which the armies stood were but gentle slopes, and between them lay the flat hollow of Broadmoor, where the long June grasses, bending their feathered crests beneath the gentle wind, ran before its impulse in soundless waves. Skippon, whose duty it was to marshal the infantry in the centre, drew them up on the northern slope of Mill Hill in a fallow field, having away to the left the protection of a hedge known as Sulby Hedge, while furze and broken ground helped his right. The site was a strong one, but to Skippon's great annoyance he was required for some reason to withdraw a little behind the crest of the hill, a position in which, it seems to-day, the range of his musketry against an advancing enemy must have been much restrained by the brow of the land.

Following the array of battle which Skippon had prepared, the infantry were as usual disposed in the centre, and the whole army was in double line of regiments, save where, trampling the clover on the right, Cromwell's regiments of horse were dressed in treble line because of the confined ground. Skippon's own regiment was on the left of the infantry, with himself at its head and the forlorn hope immediately in front. On his right Skippon had placed successively the regiments of Sir Hardress Waller, little Pickering, the stripling Montague, and Fairfax's own, and between each regiment was a section of small guns. In the second line of infantry he placed the three further regiments of Pride the Purger, the hot-headed Robert Hammond, and Rainsborough the seaman-rebel. Each regiment had its pikemen in the centre, and its musketeers on the flanks. On the right of the infantry were Cromwell's horse, numbering 3,600 sabres, and on Skippon's left, between him and Sulby Hedge, the remainder of the horse under the command of Ireton, who had but that morning been appointed Commissary-General. Further to the left, behind Sulby Hedge, were stationed Okey's picked dragoons, who, in the manner of dragoons, dismounted and lined the hedgerow with their carbines. The front was a mile in length.

The army of the King, commanded by a German and marshalled by the Spaniard Gomez, was similarly arrayed. Rupert's horse under his sky-blue banner faced Ireton's. In the centre the foot were drawn up in solid *tercios* after the Spanish manner, under old Lord Astley, that "honest, brave, and plain man." On the left, facing Cromwell's horse, were 2,000 sabres under Sir Marmaduke Langdale, the long, thin Yorkshireman, solemn of countenance, brave as a lion, uncertain of temper. Like Parliament's, the royal army was drawn in double line of regiments, but in the rear were the King himself with his foot guards and Rupert's famous foot regiment of Bluecoats. Apart from some discontented Yorkshire horse under Langdale, the King's was an army of veterans, rich in officers of experience. Parliament's on the other hand had a large number of recruits mixed with their more tried troops.

At about half-past ten, Rupert, believing from the continual shifting of the red regiments that Fairfax had no wish to fight, ordered the King's army to advance, and they came on, horse and foot, across the waving grasses, every man wearing a beanstalk in his hat. As they moved down the slope of Dust Hill, across the level bottom, and up again to mount Mill Hill, Fairfax gave them only two or three rounds from his guns, and on the crest of the hill the two armies crashed together. They touched first upon the west wing. Here Rupert's horse, though galled by the fire of the dragoons from Sulby Hedge and with all the advantage of the ground against them, charged up Mill Hill as Ireton's trotted down to meet them and at the first shock scattered the red horse with the impetuosity of their onset. Ireton himself was wounded and captured, but Rupert, forgetful still of past lessons, drove clean through his enemy and carried his charge right to the enemy's baggage lines hard by Naseby village.

In the centre, where both Fairfax and Skippon lay, a critical action was being fought between the opposing infantry. At his first onset Astley forced the Parliamentary infantry to give ground, for on their left, where Skippon's own regiment was posted, their flank had been left in the air by Ireton's rout. Shaken by the very lively attack of the royalist Welsh infantry, they fell back on the line of the reserves, in spite of their superior numbers, Skippon having some difficulty in steadying his ranks. Rupert's infantry of the Blue came up into the action, and the royalists pressed forward with fine spirit, but at the reserve line Fairfax and Skippon rallied their faltering regiments as they rode among them and bade them stand their ground, while Hugh Peters, with Bible and pistol in either hand, rode from rank to rank with strident exhortation in his office of warrior-priest. Thus for some while the two forces engaged furiously hand-to-hand. Presently Skippon, seeing that some of the scattered Parliamentary horse on his left who had lingered for pillage among the dead were caught at a disadvantage, moved to their rescue with some of his foot and charged the enemy. But in that charge he was himself struck, dangerously wounded by a shot in the left side. A bullet at short range fractured his armour and caused a piece of it to be driven into his stomach. Nevertheless, he continued to lead the charge. Fairfax, riding up to him, desired him to leave the field, but Skippon answered that he "would not stir so long as a man would stand." He accordingly stayed out the battle, remaining in his saddle for two and a half hours, and as he was the first on the field so was he the last to leave.[76]

At this crisis of the battle came the sword of Cromwell to decide the issue, as it had done at Marston Moor. As Rupert had routed Ireton on the west flank, so had Cromwell on the east driven Langdale down the hill. But while Rupert pursued the flying horse beyond the field, Cromwell, as soon as he saw that Langdale was in flight, halted his main onset, sent a few squadrons to press the defeat of Langdale, wheeled his remaining regiments to the left and fell upon the flank of the royal infantry. Okey, upon the farther wing, mounted his dragoons and did the like. The King himself, with his scant reserve, moved to their succour with a charge upon Cromwell's

---

[76] *Letter from a Gentleman*, E.288 (28); Rushworth, vi, 43; George Bishop to Lt.-Col. Roe, E.288 (38); *England's Worthies*, 55; Whitelocke, 150, 151.

flank, but Lord Carnworth, seizing his bridle, cried: "Will you go upon your death?" Someone gave the order "March to the right," and the reserve wheeled about and rode from the field.

The royal infantry in the centre were now *à outrance*. Pressed with pike and musket in front, charged in both flanks and in the rear with sword, pistol and carbine, they broke against the overwhelming odds. Regiment after regiment laid down their arms and gave themselves up to the enemy, but Sir George Lisle's regiment of Bluecoats died where they stood. Rupert, who might have saved the day if he had turned on Skippon as Cromwell had turned on Astley, had been checked at the rebels' baggage lines by a sharp fire from the guard, and now too late he rode back to the field again, to find the action nearly ended and the day lost. The royal army was irretrievably broken, and its infantry had ceased to exist. For a moment the royalist horse reformed in the rear, but seeing how sweeping was the disaster, wheeled about and sought safety in flight. For fourteen miles Fairfax's troopers swept after them in pursuit, slaughtering as they rode, till at last the walls of Leicester were reached.

No fewer than 5,000 prisoners fell to Parliament, of whom 500 were officers, together with the whole of the King's artillery train and baggage, his cabinet of papers and letters and his personal servants. Fairfax, in his dispatch to Parliament the next day, wrote:

> Major-Gen. Skippon was shot through his side, but notwithstanding continued in the field with great resolution. And when I desired him to go off the field he answered, *He would not go off as long as a man would stand*; still doing his office as a valiant and wise commander.

It was credibly reported at the time that the King himself said,

"in a kind of consolatory way" as it were, "that though he had
lost the victory at Naseby, yet Skippon was slain."[77]

The wound was in fact severe. There was a deep laceration
about eight inches long where the bullet and the fragment of
armour had entered below the ribs on the left side. Skippon,
now in considerable pain, but declaring in his hearty way that
he did not grudge it, was helped from the field by an officer
named George Bishop, who took him to a house near-by,
carried him up to a room, stripped him, and saw his wound
dressed, saying:

"Sir, your wound hath caused a little cloud on this glorious
day."

"By no means," replied Skippon, "let mine eclipse its glory,
for it is to my honour that I should have received a wound."[78]

It was a month before he could be moved, and the grateful
Commons sent down Dr. Clarke specially to attend him,
ordering a grant of £200 to be made to him and a further £200
for the doctors.[79] He also received letters of thanks for his
conduct from the Speakers of both Houses of Parliament.
When fit to travel he was placed in a horse-litter and brought
to London, but just before reaching London on July 16th a
curious accident befell him that might have ended his life.

As he was passing through the town of Islington a mastiff
suddenly ran out of a house and fell fiercely upon one of the
horses that were carrying the litter. It seized the horse by the
hindquarters, causing it "to fling and fly about, and beat and
shake the litter up and down, to and fro, in a most dangerous
manner." The litter was nearly overthrown, and Skippon was
tossed about "like a dog in a blanket." At length, all attempts

---

[77] *England's Worthies*, 55.
[78] Bishop to Roe, *supra.*
[79] Whitelocke, 152, 153.

to beat off the dog having failed, it was dispatched with a sword.

Skippon was taken to his house in St. Bartholomew the Great, and prayers were said for him in all the churches of London. He was attended by Mr. Trapham, a surgeon, who succeeded in extracting the portions of clothing which were still embedded in the wound, causing it to fester, and a perfect cure was made.[80]

During this year, when his third little book was published under the title of *The Christian Centurion's Observations*, his mind dwelt much upon that hidden sorrow of his which lies behind all these years. One feels that it is concerned with his family, though there is little evidence. The "cross" that he bears brings him nearer still to God. He speaks of "that intolerable burden (Lord, Thou knowest my meaning and necessity)"; but always "in every cross and calamity, yea, though never so grievous and desperate, even in my present misery," there is comfort in "my alone all-sufficient Saviour." He speaks with feeling also of his poverty, and prays for some happy circumstance "to relieve my wants and present feared calamities."

---

[80] *Harleian Miscellanies*, iii, 136; *England's Worthies*, 57.

VIII. TENDER CONSCIENCES

As he lay recovering from his hurt, Skippon heard the great scandal caused by the publication of the papers found in the King's cabinet that had been captured at Naseby. Here was the clearest proof of his duplicity, showing how, while he was negotiating for peace at Uxbridge, he was bargaining for the hire of foreign soldiery from the Duke of Lorraine and Papist soldiery from Ireland. He heard, too, how the Parliamentary arms continued their victorious way — how Fairfax marched into Somerset with the New Model, Skippon's regiment going with him, and utterly defeated Goring at Langport on July 10th; how they then besieged Prince Rupert in Bristol and forced him to surrender; how the King, marching north to attempt a junction with the victorious Montrose in Scotland, was intercepted and defeated in a sharp cavalry action by Major-General Poyntz on Rowton Heath on September 24th; and bow there the news came that at last Montrose himself, after almost winning Scotland back for the King, had already been overwhelmed beyond redemption at Philiphaugh on September 13th. Even Rupert had been urging the King to peace since the end of July, and after his surrender of Bristol Charles had dismissed him. The King, living in a strange, cold, spiritual aloofness, impassible and unimpassioned, made no sign that he knew the end must be near, and with an eagerness that contradicted all reality, clutched at each new straw borne down by the rising waters.

By the end of the autumn Skippon was sufficiently recovered from his wound to be employed again. There came a particular request from a body of the citizens of Bristol that the governorship of that city might be entrusted to the popular Major-General, and Parliament granted the request on December 2nd. It was the most important governorship, tantamount to command of all the western counties, but, deficient in men and in money, he found himself beset with difficulties, and in a letter to the House of Lords deplored his inability to fulfil all that was expected of him. Therefore he was perhaps not sorry when he was called upon to rejoin the army in the field, to direct the siege operations against Oxford, which Fairfax invested in May, 1646. Happily for that city, however, it was spared the ravishment of assault, for on June 20th articles of capitulation were signed, and two days later Prince Rupert and Prince Maurice rode out over Magdalen Bridge, to disappear for a little while from the English scene.[81]

Meanwhile Skippon learnt that Charles, riding through the Midlands disguised as a servant, had placed himself under the protection of the Scots, he thinking they would safely restore him to his throne, they that he would embrace the Presbyterian Covenant and cast out all bishops. But both were vain delusions, and the Scots, carrying him a prisoner to Newcastle, held him as a pledge against the satisfaction of their arrears of pay due from the English Parliament. They had no wish for him if he would not join their faith, but Westminster was less squeamish, and, anxious that the hungry Scots should quit English soil, they clinched the bargain. On the advice of Fairfax Parliament selected Skippon as the instrument of its execution, and he was appointed to command the convoy for the first instalment of £200,000, and, while continuing in the governorship of Bristol, where he had appointed his son-in-law, Lieut.-Colonel William Rolfe, as his Deputy-Governor,[82]

---

[81] L. J., viii, 153; Sprigge, 258, 266.
[82] Clarke Papers, i, 162.

to act also as Governor of Newcastle and Tynemouth upon the departure of the Scots. A few days earlier, December 5th, Skippon had himself been elected to Parliament, being returned as member for Barnstaple, but it was some time before he took his seat. The convoy of treasure left London on December 16th in thirty-six carts, and Skippon joined it at Northampton, where the army was in winter quarters. At York he issued one of his admirable and incisive proclamations, commanding his men to observe "a fair and civil carriage towards the Scots," and on January 30th, 1647, he paid over the first £100,000 to the Scots at Newcastle, and took possession of the city.

On February 3rd, the second £100,000 having been paid, the King rode out of Newcastle under the charge of the new English Commissioners, and, after a triumphal progress in which a war-weary people flocked into the streets to do him honour, he was lodged in Holmby House, Northamptonshire.

The phase which now follows is one of confused debates, proclamations, negotiations and sudden gestures, tedious in their detail, though of much constitutional interest. The land was leaderless, and though nearly all men longed to see the King at the helm once more, the people at large being indeed filled with enthusiasm for the appealing figure of a King in chains, yet the separate parties had very different views on the conditions under which he should assume his captaincy, and he for his part, with his incurable itch to outwit his opponents and to set one against another, would give no decisive answer to any party. It was a time of mental chaos in which the gusty winds of change seemed to blow from all directions, leaving ordinary men bewildered in a sea of doubt, at a loss to know how to set their sails. Age-old habits, ideas, and faiths seemed suddenly to drop away. The tremor that possessed the waters threw up before men's eyes the strangest new ideas — some exalted, some wicked, many odd, but almost all terrible or wonderful to minds either shocked or eagerly expectant. The very bases of citizenship on the one hand and of religion on the other were challenged. With Catholicism cast out and with Anglicanism suspect, there came in turn a demand that the shackles of Presbyterianism likewise should be shaken off, and that "tender consciences" who were offended by even the least of orthodoxies should have freedom to worship in any other way they pleased. So, amid the tumult of ideas, there emerged, vaguely and indecisively at first, two of enduring importance to mankind — the idea of the sovereignty of the people, and the idea of religious freedom.

We owe those ideas, not to Parliament, but to the Army, and the dominant issue in the phase that is now entered is the struggle between a narrow, bitter, arrogant Presbyterian majority at Westminster and the vital flame of the New Model. If Parliament could be said to have any leaders at all, they were such men as the younger Sir Henry Vane and Sir Arthur Hazelrig, the one a political mystic and the other a man of violent temper who had led the famous heavy cavalry in the army of "William the Conqueror." Both were obsessed with the idea of the sovereignty of Parliament, but to them it meant only the sovereignty of their own circle, and their arrogant exclusiveness had small room for the notion of responsibility to the people at large. Now under the itch of inaction the New Model Army was raising the voice of discontent. The pay of the infantry was eighteen weeks in arrear, and that of the horse forty-three weeks. The men were also deeply indignant that individual soldiers were being proceeded against in the courts of law for acts of damage necessarily committed in the stress of war. Officers and men alike held meetings of protest and submitted resolutions of their grievances. But Parliament in the pride of its victory was arrogant, and its Presbyterian majority hostile to the rising voice of the "independents," the hundred queer faiths that were attempting exact definitions of the inscrutable and that were muttering the patriarchal phrases of the Scriptures in billet and marketplace and parade-ground. They who had demanded toleration of Laud knew no tolerance of the Lilburnes or the soldier-saints who dreamed visions or passionately forswore passion. They deeply suspected Cromwell, who was championing the cause of these "tender consciences."

Yet the behaviour of the soldiers was at first carefully moderate. Though they may have had mixed motives, their grievances of pay were very real and pressing, and as one man they stood up for them. They were very far from being all of the "godly party," but it was inevitable that in such a discontent the ardent spirits should lead the singing and that the calls of piety and purse should make common chorus. Parliament treated their requests first with contempt, and then with anger. After all, they were only soldiers and must obey.

A way out of the trouble seemed to appear when Lord Ormonde, the King's Lord-Lieutenant of Ireland, gave notice that he was now prepared to surrender his charge to the Parliament. Here was an opportunity to send the bulk of the Army to Ireland; the remainder not required could be disbanded. Parliament called for volunteers, but the soldiers asked first for redress of their grievances and assurances for the future. The House not only refused to listen to their representations, but also aroused their further resentment by threatening that any who persisted in the complaints should be proceeded against as enemies of the State. At the end of March they learned that, with the single exception of Skippon's regiment, which was with its commander at Newcastle, every outlying regiment was on the march to concentrate at Saffron Walden. Accordingly, on March 29th, 1647, the Houses summoned the Major-General himself to resume his duties with the Army, in the hope that the influence of that frank and sturdy soldier would be put forth on their side, and a week later they appointed him to command the expedition to Ireland, with the title of Field-Marshal.

Skippon, however, whose son William had died a few days before in Edinburgh, was very reluctant and begged to be excused. "I am so sensible," he wrote, "of my own indisposedness of mind, inability of body, distractedness of estate and family, that I ingenuously confess myself unfit and unable to undertake or undergo such an employment."[83]

Skippon nevertheless left Newcastle late in April, leaving his Lieutenant-Colonel, Richard Ashfield, as his deputy, and on the 29th he took his seat in Parliament. He was at once strenuously pressed to accept the Irish appointment, but his reluctance was overborne only when he was told that without his acceptance the public safety could not be secured.[84] At this moment there is no doubt that he was seated in general respect higher than almost anyone in the country. Fairfax was ill, Cromwell was feared and suspected, and the common soldier's view of Skippon had been well expressed by Major Samuel Kem in a farewell sermon to his men at Bristol. "You are the happiest garrison in the kingdom," said Kem, "whilst you possess within your line that real piece of valour, humility, and sincerity, a no less noble than cordial patriot of his kingdom,

---

[83] L. J., ix, 122, 138. He had recently asked Fairfax for a commission for William (Sloane MSS., 1519, fol. 141).
[84] Cary, i, 312.

your Governor; who abhors all self-ends, and denieth attendance only for the public good."[85]

Upon the same day Skippon was visited by three troopers from the cavalry at Saffron Walden named Edward Sexby, William Allen and Thomas Shephard. They were the first of the new "Agitators," that is to say, agents, appointed by the private soldiers, and they brought to Skippon a letter signed by themselves and thirteen other agitators and asked the Field-Marshal to lay their complaints before Parliament. Their letter asked for help "from that hand that hath so often been engaged with us, and from that heart that hath as often been so tender over us," but warned him with every expression of respect that they would have to show themselves averse to serving under him in Ireland unless their desires were granted. Similar letters were sent to Fairfax and Cromwell.

Accordingly Skippon the next day produced the letter in the Commons, and we may assume that he considered this sort of thing out of accord with military discipline. The Presbyterians certainly were furious, and the three Agitators themselves were called before the House and cross-examined. They told the House that they had been engaged in Parliament's cause ever since Edgehill; that they had been at Newbury under Skippon; and that one of them when he was on the ground with five dangerous wounds had been come upon by Skippon himself, who, pitying his sad condition, had given the man five shillings to procure some relief. This Skippon himself confirmed to be true, saying "that they were honest men, and that he wished they might not be severely dealt with."[86]

---

[85] Seyer, *Memorials of Bristol*, ii, 466.
[86] Rushworth, vi, 474; Holles, *Memoirs*, ed. Maseres, 241; Cary, i, 201; *Vindication of Sir William Waller*, 114 *et seq.*; c.f. Clarke Papers, i, 431.

The Commons were now seriously disturbed, and they ordered that Field-Marshal Skippon should himself go down to the Army, assisted by Cromwell, Ireton and Colonel Fleetwood, to endeavour to quiet the distempers and to call again for volunteers for Ireland. The next few months were occupied with a continuous wrangle between Parliament and Army, and into all the details of that battle of words there is no need to enter. It will be sufficient to say that during that time Skippon was almost continuously with the Army as Parliament's chief Commissioner, and that he was the main channel by which the negotiations passed. Having himself a very natural sympathy with the soldiers, he chose the path of reconciliation when Parliament would have dictated, and if he failed it was because the "sour countenances and harsh carriage" of the Presbyterians that he disliked so much blinded them to the demands alike of fair dealing and of expediency. On May 7th and again a week later he presided, as senior commissioner, over the famous meetings of officers held in Saffron Walden church, stormy meetings in which he was hard put to keep order among the quarrelsome officers, urging them "to hear one another with sobriety," and "to speak with moderation or else be silent." But he could not fail to be moved by the ardent advocacy of John Lambert, the rising young Yorkshire colonel who championed the cause of the aggrieved, so that he reported to Parliament with his fellow-commissioners that they "found the Army under a deep sense of some suffering." Nevertheless, Skippon lost much of his great following among the soldiers, and a few days later it was said that he "is quite lost in the Army by endeavouring to please both sides." Moreover, the Commons remained blind to the danger till, Cromwell having deserted the Field-Marshal and swung over completely to the side of the soldiers, Cornet Joyce kidnapped the person of the King on June 4th.[87]

This was going too far for Skippon, who had sent 150 sabres to safeguard the King and who continued true to an allegiance that Cromwell had forsaken; but when the Presbyterians in the House were again for attempting vigorous steps, he rose and counselled them to moderation and "to bear with the infirmities of a zealous, conscientious army which had done so much good service." He urged them no longer to refuse the soldiers their full arrears of pay, and prophetically he warned the House that the soldiers were not in a temper to be provoked, for they were an organised body and might descend upon them before they were aware.[88]

"This knocked us on the head," says Holles. "Timorous men (as he knew many of those were whom he had to deal with) could make no reply to it... Fear took away the use of reason. They looked upon the army as almost at their doors, *Hannibal ad fortas*.

"By this unfortunate man's interposition at that time (to whom chiefly, and to his chaplain Marshal we must attribute all the evil that has since befallen King and Kingdom) all was dashed... For we instantly fell as low as dirt." The House voted the soldiers full pay, and resolved to expunge the offending declaration which had threatened the soldiers as enemies of the State.[89]

But the Army's demands had now grown political and they desired to reform the constitution itself. When the Field-Marshal again addressed the soldiers at a great rendezvous held

---

[87] Cary, i, 214; Clarke Papers, i, 27-33, 33-34, 47-78, 113; *Vindication of Sir William Waller*, 114-142.
[88] Clarke Papers, i, 128. Holles, 250, 251.
[89] Ibid; C. J., v, 196.

on June 10th at Triploe Heath, near Cambridge, although he was met with great respect by Fairfax and his army, he received only cries of "Justice, Justice" as he rode from regiment to regiment. When they heard that the Presbyterians were trying to raise a new army in the City to resist them they promptly marched on London itself.

They did not yet enter the City, but, taking the King with them, they sat down before its gates and carried on negotiations not only with Parliament, but also with the City, whether they should enter or not, and with the King himself, throwing themselves into the tangled forest of constitution-making under the impelling genius of Ireton. Skippon and his fellow-commissioners were now residing continually with them, like ambassadors at the court of an equal power, the significant Mr. Stephen Marshal continuing to come and go between them and Westminster. Skippon was also occupied with the affairs of Newcastle, Parliament having referred to him reports of an uneasiness in his regiment there, which had hitherto remained unaffected, and of a design to seize Newcastle for the King. He accordingly wrote instructions to Ashfield from St. Albans, where the Army had its headquarters, on June 14th, and his letter, which is in Cary's Memorials, shows that he still hopes, though not very confidently, for a reconciliation between Army and Parliament.

But on July 21st the position was so helpless that he begged the Houses, in the most pressing terms, to be relieved of his Irish appointment, and all that it entailed. He had throughout been a reluctant commissioner, for the soldiers were very much in the right, and he had no answer to the complaints voiced by Lambert and his colleagues. Nor could he with satisfaction serve any longer a Parliament that rejected the generous and enlightened proposals for the King's reinstatement made by the Army leaders and sought instead an intolerant settlement that would perpetuate their own power. In a letter to the Speaker from Reading he reminded the House of the reasons for which he had accepted the appointment, and added:

> And that it may appear I aim at no self-advantage any other way, I shall most readily lay down all my other employments at the Parliament's feet (if they so command), and either betake myself to a private life, upon my own poor means in England, or, with the Parliament's leave, seek an abiding place in some other country beyond the seas.

By now, indeed, the Irish expectation was an almost faded vision, and Skippon's letter marks the abandonment of any disagreement with the Army. Eleven of the most hostile members of Parliament, including Skippon's old comrades William Waller, Massey the defender of Gloucester, and Holles of the London Redcoats, who were not of the New Model, had been obliged to flee from St. Stephen's, and the dictates of the Army were succeeded by the shriller clamours of the mob. When on July 26th the mob broke into the House of Commons, held down Speaker Lenthall as Speaker Finch had been held down eighteen years before, and forced the members under penalty of violence to pass votes hostile to the Army; and when the Speakers of both Houses together with sixty-five members fled to the Army for protection, it was to rescue Parliament, and not to coerce it, that the Army at length carried out its threat to march upon London. When therefore on August 6th the Army made triumphal entry into the capital, escorting the two Speakers and the fugitive members of both Houses, it was led by the old triumvirate of Fairfax, Cromwell and "Major-General." For that step Skippon earned the bitter opprobrium of the Presbyterians.

The Army had indeed saved the City and the nation from anarchy, but it was heartily disliked by the whole country, save by those of the saintly party. A strong wave of royalism was sweeping the country, and the King himself was in a high good humour, chuckling to himself and his friends that it was only necessary for him to fence a little till the rebels should be themselves at blows with each other. On November 11th, 1647, he escaped from the Army's custody at Hampton Court to Carisbrooke Castle in the Isle of Wight, and though he there found he was still a close prisoner, yet he was able on December 26th to conclude the secret "Engagement" with the Scots for the invasion of England and to raise again the hopes of his friends.

These movements bore their fruit in March of 1648 in the outbreak of the royalist rising known as the Second Civil War. This is not the proper place to relate the full story of that moving phase — how Cromwell hurried off to besiege Pembroke, how Lambert in a masterly campaign held down the invading Scots till Cromwell was able to join him and crush them on the drenched fields of Preston and Winwick, how Fairfax put down the Kentish insurgents at Maidstone and swung back across the Thames to begin the terrible siege of Colchester. It is enough to say that in every encounter the splendid warriorship of the New Model carried all before it. But the key of all was London, and here, at the earnest entreaty of the Lord Mayor and Common Council, and with the active advocacy of Cromwell, Skippon was prevailed upon again, but with some reluctance, to accept the command of the trained bands and the responsibility for the City's security. On May 18th Parliament confirmed the appointment.

With the regular troops absent with Fairfax and Cromwell and with the Prince of Wales blockading the Thames with the revolted fleet, the danger to the City from without was very serious, and within its walls the streets and taverns were throbbing with unrest. In all those narrow alleys and court-yards the tradesmen and apprentices were muttering and collecting, the royalist agents busy among them. Yet through all that difficult time Skippon maintained the peace of the City, establishing an intelligence service which warned him of all movements, and, aided by his son-in-law Rolfe, pursuing his enlistments so resolutely and thoroughly that even the Common Council, always apt to blow hot and cold, tried to persuade Parliament to restrain him. When the Kentish royalists under the Earl of Norwich, in spite of their defeat at Maidstone, marched on London, seizing Bow Bridge and Stratford, Skippon was ready with his trained bands, and Norwich turned away into Essex. Skippon earned many a hard word from the plotters, being accused of estranging master from servant and father from son, and the royalist agents tried their utmost "to out" him from his post, to that end spreading a false accusation that he was concerned in a plot by a Captain Rolfe, not his son-in-law, to assassinate the King, but the Commons backed him up each time and vindicated him. Though the Presbyterians did

> besiege the Press
> With legions of your weekly lies

he nevertheless held the confidence of all moderate men, and he never performed a more valuable service than in this unspectacular duty.[90]

---

[90] C. J., v, 614, 622, 630, 648, 677, 682; E., 456, 31 (b, 4, 172); E., 457, 32 and 33; E., 525, 8 and 9; *Truth's Triumph*, Th.; Walker, *History of Independency*, i, 116, 117, 121, 131.

Thus the power of the royalists was again crippled, but it was a triumph not of any political party, but of the Army alone. Theirs was now the power. Under the shadow of the great keep at Colchester the blood of Lisle and Lucas, as they fell before Ireton's firing-party, had given augury of other blood to be shed, and the voice of the Levellers was raised against the King himself. Yet there was little exultation in the distracted country, and when Cromwell's triumphant dispatch after Preston was read in the House of Commons, it was Skippon who warned the members not to be so elated with success as to neglect the ways of peace.

Once again, therefore, Parliament opened negotiations with Charles in the Isle of Wight in the so-called Treaty of Newport, and once again Charles hedged, haggled, and procrastinated. But it was his last flight in the eddying air of political bargaining. All through 1647 the Army leaders, under Ireton and Cromwell, had been zealously anxious to effect his restoration to the throne and in the Heads of the Proposals they had offered him generous terms for a limited and tolerant monarchy. They had supported his cause for genuine kingship against the proposals of a churlish Parliament who wished him to be nothing more than a chief magistrate, a circumscribed Doge of Venice. But when he trifled by playing off Parliament and Army against one another and when he began to engage with the Scots for the invasion of England, then there came in the Army a violent revulsion, spreading from the lower ranks upwards. To the soldiers the Engagement made with the Scots, while he was yet in treaty with the English and their prisoner, seemed the utmost limit of bad faith, and it absolved them from any obligation they owed him. To them it was treason against the people of England, for if successful it would have made England a devastated appendage of Scotland, and, as was said of Skippon, not a man among them was minded to exchange the flowers de luce for the thistle.

Now the Army, its patience exhausted, again took matters into its own hands, seized the King's person for a second time, and conveyed him from Carisbrooke to Windsor their close prisoner. On December 6th, 1648, the musketeers of Colonel Pride "purged" the House of Commons of those members hostile to the Army, and all was ready for the trial of the King, "the capital and grand author of our troubles," upon which the Army was now resolved.

Again Westminster Hall chambered a memorable scene. Upon the beauty of its old stones the hand of a bitter winter struck with the chill of death, and in the face of that last call Charles in his dignity and patience reached his highest kingliness. On the freezing afternoon of January 30th, 1649, he stepped out upon the scaffold outside the Banqueting Hall of his Whitehall Palace to face the masked executioners, and before a sorrowing and angry crowd, kept back from the scaffold by a phalanx of the soldiers whom they loathed, he calmly and deliberately made with Bishop Juxon his last preparations for death, arranged his thin grey hair within a silken nightcap, and laid his head on the little block. With a single blow the executioner severed his head from his body, to send a thrill of horror through all Europe.

IX. THE SENATOR

Skippon had no part in that lamentable tragedy. He had been appointed a member of the special tribunal that under the chairmanship of the odious Bradshaw carried out the trial, but, like Fairfax and many another, he would have nothing to do with it. The remainder of his life, though spent actively and in high office in the Council Chamber, in Parliament and in the military defence of London, was without any high colours. The Centurion became the Senator. He was appointed a member of the Council of State which governed the country with a singular efficiency after the King's death, and in December, 1657, he became also a member of the new House of Lords. He was not a member of the Parliament which gave immortality to Mr. Praise-God Barebone, but in Cromwell's first Parliament after he had become Protector he was returned, on July 10th, 1654, as member for King's Lynn, in his native Norfolk.[91]

In a nation so little at one with its government, internal danger constantly threatened the Commonwealth, and whenever it did so, it was always to Skippon that men turned for the safety of the capital itself. When Cromwell marched north again to dash the Scots to ruin at Dunbar on September 3rd, 1650; again when the "Sealed Knot" plotted for the restoration of the young Charles II in 1655; and finally in the dangerous days preceding the restoration of the monarchy he found himself once more at his old post of Major-General in command of the City forces.

---

[91] Not Lyme, Dorset, as stated in the *Dictionary of National Biography*.

Though he was ranked among that veteran array of Cromwell's "Napoleon-Marshals," as Carlyle calls them, Skippon was never a compliant Cromwell man. As he had dissociated himself from the King's trial, so also he had misgivings over Oliver's second appointment as Protector, and he at first refused to take the oath of allegiance to him. Nor was he compliant when, in 1655, after the failure of successive Parliaments, Cromwell, turning to the example of Rome, divided the country into military districts, under the control of Major-Generals who were to be warrior-saints, not only maintaining order, but also stamping the heel upon vice and promoting virtuous living. It was the most unpopular of all Cromwell's measures, and though the obvious choice for Major-General of London was Skippon, the kindly old Centurion had no taste for becoming a military prefect. Because of Skippon's esteem in the City, however, Cromwell retained him in the office, but appointed Colonel John Barkstead to act as his substitute. Under his orders it was that Colonel Pride with his own hand slew the bears in the notorious bear-garden of Bankside, and that his men wrung the necks of the game-cocks in the City pits.

In the Parliament of September, 1656, when the Major-Generals were abolished, Skippon sat again for King's Lynn, and the last of his recorded utterances is found in the famous blasphemy trial of James Naylor, the Quaker who impersonated Christ in a triumphal entry into Bristol after the manner of the entry into Jerusalem.

"It has always been my opinion," Skippon declared, "that the growth of these things is more dangerous than intestine or foreign enemies. I have always been troubled in my thoughts to think of this toleration." Then he referred to the growth of the Quakers, saying that their principles struck at the root of social order. "I have been much divided in myself between duty and pity," he said, but it was clearly a horrid blasphemy. "Should we not be as jealous of God's honour as we are of our own?"[92] He spoke at length on the subject, and the House, deeply shocked, proceeded to pass upon Naylor a sentence that was typical of the savagery of the time — the pillory, the whipping-cart, the branding-iron. This was not the kindly Skippon that we have known, but "old men are testy," and in the temper of the time the provocation was great.

In these last years Skippon was become one of his country's elder statesmen, standing upon the summit of his years, the evening of his life lit with a general affection. In his last years a measure of affluence came to him. In April, 1648, in accordance with the bad practice by which the leading Parliamentarians were rewarded with the confiscated lands of the royalist nobles, the Commons had voted that he should be granted the lands of the Duke of Buckingham at Bletchley, bringing him an annual income of £1,000, but it was not until July 8th, 1651, that the Act giving effect to this decision was passed. He seems, however, to have lived in these last years at Acton. He acquired the manor of Bonyalva, in Cornwall,[93] and from his will it appears that he became at some time possessed also of "the house late the Bishop of Norwich's palace."[94] There is some justification for Walker's taunt that in these latter years he had acquired a "fat belly and a full purse," but he had done the State much service and there were few men to whom rewards were less grudged.

At the moment of crisis over the Sealed Knot, Skippon suffered a personal loss, for on January 24th, 1655, his wife

---

[92] *Burton's Diary* (ed. 1828), i, 24, 48, 101, 218.

[93] Coate, op. cit., 273

[94] No reference has been found in the diocesan records.

had died. Maria Skippon was fifty-four at that time, and she was buried in the chancel of Acton church, where a monument to her memory was erected. Ten weeks afterwards his daughter Susanna was married to Richard Meredith, elder son of the baronet Sir William Meredith, of Leeds, in Kent. Later Skippon married again, his second wife being Katherine Philips.

Now the *régime* was nearing its end. On September 3rd, 1658, the anniversary of Dunbar and of Worcester, his iron constitution worn out by his manifold anxieties, yet his spirit unfaltering to the end, Cromwell breathed his last troubled prayer. On that fateful night Skippon and other members of the Council of State waited upon Richard Cromwell, whom his father had nominated to succeed him as Protector, at Whitehall Palace, and he was one of those appointed to make the formal proclamation. But "Tumbledown Dick" had not long to stay, and England for the next many months was a prey to the clashing ambitions of rival generals. Skippon disapproved of Lambert's *coup de main* against Parliament, and together with Fairfax signed a remonstrance against the actions of the swordsmen.[95] Once again a civil war threatened the land, and once again Parliament turned to the old Christian Centurion, and, for the last time, appointed him, on July 27th, 1659, to his old post as Major-General of the London militia.

In his last hours Skippon lived long enough to see the threatened clash when Lambert marched north to confront Monck, the enthusiasm of the country as Monck crossed the border from Scotland, with the cry of "A free Parliament" ringing through the country, and behind that cry, the thought of "God save the King" in all men's minds. But he did not live to see the wheel come full circle again. He had felt the hand of death upon him, and on February 20th, 1660, he made his will.

---

[95] Rugge, 17, 18 (see Authorities under Lambert).

Ere in March the "free Parliament" met that was to declare for Charles II, Phillip Skippon, "heretofore waggoner to Sir Francis Vere," Major-General in one of the finest armies the world has seen, defender of London, senator and centurion, but above all brave and simple gentleman, passed to his rest.

AUTHORITIES FOR SKIPPON

No life of Phillip Skippon has previously been written other than the short account in the "Dictionary of National Biography" by the late Sir Charles Firth. The following are the special authorities for Skippon, in addition to the general authorities for the period and other authorities quoted in the text or notes:

The Sloane MSS.

The Rawlinson MSS.

The Clarke Papers (Camden Society and Royal Historical Society).

"Historical Collections of Private Papers of State, etc.," John Rushworth, 1721.

"The Hundred of Launditch," G. A. Carthew, 1877-9.

"The Fighting Veres," Sir Clement Markham, 1888.

"The Great Lord Fairfax," Sir Clement Markham, 1870.

"Memorials of English Affairs (Charles I)," Bulstrode White-locke, ed. 1732.

"England's Worthies," John Vicars, 1647.

"God's Ark" (Th.)

"England's Champions," Josiah Ricraft, 1649.

"Memorials of the Civil War," H. Cary, ed. 1842.

"History of Independency," Clement Walker, 1661.

"Anglia Rediviva," J. Sprigge, 1647.

"Cromwell's Army," Sir Charles Firth, 1902.

"First and Second Battles of Newbury," W. Money, 1884.

"History of the British Army," Vol. I, Hon. Sir John Fortescue.

"History of the Honourable Artillery Company," G. A. Raikes, 1878.

"London and the Kingdom," R. R. Sharpe, 1894-5.

"Bibliotheca Gloucestrensis," J. Washbourne, 1825.

"Memorials of Bristol," S. Seyer, 1821-3.

Memoirs of Denzil Holles, ed. Maseres in "Select Tracts," 1815.

"Historical Discourses upon Several Occasions," Sir Edward Walker, 1705.

"Cornwall in the Great Civil War," Mary Coate, 1933.

Diary of Thomas Burton, ed. 1828.

"Vindication of Sir William Waller," 1793.

III: ROBERT BLAKE

a true soldier appeareth, one compact at heart of sterner virtues and modesty of maintenance, mute witness and martyr of spiritual faith, a man ready at call to render his life to keep his soul.

— BRIDGES, The Testament of Beauty.

I. THE SCHOLAR-MERCHANT

NONE but the immortal Nelson himself has exercised so penetrating an influence upon the navy of these islands as Robert Blake. For that reason, since Britain owes her rise as an European and a world power almost wholly to her navy and her seafaring instinct, he has an importance to our tradition much beyond the interest which lies merely in a chronicle of stirring actions. His modesty and reserve, his tenacity, his contempt of private gain, his tactical audacity, and above all a devotion to the public service that reached to the farthest limits of selfhood are all qualities that have stamped themselves on the Service of which he was the spiritual if not the physical founder.

The English have always been a seafaring people and they quite early showed an aptitude at least equal to others for fighting at sea. But until Blake's time there had been no sea-soldiering service, though there had been assemblies of ships in the State's employ. The navy as a service began with Blake. In its annals there have been names as glorious for courage and of greater prowess in tactics — Howe, Hawke, Rodney, Hood, Duncan, and many another. But to Nelson and Blake in a special degree we owe that great development of high principles which constitutes devotion to service. Other things, too, we owe. Though the picture of Nelson has been enshrined in every seaman's heart for more than a hundred years, it is only recently that we have fully understood how much of our tradition is due to the personal example of the little Somerset man who did not go to sea till he was over fifty. In his own time and after his death many legends grew up round his name, and if to-day we must cast them aside, they serve to show how wide was his fame and how high his reputation.

Robert Blake was born of a family of gentleman merchants who by industry and prudent marriage had acquired a fair fortune and an honourable name. They were of the new gentry who had risen with the commercial prosperity which the West Country in those days enjoyed. The achievements of Elizabethan courage had thrown open to those counties a rich new field of maritime trading. Bristol was the second city in the kingdom, and a flourishing trade with the West Indies and with European ports was carried on from the many seaboard towns sheltering in the crannied coast of the South-West. A thriving woollen industry gave to "West of England" a fame it still holds to-day. Not the least of its ports was Bridgwater, which, lying in the level plain between the Mendips and the Quantocks, held converse with the sea by the brown waters of the tortuous Parrett.

The Blakes, who had formerly been settled at Bishop's Lydiard, near Taunton, had been engaged in this trade for some time, and when Humphrey Blake succeeded his father in 1592, he became master of a flourishing shipping business at Bridgwater and of good lands. His patrimony was further embellished when he married Sara Smithers, a widow who had been born Williams and who brought with her properties at Plansfield, Puriton, Woolavington, Catcott, and Bawdrip. Humphrey and Sara, says tradition, settled in that house in Bridgwater which is preserved to-day as the Blake museum, and there, beneath its oak beams and its plaster mouldings, their first child was born in 1598. On September 27th, at the old font of St. Mary's church, he was baptized Robert.

Robert was the eldest of fifteen or more children whom Sara Blake bore to Humphrey, and in due time he was to find himself, as it were, the guardian of them all. Probably the sense of responsibility grew early in him, and he was to be distinguished throughout life by his reserve and gravity, and by an immersion in duty which left him wifeless to the end. There beside those quiet inland quays, long before any thought was in his mind of voyaging out into stormier seas, he acquired the pedestrian virtues of sobriety and godliness. It is clear that the family was filled with the impulse of religion in its new Puritan urge, and there is cause to suppose that joyfulness was not always the companion of Robert's early days. The "beaded bubbles" winked seldom at the brim of Blake's cup of life.

In accordance with his station, the boy Robert attended the grammar school of Bridgwater, where he received much the same sort of education as has been shown of Hampden, save that presumably he slept at home. He took kindly to study, and in 1615 he went to Oxford, there to remain for so long that it is clear the call of commerce had less appeal for him than the voice of scholarship and the academic life. He matriculated at St. Alban's Hall, a dependency of Merton, but as Nicholas and Dorothy Wadham, of Ilminster, in Somerset, had just founded the new college to which they gave their name, it was natural that he should take an early opportunity of joining a community where he would meet so many other West Countrymen. Accordingly he entered Wadham as a commoner in 1617. It is here that we get our first picture of the man.

Blake had grown up a short, stocky, broad-shouldered man, not above five foot six in height. He was square rigged. He had strong, broad features which he kept clean-shaven, with a heavy jaw, a fine, masterful, full-curving mouth remarkable for the firm setting of its corners and for the resolute moulding of its lower lip. The brow was wide but not high, the eyes steady and deep-set, the nostrils full, and the set of the face square. In the pride of his glance and the pith and vigour of his features, it was in every inch the face of a man of action. His tenacity of purpose is plainly there. Not yet, certainly, were the features stamped with the fixed resolution that marks the inspired miniature of Greenwich, still less with the fierce intensity of the Pelly portrait, and we may imagine him at this time in the gentler aspect of the picture which hangs in Wadham College. But the general character of the man seems to have been constant throughout life, and the strength of will, the inward seriousness, the concentration on the task in hand that were his seem to have early come to him. Throughout life he buried himself in the work to which he had set his hand.

At one with his present taste for immersion in collegiate life were two further attributes that marked all his days — his simplicity of life and dress and his disregard of private gain. He always had a fair competence of his own, but he never sought to enrich himself as he might quite reasonably have done in after days. Already, too, he had shown that aloofness and taciturnity of which mention has been made. Clarendon says that "he was of a melancholic and sullen nature," and that he spent his time with serious men "who liked his moroseness and a freedom he used in inveighing against the licence of the time, and the power of the Court. They who knew him inwardly, discovered that he had an anti-monarchical spirit, when few men thought the Government in any danger."

No doubt the imputation of an "anti-monarchical spirit" owes itself less to evidence of his Oxford days than to later incidents, for when in later days he was at Cadiz he was reported to have remarked in the public square that "with the example afforded by London all kingdoms will annihilate tyranny and become republic. England had done so already; France was following in her wake; and as the natural gravity of the Spaniards rendered them slower in their operations, he gave them ten years for the revolution in their country."[96]

In like manner, so we may judge by other evidence, Clarendon certainly exaggerates in speaking of his "sullen" nature, but at the same time Blake clearly had a taciturn habit which was no doubt nourished by the austerity of life at Wadham, with its bleakness of black dress, its frigidity of daily chapel before dawn, its sobriety of "disputations" in philosophy and metaphysics. In later life, even if not at this stage, he displayed a peremptory and brusque demeanour in some of his dealings; he brooked no folly, but in like manner was keenly sensitive of every mistake of his own. Wood, however, asserts that Robert "did take his pleasure in fishing, fowling and sometimes in the stealing of swans," and on the whole one hopes that was true. Beneath his monkish disposition and his brooding taciturnity, there certainly dwelt the kindest of hearts. There dwelt also a spirit that could flash with anger for a duty ill done or a wrong committed. It needed the call of arms to reveal the essential man of action that dwelt within his damped fires.

Robert took his degree in 1618, and later attained no little proficiency in scholarship. He retained always a good command over Latin, which he used in after days when writing to the King of Spain. After graduating he endeavoured to obtain a Fellowship at Merton, but he was rejected on the grounds, it is said, of his short and stocky stature, for the Warden of Merton, unlike Caesar, liked to have tall and elegant men about him. Nevertheless, Blake continued at Oxford for ten years. In 1620 he was joined by his brother William, and among his fellow-students there were also Edmund Wyndham

---

[96] Basadonna, Venetian Ambassador to Spain, to the Doge, Venetian State Papers, xxviii, No. 457.

and Francis Blewett, both to be his enemies in the war to come. It was not till the approaching death of his father in November, 1625, soon after King Charles had succeeded King James, that he returned to Bridgwater to take charge of the family business with his brother Humphrey and to look after his regiment of brothers and sisters.

There followed a long lacuna which students of Blake call "the missing fifteen years." No authentic trace of him is found till 1640, save where, shortly after his return home, he signed a remonstrance by the congregation of St. Mary's Church against the inquisition by Bishop Laud, who then held the See of Bath and Wells, into irregularities in the form of worship which had moved the little prelate to censure. It may be assumed that in these years Robert was building up the family business, and although it is possible that that business took him to Holland, as a later story that we shall hear suggests, or elsewhere, there is no clear evidence that he ever in all that time left his native town. Most remarkable of all is that there is no word to show that he who is second only to Nelson among the admirals of England ever set foot in a sea-going ship till he was past forty-five.

If at Oxford Blake had inveighed against the licence of James I's time, it is likely that in these fifteen years under Charles his reputed antipathy to monarchy did not diminish. The signs are that he took an early interest in politics, and it is tempting to think that he was at least acquainted with the great John Pym, whose house at Carrington was only three miles away. Blake saw the struggles between a querulous Parliament and a stiff-necked King, the long years of Charles's absolutism, the melancholy failure of his attempts to establish maritime glory, the Ship Money trial, Laud's petty persecutions, and at long last the call for Parliament once again in 1640. When that call came it was Robert Blake whom the electors of Bridgwater returned as their member. That Parliament, however, as we have seen, sat but three weeks, and when later in the year the Long Parliament was elected, Blake was defeated by Edmund Wyndham, his fellow-member at Wadham and his future enemy in the field.

II. WAR IN THE WEST

When the sword was drawn in 1642 Blake was among the very first who joined the local forces raised for Parliament, taking arms as a lieutenant or captain, despite his position and influence in the county, in Alexander Popham's regiment of infantry. At first the King's cause was little befriended in the West, but presently Sir Ralph Hopton, that lion of Somerset, raven-haired and bearded like a grandee of Spain, and Sir Bevil Grenville, blue-eyed and auburn-haired, the fearless grandson of Sir Richard of the *Revenge*, the idol of his mighty henchman, Anthony Payne, and of all Cornish-men besides, raised the King's standard in Cornwall and carried all before them. They routed the Scotsman Ruthven at Bradock Down, near Liskeard, on January 19th, 1643, and at the Battle of Stratton on May 16th the audacious courage of their little number overwhelmed the Earl of Stamford on the high hill up which they scrambled in the face of formidable odds and which bears to this day his vanquished name. They secured all Devonshire for the King except for the seaport towns. Joining forces with young Prince Maurice and the Marquess of Hertford, they then swept Somerset; Taunton and Blake's own town of Bridgwater surrendered without resistance. On July 5th the combined forces met and defeated a more redoubtable foe in Waller at the desperate fight of Lansdown. In this action Bevil Grenville was slain by a battle-axe, and the next day Hopton, too, was wounded, but on July 13th he crushed Waller again in the decisive action of Roundway Down. All the South-West save Bristol and the chief seaports were now in the King's hands, and the same month his forces advanced upon the rich prize of

Bristol itself.

In all these actions nothing has been heard of Blake, though there is a natural presumption that he was engaged in some at least of the fighting. But at Bristol he comes immediately to notice.

It was the arm of Rupert himself that was now raised against the great city, where Nathaniel Fiennes was the Parliamentary Governor. When at almost the first onset Fiennes made a craven surrender on July 26th, he forgot all about the stocky little captain who, at Prior's Hill Fort, at the northern extremity of the city's defences, had thrown back assault after assault, and, not content with defence, had with the spirit that was to become typical of him sallied out from his fort to tumble a disconcerted enemy down the hill at the point of the pike. Therefore, having received no orders, Blake refused to believe the word of the enemy when they told him that the city had surrendered, and he held out for another full day before being prevailed upon to quit "by very great importunity and with much difficulty." Rupert, when he heard of this recalcitrance, was moved to hang him out of hand, but let him go on the intercession of some friends.[97] Well for him if he had not, but none could foresee that one of the boldest adventurers of the age might so soon be driven from the seas of Europe by the middle-aged volunteer captain.

After Bristol, where his conduct won him warm applause, Blake was named one of the Somerset Committee of Ways and Means and was promoted to lieut.-colonel. He was presently sent with about half a company to join the garrison of Lyme, the wind-bitten little port that clings to the picturesque coast of Dorset within a chaplet of over-topping hills. All the West but Plymouth and Lyme were now lost to Parliament and its

---

[97] "A true and full relation, etc.", E.255, 16; Clarendon, xv, 57.

possession had become of importance to that cause. In March, 1644, Prince Maurice, having failed before Plymouth, descended upon Lyme with an army of 6,000 and a strong train of artillery, confidently expecting to capture this easy prey "before breakfast," for its defences scarcely existed and the garrison was not above 1,100 men. From the heights above he had such a command over the little town and he pressed so closely upon its defences that even the ships which brought supplies into the little Cobb were within easy range of his guns.

But Maurice, the shy, tow-headed young giant with the bright blue eyes, was to be rudely surprised. Behind the flimsy earthworks and the turf redoubts, over which a man could easily leap, dwelt a spirit that was now to reveal its genius for the inspiration of men. The governor of the town was Colonel Ceeley, and the commander of the garrison Colonel Wear, the same who aroused Skippon's anger at Lostwithiel, but the heart and thews of the defence were Blake's resourceful mind and combative spirit. Maurice's first assault was thrown off with a vigour that astonished him. He was obliged to sit down to close siege operations, and a valuable field force was thus held at anchor before the "little vile fishing town" for nearly two months.

Maurice brought his overshadowing batteries up to the very fringes of the town; he flung his Cornishmen and Irishmen again and again at the thin defences; with fire-arrows and red-hot shot fired into the thatched roofs he burnt down the houses; his guns bombarded the little Cobb and sank the ships at their moorings; he broke through the defences by the sea's edge and burnt twenty vessels lying in shore. Yet he could effect no more than to give new heart to the little garrison and the staunch inhabitants from daily realisation of their ability to resist. Rightly taking aggression to be the best defence, the garrison made sortie after sortie to spike the enemy's guns or arrest his works. Wear was wounded in the stomach, and Blake, to whom command then fell, was himself struck in the foot. Scarcely a house remained undamaged, hardly a room into which a shot had not entered, scarcely a soldier was left with shoes and stockings. Townsmen and soldiers alike were imbued with the same spirit, and when in a grand assault at utmost strength Maurice pierced the defences and poured his men through into the streets, it was the women who fed the men with ammunition during several hours of desperate fighting before the invaders were evicted.

In one assault Colonel Francis Blewett, who had been at Wadham with Blake, but who was now fighting against him, was killed within the Parliamentary lines. Blake had his body shrouded and coffined and himself attended its return to the royalists, inviting the cavalier officer who received it to view the weak defences.

> Tell the Prince that if he desires to come into the town with his army to fight, we will pull down ten or twelve yards so that he may come in with ten in a breast, and we will fight with him.

On May 23rd, the Earl of Warwick, Lord High Admiral, arrived by sea to succour the little garrison, and the first recorded instance of Blake's having set foot in a man-of-war was when, at the age of forty-five, he attended a council of war which Warwick summoned in the *James*, which was later to be under his own command. Without this naval succour Lyme could scarcely have maintained its resistance, and it is likely that from this experience Blake took an early lesson in the importance of the command of the sea. Warwick, however, could do no more than aid the defenders with supplies and men to prolong their resistance, and it was not until Essex approached the town on his fateful westward march that Maurice struck his tents on June 15th and retired to Exeter "with some loss of reputation," as Clarendon tells us, "for having lain so long, with such a strength, before so vile and untenable a place."[98]

So was concluded the first of Blake's signal triumphs, a triumph from which his name soon became one to conjure with. It is to be observed of Blake's fighting career that he never underwent an experience without profiting from its lessons. As one who was accustomed to think, to think earnestly and apart in his own secret sessions, he used his brains to develop in his own way his natural talent for leadership. With Robert Bridges he would have agreed that

> Knowledge accumulateth slowly and not in
> vain.

Perhaps he had already learnt from Bristol the peril of a defensive line too long for its limited garrison, and seen that in the close-gripped rigour of Lyme's constricted trenches a greater safety lay.

Though it has small place in the history-books, there is no doubt that Lyme saw some of the most desperate fighting of the war, but Taunton was to surpass it.

In the heart of the royalist country, Taunton had considerable strategic importance. All the main roads of Somerset converged upon it and it commanded the lines of communication of any army to its westward, but it was quite

---

[98] Relation concerning the siege of Lyme, Clarendon MSS. i, 738 8; *A Letter from the Earl of Warwick*, E.51, 9; "A full relation of the whole siege of Lyme," E.51, 15; Roberts' *History and Antiquities of Lyme'*, Diary of Edward Drake (*Civil War in Dorset*, by A. R. Bayley).

unfortified. Essex having decided to maintain his westward course, and, the King being expected to pursue him, Taunton became more than ever important, and steps were taken to possess it. On July 8th, 1644, Sir Robert Pye, Hampden's son-in-law, accompanied by Blake and a few troops of horse, secured the town without opposition. Pye departed and Blake was appointed Governor and promoted to the rank of colonel, with a regiment of his own and Samuel Perry as his lieutenant-colonel and his brother Samuel Blake as one of his officers.

Save for the old castle in its midst, Taunton was an open town completely without defences, but Blake immediately began to fortify it. Barricades were thrown across the streets, breastworks were raised at all road entrances, houses loop-holed for musketry, and batteries sited. Yet, with only 1,000 men he could not hope for anything elaborate, and for the manning of the hedges, the wooden palings and the outbuildings of the town a stout heart must be his chief resource. The inhabitants were strongly Puritan and seem to have been with him almost to a man; he was in the heart of a people and a country wherein his influence was at its highest.

After their triumph at Lostwithiel the royalists determined to regain this lone rebel post isolated in the midst of a country which was otherwise wholly theirs. On his way back to Oxford, Charles despatched against the town a force of between 3,000 and 4,000 under the command of Blake's old colleague and political opponent, Col. Edmund Wyndham. Aggression was always Blake's principle, and before Wyndham could fire a gun he had sallied out from the town and taken a hundred prisoners. When Wyndham assaulted the town he twice repulsed him, but a third attack drove him back from his wooden palings and carried the town. Undismayed, Blake shut himself up in the ancient castle, and to the summons to an honourable surrender sent in by Wyndham, "your well-wishing neighbour and countryman," he returned a brusque defiance. For nearly two months, while the Parliamentary leaders at Westminster were pursuing the quarrels and the heart-searchings that followed Second Newbury, he stood out within those medieval walls until, on December 14th, 1644, he was relieved by a column under Major-General James Holborn, and that strange and vibrant genius who was afterwards to be the first Lord Shaftesbury, the young Sir Anthony Ashley Cooper.

Provisions, arms and reinforcements put new heart and new vigour into the townsfolk and garrison, whose defence, said Cooper, had been "a miracle." But the supplies were insufficient to maintain a large garrison, and it was typical of Blake that he soon dismissed nearly all Holborn's force, and stood ready to receive the enemy again with a garrison small but lion-hearted.

The defence that Blake was now to lead was one of the most gallant exploits of his crowded fighting career, and no more heroic resistance was put forth in all the Civil Wars, neither amid the flames of "Loyalty House" nor in the iron rigours of Colchester. Almost the whole strength of the royalist field army in the West was concentrated upon Taunton, amounting presently to 8,000 men, against whom Blake could oppose not more than 1,750, including both garrison and armed townsmen. The second siege began early in March, 1645. By early April the royalists, having taken some advance posts that Blake had established in the surrounding country, were entrenched within musket-shot in a complete circumvallation. Hopton, who was now a peer, presently assumed command of the royalists and, urged by the Prince of Wales to press forward, he put forth all the vigour and resource that were his. From now onwards a ceaseless cannonade shattered the town by day and night, so that at times it seemed as if the town was besieged "by a wall of fire." Lower and lower fell the provisions. The thatch was stripped from the roofs to feed the horses, and presently the horses were themselves eaten. Beds were broken up, and their cords taken to provide match for gun and musket. All the time Blake was barricading and fortifying from street to street and from house to house, so that at every step he should have a new defensive line if driven in from his outer works.

On April 30th, as we have seen, Fairfax, leading the New Model on its first march, started on his way to relieve the garrison whose stand had stirred Parliament to so much admiration, but he turned back at Blandford to invest Oxford, sending on a column of 6,000 under Colonel Weldon to relieve Blake. Knowing that relief was coming, Hopton bent up all his energies to reduce the town. Again and again he stormed the frail defences; each time he was thrown back from them by the half-starved garrison, not only with musket and pike, but with stones and boiling water. Force, guile, threats and blandishments were alike of no avail. On May 9th, having failed to lure Blake out to a fight into the open, Hopton launched one more determined attack with all the force and weight he could summon on east and west simultaneously. On the west he broke through the thin first line, but was held up by the barricades within. On the east he captured the gate redoubt, forced his way by weight of numbers from street to street, and set the town on fire.

For eight hours his men and Blake's, faint with famine, fought it out in alley and court-yard and among the shells of the shattered houses while the flames swept over the town, and when for very weariness a halt was called among the smoking ruins Blake still held the castle, the church of St. Mary

Magdalene and the market-place. All that day Blake had fought in the knowledge that Fairfax had turned back from his relief, but ignorant that Weldon was coming, yet he never flinched from fighting to the last corner. When Hopton offered honourable terms of surrender, he answered in a famous passage that he had four pairs of boots left and would eat three of them before Hopton could take the town. A further attack was made and repulsed, but Hopton then sent a more threatening summons to Blake, saying that, in default of immediate capitulation, he would put the whole garrison to the sword — save seven persons. The town was a heap of ruins, the garrison were faint with starvation and weariness, and only two barrels of powder remained to them, but the reply Hopton received was that if he would give the names of the favoured seven, Blake would send out their bodies.

It was Blake's last retort, for on that same afternoon of May 11th he observed from "a high place" through his perspective glass the distant column of Weldon's redcoats. He observed, too, the break-up of Hopton's camp, and it was characteristic of his combative spirit that he did not wait for his friends to enter, but, though his men were shattered, shoeless and exhausted, he led them out to give battle once more to the retreating cavaliers and to pursue them until his strength could no longer hold.

Weldon rode in the next day in astonished admiration of the "valiant and vigilant Colonel Blake." He found two-thirds of the town completely destroyed and all the surrounding countryside laid waste, the plundered people living furtively in the woods, but he could do no more than throw in provisions and a considerable reinforcement and withdraw part of his force (though he seems himself to have remained with Blake); for Goring came up from Bridgwater with an army of 11,000 men and nearly cornered him. Blake's continued resistance in the third siege that began on May 29th, 1645, was of great tactical value, for Goring's army was far larger than that which the King had with him at the fateful battle soon to be fought at Naseby, and with its aid he might have changed the course of history. It is Clarendon who says that Blake "disappointed all our hopes."[99]

The third siege of Taunton, however, saw little serious fighting. Goring was not the soldier Hopton was, and while he drank and ravaged the country he was boastfully confident that he could starve the ruined town into surrender by a close investment. "Dear General," Digby wrote to him, "I have nothing to add but to conjure you to beware of debauches."[100] Thus while Naseby was being fought, Blake and his men drew in their belts and kept a stout heart in their brave ruins. Not until after Naseby were Fairfax and Cromwell able at last to come to their relief and to carry their victorious campaign into the West.[101] On July 3rd, Goring retired from before Taunton under the threat of their approach, and on July 10th he was utterly crushed at the battle of Langport. To the final overthrow of the King's armies, therefore, Blake had made a great contribution, for he had held out in the heart of a hostile country for almost exactly a year, making an open country town, which no one in either army considered capable of a

---

[99] Clarendon's *History of the Great Rebellion*; Clarendon MSS., 1833 *et seq.*; *The Moderate Intelligencer*, E.271, 14; Sanford's *Studies of the Rebellion*; *Two Letters*, E.284, 9; *A Great Victory*, E.284, 11; Sprigge's *Anglia Rediviva*; Savage's *History of Taunton*; Walker's *Historical Discourses*, pp. 27, 41, 88.

[100] Digby to Goring, March 29th, 1645, Tanner MSS. Sanford's *Studies of the Rebellion.*

[101] For this third siege, see Clarendon's *History of the Great Rebellion*; Clarendon MSS.; Sprigge's *Anglia Rediviva.*

week's defence, into a major tactical stronghold. Parliament, in voting £2,000 for the garrison, voted also £500 for its commander.

The war was now all but over, and nothing remained but to clear the defiant last-ditchers. After administering relief to the destitute people of Taunton, Blake was sent with a small force in November, 1645, to reduce the castle of Dunster, where Colonel Francis Wyndham, brother of Edmund, was still holding out for the King. The episode was not spectacular and Blake did not distinguish himself. "The price of time and blood," he said, made him reluctant to force the issue and to hazard men's lives when all was really over,[102] and he did not manifest his usual boldness of purpose. His attempts to mine the castle, which was a powerful stronghold, failed lamentably, and he was himself thrown on the defensive when Colonel Finch brought in a relieving force. His earthworks and emplacements may still be seen at the rear of the "Luttrell Arms" (then known as the "Ship Inn"), where he had his headquarters. Later he was reinforced with the regiments of Skippon and Lambert, detached from Fairfax's army, and in April, 1646, when royalist hopes were completely crushed, Wyndham surrendered with the honours of war.

---

[102] Blake to the Committee of the West, E.334, 11.

III. THE CALL TO SEA

The little Bridgwater merchant had now made a name for himself, not yet nationally, but all over the West, and also among the New Model and in Parliament. His stout heart and stout Puritanism made him very acceptable in the sight of the Parliamentary leaders, and in the autumn of 1645 he was one of the group of new members who were returned to Parliament. Bridgwater was, of course, his constituency. The business of Dunster prevented him from taking his seat immediately, but he did so in May of 1646, making his first entry into the House with that Stirling republican, Edmund Ludlow.

Ludlow's, however, is the only mention that exists of Blake's participation in politics at that time. There is no recorded instance of his having opened his mouth in debate, and he took no part at all either in the ensuing quarrel between Parliament and Army, or in the second Civil War (save in organising the local levies), or in the trial and execution of the King, to which it seems, on slight evidence, he was opposed. In June, 1646, he took the Covenant, and he remained a Presbyterian to the end. Blake cannot be understood without an appreciation of his deep piety, which remained part of his essential being even when the smell of powder had roused all his fighting spirit. The spiritual monasticism he had shown at Oxford remained with him throughout life. In his human relations no man was more kindly; in spite of his peremptory manner, he was merciful and chivalrous to his enemies, solicitous for the wounded, anxious for the poor and needy, mindful of all who were near to him; his negro servant,

Domingo, was not forgotten in his prayers. Yet no man seems to have come near his soul, nor any woman into his heart. For his soul and his heart were God's. At a time when all men, including Charles I, breathed Biblical phrases as their common parlance, imputing to God's pleasure or anger the least changes of fortune, one senses in Blake a deeper feeling than dwells in the Scriptural clichés of the day. His religion, more intellectual than Skippon's, calmer than Cromwell's, unparaded and unflourished in the manner of Harrison's and Peters', was deep and unadulterated.

The disbandment of Blake's regiment was voted in November, though it was later revived, and it is probable that the merchant had given up the idea of any further soldiering, and that he spent most of the next three years in his counting-house and at local duties. Only the stir and throb of physical action could waken his hidden flame, and when stillness fell again upon the affairs of men he stole back into his haven of shy reserve. During this time he was one of the Commissioners for the sequestration of royalist estates in Somerset, and the disregard for personal enrichment that was to distinguish him all his life was made manifest by his own omission from the rich rewards that Parliamentary supporters were on all sides receiving from such sources. It was not until the end of February, 1649, after the battle of Preston and a month after the King's execution, that he was to his great surprise called once again to arms.

So far as we know, Blake had never been to sea in his life, yet in February, 1649, when he was over fifty years of age, he, Colonel Edward Popham and Colonel Richard Deane were appointed Commissioners and Generals-at-Sea for the immediate ordering and commanding of the fleet. Popham, brother of Blake's first commanding officer, had been a naval officer for some years before the Civil Wars, and Deane had also apparently been at sea in some capacity in his youth; it has therefore been assumed by some biographers of Blake that this appointment supports the theory that part of Blake's "missing fifteen years" had been spent at sea. But this argument will not do, for the appointment of landsmen captains had been a common practice for the past half-century, and it was to continue to be the practice for some time to come. Both Monck and Montague were to be similarly appointed and both were raw landsmen. Nor is the argument that Blake's early letters show a knowledge of a ship's equipment very satisfying, for such knowledge he would have acquired as a shipping merchant on his Bridgwater quays. Indeed, social position, and not technical knowledge, had been hitherto the first requisite traditionally looked for in either a military or a naval commander. It was therefore not inconsistent, when the Commonwealth adopted a sounder method of appointment, that they should be guided, not yet by technical achievement, but by a man's qualities of heart and spirit, by his aptitude for the leadership of men, and by a consideration of whether he was to be politically trusted.

One may go farther than this and assert with confidence that the three new Generals-at-Sea owed their appointments precisely to the fact that they were successful and trusted soldiers. The Commonwealth government was indeed about to place the fleet under military domination. They proposed to apply to the sea service the same principles as those upon which the New Model had been fashioned. The militarisation which Drake had resisted — a resistance which retarded by over half a century the establishment of a disciplined national navy and which contributed to the frustration of Charles's ideal — was now to be effected by men to whom the laxity and disorder of the traditional haphazard methods were unendurable. Hitherto the naval defence of the kingdom had depended, save for a very small nucleus of State ships, on what was really a maritime militia. The navy of England was its whole shipping, to be called upon in any moment of national emergency. "It was the military element that was wanting — not the chivalry and the feathers, but the element of the professional soldier."[103] Corporate discipline, the machinery of administration and the ordered manoeuvre of a fleet in battle — these were the things that seamen had refused to learn for themselves, and accordingly the soldiers set out to teach them. Paradoxical though it may seem, it was under an administration of soldiers that a heterogeneous collection of ships was to be transformed into a disciplined maritime service, a navy in the modern sense of the word.[104]

The style of Generals-at-Sea that was given to the three Commissioners itself expressed the idea that command of armed forces at sea should be of the same nature as a command of land forces. To all intents and purposes naval tactics simply did not exist before 1649. Fleets charged each other like masses of tribal horsemen, and it was common for seamen themselves to speak of "charging" the enemy. It was Blake and his colleagues who were to begin the evolution of disciplined naval tactics, and in particular to conceive the formation of line-ahead.

Let us see what this navy was like that the new Generals-at-Sea were called to command.

When the first Civil War began, the grievances of all ranks against Charles's administration were so deep-seated that the navy's adherence to the cause of Parliament had been almost

---

[103] Sir Julian Corbett, *England in the Mediterranean*, i, 190.
[104] Ibid, i, 178 *et seq.*

inevitable, and that allegiance had been retained all through the war simply by regular pay. First under the Earl of Warwick and later under William Batten, the navy's had been a vital service without which the issue might well have been reversed. The ports were kept for Parliament and the threat of foreign troops allayed. The fleet had sunk thirty-nine ships sailing under the King's commission, had taken no merchantmen trading with royalist ports, and had maintained the honour of the seas against the Dutch and the Dunkirk pirates.[105] Unlike the army, the seamen of the Civil Wars were never politically-minded, though there had been a dangerous mutiny over the command of the fleet shortly before Blake's appointment. Parliament had appointed as commander of the fleet that violent republican Colonel Thomas Rainsborough, whom, though he had been himself a professional sailor, the seamen could not abide for his "insufferable pride, ignorance and insolence." They had therefore metaphorically thrown him overboard, and in the quarrel that ensued a large part of the fleet had gone over to the young Prince Charles. However, nearly all had now returned disillusioned by his shallowness.

Thus, when Blake and his colleagues were appointed to joint command in February, 1649, the fleet had accepted the new administration; but its continued loyalty was far from certain, and after its distemper of mutiny its condition was deeply susceptible to further maladies. It was therefore important that the new commanders should be men who were thoroughly trustworthy in their loyalty to the Commonwealth. On this issue Blake was completely reliable, and his personal influence and his military record in the West Country, from which the fleet was still considerably recruited, were further aids for winning the confidence of the seamen.

---

[105] Answer of the Commissioners, June 18th, 1646, E.340 (31).

The problems of supply and administration were equally full of difficulties. Of the forty-two ships of which the Commonwealth found itself possessed nearly a half were hired merchantmen; these were manned by a civilian master and crew (who were naturally not always eager to hazard their ships in action), but commanded by an army captain and fought by a complement of soldiers. In these circumstances it is not to be expected that there would be found the spirit of service and the bonds of devotion that generate the soul of a fleet, yet the seeds of such inspiration lay there in men's hearts. The material that Blake found to his hand was as good as might be desired, for, says Clarendon, they were "a humorous, brave and sturdy people; fierce and resolute in whatsoever they are inclined to." They waited only for the strong hand of leadership and for a clean, honest and efficient administration on shore. That leadership Blake was now to provide, and that administration was to be found in the Council of State's Admiralty Committee, in which were now vested the powers of the old office of Lord High Admiral, and of which Sir Henry Vane was at the moment the guiding genius, but even more in the subordinate Commissioners of the Navy, of whom Nehemiah Bourne was outstanding for his ardent industry. The Commissioners pursued their labours with a zeal, a thoroughness and a success that has never been equalled in all the Navy's history. Generally, as Oppenheim states, our Navy has had to beat the enemy in spite of the Admiralty, but under the Commonwealth the fleet received every assistance that foresight and earnestness could give. With the co-operation of the Commissioners, Blake and his colleagues weeded the fleet of its inefficient officers, and with new blood gave it new life. Blake made, in fact, a New Model fleet. Moreover, though he infused a new military spirit into its civilian character, gradually getting rid of the hired merchantmen, there was no attempt to introduce the trappings of the soldier or the practices of the parade-ground, but rather he fostered the maritime spirit, and he gathered round him a constellation of brilliant captains.

Of the ships, only the clumsy *Sovereign of the Seas* exceeded 1,500 tons, and the *Resolution*,[106] one of Blake's flagships, was the only other ship to exceed 1,000 tons. They were of a sort that delight the model-maker to-day. The square towering stern, ornately carved and broad on the water-line, climbed upwards and inwards to the high and narrow poop. Thence, dropping by steps from poop to quarter-deck, and quarter-deck to "upper" deck, the bulwark line sloped downwards towards the bows, where it mounted slightly again to the forecastle before dropping sharply once more to the Knight-heads wherein was secured the heel of the low-set bowsprit. Broad and squat were these ships, the length of keel being little more than three times the beam. Thus, with low and rounded bows, with short and stumpy masts, they would neither go well nor work "yarely," pitched terribly in any sea, and could only with difficulty beat to windward. The masts carried courses, topsails and topgallants, while the mizzen carried a lateen-sail, and a sprit-sail was borne by a little mast often stepped on the bowsprit. Their timbers were massive, increasing their unhandiness, but making them exceedingly difficult to sink with the solid cast-iron shot that was the chief ammunition of the day. They were bare and completely without comfort.

It was just before this time that the frigate had been evolved in the pirates' dockyards of Dunkirk, which at that time led Europe in ship design. Built for speed and nimbleness, having a clean deck line and at first no forecastle, they were an immediate success. The Commonwealth, not bothering about

---

[106] The *Prince* of Charles's navy.

elephantine *Sovereigns*, set itself to practical purposes, and particularly to "outsailing the Dunkirkers," and began to build large numbers of frigates and other light vessels.

The Commonwealth ships were painted plain black, but they carried gilt figure-heads and in their rigging was a gay plumage of fluttering jacks and streaming pennants and banderolles. The flag they flew was the red cross of St. George.

No uniform was yet supplied to the fleet, but from the ships' chests seamen could buy shoes and cotton drawers, shirts, stockings, and other articles; for wet weather there were canvas coats and drawers. Blake himself, we are told, dressed as became his station, but "with a reserve of moderation." The food of the sailor was salted beef and pork, dried fish, bread, cheese, butter; water being what it was in those days, the normal drink supplied was beer, but on foreign stations when beer was exhausted it was replaced by what was called "beverage," being a cheap wine diluted with water. The victualler of the Navy was Colonel Pride, who had purged the Commons in 1648, and under the Parliament the victualling proved to be a marked advance on the previous melancholy tradition. "From the year 1641," said Richard Gibson, the seaman diarist, "the bread and beer was of the best for fineness and goodness." In later years, however, when money for paying the purveyors became more and more difficult to obtain, the victualling again deteriorated. In matters of pay, the Commonwealth Government was much ahead of Charles's, though there was constant difficulty, and the bad system by which no pay was due till a fleet returned to port, no matter how long the voyage, before long caused destitution and starvation among the seamen's families. During Blake's longer voyages these families were sometimes without means of support for more than a year, and he himself more than once had cause to complain of arrears of his own pay of £3 a day.

Such was, in brief outline, the fleet to which the three soldier-admirals were called in 1649.

It might be thought that the pinnacle of efficiency and renown that the English navy was to reach was scarcely attainable under the command of a committee of three. The arrangement worked remarkably well, however, but Blake was soon to prove himself the dominant personality. All were West-countrymen, Popham coming from Blake's own county and Deane from Gloucestershire, and all had served as colonels in the Parliamentary armies. Popham, said a brother officer, was "a gallant man, and steers as straight at sea, and marches as fair at land as any man I know."[107] Deane had distinguished himself as an artilleryman and had been Comptroller of the Ordnance in the New Model; he had carried himself ably at the Battle of Preston and had afterwards been close to Cromwell in the trial and execution of the King, for which cause his was a name hated among royalists. Scotland was soon to learn his name. He was, said Cromwell after his death, "my most near friend." It is remarkable that most of the great Commonwealth sea captains came from the West, for, in addition to these three, Monck, who succeeded Popham, came from Torrington in Devonshire, and Penn, who followed Deane, was from Bristol.

Blake was much surprised at his appointment, which he declared was "beyond my expectations as well as my merits," but he took counsel with his friend Popham, who had probably inspired the appointment and who now persuaded him to accept it.[108] Blake hastened first to London and

---

[107] Bayly, *Civil War in Dorset*, p. 72.
[108] Blake to Popham, September 16th, 1649, Leybourn-Popham MSS.

remained there with Deane for several weeks at the vast work of reorganisation that was necessary, while Popham went to the fleet. But he was soon called to action, for Rupert had now begun his career of piracy. With the aid of his mother's jewels, by the sale of the guns of the *Antelope*, and by some judicious piracy, he had contrived to assemble a royal "fleet" of seven ships in Dutch waters, and, having no hope with these to face the forces of the Commonwealth, he had resolved instead upon the plunder of English merchantmen. On January 11th, 1649, with his flag in the *Constant Reformation*, he put to sea from Holland and on January 29th established a base at Kinsale, County Cork, with the friendly Irish behind him, and began operations.

IV. THE HUNTING OF RUPERT

The news of his first raid off the Scilly Isles reached Westminster on March 24th, and on May 22nd the three admirals arrived off Kinsale and locked him up under the protection of the land batteries. Blake thus began his naval career with one of the most trying of operations, and for five months he was held down to the weariness of blockade. First Popham and then Deane departed for other duties, and Blake was left alone, the number of his ships gradually being reduced to five. While he was at this duty Cromwell in August landed in Ireland for his memorable campaign, stormed Drogheda, and, turning southward at the suggestion of the Generals-at-Sea, marched to the massacre of Wexford. Looking southward, his eye fell upon Blake, who was assuredly a man after his own heart, and he now invited him, "with much affection," to be his Major-General commanding the infantry, Skippon's old post.[109] This offer, Blake relates, came to him as an even greater surprise than his last, and he refused it, asking Edward Popham to use his influence that it might not be repeated. One suspects that, as a man who throughout his life was characterised by his humanitarianism, he was not eager to serve under one who in the past months had shown himself so ruthless as Cromwell.

Cromwell continued his conquering progress southwards and Rupert's position at Kinsale was becoming more and more perilous, but at this moment fortune came to his aid. For a storm drove Blake to leeward, and the robber prince seized his

---

[109] C. J., vi, 30.

chance to slip out of Kinsale with seven ships, and, abandoning English waters, fled from Blake to the neutrality of Lisbon.

Angry at seeing him escape, and refusing once again the command of the finest infantry in the world, Blake made haste to follow him thither when it was learnt at the end of November where Rupert had gone. Having refitted at Portsmouth, he sailed on March 1st, 1650, taking with him Charles Vane as the Commonwealth's ambassador to Portugal and Ascham of unhappy destiny as ambassador to Spain. His orders were to "pursue, seize, scatter, fight with, or destroy, all and every of the ships and vessels of the revolted fleet," as well as any foreign ships that might assist the "revolters"; and furthermore —

> Whereas the dominion of the seas hath anciently and time out of mind undoubtedly belonged to this nation, and that the ships of all other nations in acknowledgment of that dominion have used to take down their flags upon sight of the admiral of England, and not to bear it in his presence; you are, as much as in you lieth, and as you find yourself and the fleet of strength and ability, to do your endeavours to preserve the dominion of the sea, and to cause the ships of all other nations to strike their flags...[110]

Now in sole command and flying his flag in the *George*, one of James I's ships of fifty guns, Blake arrived in Cascaes Bay at the mouth of the Tagus on March 10th, and there was to follow another weary blockade, for Rupert's fleet was all within, but before he finished this new task Blake's name was to be heard, not merely in Somerset and Westminster, but in the courts of Europe. The throne of Portugal was occupied by

---

[110] Thurloe, i, 134-6.

the young King John IV and he, sharing with all Europe a shocked antipathy to the regicide republic, had not been unwilling to give shelter to the adventurous fleet of the rightful King of England. His forts denied an entry to the Commonwealth fleet and he would give no ear to Blake's demand that Rupert should be ordered out to sea. But the Council at Westminster had resolved that this situation must be handled with resolution. If King John were to be allowed to give shelter to royalist ships preying on English commerce, every ruler in Europe might do the like, and already French warships were following the example of Rupert. Accordingly, it was the whole of a hostile Europe, and not Rupert alone, with which the Commonwealth was faced at the mouth of the Tagus. As Gardiner says, it was self-preservation that drove England to become a maritime power such as she had never been before.

King John, in fact, must be coerced, but Blake, though Rupert had sought by craft to blow up the *Leopard* with an infernal machine, though his men had murdered Blake's ashore, and though Rupert had stirred up the passions of the Catholics priests and populace against the English heretics,[111] was nevertheless careful for long to take no aggressive step, even allowing two French ships that came into his power to join Rupert on the King's demand. It was not until the embarrassed John had at length definitely declared in favour of Rupert that he acted. On May 16th, as the annual fleet bound for Brazil, of eighteen ships, sailed out from the Tagus, Blake seized nine of them that were owned by English merchants in Lisbon and manned by English seamen, and these willingly took service under the Commonwealth.[112] Ten days later

---

[111] *A Perfect Diurnall*, E.277, 10 and 21; Thurloe, i, 146; Warburton's *Memoirs of Prince Rupert*, iii, 304-5.

Popham arrived from England with orders to treat the Portuguese as enemies. Hostility was now open, and the English merchants in Lisbon were thrown into prison and their goods confiscated. The task of Blake and Popham became increasingly difficult, for they were obliged to send as far as Vigo and Cadiz for water and supplies, and thenceforward duty was most trying to his ships' companies.

The months wore away and still Rupert skulked in port. At the end of July, supported now by King John's fleet, he made an attempt to come out, but to his disgust and Blake's neither his own seamen nor the Portuguese would face the Commonwealth guns, and though Blake and Popham tried to tempt them by denying themselves the weather gage, they were still disappointed. Then Popham left for Cadiz and Blake was alone. Not till September 7th did he have another chance to engage the enemy. Under cover of a patchy mist Rupert crept out. Suddenly, as the curtain of mist rose for a moment, Blake, with only two frigates in company, found himself bearing down on Rupert's *Constant Reformation* at the head of thirty-six sail. The two ships were on opposite tacks. A collision seemed certain, and Blake was three against thirty-six. But he held his course.

"Can you ram him?" he asked the sailing master of the *George*.

"Yes, but we shall hazard both ships," was the reply.

"I'll run that hazard rather than bear up for the enemy," said Blake, and he sent a broadside at Rupert's flagship. Down came her fore-topmast, and Blake's quarry seemed within his grasp. But he was to be again cheated, for the fog swept down as suddenly as it had lifted and Rupert disappeared into its folds.[113]

---

[112] S. P. Dom., xi, 91.

When the blockade had been kept up for six months, and the season was approaching when in the practice of the time it could no longer be continued, Blake had one more opportunity to teach King John a lesson. Early on the stormy morning of September 14th, 1650, twenty-three of the Portuguese fleet from Brazil, richly laden, crept over the horizon on the last stage of their journey to Lisbon. Though a gale howled in the rigging, and a wild sea smothered his lower ports, Blake made straight for his prey, and after a three hours' fight in the tumbling waters sank the Portugese vice-admiral and captured seven ships.

But now "the time of year wastes apace in which you can there ride without danger," and so, with his ships' bottoms foul after so long at sea, Blake designedly abandoned the blockade and made Cadiz, where he was received with deep respect on September 29th, for an enemy of Portugal's was a friend of Spain's; though, according to the Venetian ambassador in Madrid, he declined, with that touch of arrogance he was inclined to show to foreigners, either to lower his colours or to salute the fortress.[114]

After he had sent his prizes home Blake had but six ships remaining, but he determined to continue out yet a month or so longer, against all naval precedent, in the hope of meeting Rupert at sea. That prince sailed out from the Tagus at length, to the vast relief of the Portuguese, and, as Warburton relates, being destitute of a port, he took the Mediterranean for his harbour, poverty and despair for his companions and revenge for his guide. On his way he plundered English merchantmen and, to the indignation of the Spaniards, he violated the

---

[113] Gibson's *A Few Instances of English Courage, etc.*, B. M. Add. MSS., 11684,. fol. 2.
[114] Basadonna to the Doge, V.S.P., xxviii. No. 442.

neutrality of their harbours to burn others that had taken refuge in them. Relentlessly, Blake set out once more in pursuit, though he was so hard put to it that he had to fly his flag in a fourth-rater, the *Phoenix*. Thus it was that Blake made his notable first entry into the Mediterranean Sea, where he was to make the North Sea people an equal power among the coastwise powers and under the flag of St. George to assert for merchants the freedom of the seas. The occasion was historic, for from his experiences there was to grow in due time a realisation of the need for a Mediterranean fleet, not for strategic purposes, but for trade protection, though indeed he was soon to demonstrate that trade protection must be itself a strategic purpose. He was to show, moreover, how vital it was that such a force should have its own base in those waters, for though he might use Spanish ports when Portugal was hostile, or Portuguese when Spain was the enemy, yet such a resort was "an habitation giddy and unsure."

He had now received orders to treat French ships also as enemies. Since Charles's execution Mazarin had been permitting French privateers to engage in a ruthless piracy upon English commerce, and had given no satisfaction to the protests of the Commonwealth Government, which he could not yet bring himself to recognise though he sought favours from it. Therefore, though no war was declared, a policy of reprisals was sanctioned by the Council of State. Blake very soon picked up some French prizes and one of these was the *Jules*, commanded by the Chevalier de la Lande. Coming on board the *Phoenix* to surrender, he observed how weak the ship was and swore he had been tricked. With that queer chivalry of his, Blake thereupon sent him back to his ship to fight it out, but nothing would induce the crew of the *Jules* to do so.

Blake's chief quarry, however, was Rupert, and using Spanish ports for provisioning, he now proceeded to harry the royalists from the Mediterranean, where they were fattening on their easy prey. He captured the *Roebuck*. The *Black Prince* was run ashore and burnt by her crew. Four others were cornered by Blake and driven to ruin on the rocks of Cartagena. The destruction of Rupert's fleet was thus almost complete, but again the Princes themselves, who had adventured away with three ships to hunt the coast of North Africa, escaped the guns of Blake with that good fortune that so often favoured their audacity and found a new refuge in the French waters of Toulon.[115]

Blake had now done all he could and in February, 1651, he returned home, after nearly a year at sea, being succeeded by another great admiral in William Penn, who had a few years before fathered the child that in due time was to be the founder of Pennsylvania. Him Rupert outwitted, but when at length he escaped from Toulon with *Constant Reformation* (his flagship), *Swallow*, *Marmaduke*, and *Honest Seaman*, it was by destiny and not by Penn that the Prince was to be pursued. He set a course for the West Indies upon a career of frank piracy, but off the Azores his flagship was lost in a storm and he himself barely escaped with his life from her sinking hull; presently the *Marmaduke* revolted and declared for Parliament; and finally, the *Honest Seaman* was engulfed in the fury of a tempest that shook the waters of the Virgin Islands, taking with her to the bottom his brother Maurice and all hands.

Alone, battered by storms, goal-less, a spent force, but with his daring spirit yet uncrushed, he crept back into Nantes in

---

[115] The historical sources for the operations against Rupert are several; see especially *The Letters of Robert Blake* (N.R.S.) and articles by R. C. Anderson in the *Mariner's Mirror*, ix, 2; xiv, 4; xvii, 2; xxi, 1.

the *Swallow* in the spring of 1653 after a voyage of two years. It was the last time that he raised his active hand against the Commonwealth, but in the days to come he was to serve his adopted country more honourably as a patron of science and the arts, as the founder of the Hudson Bay Company, as a fearless admiral in the Second Dutch War — and as a notable tennis player. Stranger still, under the dissolute and irresponsible rule of Charles II he was to become himself the champion of Parliament against attempts at royal encroachments and Roman Catholic restoration.

Meanwhile Blake, on returning home, had received the thanks of Parliament and a grant of £1,000 in February, 1651. He had done much more than free English shipping of a grave threat. While Cromwell, dashing the Scots to ruin at Dunbar, had demonstrated to Europe the mettle of his soldiers, Blake had shown that England's new sea-soldiers were of equal temper. In his modest triumph there were the little beginnings of great changes. He had begun to invest the office of an English admiral with the attributes of an ambassador. He had shown a statesmanlike appreciation of the political attributes of a fleet. He had used the enmity of Portugal and France to secure the friendship of Spain, and from that proud court, so steeped in the divinity of kingship, he had won recognition for the pariah state. Portugal, too, was already "knocking at the door."

Moreover, he had already begun that vital change by which a collection of ships was to develop into a national maritime force inspired by a sense of service to their corporate spirit rather than by a thirst for adventure. The ideas of plunder and the pursuit of prizes begin to recede, and are replaced by the notion of commerce protection in all narrow waters where English vessels journey, and not only in the narrow seas at home. The lines of commerce become the lines of strategy. The distinction between the merchantman and the navy ship begins to sharpen. The merchantman ceases to count in naval defence and becomes instead the object of protection. It was the most far-reaching change in our naval history.

Blake was not the first English admiral to voyage into the Mediterranean, but his bearing and achievement were in sharp contrast to the deplorable expedition of Sir Robert Mansell in 1620-21. English shipping in that sea had hitherto been left to shift for itself against the Barbary pirates and the privateers of Spain, France or Holland. They were to suffer at those hands for some time yet, but Blake's appearance marked the beginning of a change and brought to the minds of men at home a realisation of the importance of the Mediterranean. Few seamen of that age could have thus kept the seas in distant waters for nearly a year, continuously engaged upon exacting duty and yet maintaining efficiency and a satisfied discipline. If some of the credit was due to the Admiralty Committee and the Commissioners of the Navy at home, Blake's was yet the hand that kept the organisation in working efficiency, and his was the spirit and example that breathed ardour and loyalty and corporate feeling into that empirical organism.

Immediate re-employment awaited Blake on his return. Nests of pirate royalists, like little Ruperts, had established themselves in the Channel Isles, the Scillies and the Isle of Man. Though no great glory would seem to-day to attach to expeditions against them, in former days these rocky lairs of traditional piracy were serious military objectives, and lying as they did on the main lines of commerce they provided to any enemy who possessed them fastnesses from which as a wolf he might richly raid the unguarded sheep-walks of the sea. Their possession was of the first strategic importance to Commonwealth shipping.

Blake proceeded first against the Scillies, together with Sir George Ayscue. The lonely isles of Lyonesse were held by Sir John Grenville, who with a small force of ships and men had been pillaging not only English shipping but Dutch as well. Accordingly, when Blake arrived off the Scillies he found no less a person than Marten Tromp already there with a Dutch fleet bound on the same errand as himself, but Blake was able to persuade him to leave the Commonwealth to do its own police work. So the first encounter between the two great admirals passed with peacefulness and courtesy, and Tromp even offered to help Blake root out the pirates. The expedition has little of importance beyond that first encounter, for, though his first attempt at a landing with raw and sea-sick soldiers was bungled, and though himself narrowly escaped death from the bursting of a gun, Blake had no serious difficulty in ejecting Grenville from the island of Tresco and later forcing him to a capitulation on magnanimous terms at St. Mary's, on May 23rd.[116] There Blake had his first experience of an attack upon land from sea, and there he recorded on the tablets of his memory, to be recalled when a greater occasion should require it, the uses of a smoke-screen in naval battle.

There followed now Charles II's spectacular invasion of England that was to end in the ruin of Worcester. On that fateful September 3rd of 1651, Blake, who would have been engaged in the campaign as a soldier once more, but for the death of Edward Popham, lay with the fleet in the Downs with his flag in the *Victory*. The issue on land being decided, the Council of State now turned its attention to reducing the last

---

[116] Thurloe, i, 177; Nicholas Papers, i, 255; Council of State to Blake, Int. I, 96, 130; S. P. Dom., xv, 80.

isolated fastnesses of the cavaliers in the Channel Isles and the Isle of Man, and Blake received orders in September to sail with Colonel James Heane and a military force for the reduction of Jersey and Guernsey, where Sir George Carteret and Colonel Roger Burgess respectively were still holding out defiantly.

Sailing from Weymouth with a large mixed fleet of eighty ships and with his flag in the *Happy Entrance*, he arrived before Jersey on October 20th, and Carteret, who was no easy enemy, repulsed his messenger of peace. Blake, anxious to avoid waste of blood, forbore from the peril of landing under fire before the strong defensive positions, and he sought by guile to effect a surprise landing while the vigilant Carteret watched his every move from the rocky promontories of the isle. Blake moved his fleet from the west coast to the south, and Carteret marched to conform. He sailed back again and Carteret counter-marched. Once more he moved, dividing his fleet, and the enemy was forced to do the like. In this wise, though he could not shake the resolution of Carteret, he harassed the novice soldiers of the island and by his display of strength as he sailed from point to point, firing his impressive broadsides, he played upon their half-heartedness. Blake, in fact, was using brains to save spilling of blood.

At length, under cover of night, Heane's redcoats took to the boats to attempt a landing by stealth in St. Ouen's Bay, but the unresting Carteret was ready for them. Missing the tide, Heane's men were kept in the open boats a whole day and were not able to attempt a landing till the night of October 23rd. As they leapt from the boats and floundered ashore, waist-deep in the sea, the royalist cavalry came out of the night and charged them at the water's edge. But they stood firm. The island foot militia forsook the fight, and the whole of Heane's force, including two troops of cavalry, was successfully landed. Very soon all Jersey had been taken save the stronghold of Elizabeth Castle. In that island fastness, jutting from the waters of St. Aubin's Bay, George Carteret and some 350 men of mixed nationalities, now almost deserted by the islanders, locked their gates against the invaders and held out through all the stormy month of November. It was a hopeless defiance, however. Some brilliant artillery work by Heane's gunners, and particularly the explosive bombs thrown by the mortars of Thomas Wright, "who did by his fireworks perform singular service," wrought great destruction. So that when Blake offered Carteret honourable terms, he surrendered to the inevitable, his remnant garrison marching out on December 12th with matches lighted and musket-balls in mouth.[117]

A week later Roger Burgess surrendered Castle Cornet in Guernsey, and, the Isle of Man having already fallen to Colonel Robert Duckenfield on October 31st, all the territory of England and Ireland owned the dominion of the Commonwealth. By the spring of the next year, a defeated Scotland was brought into reluctant union with England, and Sir George Ayscue's squadron had without difficulty secured the acknowledgment of Commonwealth rule by the West Indies and the American colonies. Every foot of Charles's possessions passed from him. Never was any government so efficient and public-spirited as the Commonwealth Council of State, and not often had there been any so unpopular.

---

[117] E.651, 9 and 17; E.791, 7; S. P. Dom, 1651, 441, and 1652, 578 and 591; Clarke Papers, ii, 228; *Channel Islands and The Great Rebellion*, by M. F. H. Ellis, Bulletin of the Société Jersiaise, 1937.

V. CHALLENGE TO HOLLAND

Now pirates and last-ditch cavaliers are left behind and the scene takes on ampler proportions.

For some time, despite attempts on both sides to prevent it, England and Holland had been drifting towards the rocks of war. Those who had been firm friends in the time of Elizabeth, brothers in the fight for Protestant liberty, and partners in enmity to Spain, became slowly estranged when the Dutch, having attained their independence of the Spaniards in 1609, assumed also the mantle of arrogance. Their little land, peopled by a race that was at once industrious, enlightened and brave, became a storehouse of commercial wealth, and their ships ranged the seas of the world, to bring to Europe the merchandise of Asia and America. To Holland fell Venice's ancient Oriental fee, and long before 1650 she was immeasurably the greatest maritime power in the world, for her ships carried merchandise not only to and from her own possessions, but among other nations also. That supremacy, however, was achieved not only by industry and enterprise, but also by an arrogant acquisitiveness which was encouraged by the utter degeneracy into which English maritime power had fallen under the Stuarts. They tortured and put to death English factors in the Spice Islands; they descended upon the fisheries of the North Sea in huge fleets escorted by men-of-war that attacked and sank the fishermen of other nations; they invaded the harbours and even the shores of England and with volleys of musketry repelled those who approached them; they dispossessed the English merchants of long-established foreign trade, and drove the English colonists from their fisheries and their settlements in America. The Dutch treated the clearest rights of English merchants with contempt and did as they pleased, even beneath the sentinel cliffs of Dover.

The advent of the Commonwealth, however, brought a different spirit into English administration. The new Puritan rulers were in no mood to brook any trespasses upon the rights of Englishmen. The saw the plain fact of the challenge to the flag, and they manifested the intensity of their zeal not only in an administration of high efficiency and honesty, but also in their appreciation that honour and prestige, besides being in themselves things to brood upon with ardour, have a far-stretching material import. An insult to the flag damages not only honour but also trade, "the fairest mistress in all Christendom."[118]

Accordingly, when the Prince of Orange, William II, showed his violent hostility to the new regicide government, receiving the young Charles Stuart and his exiled followers with honour, and when the Dutch allowed the murder of the Commonwealth's ambassador to The Hague in 1649 to pass unpunished the prospects of peace were not further advanced. Nevertheless, the Council of State had no bellicose intentions. They felt a kinship of blood, of religion, and of political outlook with the democratic Protestant burghers of Holland. Upon the death of William II in the autumn of 1650 and the consequent decline of the Dutch military party, the Council's hopes of maintaining peace revived, and they went so far as to send Oliver St. John, who was now Chief Justice, to The Hague in the spring of 1651, on an embassage to discuss the union of the two countries in one great Protestant democracy. St. John, however, was untutored in diplomacy, and the

---

[118] *Burton's Diary*, iii, 394, 458, promise of promoting good relations for a lasting period.

influence of the Orange party turned awry proceedings which had otherwise much St. John returned to England after a few months, angry at his treatment in Holland and deeply suspicious of Dutch intentions, and in the momentous step that was next taken his was undoubtedly the compelling influence. On October 9th, Parliament, pursuing its active government, passed the memorable Navigation Act, which prescribed that in future no goods should be brought into English ports save in English bottoms or in ships of the country in which the goods were produced. Such a step meant death to Dutch trade.

Ambassadors were at once sent to Westminster to seek some amelioration, and to discuss the whole field of relations between the Commonwealth and the Republic. The right of the English Parliament to pass such a measure as the Navigation Act could hardly be questioned, but the Dutch had some cause of grievance in the treatment that their ships were receiving from the English privateers engaged in the war of reprisals against French shipping. In pursuit of that war they searched also Dutch vessels suspected of carrying French goods, and the rough usage they had sometimes dealt out to the Dutch crews was a manifestation of the quickening temper of the English Commonwealth seamen. It was that rising temper, due to resentment at Dutch aggression and to the sense that the sap of the Tudors and the Plantagenets was once more active in their own veins, which brought them into inevitable conflict with a race of seamen who, after their long supremacy, looked upon the new Englishmen as pretentious upstarts. The right of search and the salute of the English flag were ostensibly the issues that led to the war, but these were merely symbolic. The First Dutch War is of special importance in that it marked the development of the modern economic struggle between nations. Not dynasties, but peoples, not religion, but trade, not crowns nor fiefs, but harbours and fisheries — these were the forces and the issues. Yet, on the English side, the people at large in the inland counties remained indifferent to the struggle.

While the Dutch ambassadors were still in England the States-General began preparations for hostilities. For commander they naturally called upon their national seaman-hero, Marten Tromp. That great "admiral bold and free" was at this time the first captain of the age. A year older than Blake, he had been at sea ever since he was ten years old, and had in some thirty victorious battles, notably in that over the Spaniards in The Downs in 1639, established an unequalled renown both for gallantry and seamanship. If he was the best commander to protect the commerce of Holland, he was equally the last man who would strike his colours to the English, and when asked what had been his practice on this point he replied that he only struck when meeting an English fleet stronger than his own. To Captain Tuyneman he had said on one occasion: "What did you strike for? You were as strong as they. Why were you afraid?" That which was to Englishmen a traditional right long exercised by their forefathers and which, though ineffectually enforced by the feebleness of the Stuarts, they were determined in their new spirit now to maintain, was to Tromp and the Dutch a monstrous claim in the face of their own overtopping superiority in the seas of the world.

The Commonwealth answered with similar precautions, and a day or two later General Blake was recommissioned to command the fleet and to hasten forward its preparation for sea, "for which there is extraordinary occasion." Since the expedition to Jersey he had been in London, in regular attendance upon meetings of the Council of State and the committees of it of which he was a member, but he now collected the fleet in Thames' mouth and proceeded with it to the Downs, where he was visited at the end of March by Cromwell.

Blake entered the Dutch War with a valuable experience behind him. By to-day's standards he was still little more than the inspired amateur, for he had still not yet tested his strength in a fleet action. Nevertheless, out of the treasury of his own character, in which a taciturn reserve veiled a militant energy that could hardly have been expected from the cloistered student of Wadham, he brought into English naval practice the imperishable principle, not to be abandoned until 1914, that the duty of a fleet was to seek out the enemy and fight him. "He was the first man," says Clarendon, "who declined the old track, and made it manifest that the science might be attained in less time than was imagined, and despised those rules which had long been in practice to keep his ship and his men out of danger, which had been held in former times a point of great ability and circumspection, as if the principal art requisite in the captain of a ship had been to be sure to come home safe again."

Blake was one of those men who loved battle. Like many reserved men, his bridled spirit leapt to its highest reach only, in the words of Masefield:

> When the guns are growling and the blood runs
> red.

"He was the first," continued Clarendon, "that infused that proportion of courage into the seamen by making them see by experience what mighty things they could do if they were resolved, and taught them to fight in fire as well as upon water;

and though he had been very well imitated and followed, he was the first that gave the example of that kind of naval courage, and bold and resolute achievements."

But in spite of his audacity and eagerness in battle, and in spite of the evidence of one sharp defeat he was to suffer, it is true that Blake was never foolhardy. After Captain Myngs had captured three Dutch ships singlehanded, he received from the admiral not praise but a sharp rebuke. "You think," said Blake, "that you have done a fine act, but what if they had carried you to Holland? What account could you have given the State for the loss of their ship? I do not love a foolhardy captain; therefore hereafter temper your courage with discretion."[119]

Besides this spirit of militancy that he brought, Blake gave to the fleet another teaching out of his own experience and character — the lesson of unresting vigilance. Sieges by land and blockades by sea had called for this quality above almost any other, and not the least of his contributions to naval tradition was the teaching he instilled to watch and wait in disciplined patience and with ever-open eye.

These results were not secured without a strict personal discipline. He had the manner of command, and one can observe that with the years his manner became more peremptory. He tolerated no shortcomings in duty, and did not hesitate to rebuke his captains with anger when he thought it necessary. In the manner of the time he would call a council of his captains for their advice whenever necessary, but frequently rejected it. But his hold upon the fleet was fortified by his kindness in all personal relations. He frequently used his good offices to secure employment for men who had served him, and these letters are generally written in his own hand. His old veterans of Lyme and Taunton — Thomas Adams, the one-

---

[119] *First Dutch War*, i, 12.

armed Squire, Pooke and Pelsor, to name a few — had a special place in his heart, and many of them followed him to sea. After an action he would particularly inquire how his Somerset men had borne themselves and how fared. He took the closest interest in the improvements that were slowly to be made for the treatment of the wounded and the sick.

On May 10th, 1652, in pursuance of the States-General's plans for protecting their commerce, Tromp put to sea in the *Brederode* (fifty-four guns) with forty-two men-of-war, and on the night of May 18th, having avoided Major Nehemiah Bourne's small squadron off the South Foreland because of the flag question, he anchored for the night off Dover in rough weather, ignoring the shots from Dover Castle that summoned him to salute, and insulting the Governor by musketry practice under his nose. To Blake, who was off Rye with twelve ships, his flag being in the *James*, of forty-eight guns, came a fast ship from Bourne telling him of Tromp's presence and of his orders from the States-General not to salute. Beating up the Straits, against a north-east wind, he saw the Dutch fleet early the next morning, May 19th, still at anchor in Dover Roads, and Tromp immediately on sighting him stood over towards Calais, apparently still anxious to avoid the flag issue.

On his way, however, Tromp fell in with a Dutch ship and by her captain he was told that seven Dutchmen, homeward bound with rich cargoes, had run into Blake's fleet and were in fear of search on suspicion of carrying French goods. In pursuit of his orders and not knowing that the merchantmen had been allowed to go free, Tromp immediately altered course downwind and came up with Blake four miles off Dover.

Blake, as he looked towards the French coast on that May afternoon therefore, saw a formless crowd of forty-two ships bearing down upon him in a threatening manner. It seemed, as he wrote afterwards in his dispatch, that Tromp was deliberately watching for "an advantage to brave us upon our own coast."[120] Though he had himself no more than twelve sail, he without hesitation put over on the starboard tack to front them and cleared for action. He seems to have been in happy mind, and when a little vessel joined him from Dover with forty volunteers on board he met them at the gangway, ordered Malaga to be served, an office that was performed by that useful chronicler, Richard Gibson, and joined with them in drinking.

Tromp, in fact, had not intended battle, being concerned only to inquire into the safety of the merchantmen, but with so great a superiority he equally had no intention of striking his colours to the English. Accordingly, when a shot from the *James* across the bows of the *Brederode* called upon him to strike he took no notice. A second shot alike had no result. A third shot tore through his mainsail, and in a rage, Tromp ran up the red flag of battle and replied with a broadside.[121]

Battle was joined some time after four o'clock, Blake laying the *James* alongside the *Brederode*, and the other ships of both fleets clustering about their flagships in the unorderly manner of the time. In spite of their superiority in numbers, the Dutch were roughly handled, but, in the heart of the conflict, the *James*'s mizzenmast was shot away and her sails and rigging torn to ribbons. After there had been two hours or more of warm fighting, Bourne's squadron of nine ships appeared and fell upon Tromp's rear. Tromp turned for the French coast, and as darkness fell made away from Blake's guns.[122]

---

[120] Blake to the Speaker, May 20th, Tanner MSS., liii, fol. 35.

[121] Tromp declared that Blake fired the first broadside just as the Dutch were preparing to strike, but the account here given is the one generally-accepted.

[122] For a full relation of this interesting episode see "The First Gun of

That night Blake lay at anchor, labouring throughout the hours of darkness at repairing his rigging. The little country merchant had cause to be satisfied. In his first fleet engagement, against the foremost sea captain of the age, he had come off with a clear advantage. Without losing a ship, he had compelled a greatly superior force to retire, capturing one of their vessels and leaving another a shattered hulk. Moreover, he had scored a tactical success, keeping the major portion of the Dutch fleet out of action by bearing away on the starboard tack, until Bourne came down on their rear at the right moment. A few days after the action he received a letter from Tromp personally, a soft-spoken and ingenuous letter. "My intention," Tromp wrote, "was to greet you," but when he found himself attacked he was obliged, as a man of honour, to defend himself. He begged Blake "for friendship's sake" to return the ship that had been captured, and ended by assuring him of his friendship.

Blake's reply was a masterpiece of indignant asperity, and whether he was right or not in his assessment of Tromp's intentions, it serves to show his flash of spirit and the imperious tone he often took to foreigners. This is his letter, dated May 30th, 1652:

Sir, — It is not without great astonishment that I have read yours of the 23rd May, sent to me by your messengers, wherein, though representing yourself as a person of honour, you introduce many gross misstatements; and this, just after having fought with the fleet of the Parliament of the English Republic instead of employing the customary forms of respect, which the occasion demanded, and which you yourself have hitherto employed, and having thought fit to commit an act of hostility (which you yourself style a falling

the Dutch Wars," by A. C. Dewar, *United Service Magazine*, 1911.

out with the Republic) without receiving the slightest provocation from her servants, who are thus assailed by you at a time when your Government and their Ambassadors were enjoyed in negotiations with Parliament, and in need of the friendship of the Republic of England. But God (in Whom we trust) having frustrated your purposes, to your own destruction, and seeing that we have taken some of your ships, you have thought well to demand the same of us again, as though your former proceeding had been nothing but a salute (as you assert), and failing this to follow up your former insults by your present letter; to which the only meet answer that I can return is that I presume Parliament will keenly resent this great insult and the spilling of the blood of their inoffending subjects, and that you will moreover find, in the undersigned, one ever ready to carry out their commands.

Your humble servant,
Rob. Blake.[123]

The news of the battle of Dover was received in Holland with indignation and in England with excitement. The Dutch sent over additional ambassadors, but an English court of inquiry held at Dover under Cromwell was well satisfied with Blake's action, for which he received also the approval and thanks of Parliament, and though negotiations between Commonwealth and Republic continued at Westminster until the end of June, the difference in aspirations was too wide to be bridged, and indeed the Dutch were asked to give up that which was to them the source of life. The war had in effect already begun, and on June 11th Blake brought eleven merchant prizes into Dover, Ayscue taking a further six off the Lizard on the next day.

---

[123] *First Dutch War*, i, 257.

The Commonwealth threw itself with vigour and efficiency into the task of preparing for war. The English, indeed, entered upon the coming conflict with material as well as intangible advantages, in spite of the disparity in commercial strength. They had in the first place the great strategic advantage of lying on the flank of that route by which all Dutch shipping westward and southward must pass, unless the long and hazardous route by the north of Scotland were taken. The coasts of England overhung the Channel "like an eagle's wing." A huge commerce had to be protected in its passage through these waters by the Dutch, whereas the English fleet had a relatively small commerce to safeguard. Therefore the English fleet had a mobility and a freedom to strike that the Dutch had not. Moreover, whereas the English enjoyed unity and efficiency of administration and command, the Dutch States, since the death of William II, were cursed by five separate Boards of Admiralty, whose jealous bickerings and whose muddled administration, by which ships were sent to sea ill-found, ill-armed and ill-victualled, were to prove their country's undoing.

On the same day as the action off Dover, William Penn was appointed Vice-Admiral under Blake, and Nehemiah Bourne became Rear-Admiral. Thus there came into existence a practice, previously adopted only tentatively, and copied from the Dutch, by which the fleet was divided into squadrons of the Red, the White and the Blue respectively. Bourne, the new Admiral of the Blue, was one of the most interesting of the minor characters of Cromwell's day. A freeman of Massachusetts and a ship's carpenter by trade, he had come to England when the Civil War had broken out and pledged his sword to the Puritan cause, of which he was a pious and long-winded adherent. He had served as a major in the regiment of the notorious Colonel Thomas Rainsborough, whom the fleet had refused to accept as their commander, and we have seen him already at sea under Blake in the Downs. Later on he was appointed one of the Commissioners of the Navy to attend to the equipment and manning of the fleet. Installing himself at Harwich, he gave to that work a devoted zeal which marks him as one of the ablest administrative officers the Navy has had and which in no way deterred his Puritan industry from pursuing, though with scant success, his own commercial adventures.

The Dutch ambassadors left England on June 30th, 1652, but four days before, in conformity with the strategy that had been early understood to be the right one, Blake had already set out against the Dutch herring fleet north of the Dogger Bank at the head of sixty-one ships, the largest English fleet that had yet put to sea, leaving Ayscue behind to take his place in the Channel with a small squadron. Blake's flagship was the *Resolution*, the *James* not yet having been mended of her wounds from Dover. His unheroic task was completed quickly and efficiently. On July 12th eight frigates sent forward under Penn fell upon the thirteen warships that were guarding the great fleet of 600 herring busses and captured or sunk twelve of them, taking 900 prisoners. Blake's treatment of the herring busses provides one of the best incidents in his life story, for all were allowed to return home, being bidden to return no more. In these busses the fishermen made their homes, taking with them their wives and children, and Blake would take from them neither their vessels nor even, it seems, their catch of fish.

It is in connection with this expedition against the fishing fleet that there is related a story which supports the supposition that Blake had spent some of the "missing fifteen years" in Holland, but of more interest is its testimony to the character of the man. One of the Dutch skippers having been brought on board the *Resolution*, Blake conversed with him and asked where he had been born.

"At Schiedam," was the reply, upon which Blake is reported to have said.

"I lived at Schiedam in my youth for five or six years. Come into my cabin and let us drink a glass of wine to the welfare of the town."

After a friendly conversation Blake asked the skipper to let him have two or three tons of herrings, and this was done at once. Blake desired to pay for them, but the skipper refused to accept anything, whereupon Blake threw a small packet of money on board the herring buss. He also ordered his men to throw back again the herrings that they had taken, and the Dutchman was taken in tow for the night. The next day, a few cables' lengths from the flagship, he was permitted to make a further catch of fish, and so returned home delighted.[124]

The story bears from its source the marks of truth, in essence if not in detail. Blake was subjected to some criticism at home for his lenient dealing to the fishing fleet as he had also been for his treatment of Grenville; his mercifulness, however, was not only natural and customary in him, but it also accorded on this occasion with the dictates of convenience, for he had other fish to fry. The Dutch East India fleet, homeward bound with rich cargoes, was daily expected and was known to be coming round the north of Scotland.

Tromp meanwhile had collected a great fleet of ninety-two sail at Scheveningen. He had been obliged to watch Blake sail north unopposed, but presently he set sail with a northerly wind, determined to smother Ayscue's little squadron of

---

[124] *Hollandsche Mercurius*, 1652, p. 78.

sixteen ships in the Downs, which on July 2nd had virtually destroyed a Dutch merchant fleet of twenty-seven vessels. The winds of heaven foiled him, however, in his attempt on Ayscue, and he turned north against Blake. The old hero was in an ill temper. He had mishandled the Dover affair and he had failed against Ayscue's paltry squadron. He was not used to the initiative being taken by the enemy. Heaven was to foil him again, however, for his frigates had but sighted Blake's scouts to the north of the Shetlands on the night of July 26th, when, with a sudden shift of wind, a hurricane descended from the north-west. Blake was able to round the northern extremity of the Shetlands and to find shelter, but upon Tromp, caught on a lee shore in the sound which divides the Orkneys from the Shetlands, there fell the full shock of the storm in all its rage. All night the crews battled for their lives against its ferocity, each ship for itself, and when the day dawned with the mountainous seas somewhat abated he could count only thirty-nine out of his ninety-two ships. Five had been dashed to pieces on the Shetland rocks and the remainder scattered in all directions — even to Norway. Crippled and almost without food, he turned for home, but he had achieved one purpose at least, for, chance and the wind having set them on the right course, the East Indiamen arrived safely within his arms at the height of the storm. By August 10th he was safely back in Holland. Blake had therefore missed his purpose, but the elements had struck a shrewd blow for him, so shrewd that Tromp was relieved of his command.

VI. THE KENTISH KNOCK

Blake had turned south after Tromp's departure, eager to come up with him, but, like Tromp, he had been roughly handled by the storm and, though he sent a division as far as the Dutch coast, he could not come up with the enemy. Blake accordingly concentrated at Yarmouth, occupying himself in repairing the damage of the gale and rounding up Dutch privateers that were preying on shipping. He dallied there somewhat unnecessarily, it seems, for he missed a rich prize. Another great Dutch seaman, Michael de Ruyter of the thick moustaches and the heavy jaw, had successfully made his way through the Channel with a great fleet after a sharp brush with Ayscue. In a few days Blake was back again in the Channel and moving westwards towards de Ruyter, but news that a Dutch armada was about to draw out from the Scheldt brought him back again into the Downs. Here his fleet was joined by Charles I's pride, the *Sovereign of the Seas*, now remodelled and refitted, and here, at the instance of Spain, he pounced upon a new enemy.

Dunkirk had for some time been closely besieged by the Archduke Leopold of Spain. Its fall seemed imminent and accordingly the duc de Vendôme, Admiral of France, set out to its relief from Calais on September 4th with a flotilla of store-ships, escorted by eight men-of-war. Dunkirk had been half-promised to the Commonwealth by Mazarin, but the Council of State had become exasperated by his procrastination and by the continued depredations by French privateers upon English commerce; moreover, if the siege were raised there was a danger that the Dutch might be allowed to use the port. It was at Spain's suggestion, however, that Blake received orders to frustrate the relief. Accordingly, with his flag in the *Resolution*, he pounced on Vendôme's expedition when it put out to sea, and, with greatly superior strength, overwhelmed it. Seven of the men-of-war he captured outright, and the store-ships he took, destroyed or dispersed. Dunkirk surrendered the next day, and Mazarin, brought sharply to his senses, learnt that here was something more than a pirate state, and he shortly gave it formal recognition.

The new Dutch fleet had been placed under the command of Vice-Admiral Cornelius de With, a leader of the utmost daring but of an ungovernable temper, an able seaman, but to his crews a sheer terrorist. Raging at the condition of his crews and the foulness of the beer, he put to sea with the new fleet to fight Blake, and on September 22nd effected a junction off Ostend with de Ruyter, who had skilfully avoided the English fleet. Thus united they numbered sixty-two sail, while Blake counted a trifle more.

Hostilities had now been in progress for two months and still there had been no major fleet engagement. The English had had a number of minor successes, but ever since leaving the Shetlands, Blake had been out of touch with the enemy and de Ruyter had been allowed to go free. Changeful winds and the great difficulty in obtaining reliable intelligence of the enemy's movements had been the causes, but when it was known on September 25th that de With was about to descend upon them in the Downs, excitement in the English fleet ran high. De With, for his part, in spite of his disaffected crews and bad victuals, was lusting for battle at all costs, and he remarked:

"I shall bring the fleet merrily to the enemy and. the devil may bring it off."

It was again the incalculable winds that held the balance of fortune. A gale from the south-south-west frustrated de With of his dash into English waters, and when it had abated, Blake, running before a fresh wind, had slipped out past the North Foreland into the open sea. At noon on September 28th, 1652, off the sandbank known as the Kentish Knock, which lies about fifteen miles north-east of the North Foreland, with a wind now coming from the south-west, he surprised the Dutch by appearing on their weather bow. Blake himself in the *Resolution*, accompanied by only two or three other ships, was some miles ahead of his fleet, but he was now to show his natural aptitude in the handling of a big fleet. Until the Red and White squadrons should arrive he lay to, restraining the eagerness of Penn, who would have dashed straight at the enemy, but not waiting for his Rear-Admiral, Bourne, who would thus serve as a "second wave" to strike the enemy at a shrewd moment.

Then, when both fleets were strung out face to face, like masses of cavalry preparing to charge each other, Blake filled his sails and with rolling drums and sounding trumpets, bore down before the wind with his two squadrons upon the Dutchmen as they beat against it on the port tack. Right through the Dutch fleet they "charged" and, turning, thrust through once more, like shuttles on a giant loom. As they penetrated each other's ranks the rival fleets fell on with their artillery, the Dutchmen, as their manner was, shooting high at shrouds and masts with intent to disable, the English, with their heavier guns, shooting low at the hulls to sink. "I saw nothing," wrote de With, "but smoke, fire and English." Both the gunnery and the discipline of the English were immensely superior to those of their enemy, though the lively seas sometimes drenched them to the middle. "We found," wrote de With again, "that the guns on their smallest frigates carry farther than our heaviest cannon, and the English fired smarter and quicker than did many of ours."

At the very beginning of the fight the *Resolution*, together with Penn's flagship, the *James*, and the great *Sovereign of the Seas*, grounded on the Kentish Knock in three fathoms. Apparently the *Resolution* soon got clear, but the others were slower in doing so. The apparent mishap became a blessing. As the main fleets ran clear of each other on their opposite courses, de With, having tacked, was standing to the south, but Penn had cleared himself of the sandbank by standing to the south-east, and accordingly, in Penn's own words, "fell pat to receive him." Though much outnumbered, their great weight of ordnance dealt out heavy punishment to the Dutch, and de With was no sooner clear again than Bourne's squadron of the Blue, fresh and eager for the fight, appeared upon the scene, as Blake must have intended, and continued his discomfort.

The action went on for some two or three hours when night fell and de With drew away after a severe handling. Blake had captured two ships and his prisoners included a rear-admiral. All that night his crews worked hard to repair their damaged rigging and by the next morning's first light he bore again towards the enemy. But the wind was poor and the Dutch had had enough. Though de With in his firebrand courage raged against the advice of his captains, who urged withdrawal, he was forced to give way, for the temper of his crews was uncertain, their hearts "much broken," and twenty of his ships had already sailed cravenly away. The wind turning northerly, he made all sail he could eastward to his own coast. Blake was immediately on his heels, engaging his rear at long range all through the 29th and far into the 30th, but he was unable to come up with them, and the danger of being drawn into the shoals of the Dutch coast, together with the shortage of victuals, obliged him to give up the pursuit and return to anchor in Margate Roads.

Perhaps the chief result of the Battle of the Kentish Knock was to demonstrate both the material and the moral superiority of the Commonwealth fleet. There had been little enough of tactics on either side, but Blake's victory had been due to bigger ships better equipped, guns that were heavier and better manned, and hearts that knew no discord under his steadying rule. These three were the factors that were to win the war for the Commonwealth — superior ships, superior gunnery, superior discipline. Though there had been little loss either of ships or men, the landsman admiral had worsted a fleet of experienced and renowned seamen; men whom none could call faint-hearted had, in the words of their own commander, brandished the white feather "so that we are put to shame before the world." On his return to Holland de With was received with insults, and Marten Tromp was once more placed in command.[125]

---

[125] The principal contemporary authorities for the action off the Kentish Knock, and of all other operations in the First Dutch War, including the letters of Blake, are reprinted in *The First Dutch War*.

VII. TROMP'S BROOM

Though Blake returned in triumph, he returned to difficulties. The war was unpopular with many classes. The navy was costing nearly a million pounds a year, and although it must have satisfied Blake to know that Parliament had just ordered thirty new frigates for him, they added £300,000 to the nation's bill. Blake's fleet became reduced to forty-two ships, and during the eight weeks that he remained at Margate he sent constant complaints to the Council of the under-manning and under-victualling of them. Blake's series of moderate successes seems to have given the Council a sense of security that was completely false, for which they were to be paid by one sharp lesson. The fleet became dispersed on various duties of convoy and guard in the North Sea and in the Channel, while later an expedition under Captain Peacock was ordered to prepare for the Mediterranean, where the unimpeded Dutch were holding up English shipping at will. Moreover, the King of Denmark had ranged himself beside the Dutch in open hostility to the Commonwealth, and had seized twenty English ships laden with the pitch, hemp, cordage and other materials which were vital for shipbuilding and for the supply of which England relied chiefly upon the Baltic countries.

With no section of the nation, odd though it may seem, was the naval war more unpopular than with the Army, who now dominated the nation's councils. To them, and to Cromwell with them, it seemed wrong to be waging war against fellow-Protestants. Though Parliament on November 18th passed a new Confiscation Act for the sequestration more harshly than ever of royalists' estates to pay for the war, a proposal was at the same time made for sending ambassadors of peace to The Hague. Moreover, when the new Council of State was elected on November 24th and 25th, the peace party was returned in strength, even Blake himself not being appointed. On the next day Parliament appointed Richard Deane and George Monck to be joined with Blake as Generals-at-Sea, but before they took up their duties Blake had borne on his own shoulders an action which awoke the Council to the need for harder effort.

The move towards peace was to be abruptly arrested by news which made peace impossible. Tromp, whose splendid qualities had brought new life to the Dutch fleet and prepared it once more for the test of war, put to sea on November 21st with orders to attack the English fleet "with all his force and might," but it was not until the evening of the 24th that, from the steeple of Margate Church, he was observed making sail down the straits with a huge fleet. Blake at once summoned a council, but the south-westerly wind, freshening to a gale, kept his fleet at its moorings that night, and by the next morning's light it was found that the same gale had swept Tromp beyond the horizon.

It was not until November 29th that, Tromp having again appeared, Blake put to sea, his flag in the *Triumph*. He counted forty-two sail. Tromp numbered eighty-seven men-of-war, with a convoy of 270 merchantmen bound for Bordeaux to take on board the season's wines. Yet Blake did not hesitate for a moment to put out, and he was right in doing so, for the memory of how Tromp had trapped the Spaniards in the Downs in 1639 must have been fresh in his mind. Nor did he hesitate, when the two fleets came face to face on November 30th off Dungeness, to dash straight at the massed enemy.

On the night of November 29th, the wind blowing hard from the north-west, Blake had anchored in Dover Roads, with Tromp about two leagues distant, riding apparently under the lee of the shoal known as the Varne, or Rip-raps. The next morning, the wind having moderated, Tromp weighed first and stood away towards Dungeness. Blake followed suit, "keeping the wind to the Ness to get clear of the Rip-raps before engagement," to use his own words. The grounds for suggesting, as certain critics have done, that he desired to avoid action, but was forced into it, are altogether too tenuous, and there can be no doubt that from the moment of leaving Margate he intended to fight, though he was outnumbered by two to one. The little admiral, his stocky figure keyed to the tune of the trumpet's call to action, his square face set in the lines of resolution's mould, thought maybe of Dover, and was not afraid. He might well have repeated that earlier success had he not been served in the same scurvy fashion as de With had been served off the Kentish Knock. For as Blake bore down upon the enemy with the north-west wind filling his sails, twenty of his captains "brandished the white feather" and stood out of the fight. That act of cowardice is unique in British naval history. It left the English outnumbered by four to one, in an inferiority that simple courage could not well overcome, but it resulted in one of the finest manifestations of the naval spirit on record.

Supported by the *Victory* and the *Vanguard*, Blake took the *Triumph* into the van of Tromp's triple line of ships in the early afternoon of November 30th, 1652. At once he found himself beset by twenty enemy ships under de Ruyter and Evertsen. For some hours they fought, locked together at a standstill, but though they seemed bound for destruction there were others whose condition was more desperate yet. From the deck of the *Triumph* Blake was able to observe two of his smaller ships in a death struggle with Tromp himself. As soon as the action started Captain Robert Batten in the *Garland* (forty-eight guns) and Captain Walter Hoxton in the *Bonaventure* (thirty guns) had made straight for Tromp flagship, the *Brederode*, grappled her port and starboard, and boarded from both sides. For a time it seemed as if the big flagship must be forced into surrender, but the Dutch fleet crowded round to her rescue and Jan Evertsen skilfully laid himself alongside the *Bonaventure* and ordered his crew to board. At once Hoxton called his men back from the *Brederode*, and as they scrambled over to the defence of their own bulwarks the tide of fortune was stayed. Thus all four ships were grappled together and the battle swayed from deck to deck with pike and axe and musket. When Tromp, liberated from the assaults of the *Bonaventure*'s crew through Evertsen's action, was able in turn to sweep over the decks of the *Garland*, Batten deliberately blew up a portion of his decks to check the onset of the Dutchmen, hurling scores of them dead into the air. It was a tooth-and-claw struggle to the death, no man seeking or giving mercy.

Blake, hard beset though he was himself, saw the English ships in their plight, and desperately shook himself free of his own assailants to go to their aid. But the forest of enemy ships blocked his path and his foremast was shot away. In the gathering gloom he watch their heroic resistance actually to the last man, as the swelling waves of Dutchmen flooded over their decks and engulfed their little number. Batten and Hoxton were both killed on deck, and of the entire crews of the two ships virtually every man was cut down. Not until both crews were almost annihilated were the *Garland* and the *Bonaventure* lost to the English flag, and that loss was to be as bloodily and as heroically redeemed when at the Battle of Scheveningen the same ships were to be retaken by the English as battered and sinking hulks.

It might have been supposed that the overwhelming of these ships would have shown to the English commander the hopelessness of pursuing so unequal a struggle. But Blake never took any account of odds, and never during this Battle of Dungeness did he dream of refusing the challenge of death. Therefore he still strove desperately to reach the *Brederode*, urging the *Triumph* forward little by little amid the press of enemy ships. Three times was his flagship boarded by the Dutch, and three times were they repulsed from her bulwarks. Yet had the day been longer Blake must surely have been submerged at the end. Fog and the night overcame his warriorship and compelled him to withdraw his stricken ships behind their saving shroud. Of the twenty-two that had gone into action, three had been sunk and two captured after five hours' fighting; the *Triumph* was terribly mauled, her rigging in shreds and her hull in splinters. Yet they had given the Dutch a hard hammering; one ship had been blown up by her own powder, and the flagships of Tromp and Evertsen were "miserably torn."

It was nearly midnight when Blake crept back through the enveloping vapours to anchor in Dover Roads with a bitterness of spirit upon him. The next day, December 1st, Tromp remaining still off Dungeness to bandage his wounds, Blake wrote to the Council of State tendering his resignation and praying "that I may be free from the trouble of spirit which lies upon me, arising from the sense of my own insufficiency." This his first defeat (and, as it was to prove, his only one) pressed heavily upon him, but more painful still was that "baseness of spirit" of which he complained in those captains who had shirked the fight and in those others who, being in, had fought with but half a heart. Of these his own brother Benjamin was one. He therefore asked the Council to set up a court of inquiry into their conduct and the causes of it, which indeed were not far to seek, and he mentioned specially the shortage of men and the excessive use of hired merchantmen.

To his offer of resignation the Council replied by thanking him for his gallant bearing and by reappointing him to his commission, which was due to expire on December 4th. With their usual promptness of action in such things they set up the inquiry he asked for, three commissioners being sent down to conduct it, together with Blake himself. As a result several captains, including Benjamin Blake, were found to have failed in their duty and were committed for trial or dismissed their ships.

Other results of the inquiry were more welcome, and out of this defeat a new strength was born. The pay of able seamen was advanced from 19s. a month to 24s., better provisions were made for the care of sick and wounded, discipline was strengthened, and it was recognised that the system by which privately-owned ships were engaged for war under their own masters, who must naturally be reluctant to endanger their own property, was an evil that must be ended. The old bad practice of hanging back from action had been largely due to this employment of merchantmen, and Blake's attacking tactics of which Clarendon has spoken were impossible of due fulfilment until they were eliminated. Not less important was the promulgation of a code of rules to govern behaviour in the Navy which was the foundation of all subsequent "articles of war" for the regulation of the fleet. Numbering thirty-nine articles (and so making a playground for wits), they were entitled "Laws of War and Ordinances of the Sea," and it was no doubt fitting that Article 1 should declare:

All commanders shall endeavour that Almighty God be solemnly and reverently served in the respective ships, all profaneness and irreligiousness avoided, preaching and praying and other religious duties be exercised and duly frequented, and the Lord's Day religiously observed.

The code of discipline that Blake and his colleagues formulated and administered was, by comparison with the brutality of the eighteenth century, remarkably light. Following the tradition of Charles's day, there was an appearance of basing conduct on religion. As in the royalist fleet, swearing and card-playing were forbidden, and prayers were said twice daily. Nevertheless, there was little real Puritan fervour among the seamen generally. For reasons of safety, smoking was permitted only on the upper deck, "and that sparingly." Punishment was comparatively light. Never once in Blake's time was the death penalty inflicted. Flogging was rare, being reserved only for the thief, and not till Charles II's time did it become common, and although Weale mentions later a case of "whipping round the fleet," the number of strokes was only three or four per ship. On the whole, the Commonwealth seamen were a satisfied and orderly body. It is true that Nehemiah Bourne later called them "an unruly and untamed generation," but Peter Pett, the great shipbuilder, himself a Commissioner for the Navy, considered them "very tractable." In marked contrast to Charles's day, instances of mass indiscipline were extremely rare, only two occurring between 1648 and 1653 and pay being in each case the cause of discord. In these articles that were now promulgated we may see the beginnings of professional honour among naval officers, and the beginnings of a sense of class distinction between the fighting seaman and the civilian.

The sting of defeat had not only laid bare men's hearts, but it also opened purses. On December 10th an Act was passed by which new money was allotted for the Navy, and at the same time work was pressed on with the new frigates that had recently been ordered, carpenter Bourne being now appointed a Commissioner of the Navy. In all these reforms Blake took the closest interest. The appointment of the new triumvirate of admiralty necessarily led to various changes in command before the fleet once more put to sea. In the *Triumph*, leading the Red Squadron and the whole fleet, Blake was joined by Deane, back from his spell of soldiering, and John Lawson, the Northumbrian fisherman, received a special appointment as Vice-Admiral of the Red. George Monck took the White Squadron and William Penn the Blue.

The appointment of Monck, who was now rising surely to his destiny, was highly significant, for it confirmed still further the military influence in the fleet. He had come home from Holland to fight for the King with a high reputation as an expert soldier, under whose firm hand many of the young nobility of England had been disciplined to warfare in the hard school of the Dutch wars. Soldiering was in his very marrow. He was very stout, coarse in his way of feeding, his taste in women and his manner of life; he constantly chewed tobacco, which he spat all over the deck. He had sailed as a stripling soldier in Buckingham's lamentable expeditions to Cadiz and to Rhé, but his complete ignorance of maritime matters was a standing joke among the seamen. When the quartermaster called "Starboard" or "Larboard", in action, he would reply with a cheerful shout: "Aye, aye, boys, let's board them!" He matched Blake in his taciturnity and economy of words, and the two were friends to the last.

Tromp meanwhile, however mythical may have been his mast-head broom, swept the Channel in undisputed command. He snapped up prizes, raided the coasts of Kent and Sussex to carry off cattle for his fleet, saw the merchantmen of his country safely through the narrow seas, and would have sailed up the Thames itself, as de Ruyter was to do when once again a Stuart was enthroned, had he not lacked pilots. But his domination was short-lived. The Commonwealth administration by the vigour and ability of its handling within two short months placed the Navy in that position whence it was soon to turn the lessons of defeat to the purposes of clear and decisive victory.

VIII. THE BATTLE OF PORTLAND

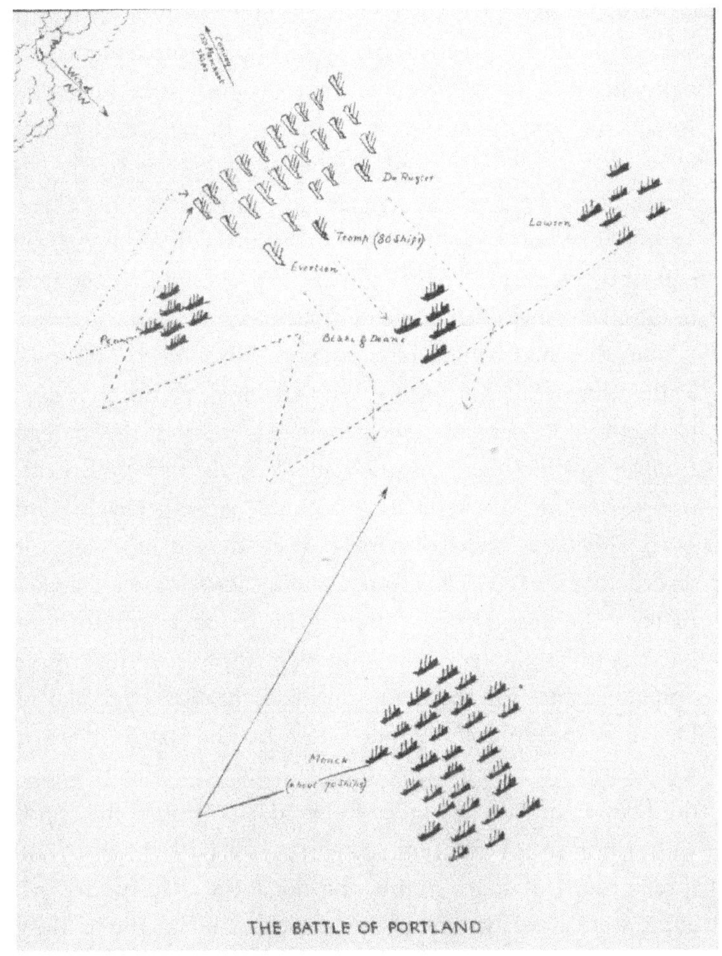

THE BATTLE OF PORTLAND

On February 10th, 1653, the fleet, reconditioned and
reequipped, dropped down the Thames to intercept Tromp on

his way back from Bordeaux with the wine fleet. In the Channel the admirals were joined by twenty more ships, so that they now had about seventy sail at their command. For several days the fleet beat to and fro across the Channel, on the look-out for the enemy. Both the Dutch and the English had but the scantiest intelligence of each other's movements, and although the English received some news from intercepted foreigners and from their own scouts of the enemy's movements, they knew only vaguely that he was on the way. Accordingly it happened that, when at daybreak on February 18th Tromp was sighted to the northward with eighty warships and 150 merchantmen off Portland, the English fleet found themselves caught at a grave disadvantage.

With the wind behind him from the north-west, Tromp was leading his great fleet before it up-Channel, compact and well in hand, but nevertheless astonished to find the defeated English so soon seeking battle again. The English, on the other hand, beating up against the wind close-hauled on the starboard tack, were dispersed after the night's sailing in disorderly array. With Tromp sailing across their starboard flank, they were strung out raggedly from north to south. Nearest to Tromp, and almost in his path, was a little group of only five ships of the Red squadron, headed by Blake and Deane in the *Triumph*. A mile astern on the starboard quarter were some more ships of the Red squadron under Lawson in the *Fairfax*, and ahead to the westward was Penn in the *Speaker*, with a portion of the Blue squadron still farther away. These three groups of ships, numbering not more than twenty or so in all, were alone within striking distance of the Dutch. Monck with the White was miles to the southward, and farther off still was a congregation of slower ships in no sort of order.

Seldom has an English fleet been discovered in a seemingly more helpless position, yet the resolution of its crews and the intelligence of its commanders turned that position brilliantly to advantage. Indeed, their very disadvantage was suited to the English purpose. For Tromp was tempted. His proper purpose was to see his wine-ships safely home, but the eagle that would have passed by a compact flock swooped to the lure of the stray sheep. His opportunity for destroying the English fleet in separate detail was too rare to be missed. Immediately before his bows was the English Admiral of the Red, Blake himself, with but five ships. Spreading his wings before the wind, he bore down upon that lonely prey.

As Blake and Deane looked out upon the seas on that cold February dawn, with the sea on all sides dappled with the filled sails of 300 ships and the great rock of Portland visible beyond the enemy, Blake must have had in mind the lesson of Dungeness. Without disgrace he could have turned to the southward to keep company with the mass of the fleet with Monck, but he must have realised that to do so might cause Tromp to refuse battle and to continue his course with the merchantmen. To bring the enemy to battle he must offer himself to the enemy's guns. Therefore Blake and Deane stood to receive the shock, without for one moment thinking of any other course. Their trumpets called the crews to action and the red flag of battle was broken at the fore.

As Tromp bore down upon him in three divisions with de Ruyter on his port and Jan Evertsen on his starboard, Blake opened fire on the *Brederode* with his heavier guns before the enemy could reach him. "I had such a welcome," declared Tromp, "that everything on board us was on fire and Blake was still unhurt." Nevertheless, the *Brederode* and no fewer than seven other ships laid themselves around the *Triumph*, and very shortly the whole group of five ships was completely surrounded. For two hours Blake and Deane received the full shock of the battle almost alone. The fight was murderous. Andrew Ball, Captain of the *Triumph*, Broadbridge, her master, and Sparrow, Blake's secretary, were all killed with more than a hundred of her crew. At least as many again must have been wounded. Blake and Deane were standing together amid the rain of shot with the masts and yards of their ship crashing about them and their friends falling on every side. Presently Blake himself was seen to fall. A shot, tearing Deane's breeches, had struck Blake in the thigh, wounding him sharply; but he "would scarce go down to have his wound dressed, nor was he out of his place all the time of service."

Meanwhile Penn's ships of the Blue to the westward had turned to the northward and were coming down with the wind upon the flank and rear of the serried masses of Dutch ships. Fighting his way through their ranks, he joined company with Blake and Deane in their gallant stand. For Lawson, to leeward in the rear, the position was more difficult. Had he hauled on a wind as Penn had done, he would have had de Ruyter bearing down upon him and barring his path to Blake. Accordingly, with great skill, he bore away to the southward, rounded Blake's flotilla, then tacked to the northward and followed in the path of Penn to crash into the heart of the battle.[126]

For many hours Monck and the bulk of the English fleet were out of action entirely. They were beating slowly up into the wind to reach Blake, but Evertsen with his division had sailed on past Blake's little group and was coming to meet him and hold him off. For yet six hours the twenty ships of the Red

---

[126] Modern naval authorities appear to agree that Gardiner, in his description and plan of this battle, has misread Lawson's movement, and that it was as here described.

and Blue squadrons held the Dutch at bay. The *Samson* was sunk and the *Prosperous* taken, but the *Merlin*, under Captain Vesay, laid alongside the captured ship, and her crew, swarming over the decks of the *Prosperous*, drove off the enemy with pike and musket and retook her. In Lawson's flagship there were 100 casualties and in the *Worcester*, eighty. In the *Advice*, Captain John Day was beset by four of the enemy and boarded, yet with thirty-five of his officers and men killed and himself and forty others wounded he repelled the boarders and sank two of the enemy.

Thus the apparently unequal fight raged all day, and it was not until 4 o'clock that the White squadron was able to reach the hard-pressed few. Monck, in the vanguard, was itching to reach the conflict with that love of fight that was always in him, and though he suffered heavy casualties he held on his arduous way against the wind and against the cannonade of Evertsen. At last, through the clouds of smoke that enveloped her, he saw the *Triumph*, dismasted and her hull in splinters, still resolutely in action. With Monck's arrival the day was saved, but more than saved, for about the same time, when the thin February light was giving place to the grey veil of approaching night, a flight of English frigates broke boldly away, and adventuring far up into the wind fell upon the Dutch merchantmen in their unprotectedness. Thus the initiative passed suddenly to the English, by whom the Dutch were now being hard pressed, and Tromp, seeing the danger to his merchant convoy, broke off the action and drew off his fleet to the north-east as darkness fell. He had indeed suffered a severe hammering, in spite of his great superiority of numbers, for the *Vogelstruis*, a great ship of 1,200 tons, had been captured and seven others of his ships sunk.

That night, as they tossed in the Channel, Blake lay below deck suffering severely from a wound that was to leave its sharp sting upon him throughout life. Eager to press on with the battle by the morning's light, the fleet spent the night in repairing their ships, in dispatching their wounded to port, and in matching up the crews of the ships that had most severely suffered. But in the Dutch fleet an anxious council of war was being held. Their failure to defeat the English fleet had been rendered the more serious by reason of their shortage of ammunition and provisions, which had become more acute by the day's fighting, for Tromp had neglected to reprovision his fleet since he left Holland before Dungeness. Though the old hero was ready enough to fight again, for the sake of his merchantmen, there was now nothing left but to run for it.

So, when the English admirals stepped upon deck at dawn on February 19th, they saw the great fleet of Dutch merchantmen on the distant horizon to the north-east, with their protecting warships spread out astern in a sweeping crescent. The admirals immediately gave chase, but so light was the wind that it was not until two o'clock that the English fleet was again able to bring the Dutch to battle just south of the Isle of Wight. Blake was in great pain from his wound, but he seems to have continued all the time at his post, though he must certainly have been unable to stand. All the afternoon the fleet strove to break through the crescent of Dutch warships. Tromp, however, maintained his line unbroken, but before darkness fell again the tide had turned surely against him, for some of his captains were now running from the fight, while Lawson, slipping his greyhound frigates, ran up from his right wing, capturing two of his warships and six merchantmen.

February 20th was a Sunday, and at nine on that morning the action was renewed with the Dutch fleet in roughly the same formation, but now they were in a sorry plight, which is best described in the plain and frank words of Tromp himself in his dispatch to the States-General:

> In the morning of February 20th the wind was N.W. and about nine o'clock the enemy renewed the attack with great vigour, and before we had fought more than two hours we calculated half our ships must have exhausted all their powder and balls; several, therefore, made all sail and took to flight; we fired several shots after them to signal to them to come back which they did; I enquired if they were going to fly like knaves; they replied they had neither powder nor balls left; upon this I commanded them to remain a little distance off, in the centre of the fleet, and not to betray the slightest sign of fear; and that those of us who had powder and ammunition still left would defend both them and the merchantmen. And then with about twenty-five or thirty ships that still had powder and shot we defended the whole of the fleet from noon until evening after sundown.[127]

No longer was he able to defend the merchantmen, however, and Penn, slipping through with a number of nimble frigates, "gleaned up merchant ships above forty." The rest, and many of the warships, were scattered in all directions, and the English fleet likewise scattered to pursue them in numerous individual actions. As dusk drew down, the generals called them all in, and, just as Tromp was expecting a final assault that must surely have destroyed him utterly, the action was halted. Tromp was now close under the rocky cliffs of Cape Gris-Nez, with the English to windward. The English generals, on consulting their pilots, were advised that it was impossible for Tromp to weather that headland with the wind in that

---

[127] Tromp to the States-General, February 22nd.

quarter and the tide on the ebb. By virtue of the same advice, the English fleet cast anchor where it lay to avoid being carried on to the lee shore, deeming that the morning's light would reveal an enemy at their mercy.

But the old sea-dog of Holland, who knew that coast as a fox knows his coverts, cheated them. For during that Sunday night, with his lights extinguished, he crept past the perils of Gris-Nez, and by magnificent seamanship led his shattered navy safely within the fastnesses of their own Dutch shallows. The Battle of Portland was that night ended.

By his resource and skill, by the personal example of courage that he had shown to a wavering fleet, Tromp had saved himself from destruction, but the command of the Channel had passed once again to his enemies. In the three days' continuous fighting he had lost nineteen warships and fifty-six merchantmen. In personnel he had lost upwards of 4,000 killed and wounded, including many of his leading captains, and 1,500 seamen and officers had been taken prisoners. Says *Mercurius Politicus* of February 22nd:

> All the men-of-war who are taken are much dyed with blood, their masts and tacks being moiled with brains, hair, pieces of skulls; dreadful sights though glorious, as being a signal token of the Lord's goodness to this nation.

Against this heavy loss, the English had suffered but one ship sunk and 1,200 men killed and wounded — nearly all in the first few hours' desperate fighting on the 18th around Blake's flagship.

Blake himself was put ashore at Portsmouth a very sick man. Besides his wound, he had contracted a severe cold. Moreover, at the age of fifty-four, he had now been at sea almost continuously for nearly four years on exceedingly trying service, in which he had endured the weariness of blockade, the buffeting of the great northern storm, the rigour of three pitched battles, the tribulation of defeat, and the fret and burden of daily directing a great service which until his time had been served by only the crudest administrative machine. He was never the same man after the Battle of Portland, and for the rest of his life was in continual suffering. Amid the applause for the victory, there was deep anxiety for his health. It was said, for example, that he might "never go to sea again, for one of his hamstrings is broken, and he has a continual rheum that falls down into his eyes which almost blinds him." The Council of State accordingly sent Doctors Prideaux and Bates by the earliest night coach to care for him, and he was also attended by Dr. Daniel Whistler, one of the leading physicians of the day, who had been despatched to look after the sick and wounded in the fleet. For long his condition remained serious, and nearly a month later Whistler was still sending the gloomiest report, though cloaked in the garments of the authentic high Puritan.

> "General Blake I hope mends," he wrote to Sir Harry Vane, "but I am checked from too presumptuous prognostics by that maxim *de senibus non temere sperandum*. It is the prerogative of the great physician in heaven to presage life or death according to His secret decree, a ray of whose all-seeing knowledge appears but dimly to us through narrow crannies of conjectural guess."[128]

Nevertheless, Blake continued to give close attention to the affairs of the navy, and on March 29th, there were published over the signatures of himself, Deane and Monck, two codes of instructions for "the better ordering of the Fleet" in sailing

---

[128] Cal. S. P. Dom.

and in fighting. They are of great importance in naval history, for the instruction on fighting prescribes for the first time the "line ahead" formation. It has been maintained that Monck was the inspirer of this far-reaching advance in tactics, but the probabilities are strongly against it, for Monck had been to sea only a few weeks and the formation was the very opposite of that which he had been used to on land.

The notion of line-ahead was one of the Commonwealth's prime contributions to the navy. It was the typical product of the Puritan soldier, for ordered and controlled movement was of the very substance of the New Model teaching. It was as important for Blake to keep a firm rein on all his ships as it was for Cromwell to arrest a victorious charge with all his troops well in hand. Blake had seen in these naval mass charges how the strength of a fleet was dissipated by individual captains breaking away to conduct separate actions on their own account, and in these fighting instructions made a great step forward towards enforcing unity of command in action. In due time he was to demonstrate that principle with brilliant efficiency.

Before the end of April, though still poorly, Blake was well enough to go to London, where the ship of state was in troubled waters. For on April 20th Cromwell had at last turned the Long Parliament out of doors and had become by virtue of circumstances dictator of the three kingdoms. It was said that there were some who at this moment turned their eyes towards Blake to lead the nation, but in fact he had no disposition towards political faction. Convincing evidence of his feelings towards Cromwell's *coup* is not available, but there is not much doubt that he disapproved of it and of Cromwell's subsequent appointment as Protector. The *Newsletter* of April 29th, said that Blake "is come to town highly discontented. He is much for the Parliament." There were other similar references, and the arguments sometimes adduced that his views were otherwise are not satisfying. Blake's signature is absent from the manifesto to the navy supporting the new regimen issued by Deane and Monck, whose long associations with the army disposed them on the side of Cromwell. Moreover, Blake was not appointed one of the new Council of State. Nevertheless, he took the course of action which to-day would be considered the only right one, and, as Gardiner says, "mastering his dissatisfaction, accepted the principle of non-political service."

"It is not for seamen," Blake is reported to have said to a gathering of officers, though possibly at a later date, "to mind State affairs, but to keep foreigners from fooling us."

By May 12th he was back at work at the Admiralty offices. For some time his bad health kept him ashore, but it was not long before the sound of the guns lured him back, sick as he was, to their ocean platforms. The Dutch, though run out of the Channel, had an "indefatigable quantity of fight" in them, as a great American has said of the English. Though their trade had already been nearly crushed, though the grass grew in the streets of Amsterdam, and though their ships rotted in the harbours, they would not bow to the severe terms that the Commonwealth demanded as the price of peace. They worked feverishly to repair and strengthen their fleet, while the Commonwealth did likewise, and before long Tromp was again at sea, giving the English the slip by escorting a convoy of 200 merchantmen by the far Shetlands and returning with another. Deane and Monck were out after him, but, so difficult was it in those days to have sure knowledge of an enemy's movements, that for weeks the two fleets were chasing each other's shadows to no purpose. While Tromp was in the Downs wasting good ammunition in a bombardment of Dover Castle, Deane and Monck were in his own waters. Yet they were two of the greatest fleets that have ever put to sea, both over 100 ships strong.

At length, however, they came face to face in the afternoon of June 1st, 1653, off the Gabbard sandbank, which lies some 40 miles east of Harwich and roughly north-east of the North Foreland. On that memorable day, in a motionless sea and under a wind scarcely sufficient to stir the drooping pennants or to move the crowded sails spread to catch its lightest breath, 105 English ships faced 104 of their enemies. So light was the wind that they could not come to grips that day, but at dawn on June 2nd shots from the long-range English guns began to hammer the timbers of the Dutch. From dawn till dusk the two great maritime powers were joined in one of the grandest of all sea fights, in the first hours of which Richard Deane fell dead upon the deck of the *Resolution*, mangled by a chain-shot and drenching with blood his brother admiral at his side. Monck, it is recorded, calmly covered the body with his cloak and sent it below, lest the crew should be discouraged by that loss, and, though he had been at sea not yet five months, he with quiet efficiency continued alone in command of the great fleet. By nightfall, spite of Tromp's attempt "to break the line," the shadow of defeat had begun to creep over the Dutch, whose lighter armament was no match for the heavier English ordnance that pounded their hulls. By nightfall the two fleets, still in close contact, were lying off Nieuport.

Meanwhile, Blake, having visited Portsmouth to see personally to the refitting of the troublesome *Sovereign of the Seas*, had come into Thames' mouth to attend to the refitting of a small squadron there. He was still a sick man, admitting in a letter to the Council that his infirmity grew upon him daily.

But on June 2nd came word from Deane and Monck to the captains of the ships in the Thames, where Blake was inspecting them, that an engagement with the Dutch was imminent and calling on them to sail with all speed. It was a call that Blake could not resist. Not only did he order the ships to prepare for sea at once, but he also resolved to go with them himself. There and then he hoisted his flag in the *Essex*, and led out the little squadron of thirteen ships, making all speed he could against a contrary wind for the Gabbard.

When he arrived upon the scene of action off the Flemish coast on the afternoon of June 3rd the fight was at its pitch. Tromp, again nearly exhausted of ammunition, was fighting hard to hold his own at long range, but when Blake appeared on his port bow, and when the admiral's nephew Robert broke through their line in a fast frigate and brought to the cheering Englishmen the news that Blake himself was come, then were the Dutch overwhelmed by an impassioned onset. Blake threw his new ships vigorously into the fight. The *Brederode* herself was almost captured as Penn's crew boarded and swarmed over her decks, and only by blowing up part of his own decks, as Batten had done at Dungeness, did Tromp save his flagship. Overcome by sheer gun-fire and the vigour of the attack, Tromp was forced back, fighting all the way, to the refuge of his own shallow waters. Throughout that night the rout continued and when at last Tromp was safe his losses had amounted to nineteen ships captured or sunk and 3,000 good seamen killed or wounded. Monck had not lost one ship.

It was nearly the end. Blake and Monck proceeded to a close blockade of the Dutch coast. With de With held fast in the Texel and Tromp separated from him in the Scheldt, the English remorselessly pressed on with their strangulation of that commerce which was the life-blood of Holland. Tumult and starvation were at the doors of their cities, and their people had reached "the climax of embarrassment and distress." Three thousand houses were vacant in Amsterdam, the great herring fishery was brought to complete stagnation, the once opulent banks in their empty silence were darkened with the shadows of bankruptcy.

A gleam of hope came when after a month some unnamed epidemic swept the English fleet, and sent the greater part of it back to Southwold, on the Suffolk coast, to seek relief. With it went Blake, whose sickness throughout the month of blockade had grown gradually worse. He was landed at Southwold on July 5th, suffering acutely from the pains of gravel in the kidneys, and was too ill to sign a dispatch that was written on that day. Presently he was moved to Walberswick near-by, and while he lay prostrated vital and moving news came to him.

Monck returned to the blockade with a refreshed fleet. He had been back little more than a week when Tromp, luring him from his station by a feigned retreat, reunited with de With, and with him made a dash to regain the freedom of the open sea. It was their last stroke. On July 31st the English fleet fell upon them off Scheveningen, and in the bloodiest battle of the war finally devastated the hopes of the Dutch. The *Garland* and *Bonaventure*, which had been captured by the Dutch at Dungeness, were recaptured by English boarders after a struggle of extraordinary ferocity, but only to be scuttled as shattered hulks. In the hour of defeat Tromp himself, the best and bravest sea captain that ever faced an English fleet, was fatally struck down by a musket shot on the deck of his flagship.

It was the end of the war, and peace negotiations were opened, though they were not concluded until April, 1654. The terms were less severe than those which the Commonwealth had previously demanded, the Dutch Republic being saved from a compulsory union of the two nations. Nevertheless, the vanquished were required to pay reparations of nearly £1,000,000, together with indemnities for the Amboyna massacre of thirty years before, and they were compelled to recognise the British sovereignty of the British seas and to salute the flag of St. George. Moreover, the English fleet had during the war captured no fewer than 1,500 prizes.

The first Dutch War is one of the few examples in history of a conflict brought to a firm conclusion by naval action alone; at no time were any land forces engaged, nor was there any attempt to annex territory. The real value of the victory to the Commonwealth lay in the recognition by the nations that England had become the first sea power, and that her voice, which had sunk to so ineffectual a whisper under the Stuarts and which was to fall to the same low pitch when again the Stuarts were restored, was one that the kings and cardinals of Europe must listen to with circumspection and respect.

Blake recovered slowly from his complaint. When he was well enough to leave Southwold he quite likely took the cure at Bath, for a letter from him of September 30th says that he was on his way from there to London. On October 10th he took his seat again in Parliament, and for the next few months he was busy with naval administration. In January, 1654, he was again at sea in the *Swiftsure*, maintaining such hostilities against the Dutch as were still necessary until the signing of the peace, and sweeping up a few overbold pirates and privateers under the colours of the French. In July he and John Lambert were jointly appointed to the office of Lord Warden of the Cinque Ports and in the same month Blake was returned as member for Bridgwater in the first Parliament of the Protectorate that was to assemble in September.

The Blake who emerged from the Dutch War was a different being from the inspired amateur who had begun it. In the exploits that remained to him he was the acknowledged master. Throughout his fighting career he progressed by the ladder of his own experience, until at the end we see the hand of the master executing his work with a sure instinct and a perfection of detail. Wherever he went in his last two famous voyages in southern seas his great name went before, breathing hope or fear, and wherever he passed there gathered about his memory legends and traditions that history has not been able to probe, but which testify richly to the power of his personality and the great new fighting machine that he had fashioned. Not only had he taught the fleet certain lessons of his own inspiration — vigilance, aggression, corporate loyalty — but he had also learnt much for himself; he had learnt to keep his fleet together, to plan every detail of an enterprise with care, and to gather the fullest intelligence of the enemy's movements.

Blake had never flown on "wings of high desire." He did not, like Nelson, resolve to be a hero. He had not what Southey calls Nelson's "second sight of glory." He never sought office or appointment, and he achieved greatness by having office thrust upon him. Medals and gold chains were at most his only rewards. In the last phase upon which he now entered he was led still by the sense of public service that had brought him onwards. But he was a changed man. For his last years he was in constant suffering and he became at times testy and irritable, at others he was filled with a clear spiritual calm. He was, it seems, regarded with no little awe, and certainly with reverence. Physically, he retreated yet farther into his natural fastness of solitude. He had always been of the simplest modesty, avoiding all public show, and on his last voyage in the Mediterranean he "never shows himself even in his own ship, except when the sun shone, and although invited he would never go on shore on a single occasion to see the place and gratify his own countrymen."[129]

But though the years stole vigour from the limb they did not steal fire from the mind. For yet a little while his shrouded heart could leap

> When glimmers down the riotous wind
> The flag of the Adventurer.

The smoke of battle was still sweet to his nostrils.

---

[129] Sarotti to the Doge, Venetian State Papers, xxx, No. 25.

IX. "I RIDE THE ROLLING TIDE"

Peace brought with it the problem common to all wars concluded. The Protector found himself with a great fleet of nearly 160 fighting ships with no work to its hand, its idle seamen beginning mutinously to clamour for their long arrears of pay. Cromwell set himself quickly to work to remedy that defect. The eyes of all Europe were upon him, anxious to discover where he would place his friendship and where his hostility. Profitable treaties were effected with Denmark and Portugal. France and Spain, at war with each other, courted him like rival lovers, ambassadors and plenipotentiaries waited on him with protestations of friendship, but no man could learn his mind. With France a reckoning was long overdue for the damage caused to English shipping by years of privateering, and Spain hoped much from the friendly help that she had given when Blake was pursuing Rupert. But Cromwell was considering, not rewards and punishments, but needs and opportunities.

Accordingly, at a Council meeting in June, 1654, it was resolved to undertake two enterprises. One was to be to the Mediterranean, where English commercial shipping, particularly of the Levant Company, had long cried out for protection against French privateers, Dutch men-of-war and Barbary pirates, and where, in spite of what had been accomplished in the North Sea, the English had come to be regarded since Blake's departure after the Rupert hunt as "a nation undone." The other, undertaken against the advice of John Lambert, was to be to the West Indies, where, on the excuse of the sovereignty over all those coasts and waters to which the King of Spain pretended, English settlements had been ravished by the Spaniards, English ships captured or despoiled, English colonists, merchants and seamen put to the sword or enslaved in the plantations.

Both projects were legitimate, both were indeed necessary in the modern conception of a state; but the manner in which the Protector set his hand to the West Indies project, or the Western Design, as it was called, did no credit to him. For he struck in secret even as he was parleying, seeking to cozen the Spaniards with the notion of his friendship and obtaining their ready help for his Mediterranean project while Penn and Venables were sailing to the attack of Hispaniola. Neither did the Western Design do him credit in its results for, though the expedition took Jamaica, it failed to win the richer prize of Hispaniola, the regiments that accompanied it being of such wretched stuff and being by Disbrowe so ignorantly equipped against the tropic sun, having not even water-bottles, that they perished in hundreds from fever and ran shamefully from, the spears of the half-caste cowmen who faced them.

To Blake was fortunately assigned the Mediterranean expedition, one that was destined to become memorable in naval annals. Flying his flag in the *George*, a second-rater of sixty guns and 350 men, he set sail from Plymouth on October 8th, 1654, at the head of one of the most stouthearted companies of men that have put to sea. His little fleet, all specially sheathed for a long voyage, numbered twenty-five men-of-war, for the most part fourth-raters or less, with not more than forty guns, but fully manned and fully equipped after determined pressure by the admiral.

His vice-admiral, in the *Andrew*, was old Richard Badiley. That sturdy and lovable old sea-dog, who was said to have begun life as a cabin boy and to have served his hard term before the mast, was the authentic "heart of oak." He it was who, with a handful of men, had boarded the *Antelope* in Dutch waters and burned her under Rupert's nose. He had been one of Blake's captains in the old days of the Rupert hunt and had afterwards striven with courageous resource to uphold the flag of St. George in the Mediterranean with insignificant forces until he had at last been driven out by the unequal odds. He had been chosen, no doubt, for his knowledge of those waters. Joseph Jordan, one of the new and most brilliant reputations of the Dutch War, was rear-admiral. Another old friend, who had been with Blake at Lyme and Taunton and in his early fights against Tromp, was stout Thomas Adams, commanding the *Maidstone*, a little fourth-rater of thirty-two guns. His other captains included his nephew Robert, commanding the *Hampshire*, and the debonair Richard Stayner, who was so soon to rise to fame.

Blake's second voyage to the Mediterranean was begun under orders that are lost to history. As he had reason later to observe, they were ambiguous orders — ambiguous because the Protector was still uncertain of his own course of policy. But this ambiguity may well have been the measure of Cromwell's faith in his admiral, and Blake was to show that, following the broad lines of an understood policy, he knew how to determine his own courses of action and, where need be, to pick his own targets. His first movement, however, was clearly to be against the French, who were fitting out an expedition under the duc de Guise for the conquest of the Kingdom of Naples. For that reason Blake received a cordial reception in Spain; and off Cadiz the admiral of a Dutch squadron struck his ensign and his topsail as he entered.

In the Straits of Gibraltar Blake spread out his frigates under Stayner to look for the French Ocean Squadron that was on its way from Brest to join the duc de Guise in the Mediterranean. After three days of reconnaisance Stayner returned, and, coming on board the *George*, reported to the admiral that the enemy was not to be found. His answer was a sharp reprimand from the admiral, who angrily ordered him out again. The French, however, in no way anxious to exchange broadsides with the victor of Portland, had taken refuge in Lisbon, and Blake was delayed for three weeks in a fruitless wait.

Thus Guise likewise eluded him, for when he arrived at Naples he found that the feather-brained duke had abandoned his design of conquest and made away. At Naples Blake was hailed as the nation's saviour, but, according to the Venetian Resident at Florence, he did not invite the envoys sent to greet him in his flagship even to be seated and they remained standing before him with their hats off.[130] Guise had made for Leghorn and thither Blake chased him only to find that he was again too late and that Guise was safely back in Toulon. It was thanks only to these mischances that war with France was avoided, but, in fact, those weeks of watchful inaction marked the most significant phase of the whole of this famous voyage to the Mediterranean, outweighing the spectacular exploit that he was soon to launch against the walls of Africa. For in those weeks of waiting in the Straits of Gibraltar, when he had denied to Guise the support of the ocean squadron on which he was relying, thereby ruining French hopes, Blake had demonstrated that to hold that corridor was to hold the Mediterranean, to shackle France and to handcuff Spain. Not the Atlantic seaboard but the Straits of Gibraltar became the key to domination of the seas of the world.

At Leghorn Blake re-provisioned, and, in spite of the efforts of Genoa to stir up a quarrel, he maintained the friendliest

---

[130] Sarotti to the Doge, V.S.P. xxx, No. 3.

relations with the Grand Duke of Tuscany, conveying to Ferdinand a request from the Lady Protectress, which was readily granted, for portraits of the grand-ducal family, and receiving a present of the choicest wine of Tuscany. Many legends have grown on Blake's voyage to Italy — how Tuscany and Naples trembled at the news of his approach and how the Pope himself was humbled. They have little truth in them, but nevertheless it is true that the conqueror of Tromp, de Ruyter and Vendôme was received everywhere with the utmost respect, and that from the moment of his entry into the Mediterranean his mere presence changed the prestige of Englishmen and gave a stimulus to the English merchants in its prosperous ports. Wherever he went upon the seas he was saluted, and the Venetian Resident at Florence tells us that "men remark upon the headlong progress with which the English display their supreme power in these waters."[131]

His purpose towards the French peacefully achieved, the admiral turned next towards the Barbary coast, to seek from the Turkish overlords of those parts the liberation of Englishmen, who, having been captured by the pirate ships, had been sold into slavery. The condition of these unhappy men in Tunis, Tripoli, Sallee and Algiers had long demanded redress, but it was something more than that service that Blake hoped to render. For as he set sail for Algiers in January, 1655, a violent storm drove him back to Leghorn, and there he was told of a great concentration of Turkish ships taking place at Tunis for a renewed attack on Crete, where the gallant Venetians, friends of the Commonwealth and the cynosure of Cromwell's admiration, supported by that haughty cavalier, Marmaduke Langdale, and some other Englishmen, had for

---

[131] Ibid.

long been upholding the Christian standard against the infidel waves.

To Blake it was plainly the hand of God that had raised the storm which drove him back to receive this clear call. He could strike a blow, not only for England, but also for the faith. Ill though he was in body, his spirit leapt to obey the summons. It was one of Blake's moments of dramatic inspiration. All the crusader in him rose. As soon as the storm would let him he dashed straight for this hoped-for prey. He had no commission to attack the Turks in their own ports, and he was in fact exceeding orders. But, again like Nelson, he was able to decide for himself when a bold stroke of his own choosing would fit the policy of his political chief at home.

He was to be deeply disappointed; for when he arrived before Tunis on February 8th, 1655, he found his news was false. There was no general concentration, but there was instead an assembly of nine warships of the Dey of Tunis in the harbour of Porto Farina near-by. If he was denied a service to heaven there was still a practical mission to his hand. He therefore addressed himself to the question, of piracy and requested from the Dey the liberation of some English sailors recently captured, but the Dey, who bore the English a grudge for a scurvy trick played him four years before by a sailor, gave him a downright refusal. Blake then made for Porto Farina, since Tunis itself, lying back from the great fortified lobster-claws that stretch out before it into the sea, was unassailable.

At Porto Farina he found the Dey's warships hauled inshore under the protection of the castle and of powerful batteries sited on its flanks, with large bodies of Barbary warriors, horse and foot, drawn up in expectation of an attempt at landing. The position appeared much too strong, however, and Blake contented himself with exchanging a few shots with the shore batteries, from which he learnt that the Turks, then as now, were no gunners. Leaving a few frigates to blockade the gulf, he withdrew, "meaning to give them a more sudden and hotter visit" presently, and returned to Tunis in a further attempt to negotiate with the Dey. The Turks, however, were "more wilful and untractable than before, adding to their obstinacy much insolence and contumely, denying us all commerce of civility." They refused Blake permission to water and fired on his boats. "These barbarous provocations," said Blake, "did so far work on our spirits that we judged it necessary for the honour of our fleet, our nation and our religion, seeing they would not deal with us as friends, to make them feel as enemies."

To deceive the Dey as to his intentions he turned about again and sailed over the horizon, but only to take in water in Sicily, and on April 3rd the fleet was again before Farina. Blake was still troubled that his orders did not expressly authorise him to raid the Barbary harbours,[132] but a council of war held on board the *George* had resolved upon the hazardous exploit of assaulting the ships and forts, challenging the accepted maxim of then as of to-day that naval forces cannot subdue land batteries. It was the first time in history that such an exploit had been dared,[133] and Blake made his plans with immaculate detail.

"He was the first man" says Clarendon, "who brought the ships to contemn castles on shore, which had, been thought to be very formidable, and were discovered by him to make a noise only, and to fright those who could rarely be hurt by them."

---

[132] Blake to Thurloe, Rawlinson MSS., xxiv, 235.
[133] The exploit of Leveson and Monson in 1602 was for various reasons not comparable.

At dawn the next morning, having earnestly "sought unto the Lord" upon his knees, Blake slowly closed in upon the harbour with fifteen ships under a gentle breeze blowing off the sea. The frigates, in line ahead under Nathaniel Cobham in the *Newcastle*, bore down immediately upon the enemy galleys in the face of a clamorous fire from ships and shore. Close behind followed Badiley, Stayner and finally Blake with the heavier ships. Without pause they sailed straight up to within musket-shot of the castle, anchored, swung round to use their broadsides, and opened a devastating bombardment of the castle and batteries. Meanwhile, the frigates had been sharply engaging the enemy's ships, and the cannonade all along the line was at its height. In its midst, and screened by its smoke blowing on-shore, after a fashion that recalls the experience of the Scilly Isles, a force of boats quietly put off from the English ships under John Stokes, captain of Blake's flagship, and, in "blinding clouds of smoke rolling on the enemy," rowed towards the doomed galleys. At their approach the crews of the galleys, seized with panic, leapt overboard and floundered ashore, but a storm of musketry from the troops ashore burst upon the English raiding party. With men dropping at their oars, Stokes's force kept on its way, however, reached the galleys, swarmed over them, and fired them. By eight o'clock they were a sheet of flame. As the boats' crews drew off the enemy crews moved to return to the blazing galleys, but a hail of shot from the English ships sent them reeling back again.

The gun-fire from the shore batteries had by now been completely silenced by Blake's cannonade, and that of the castle was also suppressed. The purpose of the expedition had been achieved. Accordingly, when Stokes's "boats of execution" returned from their task, they put warps to their parent ships and towed them out with as much coolness as they had entered. Stout old Badiley, the first to anchor under the castle's guns, was also the last to weigh. The enemy ashore made one last despairing attempt to reach their burning ships, but another peremptory burst of gun-shot fired into the blazing hulls again denied them recovery. The action was all over well before midday, but the galleys remained blazing all day and far into the night.[134]

Thus was executed what Mr. J. R. Powell aptly describes as a "complete and artistic victory." If the exploit was daring it had also been designed with minute care and precisely executed. It had been founded upon Blake's realisation of the enemy's inferior gunnery, and against more efficient gunnery it must have been a disaster. The English casualties amounted to only twenty-five killed and forty wounded, nearly all sustained by Stokes's boat parties from the musketry fire from the shore. But, as Gardiner says of this action, "it is the incommunicable attribute of genius not to be the slave of theoretical rules," and superior gunnery and superior discipline gave Blake his chance. The action of Farina was in the authentic Nelson manner. In the words of Weale, one of the officers present, it was "a piece of service that has not been paralleled in these parts of the world,"[135] and in the words of Clarendon it "made the name of the English very terrible and formidable in those seas."

Nevertheless, Blake's dispatch after the action[136] shows that he had some misgiving at the over-stepping of his instructions, for he wrote that he expected "to hear of many complaints and clamours of interested men" who were engaged in trade with

---

[134] Blake to Thurloe, Rawlinson MSS., xxv, 503; *Letters from the Fleet*, April 9th, 18; *Perfect Diurnall.* E.840, 11; *Weale's Journal*, Sloane MSS. 1431, fol. 26.
[135] Ibid.
[136] Blake to Thurloe, Rawlinson MSS. xxv, 503.

Turkey. "I confess," he wrote, "I did awhile much hesitate myself, and was balanced in my thoughts." But he need have had no fear, for Cromwell was delighted with this bold stroke which had so far advanced the renown of the English name. "You have done," the Protector wrote to him, "a very considerable service to this Commonwealth."

However, it had no effect upon the obduracy of the crafty Dey of Tunis, who, trying to frighten Blake with the notion that he must now face the fury of the Sultan of Turkey himself, still refused to give up his English captives. Tunis was too hard a nut to crack without land forces. Nevertheless, Blake's exploits in Southern waters in the next two years so elevated the reputation of the English navy that after his death his successors, Stokes and Whetstone, riding the Mediterranean in undisputed mastery, were able without fighting to secure from Tunis and Tripoli not only the release of captives, but also the freedom of English shipping from further molestation.

Blake now proceeded on a similar mission to Algiers, anchoring before its white facade on April 28th. With the Dey of that territory easier relations existed, nor was he unheedful of the prowess of the English fleet, to which he extended a reception of marked respect, and Blake had no difficulty in ransoming all the remaining English captives or in obtaining all the provisions he asked for. The occasion was much more notable for an incident that showed the temper and character of the men whom Blake had now shaped into the New Model of the navy. After the liberated Englishmen had been taken on board, the fleet was astonished by the sight of forty men swimming out to them and begging to be taken on board. They were Dutchmen who had been enslaved and who had now made a concerted escape for liberty. Blake was in a quandary. To sail away with them would have been to play a scurvy trick upon the Dey; to send them back would have been treacherous to men of his own faith and kind. It was Blake's seamen who found the honourable solution; for they offered to provide ransom for the Dutchmen by subscribing one dollar out of their pay from every seaman in the fleet — an offer that was readily accepted by the anxious Algerians.

Meanwhile, the direction of Cromwell's mysterious foreign politics was gradually being guided by the course of events themselves. Hitherto, Blake's instructions on his Mediterranean commission had naturally led him to suppose that France was to be the enemy and Spain the friend, but while he was at Algiers, as now appears from his letter to the Commissioners of June 12th, he received secret instructions from home saying that Spain and not France was to be the enemy.[137] Accordingly, having withdrawn to the Balearics for provisions, he despatched the *Amity* and the *Hector* to Alicante and Cartagena to collect the guns and anchors from Rupert's wrecked ships that had been lying there since 1650, and sailed for Cadiz Bay to re-victual from the store-ships sent from England. Thence he put out to sea on June 4th. His new orders were to intercept the Plate fleet homeward bound to Spain with treasure, and presently he had further orders to intercept also any assistance going out from Spain to the Spanish force who had been resisting the assaults of Penn and Venables; for it was not yet known that the Western Design had already shamefully failed.

All through the summer of 1655 Blake ranged the Atlantic seaboard of Spain and Portugal seeking for a prey that did not come, for it had wisely turned back to safety. He was in an unhappy state. He was ill and a feeling of loneliness was upon

---

[137] Add. MSS. 19367, 7. This, as Mr. Powell observes, was the little point on which Gardiner and Corbett were in doubt; see *Letters of Robert Blake*, p. 275.

him. His ships were foul-bottomed and stubborn to handle. He was hard pressed for victuals and stores, the Protector's policy having left him without any friendly port in those waters, and on July 6th he begged Cromwell "to lay your quickening commands upon the Commissioners of the navy."

In one of the most vivid passages of all his correspondence he wrote to Cromwell:[138]

> Our condition is dark and sad, and (without especial mercy) like to be very miserable: our ships extreme foul, winter drawing on, our victuals expiring, all stores failing, our men falling sick through the badness of drink, and eating their victuals boiled in salt water for two months' space, the coming of a supply uncertain… and though it come timely, yet if beer come not with it we shall be undone that way. We have no place or friend, our recruits[139] here slow, and our mariners (which I most apprehend) apt to fall into discontents through their long keeping abroad. Our only comfort is that we have a God to lean upon, although we walk in darkness and see no light. I shall not trouble your Highness with any complaints of myself, of the indisposition of my body or troubles of my mind; my many infirmities will one day, I doubt not, sufficiently plead for me or against me, so that I may be free of so great a burden, consoling myself in the meantime in the Lord and in the firm purpose of my heart with all faithfulness and sincerity to discharge the trust, while reposed in me.

Moreover, he was in a perplexity of mind over the conduct of an irrational policy. A clear-cut state of peace or war would have left no ambiguities, but no declaration of war had been made and he had had orders to attack only two targets — the

---

[138] Blake to Cromwell, Rawlinson MSS., xxix, 336.
[139] i.e., replacements.

homeward Plate fleet or an outward-bound relief expedition to the West Indies. He was therefore faced with a pretty problem when he encountered a Spanish fleet that was not quite either of these, but was a naval escort for the expected treasure fleet. His forbearance and the shyness of the Spaniards preserved the precarious peace, and it is to his credit that during those trying months he did nothing to exacerbate the threatening rupture and, to Cromwell's regret, so guided his actions as rather to encourage peace.

At last, with supplies further failing and the need for repairs growing more urgent, he headed his weather-beaten fleet northwards for home, and arrived with thanksgiving at Portsmouth on October 7th.

It was a year all but a day since he had set out, and in that time Blake had begun a new page in the history of nations. He had opened the gates of the Mediterranean to the English ensign and had so established its repute in those waters that the way was now open to that dominion which was to be so vital to the people of these islands and those of them who were to seek the new lands in more distant seas. He had opened this gate not with sword and battery, but by the strength of his presence, the dignity of his bearing, the restraint that earns respect. Save for the merited punishment of the Barbary pirates and the cutting out of a few French privateers, his guns had remained silent, and he had given to the office of a British admiral the attributes and functions also of an ambassador. In 1655 the navy passed out of the uncertainties and growing pains of adolescence and attained manhood.

X. THE LAST MERCY

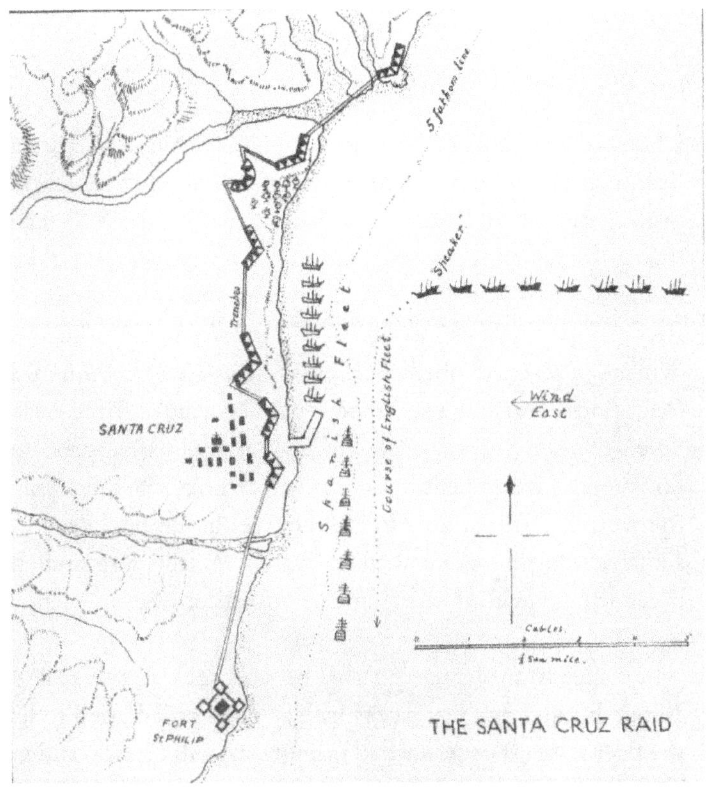

Blake longed for rest and retirement. He who had loved the tranquillity of Oxford's court-yards and Bridgwater's quays looked for repose and solitude after nearly thirteen years of warfare. He was fifty-seven and had too long endured the privations which were inherent in a seaman's life of that day. Behind the frequent references to his sickness that occur in his letters there seems a yearning for the solace of home, and, though his compelling sense of duty still drove him onwards to its inescapable bourne, in his heart was that sense of spiritual solitude of which Masefield has written:

> Weary the cry of the wind is, weary the sea,
> Weary the heart and the mind and the body of
> me.

Under the stress of his increasing infirmity his natural brusqueness had developed into a note of asperity. He had grown, we are told, "a very touchy and particular old man," treated his captains severely, and to foreigners was curt almost to the point of incivility.[140] Alike by foreigners and by his own fleet, he was held in no little awe, and from his officers he demanded an exact obedience. He is now as we see him in the Pelly portrait — intense, imperious, not a little fierce. For a little while some rest was now indeed his, and perhaps the next few months were spent in his native pastures, when the fall of the year yet left him time to see the trees in the final beauty of summer's green mantle and to watch for the last time the perennial miracle of their aureate investiture before winter's long sleep.

But already by January, 1656, he was back at work at the Admiralty, and in a few weeks he was again called upon to lead the fleet to sea. For peace had been made with France, and war declared by Spain. Before he sailed, however, as if he had had the same vague premonition as Nelson was to have before his last voyage, he made his will. In it he left bequests to his various brothers, nephews and other relations, to the poor of Bridgwater and Taunton, to his two servants James Knowles

---

[140] Sarotti to the Doge, V.S.P. xxx, No. 3; the same to the same, xxx. No. 13.

and Nicholas Bartlet, and £50 was set aside for Domingo for his "better education in the knowledge and fear of God."

During January and February a new fleet was preparing at Portsmouth, and none but Blake was possible as its leader. Obediently he undertook to assume the charge laid upon him, but now he asked the Protector for a colleague to help him share the burden. The request was granted, but some surprise was occasioned by the appointment of young Edward Montague, who at thirty-one was one of the Protector's most intimate friends, an 'eager genius who knew neither fear nor repose. At twenty he had commanded a regiment of the New Model at Naseby. He was to become in due time the first Earl of Sandwich and the patron of Pepys before he met a heroic death on the deck of his ship when it was overwhelmed by the Dutch at the Battle of Southwold Bay in 1672.

It was the common talk that the taciturn veteran of Taunton and Portland took very ill the appointment of this high-mettled young aristocrat who had never been to sea; "the old commander," reported Giavarina, the Venetian Resident, "is disgusted and unable to digest so bitter a pill."[141] According to Ludlow, Cromwell, suspecting that Blake was dissatisfied with his Protectorship, had appointed his favourite in order to gain experience of the sea, win the interest of the seamen and take away some of Blake's glory.[142] However, there is no real evidence that anything but friendship existed between the old sea-horse and the colt. Nevertheless, it seems true that Montague was more interested in the hopes of prize-money than in the purposes of serious war, and more than once Blake had need to check his eagerness for promising adventure.

---

[141] Giavarina to the Doge, Venetian State Papers, xxx, No. 339.
[142] Ludlow, 603.

There was trouble in other directions, however. Political unrest was moving among sailors and soldiers alike, the constant prey of every kind of agitator. Lawson, who was appointed Vice-Admiral of the new fleet, was deeply suspect, and one of Montague's tasks was to keep an eye on his covert royalism, but fortunately Lawson resigned before the fleet sailed. There was trouble likewise with the manning of the ships. The men who had come home with Blake from the Mediterranean had had no pay for twenty months. But, in spite of all, the fleet was able to set sail from Portsmouth on March 28th, 1656, as a fine fighting unit. The two Generals-at-Sea took as their flagship the *Naseby*, a splendid new frigate-built first-rater of 1,634 gross tonnage just built by Charles Pett at Woolwich and mounting eighty guns. Badiley was Vice-Admiral in the fine old *Resolution*, and John Bourne, brother of Nehemiah, carried the flag of the Rear-Admiral in the *Andrew*. The fleet numbered forty-eight ships.

Its immediate purpose, as before, was to intercept the homecoming Spanish fleet from the Plate, but the delays of discipline and supply had been such that when they arrived off Cadiz, Blake and Montague found that they were too late and the treasure had been banked. An attempt on Cadiz itself was then discussed by the two leaders, but the Spaniards had taken care with chains and block-ships that the exploit of Drake should be impossible of repetition. The fleet accordingly set itself to the task of blockading the whole of the Atlantic approaches to Spain. Here was another task never before attempted in naval history, and the efficacy with which that trying service was conducted, at a time when ships were built chiefly for fighting and not for long habitation, when facilities for storing even the barest necessities of life were of the most primitive, when the nearest base was 1,200 miles away, showed an understanding of the use of sea power which was entirely new in its day and which has been a pattern ever since.

For months the tedious work of blockade of an enemy who would not face them continued. Other work also kept the fleet arduously occupied. In the manifest need for a port and fortress of their own in these waters they cast far and wide. They reconnoitred Gibraltar, but that stronghold had to wait for forty-eight years before the skill and gallantry of Rooke secured it; they voyaged again into the Mediterranean, raiding Malaga and repeating the exploit of Farina to burn nine ships in harbour there; they called at Sallee in another attempt to release English slaves; they rode out a great storm which mightily impressed young Montague by its fury and in which only a "singular mercy" preserved the *Naseby* from destruction; and they brought the inspiration of their presence to Lisbon again to overcome the reluctance of King John to fulfil his treaty obligations, giving occasion for Montague's flashing anger to break upon the undeserving head of the English ambassador, until it was hushed by Blake's calmer understanding.

When at last a treasure fleet appeared Blake was robbed of the prize, though not of great glory. While the fleet was watering at Lisbon, Stayner, who had been left with eight ships before Cadiz to maintain the blockade, was visited by a violent gale on September 8th which scattered his squadron beyond the bay. The apparent misfortune became a blessing. In the evening he sighted eight Spanish ships and, following them throughout the night, engaged them the next morning and utterly shattered them after a seven-hours' battle. They proved to be a fleet of merchant galleons homeward bound from the Indies, ignorant of Blake's continued presence, and they provided Stayner with a huge booty amounting to 4,000,000 pieces of eight and quantities of merchandise and plate. On board the great *Capitana* was the Marquis de Baydes, who was returning home with his wife and family after his governorship of Peru. The great galleon fought desperately for six hours before she began to sink in flames, and as the flames spread the marquesa and one of her daughters swooned and were burned to death. The Marquis chose to die with them, throwing himself across their dead bodies in a Roman sacrifice. His two young sons, however, were rescued from the sea by the English sailors,[143] and were taken home by Montague, who looked after them with affection before they were returned to their own country.

With the approach of winter, it was decided not to continue to maintain so large a fleet in distant waters, and some of the heavier ships were sent home. At Cromwell's desire Montague, who was nothing loath after so tedious a sojourn with disappointing profit, came home with them. Blake, however, suffering in health though he was, was called upon to spend one more winter at sea, for he had information both that the Spanish fleet was preparing to put to sea and that another treasure fleet was expected from the Indies. He was suffering from scurvy, living entirely on broths, jellies and cordials. He had moods when he was testy and irritable, and spoke sharply to his captains. Yet he once again declared the "ready faithfulness of my spirit to submit myself thereunto as the Lord shall enable me."

With Montague, Blake lost also trusty old Badiley and the *Naseby*. He now transferred his flag to the *Swiftsure*, of sixty guns, and John Bourne was promoted Vice Admiral in place of Badiley, Stayner becoming Rear-Admiral. With six fresh ships that the Protector sent out to him, his fleet now numbered

---

[143] Thurloe, v. 433 *et seq.*

twenty-nine sail. Through all the storms of winter he pressed without respite that hard blockade, but the rigours of the service told severely upon his body and spirit and upon his men. "This place," he wrote to Montague, "is a prison to me." Never before had a fleet been called upon to maintain itself at sea throughout the winter far from any port of its own, and though Lisbon was now available since the settlement with Portugal, its resources were scanty and John an uncertain friend. The ships were streaming with seaweed and could scarcely make headway through the water; masts and sails had been swept away by storms and many ships rode jury-rigged; timbers had been shattered by the force of the Atlantic's winter blows, so that men laboured at the pumps day and night to keep their comfortless homes afloat; crews were reduced to skeleton numbers by sickness and death; the *Swiftsure* became so foul that Blake had again to change his flagship, removing into the *George*, a ship, he said, "much unfit to bear the Standard of England." Yet, writing again to Montague on February 9th, 1657, he uttered those memorable words of a spirit that never knew dismay:

> Notwithstanding the great tempests of wind that we have encountered, without the Straits and within, we are all together and behold one another's face in comfort.[144]

No wonder that that feat of maritime endurance made a profound impression throughout Europe. No other navy had ever attempted so arduous a service. No other commander had so enlarged the conception and the uses of sea power. It was with no vainglory that Waller might declare:

> Others may use the ocean as their road,
> Only the English make it their abode.

---

[144] Lord Sandwich's MSS.

The last scene opens. It fits the hero that the scene is the most glorious of all. He marches again with Nelson in this, that his last exploit was his greatest and that his spirit and his intellect rose to their highest achievement when the body was sunk in suffering.

In the midst of their dreary vigil, blown off their station by a violent storm and struggling back on reduced rations, came news that quickened all hearts and lighted up scurvy-stricken eyes. David Young, master of the merchant ship *Catherine*, was bound from Barbados to Genoa when in February, 1657, he sighted a fleet of Spanish galleons making for the Canary Isles. This was the treasure fleet from Havana to which Blake had been so long looking forward. Now Young had served in the famous little *Amity* under Blake and had lost a hand in fighting against the Dutch, and his thoughts flew at once to his old commander. Without hesitation he turned aside from his course, his commerce forgotten, and sought out the English fleet. Blake celebrated the good news with a salvo of guns and instantly summoned Bourne and Stayner to a council on board the *George*.

Their advice, fortified by that of the ships' captains, was that, the fleet having short rations, six or seven of the best frigates should be fully provisioned and dispatched to find the Spaniards. Blake rejected that advice, for he was expecting the Spanish fleet in Cadiz to come out and fight, and since Dungeness he had rightly shown the strongest aversion to dividing his fleet; moreover, de Ruyter had just arrived before Cadiz with a Dutch squadron, and an attempt was being made by the Spaniards to recruit his support. "The admiral," said Stayner afterwards, "was very angry with us, and said he would not part the fleet."

Reluctantly, and to the disappointment of a fleet eager for a fight and for prize money, he decided to remain on his station, to wait the arrival of a convoy that was expected shortly with fresh provisions. It was not until the end of March, however, that the convoy arrived, and when it did the transference of stores took place in record time, so eager were the men for action. The fleet now had six months' provisions, and again his captains urged him to make for the Canaries. Still the admiral was adamant, for he gave no thought to prize money, and he considered that the warships of Cadiz were now bound to come out to the help of the treasure fleet. To destroy Spain's battle fleet seemed to him more important than the capture of treasure ships.

When after re-victualling he arrived again before Cadiz, however, he found the enemy in no shape to put to sea, and messages began to come in one after the other telling him now that the treasure ships were anchored at Santa Cruz in Tenerife and had landed their treasure there with no immediate intention of bringing it on to Spain. At last, in April, there arrived one William Sadlington, captain of an English privateer, who repeated the same facts, telling Blake he had actually exchanged shots with the ships as they lay at Santa Cruz. Immediately calling his captains together, Blake sailed that same night for Santa Cruz, and with twenty-three ships "heeling under a freshening gale from the north-east, swept westwards out of Cadiz Bay."[145]

He had appreciated rightly that the task, if to be attempted at all, was not one merely for a few frigates; moreover, it was freely reported that de Ruyter had contracted with the Spaniards to escort the treasure from Santa Cruz to Flanders. Therefore Blake kept his fleet together, leaving only half a

---

[145] Dewar: *Blake's Last Campaign.*

dozen frigates to watch the Spaniards at Cadiz. With a fair wind behind him all the way, he sighted Tenerife on the evening of April 18th, and on the evening of the next day he lay off Santa Cruz itself preparing for battle, sending two frigates to observe the disposition of the enemy. During all these days he was very brusque to his captains, rejecting their advice so often that at last they shrank from giving it. Worn out by scurvy and by dropsy, he was already "wrestling on the world's edge."

The problem that presented itself to him was very similar to Porto Farina, but a much harder one. It could be no affair of boats, and no other commander in the world would have attempted it, the Spaniards laughing contemptuously at the Dutch captain who lay in the harbour and, knowing something of the mettle of the English leader, asked leave from the Spanish commander to put to sea. "Go if you will," replied the Spaniard, "and if the English fleet dares to come we will serve them as we served them at Hispaniola." The Spaniards, said an English prisoner on the island, "derided us among themselves, laughed our intentions to scorn, drank health to our confusion, and were (of Spaniards) very jolly."[146]

They had cause for such confidence. "Of all the places which ever came under our inspection," wrote one of Nelson's officers, "none we conceive is more invulnerable to attack or more easily defended." Santa Cruz lies in a sheltered roadstead with a coast of a shallow crescent shape, open to the sea to the east. Steep and rocky hills form a wild skyline behind it. At the southern extremity of the bay stood St. Philip's Fort, armed with forty guns. Northwards stretched a line of seven stone-built forts, connected with each other by a triple line of breastworks. Under cover of St. Philip's Fort lay seven of the

---

[146] *Mercurius Politicus*, p. 7826.

great treasure galleons, broadside to the sea, and about the centre of the bay nine smaller ships lay close in-shore.

At six o'clock on the morning of Monday, April 20th, 1657, Blake summoned his captains to a council. There in the oaken cabin of the old *George* the little invalid admiral, rough-hewn, monolithic, scored by the winds of time, the flame of battle and the creeping hand of sickness, yet still with his spirit bent up to its full height at the thought of action, held his last council of war with his silent captains around him. He was propped up in bed with great woollen cushions, Giavarina tells us, and in that position went into battle and gave all his orders.[147]

Stayner urged an expedition by frigates alone, but Blake decided to strike with his whole force. He saw every detail clearly. Following the same design as had succeeded at Farina, he ordered that a force of frigates should engage the enemy ships in harbour at close quarters, while he himself with the heavier ships bombarded the land batteries. He picked four frigates each from the Red, the White, and the Blue Squadrons for the first duty, and the command of these was accepted by Stayner "with all my heart."

Therefore, while the African sun was still low in the sky and with a favourable wind blowing into the bay, Stayner spread his canvas and led in his division of frigates in line ahead. They were greeted by a storm of gun-fire from the Spaniards. Silently they bore on, making no reply to the cannonade, save for two shots fired in error. Leading the line in the *Speaker*, Stayner placed himself in the forecastle, looking for the most dangerous position for himself. He found it between the Spanish admiral and the vice-admiral, and to that spot he steered.

---

[147] Giavarina to the Doge, V.S.P., xxxi, No. 52. Stayner does not confirm this.

As his division came up after him, having anchored and veered, they laid themselves one by one alongside the big galleons at a distance of a few paces, and not till then did their guns speak. "The gunners went to it in earnest." By their very boldness they profited, for the high galleons were now a shelter to them from the guns of the forts. "They were my barricadoes," said Stayner. So for four hours they hammered each other ship to ship. More and more the English gunners asserted their mastery. Soon after the sun had reached his full height the ships of both the Spanish admiral and the vice-admiral had been blown up, and nothing remained of the flagship but her carved and gilded stern floating upon the water.

As the English ships gradually mastered the Spaniards by their gunnery, each of them lowered away boats with boarding parties. The Spanish crews, firing a last desperate broadside at the boats pulling through the smoke, thereupon fled from their ships, dropping overboard on the landward side and seeking safety ashore. Swarming aboard, the English, though met by volleys of musketry fire from the shore, set fire to the galleons and dropped back to the boats ready to warp their own ships out of the bay.

But as the enemy ships went down one after another, so did the English become exposed to the fire of the shore batteries, and they were so close in that the exposed boats' crews felt also the sharp sting of the musketry from the trenches ashore. Blake, however, waiting till there was a real need for him, had by midday followed into the bay and was now bombarding the shore batteries with every gun at his command. So excellent was his gunnery that, as at Farina, several of the Spanish batteries were actually hammered into silence or deserted by their garrisons. The whole bay was filled with flame and with the smoke of guns and burning ships rolling in clouds upon the shore before the wind, while the roar of guns, the deeper shock of explosions and the crackle of musketry reverberated back from the rocky hills. For three hours this bombardment was maintained while Stayner was completing the annihilation of the ships, and it was then that the most critical moment of the action arrived. For, having got themselves in with the wind, they must now get themselves out by boats against it and under fire. Only five of the enemy ships remained above water, and these had been taken in tow as prizes by the frigates, but the Spaniards were now sending up fresh troops to man the defences ashore. Blake never gave thought to prize money, and observing that the prizes would encumber the frigates in their withdrawal, he signalled that they should forthwith be set on fire and abandoned. The order had to be given three times before it was obeyed.

With shot falling all round the open boats as the men pulled at the oars, the fleet was slowly warped out of the bay; but the frigates, lying close in under the enemy guns, had been heavily hammered, and it was seven o'clock in the evening before the crippled *Speaker*, first into action and last out, had crept out of range of the batteries ashore. Her yards and main topmast gone, not a whole rope or sail overhead but spritsail and spritsail-topsail, the holes rent in her hull covered with hides and barrel-staves to keep her from sinking, and with every gun ashore concentrated on her, she was almost a wreck. Blake ordered Bourne to take her in tow. The vice-admiral did so, but for some reason cast off again, leaving the stricken ship struggling alone. "They paid us extremely," said Stayner. All her masts were now down, yet her guns were still speaking, and by a lucky shot she blew up a magazine in St. Philip's, reducing the whole fort to silence. The *Plymouth* now came to her rescue and at last towed her into safety.

So ended an exploit that was to amaze Europe and strike the English Parliament dumb with momentary unbelief. In twelve hours' furious fighting the whole Spanish fleet had been completely destroyed without the loss of a single English ship. So miraculous seemed the successful withdrawal of the fleet that, in order to explain it, a legend was invented that God not only caused the wind to blow on-shore to carry the fleet in, but He also caused it to veer at the right moment to carry it out again. The legend became history, and Nelson himself in his own unsuccessful attack on Santa Cruz said: "I do not reckon myself equal to Blake, but if I recollect aright he was more obliged to the wind coming off the land than to any exertions of his own."[148] The blow was felt throughout the Spanish Empire. In Spain and in the Americas prices rose; Spanish arms were frustrated in their attempt to conquer Portugal, and in Flanders the armies of Turenne were victorious. Cut off from her colonies and the silver-mines that paid her soldiers, she was for the time crippled as a European power.[149]

Santa Cruz was Blake's supreme exploit; all the vigour, the dash and the imagination of his fighting spirit were there in its undying youth. But the hand of death was upon his body. In

---

[148] *Despatches and Letters*, ed. Nicolas, ii, 379.

[149] The chief authorities for the Battle of Santa Cruz and the events leading up to it are: *The Thurloe Papers*; Blake's despatch; *Weale's Journal* (Sloane MS., 1431); Stayner's narrative (Add. MS., 32,093, fol. 372); letters from several officers in *Mercurius Politicus*, pp. 7822-6; Thomas Lurting's *The Fighting Sailor Turned Peaceable Citizen*. The accepted accounts of the whole exploit, splendidly told, are those of the late Sir Charles Firth in the *English Historical Review oi* 1905, reprinted in the same author's *Last Years of the Protectorate*, Vol. I, and Capt. A. C. Dewar's article, "Blake's Last Campaign," in the *United Service Magazine*, 1911.

June he began his last journey home, taking from his battered fleet those ships that most urgently needed repair. One last useful function remained for him, however, for on his way he called at Sallee and successfully treated for the release of all the English captives.

On July 17th he set sail from Lisbon on the last stage. "The General," wrote the English Consul, "is very weak; I beseech God to strengthen him." But Blake knew that the end was near, desiring only that he might be spared for a few days to see his native land again and to settle his estate. He grew daily weaker, however. On the night of August 6th, 1657, the Lizard having been passed, he called John Bourne and some of his captains to his cabin in the *George*, and, mindful to the end of the great service to which he had utterly given himself, he charged them to represent to the Government the necessitous state of his seamen. He died the next morning within sight of Plymouth Sound while the expectant people were gathering to receive him.

His intestines were buried at St. Andrew's, Plymouth, and his body, after lying in state at Greenwich, was borne up the Thames on September 4th in exalted pomp, with salute of guns, with his banner and guidon before, with Protector, Council, Lord Mayor and his own good regiment following; and with volleys of musketry from all the regiments in London he was buried in Westminster Abbey.

But even the grave brought him no rest, and better for him had been the simplicity of a sailor's undiscoverable tomb, with the sea as winding-sheet and plain round shot at his head and his heels. For he had rested but four years, when, by order of the chivalrous heart of Charles II, his body was disinterred with Deane's and sixteen others and flung into a common pit

between the Abbey and St. Margaret's. There he lies — within
a few yards of Raleigh.

PRINCIPAL AUTHORITIES FOR BLAKE

Two or three worthless lives of Blake have been written. Perhaps the best is that by Colonel Beadon, a painstaking study dealing with operations at some length. For the last phase nothing exceeds Sir Charles Firth's essay on Santa Cruz in the "English Historical Review," reprinted in his "Last Years."

Besides the general authorities for the period, the following are the special authorities and sources for Blake, in addition to those quoted in the notes to the text:

"The Letters of Robert Blake," edited by the Revd. J. R. Powell (Navy Records Society), 1937.

"Letters and Papers Relating to the First Dutch War," edited by S. R. Gardiner and C. T. Atkinson (Navy Records Society).

The Thurloe Papers.

The Rawlinson MSS.

The Venetian State Papers.

Weale's Journal in the Sloane MSS.

"The Administration of the Royal Navy," M. Oppenheim, 1896.

"England in the Mediterranean," Sir Julian Corbett, 1904.

"The Naval Side of British History," Sir Geoffrey Callender, 1924.

"The Royal Navy: A History," Sir William Laird Clowes, 1897-1902.

"The Navy under the Early Stuarts," C. D. Penn, 1913.

"Last Years of the Protectorate," Sir Charles Firth, 1909.

Narrative of the Battle of Santa Cruz, Sir R. Stayner, ed. Firth

(Navy Records Society, Naval Miscellany, Vol 2, 1910).

"The Fighting Sailor Turned Peaceable Citizen," Thomas Lurting, 1816 edition.

"Memorials of Sir William Penn," Granville Penn, 1833.

"Anglo-Dutch Rivalry During the First Half of the 17th Century," G. Edmundson, 1911.

"Robert Blake," R. Beadon, 1935.

"Blake: General-at-Sea," C. D. Curtis, 1934.

"Robert Blake, General-at-Sea," Revd. J. R. Powell, 1932.

Studies in *The Mariner's Mirror* — "The Royalists at Sea," 1648-50, R. C. Anderson; "Blake's Reduction of the Scilly Isles," J. R. Powell; "Blake's Reduction of Jersey," J. R. Powell.

"The Siege of Taunton," Emanuel Greene.

IV: JOHN LAMBERT

Be bolde, be bolde, and everywhere be bolde.
— SPENSER, *The Faerie Queene.*

I. INITIATION

THE man who might have been king brings us to a very different gallery from the high-principled servants of the State we have seen in Hampden, Blake and Skippon. Unlike those older men, who had been born beneath the trailing clouds of Elizabethan glory and had watched their skies grow pale in the spiritless Jacobean air, he was only twenty-two when the Civil Wars began, and no doubt they came to him as a great adventure. He was a child of the unrest. Well-born, handsome, cultured and brave, he did not belong, like those others, to the school of godly warriorship. He was vain, ambitious and daring. Nevertheless, he was far from being the unscrupulous self-seeker the world has generally supposed him, and the follies of his later years were due rather to his impulsive nature, his rash judgment, and the faults of a political education in the stormy school of rebellion. Had his greater qualities — his physical and moral courage, his driving power, his tolerance and his generosity — been balanced by some political acumen, and had he sought to emulate Cromwell otherwise than by imitating him, he might well, since he had an immense following in the Army, have attained that high seat to which his ambition aspired.

Lambert's is the story of the war in the North, and in all those vivid actions his sword gleamed in the first rank. He was a Yorkshireman, and in that county of divided allegiance he marched with fine friends against gallant adversaries. Under the knightly Fairfaxes he learnt his soldiership and against the grim visage of Marmaduke Langdale he set his spur. They were Yorkshiremen all. When later he marched to the conquest of

Scotland, it was with a colleague of a larger destiny, for George Monck was his friend and colleague before he became his opponent in a day of higher ambition. Few young men have joined arms with such sterling and such fateful companions.

John Lambert came of a family long settled in the Craven country near Skipton at the foot of the Pennine Range — though some of his forbears were of Durham — and he could claim with some confidence a lineage as far back as Sir Thomas Lambert in the days of Henry III. The Lamberts' was, however, a modest inheritance until the time of Henry VIII, when the John Lambert of that day acquired by acumen and influence much of the valuable lands of the famous Bolton and Fountains Abbeys of which they had been stripped by Henry. Bred to the law, he held, among others, the offices of Vice-Chancellor of the Duchy of Lancaster and Steward of the courts of the Prior of Bolton. Profiting from that training and those connections, he acquired the lands of Airton, Scosthrop, Hanlith, Otterburn, Malham and Calton, besides others, and he moved into the principal mansion house of Malhamdale, known as Calton Hall, which for a hundred years was to be the family residence and which is still inhabited, though little remains of the old Tudor house. His son added further to these properties.

In due time the property descended to his grandson, Josias Lambert, and to him, by his second wife, Anne Deane, a son was born at Calton Hall in the autumn of 1619. On November 7th he was baptized John.[150]

Josias did not sustain the prosperity handed down to him from great-grandfather John, for he was constantly raising substantial loans on the security of his property to pay debts.[151]

---

[150] Morkill: *The Parish of Kirkby Malhamdale*, p. 138 *et seq.*, c.f. Whitaker, *History of Craven*, pp. 256-8.

He died in September, 1632, leaving to his widow the care of his son, now nearly thirteen, and several other children. The youthful new owner of Calton was therefore born to a substantial competence but not to riches, and the circumstances of his early life gave much to the formation of his character. The fair-haired, bright-eyed boy, living remotely in the country and deeply rooted in its strong soil, the titular head of generous acres, roaming its windswept uplands and its lonely sheep-walks or high beside the shores of its secret-hearted tarn, acquired an assurance and a self-reliance which were to give him a natural habit of command when he stepped out into the world of men, but which proved too fertile a soil for an ambition later grown restless under the restraint of peace. The brisk moorland winds that whipped his cheeks brought also a sparkle to his eye and stirred within him the springs of high desire.

So may we picture Jack Lambert in his boyhood. Amongst horses and dogs, in a country where the deer was freely hunted, he grew up a natural cavalryman. He was a young gentleman of the county, armiger, on friendly terms with the Listers and with the Asshetons, whose land marched with his. He was brought up in the established Church, and there is reason to believe that his family was among those who were moved to some hostility to Archbishop Laud.[152] Unlike the rest of our gallery, however, he was never one of those who were deeply stirred by religious cries, though it is quite untrue to represent him, as has been done, as "irreligious." He grew up into a young man of very handsome appearance. He was, in Gordon's words,

---

151 Morkill, 155-6.
152 Whitaker, *supra.*

iron-sinew'd and satin-skinn'd,
Ribb'd like a drum and limb'd like a deer,
Fierce as the fire and fleet as the wind.

Clean-shaven, with fair brown hair flowing to his shoulders, he was proud and upright in bearing, his features lit by the glow of an ardent and eager spirit within. Here are the keen eye, the stout heart and the cool head of Macaulay's natural soldier. Here, too, is the fallible strength of Lucifer, son of the morning. For Lambert was one "born to be a rebel," a soul filled with "high hopes and unknown flying forms of powers," a spirit warmed by the flame of a passionate restlessness.

To this comely frame and this impulsive spirit were matched a winning grace and a charm of manner that, where-ever he went, made Jack Lambert instantly popular. His manner was gay and he wore an "atoning smile." He was generous and gentle. He had a natural culture, and, alone among those who were to be his companions in a robust and masculine society, there ran in his veins an instinct for the arts and for science. He had a convincing and persuasive speech; he was "brave Lambert, that carries charms on the tip of his tongue."

Such was the character that grew to young manhood on the eve of the Civil Wars, and nothing that he did in life was more momentous than the choice that he now made of the woman to be his mate. On September 10th, 1639, at the age of nineteen, he married Frances, daughter of Sir William Lister, of Thornton in Craven.[153] She was not only a woman of beauty and of good family, but also of vivid personality. She was one of the most striking women of the Commonwealth era and was to exercise an abiding influence upon her husband, whose career became to her a passion and to whose ambition she was

---

[153] Ibid.

the unresting spur. Proud, vivacious, "elegant and accomplished," she took a lively interest in public affairs, following closely the progress of her husband's campaigns and becoming afterwards his active prompter in the more dangerous game of politics. It was later said on several sides that she was a special favourite of Cromwell's, who called her his "jewel," and she was courted by all who sought to enlist her husband's sword on their behalf. If she was responsible for the eclipse of his glory, she was nevertheless unswervingly loyal to him, and in the last days when he was eating the bitter bread of banishment she sought no other fortune than to be at his side.

Already in the year of his marriage John had seen the clouds of war gather in Yorkshire. In that year Charles had made his attempt to invade the Scots and force the English Liturgy upon them, and the Yorkshire gentry and trained bands had answered to his summons, but with small enthusiasm for the cause. Nevertheless, when the Civil War at length broke out in 1642, most of the gentry rose for the King against Parliament, but young John Lambert from the first moment ranged himself with the Parliamentary party, and at the meetings which took place at York on Charles's summons in May he was among those who were opposed to raising a guard for the King. An attempt was made to save the county from bloodshed by a treaty of neutrality, to which Frances Lambert's father, Sir William Lister, was a party, but as the summer months went by neutrality became impossible.

The command of the Northern Parliamentary forces was given to Lord Fairfax, second of that title, but it was in his son Sir Thomas Fairfax that Parliament's cause in the North was to find its inspiration and its spear-head. Something has already been said of that splendid character that shines with so steadfast a light among the many flickering lamps in those days. In every point he was the chivalrous gentleman, and he was matched against one who was no less so, the princely Earl of Newcastle. The Earl, however, was fit rather for the poet's bower than for the rigours of the camp, and though he brought into the field an army far larger than the Fairfaxes could muster, including his own magnificent regiment of Whitecoats, he never knew how to use them best.

"Young Tom," or "Black Tom," as the younger Fairfax was sometimes called (like Strafford), was appointed general of the horse in his father's command, and it was under his inspiring leadership that John Lambert took arms as a cavalryman. The greater issues to come permit only a passing reference to the actions of the northern war, full though they are of the colours of ardent battles, the swift dashes of Tom Fairfax's white horse, the courage of half-naked soldiers struggling through bitter snows. Of John Lambert nothing authentic is heard until the autumn of 1643, when, at the siege of Hull, twenty-three but already a colonel, he earned good report by having "carried himself very bravely" on October 11th in a sortie against Newcastle's besieging forces — a sortie so vigorous that it ended the siege.[154] That experience, one may think, was to make a lasting impression on Lambert, for all through his career in arms it was to be his special characteristic to come out from a defensive position and strike for a decisive result. He distinguished himself again on January 25th, 1644, when Fairfax, having marched through the snows to relieve Sir George Booth, besieged in Nantwich, met "Bloody Byron" at the head of the King's green-coated regiments from Ireland in the icy swamps of the Weaver, and, after one of the sharpest actions of the war, utterly defeated him. Here one Colonel George Monck, whose destiny was to be so closely linked with

---

[154] Meldrum to the Speaker, *God's Ark*, 40.

Lambert's, was taken prisoner by Colonel Bright's regiment. Again John won special commendation.[155]

Then followed Lambert's first independent command. Lord Leven's Scots having crossed the frozen Tweed and Newcastle having hurried to confront them, the young colonel was sent to rescue the faithful clothing towns of the West Riding from Colonel John Bellasis, who was his wife's kinsman. He took with him his own regiment of horse, in which William Fairfax was his major, and Bright's regiment of foot, with which marched the stout John Hodgson, and he was now to demonstrate in miniature those instincts for tactics and for leadership which marked him out as a natural soldier, for in a mere month he scored three sharp victories. First he met Bellasis and Sir Charles Lucas outside Bradford on March 5th. After a long fight Lambert found his musketeers desperately short of ammunition, having but two bullets left to each man. He therefore put his horsemen to charge with the sword, and as the enemy shook under the impact he shrewdly brought in his pikemen and turned a doubtful battle into an utter rout.

Lambert then entered Bradford and garrisoned it, and when Bellasis returned with fresh and superior forces he retired within its weak defences. Having beaten off again and again their attacks on the earthworks, at the moment of their exhaustion he sallied out from his trenches and sent them flying from the field. He engaged Bellasis yet a third time at Kirklees, decoying his brigade by a stratagem into an ambush where he sharply punished them and obliged them to surrender in large numbers.[156] Joining then with the Fairfaxes,

---

[155] Rushworth, v, 302; Carte, i, 36-40; Ed. Burghall, "Providence Improved" in Ormerod's *History of Cheshire*, 112; *God's Ark*, 142; Whitelocke, 81; Hodgson's *Memoirs'*, Fairfax Corr., iii, 74; Clarendon, vii, 403.

[156] *God's Ark*, 168, 170-1, 199; Slingsby, 103; Burghall, *op. cit.*, 125.

he took part in the storm of Selby, perhaps the most vital minor action of the Civil War, on April 11th, when Bellasis was taken prisoner.

Now the way was opened to an ampler scene, in which the winds were rising fast for the Roundhead cause. The Fairfaxes, and John with them, united with Leven's Scots and with the army of Lord Manchester, in which Oliver Cromwell, gaining daily in renown, was lieutenant-general of the horse. Together this great army besieged Lord Newcastle within the walls of York, and to Newcastle's cry for help the swift arm of Rupert, having relieved the gallant Countess of Derby at Lathom House, swept eastwards in answer. Outwitting Fairfax's attempt to intercept him, Rupert relieved York, joined forces with Newcastle and with Goring's army from Lincolnshire, and upon Long Marston Moor on July 2nd, 1644, sighted the rearguard cavalry of the united Roundheads as they marched away towards Tadcaster.

Their far vanguard recalled, the Roundheads turned about, and all through the morning Lambert watched them marshalling, 27,000 Scots and English, upon Marston Moor among unenclosed fields of ripening corn heavy with rain, for the air was burdened with thunder, and constant showers drenched the armies between the bursts of sun. The Roundheads were under the command-in-chief of Lord Leven, the "little crooked old soldier" freshly home from the service of Gustavus Adolphus. Their right wing of cavalry, composed mostly of raw lads from Lancashire and Yorkshire, but supported by veteran Scottish lancers and swordsmen wearing the blue bonnets of the Covenant, was commanded by Thomas Fairfax, with Jack Lambert at his right hand. As the young colonel rode through the trampled crops to his allotted place, he saw before him the gathering royalist armies, 18,000 strong, forming up east and west behind the shelter of a hedge and ditch that ran across their entire front, and immediately facing him, on the royalist left wing, protected and flanked by rough ground cut up by deep runnels and covered with furze and thorn, he recognised the cavalry of Lucas and Dacres under the command of Goring.

All that afternoon the two armies stood at gaze across the dividing ditch in a "fearful, ominous silence," each expecting the other to attack. The thundery summer day wore on in strained expectancy with frequent showers, till on the early evening air the chant of psalms arose from the Puritan regiments knee-deep in the sodden corn, and the royalists, believing there could be no battle that day, sat down to eat their evening meal.

But the moment of their unpreparedness was the instant Leven chose to strike. Away on the far left, where the summer sun was declining to the oncoming night, Lambert heard the sound of guns and the sharp rattle of pistol-fire. The action had begun, and at seven o'clock, as the whole Parliamentary line went forward with white handkerchiefs in their hats as their distinguishing badge, John put his horse to the trot at the head of his raw yeomanry.

A shower of musketry and gunfire broke upon them from the hedges and furze ahead, but they rode forward steadily across the dividing ditch, and with sword and pistol attacked the hidden musketeers and drove the gunners from their pieces. Emerging into the clearer ground beyond, John reformed his ranks and moved forward again with his men dropping one by one under musketry-fire, and in a moment there came down upon them the full shock of Goring's horse. For a moment the raw levies held their own, but they were winnowed with so rough a wind that they broke and fled.

Charles Fairfax fell mortally wounded beside Lambert, and his major, William Fairfax, went down with thirty wounds; Lambert found himself cut off from Thomas Fairfax, but, each with a few troops of horse, they separately cut their way forward right through Goring's wing, though Fairfax's cheek was laid open by a sword-cut and Lambert's horse was shot beneath him.

When they turned to re-form, however, they saw that disaster had overcome the Parliamentary right and centre, and that crisis was over all the field. Fairfax's cavalry were streaming from their pursuers, and his father's infantry in the centre had broken in hopeless rout. Only a few Scottish regiments stood firm around their banners of St. Andrew in a desperate resistance to Goring's horse and Rupert's Bluecoat infantry. Even Lord Leven and the old Fairfax were themselves flying from the field. The shadow of defeat seemed to mingle with the lengthening shadows of departing day, but as Lambert and Fairfax looked yet further towards the sunset they saw that all hope was not let lost. For there they saw that the Eastern Counties infantry had overwinged Newcastle's Lambs, and beyond them again the horsemen of Cromwell had by the help of a flank attack by David Leslie's Scots overcome by a hair's breadth the imminence of utter rout as they reeled under the shock of a charge by Rupert himself, and were steadying themselves for the supreme effort of their counter-charge. Here, therefore, was still work for the swords of Lambert and Fairfax, and, undismayed by the ruin around them or by their own peril, they resolved that, alone though they were, they would ride right through the heart of the enemy's army and lend their swords to Cromwell and Leslie. Plucking the white favours from their hats, they turned their horses' heads to the left, and, accompanied by only a handful of troopers, drove boldly and unscathed across the stricken field to the farther wing.

It was now about eight o'clock. Cromwell, dazed and sick through a wound in the neck, had joined with Leslie in the devastating last charge that sent Rupert reeling from the field, with his favourite dog lying dead in the path of his ruin. From Fairfax Cromwell learnt of the disaster to the right and centre and of the fate that threatened Baillie's hard-pressed Scots, so, leaving the Eastern Counties infantry to hold the Whitecoats, Cromwell, with Fairfax and Lambert riding beside him, swung his cavalry to the right, swept down upon the other wing and cut to pieces the Bluecoats and the cavalry of Goring. In half an hour the fortunes of the battle had been changed. Only the Whitecoats remained undefeated, and as Lambert swung north for yet another charge the gallant Northumbrians retreated to a stone sheepfold, and there, disdaining quarter, they stood with their pikes in their hands against charge after charge and as the grey shapes of approaching night clustered about their heaped dead, they died to a man.

By the Battle of Marston Moor the power of the royalists in the North was virtually extinguished. The stricken countrymen buried more than 4,000 bodies, most of whom were the King's. More than 1,500 prisoners were taken, Newcastle's army was wiped out and the proud Marquess himself, deeply offended by the overbearing Rupert, fled overseas.[157]

---

[157] Since Marston Moor has only a minor part in this story it has not been dealt with in detail. For the best account, see Mr. Buchan's *Oliver Cromwell*. A full review of the authorities on the Battle of Marston Moor is given by Sir Charles Firth, "Trans, of the R.H.S.", 1898.

II. THE FULFILMENT OF PRESTON

What remained of the royalist army of the North was shut up again in York, but was obliged almost immediately to capitulate, and Lambert was one of those deputed to arrange the terms of surrender. At the end of this first phase we find him gaining rapidly in reputation, already well to the fore in spite of his youth and easily the most able of the northern colonels. His conduct at Marston Moor had been of the highest soldiership, and he had shown already that superb courage which was to become remarkable even among a body of men in whom daring was a common quality. Though impulsive by nature, he had shown also that in the element of battle for which nature had so fitted him his faculties found perfect form and balance. He had brains as well as courage. He was no headlong hell-rider, but watched his quarry before he struck — and then struck hard. He understood surprise, and knew when to retire. In the hard-fought little battles of the northern war was a splendid schooling for his natural aptitudes, and he was now to experience another similar campaign of skirmishes and brisk expeditions. His bright sword was seen at Plumpton, before the lofty stronghold of Pontefract and at the storming of Knaresborough. In a brush with Marmaduke Langdale marching to relieve Pontefract he was slightly wounded and repulsed. When he heard that a royalist garrison, sallying out of Skipton Castle, had beaten up Colonel Brandling's quarters and was making away with a hundred prisoners, he lay in wait, dashed in among them like a wolf among deer, rescued the prisoners and chased the royalists back to the gates of Skipton. In the winter of 1644-5, in ill health, he was in London with his wife.[158]

When Fairfax went south to command the New Model, he left the young colonel for a while as Parliamentary commander in the North, until Colonel Poyntz, the hot-headed victor of Rowton Heath, was named in his stead, so that Lambert missed Naseby and the splendid action of Lang-port, when a handful of cavalry and musketeers vanquished Goring's 10,000. But when at last Skipton Castle fell, after an intermittent siege of three years, of which unhappily no good records exist, then John was at last free to come south, and he, donning the red coat of the New Model, was given command of young Edward Montague's regiment of infantry in the New Model. Under Fairfax he helped to quench the last glowing embers of the war in the Southwest, attending the capture of Dartmouth in January, 1646, the surrender of brave old Hopton at Truro, the capitulation of Exeter and finally the siege and fall of Oxford, of which he was made temporary governor. We see him in these months of 1646 advancing further in the reputation of the Army and gaining a name for semi-political gifts. Already at Oxford, Whitelocke speaks of him as one of the "great commanders." At York, Truro, Exeter and Oxford he had been one of the Army's commissioners to arrange terms of surrender, and it is likely that in these parleys he had already shown that aptitude for dialectic and for negotiation which was soon to bring him right to the front in the big word-battle to come between Army and Parliament.

In that spirited duel, which has already been briefly reviewed in the memoir on Skippon, Lambert became at once a leader. He had met Cromwell, and the tinder within him had been lit by the flame of that contrary genius. If thus far Lambert had

---

[158] Vicars, *Burning Bush*, 44; Whitelocke, 132, 136; *Mercurius Aulicus*, 1396, 1405-9; Fairfax Corr., iii, 177.

been no more than the dashing young cavalryman, he now showed himself the born revolutionary, whipping men with his words, banding them into a determination to stand up for their rights, feeding all the time with this inflammable fuel the yet unlit beacon of his own advancing ambition. Cromwell grew to love him "as his son," calling him his "dear Johnnie," and between these two so different men, the one handsome and young and flamelike, the other plain, boorish and given to weeping paroxysms of religious hysteria, there grew up a friendship that was not to be broken until the pupil strove to be too much like the master.

There is no need to go again into that fervid quarrel between Army and Parliament. It will be enough to say that Lambert's role was the opposite of Skippon's, and when the bluff and simple old Centurion and his colleagues addressed the assembled officers in Saffron Walden church it was young Jack Lambert who answered for them. As well as Cromwell, he had now also met Henry Ireton, the lawyer-soldier who became Cromwell's son-in-law, and was the brains of the Army's council of officers, and in Lambert Ireton found his ablest collaborator, for the young Yorkshireman had, says Whitelocke, "a subtle and working brain." Together they drew up the Declaration of the Army, by which they claimed an equal voice with Parliament in the settling of the kingdom, and claimed, too, a reform of Parliament itself; together also they drew up a more notable document, "The Heads of the Proposals," in which, framed as the terms of a treaty of settlement directly with the King over the heads of Parliament, they foreshadowed in outline the future constitution of Britain. His association with Ireton in the creation of that remarkable state paper, with its scheme of a limited monarchy, had the deepest influence upon Lambert and was to provide him with the inspiration by which in due time he was to evolve the Cromwellian constitution. During this period he met the King himself.[159]

While these disputations were going on, with the Army preparing to enter the City and the mob breaking into the Houses of Parliament, an angry wind had swept the troubled habitations of the North. Poyntz, commanding the forces in the North, was not the man to maintain discipline among a discontented soldiery nor to gain the confidence of a harassed population. He had stood out for Parliament against the Army's demands, and on July 8th, 1647, his soldiers mutinied, dragged him bootless from his lodgings, and sent him a prisoner to Fairfax. Young though he was, Lambert was chosen to succeed that violent man, as major-general, and he therefore quitted the military council chambers to return to his familiar dales. By going he lost his New Model regiment of foot, which was given to Sir William Constable, but took over instead a regiment of horse in Yorkshire. Sullen looks, frowns of discontent and the murmur of mutiny met him from idle soldiers who could not learn the discipline of inaction under the smart of political injustices and long unpaid wages. Supernumeraries would not lay down arms until they saw their pay assured, and the civilian population, weary of soldiers and fretting to make good the wastage of war at their looms, their pastures and their flocks, muttered rebelliously at any longer providing free quarters for the soldiers.

But as John rode from garrison to garrison his compelling personality and his willing sympathy restored the soldiers readily to their allegiance, and at a general rendezvous on Peckfield Moor on August 8th, 1647, he was received by the

---

[159] Whitelocke, 254, 257; Clarke Papers, i, 33-44, 47-78, 80-82, 197, 212, 217; *Vindication of Sir William Waller*, 114-142.

5,000 soldiers with acclamation. To such as still remained refractory he dealt out "exemplary punishment."

With the civilian population he was equally successful by his "fairness, civility and moderation," and by his "endeavouring (now that the sword is sheathed) to win and overcome by love." At Pontefract he was warmly greeted, at York he was entertained to dinner with ceremony by the Lord Mayor, and in Richmondshire the hostility of the people was overcome by his "sweetness" and his "atoning smile." He sent fresh forces to the garrisons of Newcastle and Hull, and, answering the cries of the border homesteads, rode north to suppress the Scottish moss-troopers who were raiding, burning, murdering and pillaging this side the Cheviots.

In November he was at home in Craven for a spell, and there he received a letter from Fairfax, telling him of the King's escape from Hampton Court and ordering him to watch all roads and to arrest the King if he went north. In the spring of 1648 he was out again at the work of pacification, but it is not surprising to find him writing that: "I find this business something tedious."[160]

From this period, we may note, dates Jack Lambert's significant association with Thomas Harrison, one of his colonels in the northern brigade. Harrison was a superb and erect soldier, a man fearless to the point of folly, but in whose inflamed mind this war assumed the monstrous semblance of a merciless crusade against the powers of hell and who believed his sword to be the weapon of God's wrath hungry for the blood of the enemies of Puritanism. He did not fail in that pursuit. He lived in a continual state of religious intoxication,

---

[160] Baynes MSS., 21417, fol. 49, 69; Fairfax Correspondence, 36996, fol. 149; Whitelocke, 265, 269, 270-3; Rushworth, vii, 777, 808, 824, 831-3, 859; Clarke Papers, i, 418 and ii, 252; Tanner MSS., lvi, i.

being of such exuberant vivacity and hilarity that it seemed always as though he had "drunken a cup too much." But he was honest and upright, and as a soldier had a splendid skill and energy.

The bonds of peace did not long unite a restive people. Parliament and Army were at odds; and the King's attempts to play off the one against the other, his refusal of the lenient and enlightened Proposals by the Army, and his new entanglement with the Scots had kindled fresh fires in the ranks of the New Model and around their flames the sinister voices of the Levellers rose to an angry pitch. Constitutional opposition developed into a revolutionary assault upon the essence of monarchical government, and Puritanism, which might have become bracing and humanising, became instead bitter and astringent. But men had not fought the King in order that he might be replaced by a Parliament of sour faces, still less by a junta of Ironside soldiers, of Cromwells and Iretons and Rainsboroughs, who threatened to overthrow so much that was embedded in the hearts of Englishmen,

> And cast the Kingdoms old
> Into another mould.

So much of sentiment, so much of rapturous vision, so much doubt, perplexity and despair blew into the quick forge and workhouse of men's thoughts that few save men like Ireton could think clearly, few could remember what the King had been or see what Parliament might become.

The smouldering embers flamed at last. In March, 1648, John Poyer gave the signal for the royalist rising by seizing Pembroke for the King. All over the country there were little outbreaks by the Cavaliers. But the worst danger was from the North. On April 28th Marmaduke Langdale, marching out of

Scotland, surprised Berwick, and a day or two later Carlisle was seized by Sir Philip Musgrave.

But behind the little English forces of Langdale and Musgrave there lay the greater threat of an impending invasion from Scotland. Imbued on the one hand with the tradition of royalism, but on the other with a passionate determination to maintain Presbyterianism, the Scots resolved in March to deliver Charles from his captivity and to suppress in England the tender consciences who were daily casting off the prescribed orthodoxy of Presbyterianism for the queer garments of newer faiths. Such was the fruit of the secret "Engagement" made with Charles in his captivity at Carisbrooke on December 26th of the previous year, and in fulfilment of it the Duke of Hamilton, who represented a moderate left or centre party, having secured a majority against the party of the Marquess of Argyll, and supported by the brigade of English cavaliers already in the field under Langdale and Musgrave, began to assemble an army for the invasion of that country where they had so lately fought as the allies of the Roundheads.

Thus there was sudden crisis over all Britain. Cromwell was tied to Pembroke, Fairfax was engaged against the Kentish rebels and soon to be held fast before Colchester, and to Major-General Lambert, not yet twenty-nine years old, fell the critical task of the defence of the North. He had, scattered over five counties, a command of not more than 5,000 men, and although among them were three or four of the finest regiments in the New Model, including the cavalry of Robert Lilburne and Harrison and some of Cromwell's own, the remainder were local levies.

Seldom has so young a commander been set a more difficult strategic task, for, not knowing which route the Scots might take, he had to defend the whole breadth of northern England from sea to sea, and the gateways to the two only roads — Berwick and Carlisle, seventy miles apart on opposite coasts — were both in the hands of the enemy, open to the gathering forces of Hamilton's "Engagers." Hamilton's army soon rose to more than 10,000, but it was not of the same stuff as Leven's army that had helped to save the day at Marston Moor, ill-organised, poorly provided, without artillery, and led by quarrelsome and jealous generals under a weak and vacillating chief. His best troops, until Monro joined him, were Langdale's English. Moreover, the threat of invasion by their old northern enemies roused the national spirit in many Englishmen, who though they might be royalists at heart, had no mind to submit to a Scottish domination.

Lambert did his work brilliantly. He set himself to raise new levies in Yorkshire and Lancashire, then he marched against Langdale, who was aiming at getting through to his waiting friends in Yorkshire, forced him to turn back towards Carlisle, and although Langdale sought to avoid action, he struck him again and again, harassing him by day and by night, and cutting up his rearguard in their quarters. He re-took Appleby and four other castles and finally shut Langdale up in Carlisle. This was in June, 1648, and John established himself at Penrith, having now made fairly certain that his tactics would succeed in obliging Hamilton to march at first to Carlisle in order to unite with Langdale's 4,000 English.

He had no sooner turned North against Langdale, however, than the Yorkshire royalists behind him took advantage of his preoccupation. On June 1st Colonel John Morris, having guilefully cultivated the friendship of the governor of Pontefract Castle, sharing his bed with him and having the freedom of all the defences, had gained admission by stealth for a party of his friends disguised as countrymen and, with the object of giving Langdale a focal point for a new rising, seized the castle for the King. Lambert's position, and that of the Parliamentary cause were full of danger. Militia troops had to be sent against Pontefract and Robert Lilburne had to be sent off to crush a force under Sir Richard Tempest.

On July 8th Hamilton crossed the border with his blue bonnets and his banners of St. Andrew and sent his trumpeter with a letter to John at Penrith, urging him not to oppose the royalists in the "pious, loyal and necessary undertaking" of rescuing the King, enforcing the Presbyterian Covenant and freeing the English Parliament from the soldiers, but John sent the trumpeter back forthwith with an answer that neatly exposed the shallowness of these pretexts, and declared that if Hamilton invaded England he would oppose him "to the utmost of my power."[161]

These were only the formal civilities of the time, and both sides prepared for the struggle. For John the position was full of perplexity. With his mere brigade he could not hope to meet the royalists in pitched battle, and he had had to detach some of his best troops to invest Pontefract. The Engagers might still make across towards Newcastle, or, if they kept to the western route, might turn left across the Pennine Range by one of several passes to make for Pontefract, which John was convinced would be their first objective, since it would afford a rallying point for all the North.

The young general had to resolve how best he could frustrate that purpose without an open battle, which if he were defeated would leave Hamilton with an open door to all the North and Midlands. The way in which he accomplished that design provided the first instance of real military strategy in the Civil

---

[161] Rushworth, vii, 1193-5; Whitelocke, 321-2.

Wars, and was not unworthy of Davout or his imperial master himself.

The course on which he resolved was, not to retire in face of them, but to pin them down to the west coast road, to threaten their flank continually and to deny them any help from their friends in Yorkshire, to be ready to fight them in the narrow passes of the Pennines if they should try to cross them to their friends in Yorkshire and otherwise to keep his army intact until help, for which he now sent to Parliament an urgent call, should arrive from the South.

It was a season of exceptional violence. For the ensuing six weeks the rain fell in an almost continuous downpour and frequent storms swept the whole of the North. From the overcharged rivers and ditches floods spread over the valley ways, and in the hills the trivial roads became often impassable for deep mud. As Hamilton advanced in the rain, with the eager Langdale's English in the van, Lambert, after a further exchange of letters, retired before them, bending south-eastward from Penrith to Appleby, with Harrison's regiment of horse in the rearguard.

At Appleby John remained for the week-end, and on Sunday his cavalry stood-to all night in pouring rain expecting an attack. None came, and with the daylight they were dismissed to their quarters for rest. But at eleven o'clock of a dark and rain-swept morning, Langdale's horsemen and some Scots appeared suddenly on the hills and swept down upon the town. Lambert sprang to arms, and in a vivid action lit by the fiery courage of Harrison, whose grasp upon an enemy's colours three sword cuts could not unloose, he not only beat off the enemy decisively, but, turning defence to attack as he had done before, moved out from his ground and drove the enemy back upon their main body.[162]

Continuing his retreat, he left a garrison in Appleby Castle to delay the enemy further, and Langdale was occupied for two days in front of it before the garrison surrendered on honourable terms. From Appleby, his men in rags and "shod with blood" but sustained by a splendid discipline, John bore away almost due east through the Stainmore Pass, in order to deny the enemy that entry into Yorkshire if they should attempt it, stopping all passages towards Stainmore, delving trenches and diverting the flooded ditches to hinder their approach, and preparing to fight if they should attempt that way. His resistance at this point persuaded the Engagers to continue still by the westerly road, as he desired they should, and he did not hesitate then to draw right way from them still farther east as far as Barnard Castle, just within the borders of County Durham, on July 17th. As he rode through those desolate hills a great storm raged from the north-east, the floods and the driving rain carrying away the mown hay, drowning the ripened corn, sweeping away trees by the roots and flooding the coal mines.[163]

Indecision, foul weather, and frequent quarrels among his generals made Hamilton's march fatefully slow, and it was not until August 2nd that he arrived at Kendal, where he was joined by Sir George Monro and 3,000 veteran Scots from Ireland, so that they now were an army of 21,000 men. On the other hand Lambert had been joined at Barnard Castle by Cromwell's cavalry, which had been hurried up from Wales by forced marches, and he now knew that Oliver himself, released by the fall of Pembroke on July 11th, had been ordered by

---

¹⁶² *Perfect Diurnall*, letter from an officer (E., 525, 8); Hodgson, 112-113; Rushworth, vii, 1201.
¹⁶³ *The Moderate Intelligencer*, E.457, 33.

Parliament to answer his call for help and, at Lambert's urgent request that he should hasten, was hurrying north.

Learning next that from Kendal a strong royalist force had been thrown out eastwards past Sedbergh and Dent which might surprise him through the Wensleydale pass, Lambert moved on August 3rd down to Richmond. He was now forty miles away from the enemy, yet he was fulfilling his purpose as effectively as if he had been in close contact. He had his scouts among them constantly and was kept always advised of their numbers, their route and their demeanour. He intercepted their letters almost daily and sent them up to London. Oliver had sent him a message not to engage until he arrived, and he knew that he must hang on somehow till Oliver came. Moreover, he knew that Cromwell was coming, not directly towards the royalists' line of march, but up through the centre of England, in order to obtain supplies from the Midlands for his shoeless men and ordnance from Hull, and because John had informed him of his expectation that the royalists would turn into Yorkshire.

At Richmond John received intelligence which showed that Hamilton would not advance through Wensleydale, but by Ribblesdale and the valley of the Aire through his own Craven; he therefore bent his march southward to Knaresborough to cover Pontefract, and at last, near Knaresborough on August 13th, Cromwell and Lambert joined hands.

Forthwith on the next day they turned together westward, still expecting to have to fight in Craven. But they passed through Lambert's country still without meeting the enemy, and, crossing the Pennine range by the valley of the Ribble, dropped down into the plain of Lancashire, to find that Hamilton's main body lay straight ahead at Preston and that they were riding down right upon his flank.

From their scouts they learnt that the Engagers, an ill-knit and quarrelsome company, had after much wavering decided still to continue by the western road, but were strung out over a space of twenty-five miles without coherence, yet so placed that they might, by any one of two or three tactical moves, have placed the Puritans within the jaws of destruction. Hamilton himself was at Preston; thrown out on his left flank to watch the passes into Yorkshire, and now immediately in Cromwell's path, was Marmaduke Langdale with 3,600 good English; Monro, having disloyally refused to serve under Baillie and Callander, wasted his splendid regiments as a rearguard a full day's march behind with some English cavaliers under Sir Philip Musgrave; Baillie with the main body of Scottish foot was about to cross the Ribble on his southward course ahead of Hamilton; and the cavalry was straggling, "like a flock of sheep ill-knit," for fifteen miles ahead along the road to Wigan.

Cromwell was therefore confronted with two strategic alternatives. On that day, beside the bridge that spanned the river Hodder just above its junction with the Ribble, he held a council of war with Lambert and his colonels. He could either turn south and place himself across the head of the enemy's long column, or he could cross the bridge and strike into the enemy's flank at Preston. By the first plan, if he were defeated he would have a retreat to the Midlands, but if he were victorious so also would Hamilton have a retreat into Scotland. By the second plan there was scarcely hope of escaping destruction if he failed, but if he succeeded he would cut the retreat of all the royalists except Monro's rearguard and, by driving them southwards, not only defeat them but destroy them.

He chose the second course.

It was typical of Cromwell that he should thus "put it to the touch, to win or lose it all"; and one must pass by the temptation to surmise whether that "deliberate advice" may not have come from the "subtle and working brain" we have seen throughout this campaign and that we shall see again…

So Oliver and John lay that night of August 16th at Stonyhurst Park, nine miles from Preston and three from Marmaduke Langdale. Save for Ralph Ashton's Lancashire levies, their troops were all superb regiments of the New Model, but they numbered no more than 8,600 against Hamilton's 21,000. Therefore, when Hamilton the next morning heard that Langdale was being furiously attacked, he held back only two of Baillie's Scottish brigades and 1,500 cavalry to cover Preston, not knowing that it was Ironside himself who was upon him.

But it was indeed Ironside at his most terrible. Early on that summer morning Cromwell and Lambert, with John Hodgson at the head of the forlorn hope of foot, advanced over Ribble Moor in a deluge of rain and threw the finest regiments in the world upon Langdale's few. They found that that grim soldier, giving them no opportunity of repeating Naseby, had skilfully lodged his infantry in a web of hedges spread over ground which under the heavy rains had become a swamp. To clear that bristling fortress of hedges was the work of infantry, so Lambert took a pike and fought that day on foot at the head of Bright's regiment. For four hours the infantry wrestled among the dripping hedgerows, Bright's regiment being often at push of pike and earning Cromwell's special praise. At length Langdale's men, after one of the most courageous stands in the Civil Wars, were driven back inexorably to the outskirts of Preston. There Cromwell's horsemen dashed in among them and among the reserve brigades with Hamilton, turning the defeat into hopeless rout, and swinging so from the right wing that the royalists, save for a few flying horsemen who galloped northwards to Monro, were thrown headlong southwards, surrendering in thousands to a remorseless cavalry from which there was no escape.

But this was only the beginning. Hard by beyond the Ribble Baillie's 7,000 Scottish foot had not raised a finger to succour Langdale, and now the Puritans, with their ranks facing south, seized the bridge over the river, fell upon Baillie's men, and under the weeping grey skies of that summer's evening drove them still farther south over the Darwen, for they in their turn were denied the help of their own cavalry. Night fell to grant a little rest, and as Lambert floundered through the mud to a council of war with Cromwell, he knew that, spite of their sweeping victory, they still had ahead of them an army much larger than their own, and behind them Monro's threatening rearguard.

But when the next day dawned Hamilton was gone, in hopeless flight. So throughout that Friday, August 18th, with the rain ringing on his armour and his standard clinging to its pole, Lambert joined in a remorseless pursuit, every hour adding to the huge toll of drenched and weary prisoners in spite of repeated charges by the Scottish cavalry, while Monro in the rear played a coward's part and turned for Scotland.

On the morning of the 19th, passing through Wigan, Cromwell was again hard upon the Engagers' heels, and at Winwick, three miles from Warrington, he forced Baillie's infantry to turn and fight and utterly crushed them. It was now a frank rout. For mile after mile Cromwell's few horsemen, their mounts so tired that they could move no faster than a walk, pursued the blue bonnets across the flat Mersey plain, their swords ever rising and falling, and prisoners coming in "in drifts." Many had had no sleep for four nights save what they could snatch on horseback. At Warrington there was a last scuffle, and here, on Hamilton's order, Baillie with all the remaining Scots infantry surrendered.

Hamilton himself made away into Cheshire with 3,000 horse, hoping to join Byron from Wales, but now Lambert was left in charge of the pursuit by Cromwell with four regiments, while Oliver himself turned north towards Scotland. John, no less exhausted than the enemy, could do no more than follow in their path, but it was only a matter of time. Hamilton drifted away into Staffordshire, but every man's hand was against him and the trained bands turned out as he passed to harass him; for, says James Turner, "there was no visible party for the King in England to join with."

Coming to Uttoxeter on the 22nd in tempestuous weather, Hamilton's troops mutinied and Callander rode away from him after a stormy quarrel. Hamilton began to treat for surrender with the governor of Stafford, but on the 25th Lambert rode into Uttoxeter out of the mire and claimed him as his prisoner of war. "We found him," says Turner, "very discreet and his expressions civil enough." Anxious to save Hamilton from arrest as a political prisoner by Lord Grey of Groby, whom he knew was approaching, Lambert secured the royalists' immediate signature to articles of capitulation as prisoners of war by which they were assured of their lives. The articles had no sooner been signed than Grey rode up and seized the person of Hamilton. Lambert, however, would not countenance this high-handedness and insisted on the observance of the articles which had been signed as between soldiers. It was not his fault that they were afterwards shamefully forsworn by Bradshaw's court and that Hamilton, with Norwich, Holland and others fell to the headsman's axe.[164]

Preston was thus far Cromwell's most splendid military achievement; his dispositions in his initial attack upon Langdale and his subsequent sweeping movement southward were masterly. But his opportunity he owed entirely to Jack Lambert. His had been the subtlety. His had been the "working brain" that had realised the strategic issues from the first moment, and, using the configuration of those northern highlands to brilliant purpose, had persuaded the enemy into a bad strategy first by denying him an entry into the North Riding plains, and then, discarding the obvious course of a frontal opposition, had from a distance continually threatened his flank and pinned him down to the straitened path of the western defile.

The results of the battle were shattering. The Engagers' army had ceased to exist, and Cromwell's forces, which never exceeded 8,600 men, and for the greater part of the action were considerably less, had taken over 10,000 prisoners. The disposal of them was a serious problem, but Parliament solved it by releasing all soldiers who had been pressed, and shipping those who had volunteered off to the West Indies as slaves.

----

[164] The chief authorities for the Preston campaign, from which this account is taken, are:

On the royalist side — Burnet's *Memoirs of the Lives of the Dukes of Hamilton*, 1677, 354-364; Sir James Turner's *Memoirs*, ed. 1829; Langdale's narrative in *Civil War Tracts of Lancashire* (Cheetham Society, 1844); *Letter from Holland*, E.467, 21.

On the Parliamentary side — Cromwell's *Letters and Speeches*, i, 329-47; Hodgson's *Memoirs*, 112-123; several newspapers of the day, particularly *The Moderate* (E., 457, 21), *The Moderate Intelligencer* (E., 457, 33), *Perfect Diurnall* (E., 525, 8 and 9), and *Perfect Occurrences* (E., 525, 15 and 17), which give generally reliable accounts of Lambert's flank march; Clarke Papers, ii, 20-22, 195-7; Fairfax Correspondence, B.M., 36996; Rushworth, vii, 1148- 1238, *passim*; Whitelocke, 308-324, *passim*.

III. ONWARD TO DUNBAR

Cromwell was never a man who failed to make a victory twice itself by following it home to the heart. If Hamilton's Engagers had been crushed there yet remained Scotland itself, and in September, though leaving stubborn Pontefract still undefeated, he was upon the Scottish border, ready to step over. But Preston scattered Hamilton's cause in Scotland as well as in England, and the Marquess of Argyll had already one foot in the stirrup and was only too glad that the English should help to swing him safely into the saddle. When he asked for troops it was to Lambert, so high had his reputation grown, that Cromwell entrusted the important mission, and thus, just after his thirtieth birthday, the major-general rode forward to Edinburgh with seven regiments of horsemen, and was received with every honour. Cromwell followed him into Edinburgh on October 4th, but three days later returned to England, leaving Lambert to support Argyll with the regiments of Robert Lilburne and Philip Twistleton.

The Scots did not like Oliver, whom Robert Blair described as "an egregious dissembler and a great liar," but John's charm of manner and his handsome soldierly person won them at once, though they made murderous attacks on his men in the streets. They were pleased by his "discreet, humble, ingenuous, sweet and civil deportment," and Turner, to whose wife he showed kindness, says he was so well entertained that when a different summons came two years later he looked forward to returning.

His work accomplished, John took leave of the Scots on November 6th with many expressions of thanks from the

Committee of Estates, and on November 13th he joined Cromwell's forces in the siege of Pontefract Castle, where the audacious Morris was still defiantly holding out for the King, and where a week earlier had been perpetrated a deed of blood that was already crying out for a bloodier revenge. Hearing that the fiery Thomas Rainsborough, the seaman-colonel so hated of royalists, was lying at Doncaster, Capt. William Paulden stole out of Pontefract Castle with twelve horse on the night of October 28th, and coming by devious ways to Rainsborough's lodging early the next morning, summoned him from his bed under pretext of being messengers from Cromwell, and ran him through the body.

So a turbulent career was brought to its rude close, but Morris's men had served their royal master an ill turn, for the blood of Rainsborough, the idol of the proletarian Levellers, raised a cry throughout the army for the blood of him who was deemed the grand author of all these crimes. "*Avenge, O Lord, Thy slaughtered saints!*" The mutual good feeling and chivalry of the first war were gone. Men who had been content after Naseby and Langport that clemency and forbearance should be extended to those who differed honestly from themselves now felt a ferment of resentment that the settlement of the country should have been bloodily disturbed by those who had given their parole to sheathe the sword, by those others, who, like Morris and Poyer and Henry Lilburne, had in 1648 changed sides and risen against their old friends, and above all by him who politically was inconstant and changeful as the winds.

The fervent brain of Ireton was even now hatching the final sorcery. Fire burned and cauldron bubbled; and as the vapours gathered about the head of the doomed king Cromwell himself hastened to London to be ready for the tragic deliverance. He left Lambert in command of operations in the North, but

Lambert's army, like the rest of the New Model, was now seething with the frenzy of politics. News came to them of Ireton's fateful "Remonstrance of the Army," in which he had demanded that the King should be brought to justice and had outlined a future government of the country by freely-elected Parliaments. Lambert's officers thereupon assembled at a meeting at Pontefract on December 12th, appointed their own Council of Officers, named deputies to sit with the general Council of Officers at army headquarters, and drafted its own "Remonstrance." This document, which was sent to Fairfax under a covering letter signed by Lambert, made no specific reference to the trial of the King, but nevertheless urged that Ireton's "Remonstrance of the Army" should be speedily acted upon.[165]

This is the only evidence of Lambert's attitude towards the trial of the King, and though he was active in persuading officers to join in the declaration, there were suspicions that he was not whole-hearted.[166] When the monstrous "court" was presently appointed John was named as a member of it, but like Fairfax, Skippon and many others who regarded that method of procedure with horror, he took no part in it, remaining at his military duties. When on January 19th, 1649, his Council of Officers met again at Pontefract and wrote to Fairfax applauding the trial, Lambert's name was not associated with it, for he was away in the East Riding.[167]

His time was occupied again riding throughout Yorkshire and Lancashire enforcing unwilling disbandments of the militia — "a difficult and troublesome business," he wrote — and again the same praise of his personal qualities is heard. Not till

---

[165] Rushworth, vii, 1366, 1367.
[166] Clarke Papers, ii, 70 (Margetts to Clarke).
[167] Rushworth, vii, 1399, 1400.

these disbandments were over was he able to concentrate upon the siege of Pontefract, "this unlucky hole" as he called it. His presence at once gave a new vigour to the siege. The town was in his hands and he pressed so close upon the castle that the garrison killed many of his men with stones. On its lofty rock the place was almost impregnable even against the heavy mortars that were brought against it, but at long last, when all hope for the King's cause seemed dead and when Charles had been nearly two months in his grave, the defenders, after a nine months' siege, surrendered on March 21st, 1649, to terms in which John gave freedom to all but Morris and five others concerned in the murder of Rainsborough; even so the resourceful defenders contrived by mock sallies that the six should escape, though Morris was ultimately captured and executed.

So was brought to a successful close Jack Lambert's second campaign, and on instructions from London he destroyed the castle that had given such trouble to Parliament during four years. On March 27th, on the earnest recommendation of Fairfax, a grateful Parliament voted to him and his heirs £300 a year out of the demesnes of Pontefract, which were part of the Queen's jointure, in recognition of his services and of the fact that he had not received any pay as a major-general. He found the revenue from these demesnes "a very distracted thing," but he was also granted some part of Marmaduke Langdale's Yorkshire estates.[168]

For the rest of the year 1649 Lambert pursued quieter ways. He did not go with Cromwell on his memorable Irish campaign, and for some time was still busy at disbandments. In

---

[168] C. J., vi, 174, 406; Baynes MSS., 21417, fol. 98; Yorkshire Archaeological Society, Record Series, Vol. XX, No. 550, p. 159. See also the interesting draft in Baynes MSS., 21,427, fol. 125.

May came to him news that Parliament, rejecting the rule of kings, had "declared and enacted" that "the people of England, and of all the dominions and territories thereunto belonging, are and shall be, and are hereby constituted, made, established, and confirmed, to be a Commonwealth and Free State."

In June Lambert was in London, where for a while he occupied Holland House, the splendid residence of the peer who had recently been executed. Very shortly, however, he moved to the little thirteen-acres estate of Coldhern, in the hamlet of Earl's Court, which his wife had inherited by the death of her father the previous year. This for the next four years was the home of the Lamberts, but in a bare twelve months the drums called John himself once more to horse and led him to the field of his greatest exploits.[169]

For, in May, 1650, the young Charles Stuart had decided at last that Scotland was well worth a Covenant, especially if the Scots would lift him into the richer throne of England. The unhappy youth, who surrendered his conscience when, at the price of betraying the Church of England, he set his insincere hand to that document, surrendered also his honour when he thirled himself to the bondage of a bigoted kirk and embraced the extremist party which had not only aided in his father's destruction but which now also flourished before his eyes the mutilated limb of one who had lost all for his cause; for the severed arm of Montrose, Montrose hanged and dismembered by that party which called Charles back from exile, hung rotting above the gate of Aberdeen as he passed.

In truth the Covenanters who drove this cynical bargain with Charles were no less hypocritical than he and had small respect for the lad with the crooked smile, for in Scotland intolerance now had the upper hand. He was little more to them than a

---

169 Lysons, *Environs of London* (1795), iii, 205.

trade-mark for their nationalism, an emblem under which they might rouse the people to do battle with their traditional enemy beyond the hills and under which the narrow-minded clerics who now dominated affairs might call upon all good Presbyterians to unite and to trample upon the atheistical saints of the unorthodox. He should lead them again against the English and the Anabaptists. But beyond the Cheviots was now a government that was unequalled in the world for its swift efficiency. Energy, discipline and foresight were theirs. They were intensely proud of being Englishmen, whom they knew to be God's chosen people, and they were ready to stand up for the rights of Englishmen against all the potentates of Europe. Those who set out to establish their authority in the farthest bounds of the Atlantic and to challenge the supremacy of the world's greatest sea power were not likely to be complacent under the threat of a Scottish invasion. They resolved to strike first. Not England but Scotland should be invaded.

To this Fairfax, who was still commander-in-chief and who had now succeeded his father in the peerage, demurred. He put forward technical scruples against invading Scotland, but they were but a cloak to hide his deeper moral repugnance to the whole new regimen. Lambert was one of those deputed with Cromwell to endeavour to overcome his objections, but their famous meeting with him at Whitehall on June 24th was fruitless, and he therefore resigned his commission. Thus at last Cromwell came to the command in chief as Captain-General, and it was not surprising that for his major-general of foot and second-in-command, he chose his splendid lieutenant of Preston — dear Johnnie Lambert. Charles Fleetwood was his lieutenant-general of horse. Four days later they started for the North.

As they rode out by the Oxford road and turned right on the way to Edgware, passing the Tyburn gallows, a prophetic conversation took place that Lambert was to recall in the unhappy circumstances to come. The people were shouting and wishing them success as Cromwell and Lambert rode by with a body of officers, and John observed to Oliver:

"I am glad we have the nation on our side."

To which Cromwell answered prophetically:

"Do not trust to that, for these very people would shout as much if you and I were going to be hanged."[170]

As they marched, picking up the regiments stationed in the North, the army grew to a total of 16,400 men, of whom two-thirds were infantry, and it was perhaps the finest English army that has ever been put into the field. Its eight regiments of horse were Cromwell's own, Lambert's own, Edward Whalley's, Francis Hacker's, Robert Lilburne's, Fleetwood's, Twistleton's and Okey's famous dragoons; its infantry were the regiments of Cromwell, Thomas Pride, Mauleverer, Charles Fairfax (Thomas's uncle), Coxe, Daniel, Overton, and John Bright. Veterans all, and several of them regiments that had fought under Lambert in the North. Already there had become apparent a marked change among its officers; Fairfax was not the only man of gentle breeding to leave its ranks, and the men who were coming to the front more and more were men like Hewson, the one-eyed cobbler-colonel, Pride the drayman, Okey the chandler.

On their arrival at Newcastle Colonel Bright threw up his command, and Cromwell was minded to give his regiment to George Monck, who, having taken arms as a royalist, had been taken prisoner at Nantwich by this very regiment, had been

---

[170] Clarendon S. P., in, 735; Burnet, *History of Own Time*, ed. 1833, i, 155.

imprisoned in the Tower, but had lately taken service with the Commonwealth. Cromwell therefore sent some colonels to address Bright's regiment as it was paraded at Alnwick and to ask them whom they would have as colonel, but they replied they knew not whom. The colonels asked if they would have Colonel Monck?

"Colonel Monck!" exclaimed some of them with prophetic vision, "What! to betray us? We took him prisoner not long since at Nantwich; we'll have none of him."

The next day the colonels came again, and, instructed by Cromwell, asked if they would have Major-General Lambert as their colonel, at which all threw up their hats, and shouted:

"*A Lambert! A Lambert!*"[171]

So the young general, in addition to his cavalry, took as his own a regiment he had so often led into battle, and Monck was provided with a new regiment made up partly from Hazelrig's regiment at Newcastle and partly from Fenwick's; thus was born the oldest existing English regiment in the British Army — the Coldstream Guards.

On July 22nd, after issuing various friendly declarations to the Scots, Cromwell crossed the border, entrusting the vanguard to Lambert. His plan was to march straight on Edinburgh, and, since he would be in hostile country, to provision his army from the little ports of Dunbar and Musselburgh, to which command of the sea gave an assured access for the Commonwealth ships. As John advanced through Berwickshire and East Lothian the beacons flamed from hill to hill. He found the villages emptied of men save the very old, and, as his regiments passed, pitiful women, "sorry creatures, clothed in white flannel," bemoaning that the lairds had forced their menfolk "to gang to the muster," shrank back

---

[171] Hodgson, 139; E. 609, 1.

from them, fearful that, as the Kirk had told them, Cromwell's soldiers would thrust red-hot irons through their breasts. Farm and cottage were swept bare of provisions, and cattle driven off.

The Scots had prepared for the challenge with energy and astuteness, and had assembled at Edinburgh an army of 32,000 men — just twice the strength of the English — under the nominal command of old Lord Leven, but actually led by the same David Leslie who had charged beside Cromwell at Marston Moor and who was now to manifest a generalship of high order. But from the beginning the unfortunate Leslie was cursed by the stridulations of the clerics who dominated military as well as civil councils and demanded that the army should be purged not only of all the old royalist "cavaliers," but even of Hamilton's Engagers.

No attempt was made to stop the advance of the English until, marching by Musselburgh and the old battlefield of Pinkie, they found Leslie impregnably entrenched across the flank of Edinburgh, from Canongate to the sea. After an attempt on St. Leonard's Hill Cromwell was forced to draw off, and that night his men spent shelterless and sleepless in a tempest of driving rain. On the next day, the 30th, wet through and unfed, they began to march back upon Musselburgh for rest and refreshment, with Lambert now entrusted with the rearguard, but no sooner had they turned about than Leslie's men were upon them, "swarming out like bees, horse and foot" to harass the rear.

From right and from left bodies of lancers swept down under the eyes of the boy King, with cries of "Remember Pontefract" from Morris's English cavaliers who charged with them. Upon Lambert's cavalry and two other regiments fell their full impetus. Cromwell's regiment charged and checked them, but a fresh onslaught put even the Ironsides into jeopardy. Whereupon John, having repulsed the attack upon himself, wheeled his cavalry about and with Whalley riding beside him threw himself upon the enemy as they harried Cromwell's men, shook them off and pursued them to their own trenches.

But in that charge, or in a counter-charge by the swarming lancers, his horse, shot in the neck and head, went down beneath him. As he stood unhorsed a lance ran him through the arm and another through the thigh. He was taken prisoner. He was dragged back towards the Scots lines. But Lieutenant Empson, of Cromwell's regiment, had seen his red sash go down. Collecting a handful of men, he spurred forward in pursuit, cut down Lambert's captors and repaid his regiment's debt. John was brought back to the safety of his own foot regiment, where he was placed on a fast horse.[172]

He made his way into Musselburgh and for a fortnight was incapacitated. Cromwell retired to Dunbar to provision, returning to Musselburgh on August 12th, and here Jack Lambert rejoined him.[173] Oliver now began a new attempt to reach the Scottish capital, but for the first time in his career he was faced by a general of real ability, a general accomplished in Fabian tactics, and he was being outpointed. Leslie knew his Cromwell. Oliver wanted a swift rough-and-tumble, but Leslie forced him into the harder trial of chess. Cromwell, seeking a new approach, moved round Edinburgh southwards by Braid Hills and so gradually to the west, but at each rook's move Leslie side-stepped to conform, steadily refusing action and

---

[172] Cromwell, cxxxv; Hodgson, 132-4; *Large Relation of the Fight at Leith*, E. 609, 1; *True Relation of the Proceedings of the English Army*, E. 608, 23.
[173] E. 778, 21.

keeping himself on the high ground between the English and the sea, with lake-land and bog as his bastions; for it was again a very wet August, and the driving rain made every hollow a swamp. Dysentery began to ravage Cromwell's ranks. There was frequent skirmishing, and a half-hearted attempt to seek peace by negotiation. The Scots had small trust in their new King, whom the merciless Kirk had now pressed into signing a humiliating acknowledgment of his father's iniquity and his mother's idolatry. On August 20th Lambert himself had a conference on the hills with Archibald Strachan, the vanquisher of Montrose and a rigid Presbyterian deeply distrustful of Charles, but the meeting was fruitless.[174]

Frustrated, and with his army ravaged by dysentery, Cromwell fell back again upon Musselburgh on August 28th, with Leslie treading sharply on his heels, and there he embarked 500 sick. The rain fell incessantly, as it had done just two years before. On August 30th Lambert attended a council of war at which it was resolved that they must retreat once more to Dunbar. On the 31st, with "a poor, shattered, hungry, discouraged army," now only 12,000 strong from the wastage of sickness, they struck camp, and the next day, with Leslie's horsemen tearing at their heels, arrived in a downpour at Dunbar.

---

[174] E. 610, 8; E. 612, 14. Though Charles had signed the Presbyterian Covenant, he yet assured the Irish that he was "a true cavalier" and "a true child of the Church of England."

IV. TRIUMPH ON DOON HILL

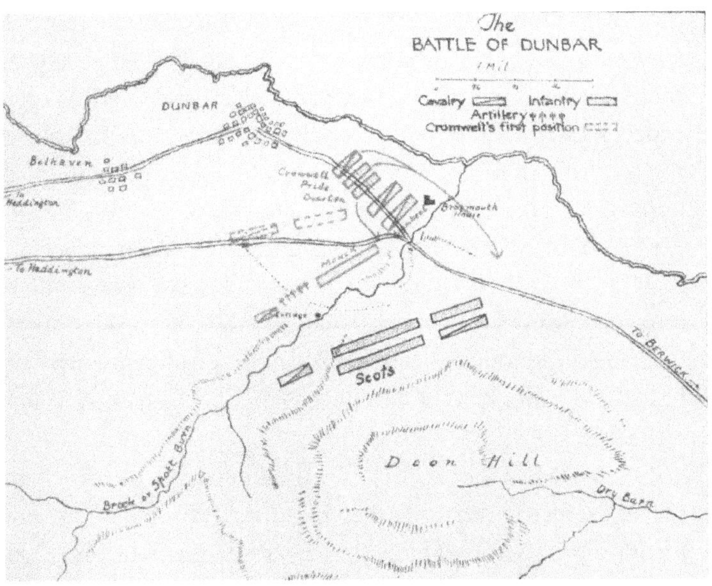

Dunbar lies on the flank of a squat promontory where the coast of Scotland looks roughly to the north. To the southward the rolling Lammermoors dominate it. Save for the sea, Cromwell's only road to the safety of England was the Berwick road issuing south-eastward close to the coast. Crossed by this road, and flowing into the sea a mile or so east of Dunbar, was the Brock, or Spot, burn, flowing through its inland course in a deep gorge, but emerging between shallower banks at a point about a mile and a half from the sea. Between this point and the sea the Brocksburn was fordable at three points, and near its mouth, on the Dunbar side, stood Broxmouth House. South of the Brock lay the height of Doon Hill, a spur of the

Lammermoors, crossed at its northern instep by the Berwick road.

High on this hill Leslie implanted his army of 22,000 men, with his front diagonally protected by the Brock ravine, his right flank dominating the Berwick road that was Cromwell's only escape. The English lay far below him floundering in the water-logged ground of Dunbar fields, and drawn up in expectation of attack, their left flank resting on Broxmouth House, and their ranks stretching obliquely away from the burn, facing south across the shoulders of the Dunbar peninsula. Their strength "as to sound men" was now no more than 11,000. They were, as Cromwell himself noted, in the same predicament as that by which Essex and Skippon had been encompassed at Lostwithiel six years ago to the very day. Leslie had trapped them in a corner from which there was no tactical escape.

But just when he in his own turn intended to give battle, Oliver refused. Instead, he began preparations to build fortifications before Dunbar and to sit down behind them, with the friendly sea for his communications, until help should come from England. This did not at all suit Leslie. He had no relish for the idea of a winter siege, lying out upon the bleak Lammermoors in a country stripped of all food. Moreover, the ministers of the Kirk, chanting upon that Sabbath the war-cries of the priests of Israel, thirsted for the destruction of the Moabites. On Monday, September 2nd, Leslie came down from Doon Hill.

All day high winds blew with a tempest of rain. Having dined hurriedly in Dunbar, Lambert stood in the grounds of Broxmouth House with Cromwell at about five o'clock that afternoon and watched the descent of the "Jockies." Blue bonnets, banners of St. Andrew, moving spinneys of up-pointed pikes, squadrons of gleaming lances, crept down slowly under the driving rain in solid cubes across the glowing heather. They settled at last in the stubble of the sloping fields studded with the shocks of gathered corn, with their left wing resting securely on the deep ravine of the burn in its upper course and their right upon the Berwick road. Here to-morrow they would attack the English and drive them into the sea. Their horses on the wings began to munch the corn, and in the centre the infantry took shelter from the rain beneath the standing shocks.

But the quick eye of Jack Lambert had seen at once the chance of an advantage against them. He saw that although Leslie's left wing on the burn was cramped and crowded, his right wing had not been extended to the sea. In that space of a few hundred yards a bold commander with skilled soldiers, by a swift knight's move, might surprise the enemy flank, and, with the cramped left wing unable to manoeuvre, roll up the whole army from right to left. Beat the right wing and the whole Scots army would be in confusion. But such a plan involved a difficult manoeuvre by the English forces, for it meant that several regiments, particularly the cavalry of the right wing, must be edged sideways and forward in the face of the enemy. It was the manoeuvre that in its failure had brought the Covenanters to disaster at Kilsyth from the swift hand of Montrose.

The same thoughts were apparently also in Cromwell's mind, for he records that, having observed the new posture of the Scots, he turned to John and told him:

I thought it did, give us an opportunity and advantage to attempt upon the enemy, to which he immediately replied, that he had thought to have said the same thing to me. So that it pleased the Lord to set this apprehension upon both our hearts, at the same instant.[175]

George Monck, stolidly chewing his quid of tobacco, was called for, and they put the notion to him. That evening a general council of war was summoned. Several of the colonels were for embarking their foot while the cavalry cut their way through as Balfour had done at Lostwithiel. Lambert, however, argued vigorously for the flank attack, showing how it could roll up the Scottish front sideways and adding the further suggestion of an artillery concentration on the other wing. His arguments carried the council, and afterwards someone asked that Lambert "might have the conduct of the army that morning, which was granted by the General freely."

Accordingly it was planned that Lambert, having first prepared the order of battle as major-general, should direct the concentration of artillery on the right wing, and should then, although Fleetwood was the lieutenant-general of horse, ride over to command the cavalry on the critical left wing. He was to have six regiments with which to ford the Brocksburn at a point near its mouth.[176]

Behind this shock division was to be assembled a special force under Cromwell himself, consisting of two regiments of horse, including Cromwell's own, with Pride's and Overton's brigades of infantry. These were to follow Lambert across the Brocksburn, and then, inclining to the left along the coast, were to come into action beyond him and swing inwards to attack the Scots in flank and rear.

Monck, with a selected brigade of three and a half battalions of infantry was to command in the centre, where there was

---

[175] Cromwell, cxl.

[176] The regiments were: Lambert's own, Fleetwood's, Whalley's, Twistleton's, and probably Lilburne's and Hacker's.

another ford where the Berwick road crosses the burn. On the right, where the ravine was deep, were to be only a few cavalry with the massed batteries of guns to distract the enemy horse opposite. In preparation for the attack the whole line was immediately to effect a half-left wheel and form up close to the brook. It was a complete departure from the traditional battle formation.

So upon that wild night began the knight's-move to the left. The Scots, shivering in the rain among the stooks of corn, suspected no peril, for the English seemed at their mercy. Officers went to seek shelter; musketeers extinguished their matches save for two in every company. But behind the curtain of night and unheard above the cry of the wind and the surge of the sea, the veteran army beyond the brook was executing its deadly check-mate.

Quietly Lambert was ordering the regiments in the dark to the appointed places, swinging the right wing forward to the burn and shunting to the left the regiments to be massed for the essential battle'. Both his own regiments were there on the left — his horse in the van of the cavalry, his foot in Cromwell's flanking force.

Then, while a cornet of horse burst into prayer which gave new hope of deliverance to John Hodgson, Lambert rode over to assemble the artillery on the right. He found it difficult. The ground was boggy, and to move heavy pieces over drowned land is the hardest of labour. To site gun positions in the dark cannot be quickly done. The night wore on, and on the other wing Cromwell, riding on a little Scottish nag and biting his lips till the blood ran, and filled, as he often was before battle, with the boisterous ecstasy of a schoolboy on the eve of a holiday frolic, grew impatient. There were sounds of movement in the

Scottish lines. A trumpet sounded. At the hour of four the flying night-clouds parted, and the surprised moon,

> gleaming upon the random of the wind-swept night,

discovered an army still in some disorder. But in a moment the uneasy peace of night was shattered as the English guns spoke on the right. Under the cover of their fire Lambert sent forward a forlorn hope of cavalry to scramble across the ravine by the third ford and launch a feint attack upon the enemy beyond. That done, he rode hard to the left wing, and, placing himself at the head of the massed cavalry, gave the order to his trumpets and plunged forward over the stream.

Now over all the burn the line moved forward, and answering trumpets beyond the night anxiously called the soldiers of the Kirk to arms. Beyond the burn the English regiments re-formed from column into line of battle and drove in the Scottish outposts. About five o'clock, as the shadowy forms resolved themselves in the grey of approaching dawn, battle was joined. Surprised as they were, the Scots met the sudden attack with all the resourceful courage of their race. In the centre Monck met a force that outnumbered him by three to one, and though their matches were out they met the English with rigid pikes and with their deadly short swords. Monck was repulsed, and he drew back beyond the burn to re-form. On his left stirring things were happening. Lambert with his 2,500 sabres threw himself against twice that number and against the concentrated metal of the royalist guns. He threw them into instant confusion. But as he pressed his advantage there fell down upon him with all the impetus gathered from the hill-side the full weight of the Scottish lancers, and under the shock of that impact Lambert recoiled.

Behind him, however, and masked by his body of cavalry, were coming up the rear-guard brigades of foot and Cromwell's regiment of horse. Seeing the danger to Monck, Cromwell's foot regiment inclined to the right, coming in between Lambert and Monck, and at push of pike with great gallantry "did repel the stoutest regiment the enemy had there."[177] At the same time Lambert gave the word to the remainder of the flanking force, with Oliver himself at its head, to incline to the left, and they did so, their manoeuvre concealed in the dim dawn behind Lambert's own brigade. As they came up alongside him and turned inwards upon the enemy to the drums' beat John gathered his cavalry together again, sounded his trumpets, and swept once more up the hill.

His success was immediate. As with his swordsmen he drove through and through the massed regiments, the Covenanters' wing was shivered into ruin. The enemy, ran Cromwell's memorable dispatch, "were made by the Lord of Hosts as stubble to their swords." On Lambert's left, too, the advance of Cromwell's flanking force was only for a moment delayed; here the Highlanders of Lawers stood fast, fighting "at push of

---

[177] Cromwell's own foot regiment, I think, was more likely to have been with Overton's brigade than Pride's; otherwise it seems difficult to reconcile Cromwell's own report of how the regiment went to the relief of Monck with the operations of the flanking force. I think the whole of Overton's small brigade must have been thrown in between Monck and Lambert, and that the only troops in the flank attack were Pride's brigade and Cromwell's regiment of horse, and perhaps Okey's. Mr. Buchan does not mention this operation of Cromwell's foot, but in this point I have read the action in the same way as Sir Charles Firth, who, however, appears to think that Pride's brigade also came in at this point and that the only troops in the flanking force on the extreme left were Cromwell's horse and Lambert's foot — not so Mr. Buchan.

pike and butt end of musket" till a troop of horse charged through them from end to end.

Then, Cromwell having ordered Lambert's foot regiment still farther to the extreme left, there came swift and utter destruction. "I never beheld," wrote John Rushworth, "a more terrible charge of foot" than was given by Lambert's and Pride's battalions. From east to west the army of the Covenant rolled up and collapsed in confusion, the driven horsemen riding in squadrons over their own foot. Monck's infantry charged again in the centre, pouring in through the gaps of the broken regiments to complete the devastation. As the sun rose out of the sea in a red dawn, revealing the utter destruction of an enemy caught between the steep hillside of Doon and the inexorable steel flails that threshed them, the voice of Oliver, close behind Hodgson, was heard to cry:

"Let God arise, let His enemies be scattered!" and again in exultation:

"I profess they run!"

By six o'clock, after no more than an hour's fighting, the rout was complete. Lambert's foot regiment on the extreme left pushed right to the top of Doon Hill to prevent the scattered Scots from reforming, and down below pike and sword and musket went to it till whole regiments surrendered. The Scottish left wing, helpless between Brocksburn and the steep flank of Doon, fled with scarcely a blow.

After victory, prayers, and then pursuit. For a moment the Ironsides gathered about their General, and sang a brief thanksgiving in the words of the 117th Psalm, "for His merciful kindness is great toward us"; then into the saddle again with sword and carbine to complete God's work for eight miles. Cromwell lost no more than a score or so of killed, one of whom was Rokeby, Lambert's major of horse. Of the

Scots three thousand were slain. Ten thousand were taken prisoners, with two hundred colours and the whole of the artillery and baggage. Leslie himself flew straight to Edinburgh, and as the reverend Mr. Haig was joyfully telling his congregation in the capital that the Moabites had at last been driven from Scotland's soil, there staggered in through the doorway a broken horseman, his face white with the ashes of defeat.[178]

Now arises a point to which chroniclers, preoccupied with the great figure of Cromwell, have not all done full justice.

Dunbar was of course a battle for which the commander-in-chief could claim large credit, but on a close examination of all the available evidence it must stand out also as a great personal triumph for John Lambert. There is not sufficient evidence for saying, as has been said, that the plan and direction of the battle were wholly his. John Hodgson, our most reliable informant, says nothing of Lambert's having conceived the flanking plan — only that he urged it at the council of war in the face of opposition and that he was chiefly responsible for its adoption. It is only internal evidence, so to speak, that

---

[178] The following are the principal authorities relied upon for Dunbar and the campaign preceding it:

Cromwell, *Letters*, cxxxv to cxl; Hogsdon, 125-149; E. 608, 23; E. 609, 1 and 3; E. 610, 8; E. 612, 7, 8, 9, 10 and n; E. 777, 20; E. 778, 7 and 21; Cadwell's account in Carte's *Original Letters*, i, 380 — these on the English side.

On the Scottish side: Sir James Balfour's *Annales*, vols. 3 and 4; Robert Baillie's *Letters*, iii, III; Maidment, *Collections by a Private Hand*; John Nicoll's *Diary*, 27-28; Sir Edward Walker's *Historical Discourses upon Several Occasions*, 180. Various minor details are found in other places. For modern accounts see Buchan's *Oliver Cromwell'*, Firth, *Trans. Royal Historical Society*, 1900, in which all the sources of information are analysed; Gardiner, C. & P., Vol. 1; and Douglas's *Cromwell's Scotch Campaigns*.

strongly supports the idea that the scheme was Lambert's, for a study of the man shows that from the outset of his career, from Bradford onwards (and indeed he had learnt the lesson even earlier at Hull under Meldrum), it had been his special characteristic to sally out from a defensive position at the timely moment and strike to destroy the enemy. In any event it must be evident on a close examination that Lambert was at least the outstanding figure of the battle. We see him, after urging a particular plan of action, as the chief agent in the execution of it. We see him being put forward to have "the conduct of the battle." We see him ordering the artillery on the right and we see Cromwell waiting for him to arrive on the left and lead the main attack. We see him, though major-general of the foot, leading the cavalry instead of their own lieutenant-general, Fleetwood. We see him, before his second and decisive charge, giving the word to the "rearguard" when it should incline to the left for its allotted task on the flank — the vital manoeuvre of the whole action.

To have "the conduct of the battle" has puzzled some people, but it probably meant to lead into battle, which itself implied, in a battle of manoeuvre, something more than heading the first charge. It meant, no doubt, that from him the whole army should "take their time," in the modern drill phrase, that he should be their pacemaker as it were. His was to be a part comparable to Stayner's at Santa Cruz, and the circumstances in which each was called upon to lead the van are closely analogous. It is quite clear that Oliver himself was but with the rearguard, Hodgson being close to him throughout. The rearguard was, of course, to become the critical flanking force, but it was not in action until the final phase. Having the fullest confidence in his major-general, it is probable that Cromwell was content that Lambert should carry into effect the agreed plans, while he himself, riding in the rear in the dim light of dawn, chose the special task of leading the flanking force. It is clear that, whoever was the author of the plan, Dunbar was in a very special sense Lambert's battle.

This view is in no way inconsistent with Cromwell's own despatch, is in fact confirmed by what can be read between the lines. One may note especially on this occasion that Cromwell's frequent reluctance to attribute credit to another is neatly clothed in the modesty of heroes-all. "I know they look not to be named," he said, "and therefore I forbear particulars." But of that to which Cromwell leaves us veiled John Hodgson fortunately gives us his sunlight glimpses.[179]

---

[179] The more one studies Hodgson, who was far from being the "pudding head" that Carlyle called him, and compares him with other informants the more one is impressed with his trustworthiness. Firth (op. cit.) emphasises the several glimpses from various authorities that we have of Cromwell at Dunbar, but only one of them is in relation to the operations of the battle, and if, as he says, there was evidently a single brain at work it might well have been some other brain than Cromwell's. Nor does it seem sufficient to answer that Lambert himself never claimed the credit for Dunbar, for, as far as is known, he did not claim credit for any specific exploit. See also *The Case of Col. John Lambert*, 1661.

V. INVERKEITHING AND ITS FRUITS

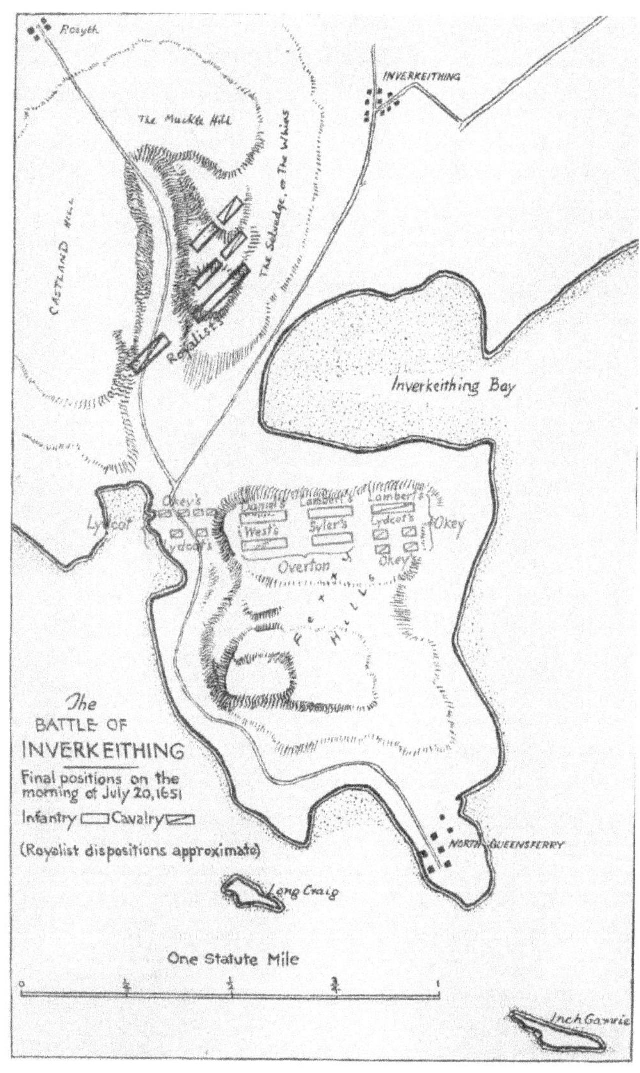

Crushing though it was in its immediate military issue, Dunbar was little more than a brilliant example of the old maxim that attack is the best defence. The English were fighting for their lives in a desperate situation. Strategically it achieved little, for the Scottish nation remained undefeated, and Leslie, though he was forced to abandon Edinburgh and to place himself once more on the defensive, soon gathered a new army almost as strong as before. Nevertheless, Dunbar shook to its foundations the domination of a people by a theocracy of bitter-lipped ministers, and it saved England from the imminent threat of a like bondage. The army was freed from the thirlage of the clerics, who, discredited as national leaders, shrank back into painful searchings of their acrimonious hearts.

Cromwell, seeking first the path of persuasion, himself plunged into a controversy with these same clerics in the high language of Zion. But he did not neglect to support persuasion with the more persuasive sword. Lambert, again in the van, went forward to occupy Edinburgh and to seize Leith, and on November 8th, with George Monck spitting tobacco-juice beside him, he stormed and took Dirleton Castle, near Haddington. Leslie retreated to the strength of Stirling, employing again his canny Fabian tactics, the royalist North solidly behind him. Richard Deane arrived with a portion of the English fleet in Scottish waters, where he was to play a vital part in holding the Scottish coasts secure against foreign help, while Blake was harrying Rupert in the Mediterranean.

To John was now assigned the trying tasks of reducing the Lowland castles that held out defiantly and of suppressing the bands of freebooters that harried the English communications and raided the border counties. He and his colonels, ranging far and wide in those wild vales, fought again the battles of the old border ballads in sudden ambushes and fierce assaults and swift night-raids. Himself, sweeping up to the fortress of Blackness, against which Monck had been sent, rescued "honest George" from the threat of imminent destruction by Edward Massey, once the Parliamentary defender of Gloucester, and sent the royalists into precipitate retreat.

When Strachan and Gilbert Ker, the ultra-Presbyterian "Remonstrators," broke out into a little war of their own in the south-west, Cromwell marched against them and ordered Lambert, who lay at Peebles, to join him at Hamilton with 3,000 sabres. Delayed by the floods and the rain, for the Clyde was in spate, John Lambert, accompanied by Whalley, was nearly a day late at the rendezvous, and he found that Cromwell had with due caution withdrawn. John nevertheless "came cranking in" alone, and on the night of November 30th lay in Hamilton. Ker, seeing an opportunity to destroy him, fell upon him at four o'clock on Sunday morning, December 1st. But Lambert was ready. Warned either by his outposts or by informers, he sounded to horse half an hour before, and in the streets and ditches on that dark winter morning threw off the attack, and, as his manner was, strode forward to deal a decisive blow.

At a cost to himself of but six men, he pursued and scattered the enemy, killing a hundred and capturing a hundred more, including Ker himself. Strachan rode up from near-by in an attempt to rally, but surrendered himself to Lambert instead, soon to die of religious mania. The skilful little action had important results, for the Remonstrators were completely dispersed.[180]

But the sword did not engage John's whole attention. Cromwell found that, of all his captains, Johnnie had not only

---

[180] Cromwell, cliii; Nicholl, 36; Baillie, 124-5; Douglas, 177-187.

easily the keenest and most enterprising military mind, but that, as one who carried "charms on the tip of his tongue," he had a special gift for negotiation and debate and was well fitted to skirmish with men who had "lived long on the almsbasket of words." He called him in therefore to help in his interminable battles of words with the Presbyterian clergy, designed to persuade the Scots to abandon their allegiance to young Charles, and in April of 1651 he and Lambert engaged in a formal "disputation" of theological politics in Glasgow with James Guthrie and Patrick Gillespie. It was the beginning of a long friendship between Lambert and Gillespie, a queer, oddly-assorted friendship, which was to reach forward into the years of trouble ahead when disgrace fell upon the one and ill-favour upon the other.

All the while young Charles's army, under Leslie's harassed command, avoided every attempt to be brought to battle. It lay secure on the hills south of Stirling, guarded by the bogs and the floods from the Carron and the Forth. The young King, owning but half a kingdom, was crowned at Scone on January 1st, 1651, and gradually there gathered round him all those elements that were royalist in their different ways. With the clergy largely discredited as military advisers, Presbyterian piety was no longer the first qualification for bearing arms, and men who swore good round oaths, in English as well as in Scots, were again suffered to bear the King's commission. From the Highlands the rough mountaineers began to come into him with their long kilts, their bows and arrows and their eldritch music.

In June of 1651 Mrs. Lambert arrived in Edinburgh to join the little group of officers' wives who had gathered there. She followed all the actions of her husband with an intelligent and accurate interest, and in the few letters of hers that remain shows her deep affection for him.

"For some days," she wrote to Adam Baynes on July 1st, "I happily enjoy my dearest friend, but now he is gone into the field." Twelve days later, when it is thought the army will be returning to Edinburgh, she writes: "I begin to be much more satisfied in my stay here than I was some few days since, for now I hope to see my dearest very shortly." Like her husband, she was not one of the new sobersides, and one little touch in these letters reveals in her the unchanging woman of the ages. She had written twice to England urgently for some French lawn (which must be of the very finest) — "for" wrote she, "I have nothing to wear about my neck, and I dare not go bare, for fear of giving offence to tender saints." She is one of the few women whose qualities come dimly to light in the battle gloom of those warring days.[181]

That summer Cromwell, recovered from a trying illness, made fresh efforts to bring Leslie to action. Frustrated in his attempts to fight him face to face, he resolved to attempt an attack in flank, but the difficulties of terrain were serious. Leslie lay across the narrow loins of Scotland with bastions of water to right and to left. But Cromwell had now been in Scotland nearly a year, and he felt that at all risks the issue must somehow be brought to a decisive finish. The great commander was now at the pitch of his powers, displaying in the coming phase of the campaign a restless energy of brain and body which resulted in his most brilliant manifestation of the military art, and calculating with instinctive psychology every movement of his opponent's brain.

Throughout this phase John Lambert continued close at his side, the chief instrument of his designs and the first lieutenant

---

[181] Letters of Roundhead Officers, Nos. 57, 60 and 64.

of his brain, for in the realm of action both men thought extraordinarily alike, though it is true to say that Lambert, as the younger man, responded more immediately, more impulsively, to the inspiration of a moment. "*Aussitôt qu'on y touche, il résonne.*" Of that the brisk affair at Hamilton had been a miniature example, and in the action to come Lambert was to manifest the true Cromwellian touch.

Since there was a landward approach, Cromwell decided to attempt first a movement round Leslie's western flank. He therefore sent Lambert out upon a difficult reconnaissance to find a way. At noon on July 8th John rode out from Glasgow with his own, Lilburne's and Alured's regiments of horse. Marching by Killearn, where he captured a laird's house, he came to the neighbourhood of the lake of Menteith, crossed the fords of Forth, and in less than three days after a splendid march was back in Glasgow reporting that the route was practicable save for guns and baggage. The plan, however, was not adopted. A forward move by Leslie to Kilsyth gave Cromwell fresh hopes of a frontal attack, and he moved against him only to be again frustrated by the bogs. Therefore he moved his army to Linlithgow, and there a new and more audacious enterprise was resolved upon.

This time it was decided to cross the Firth of Forth in boats, land upon the shores of Fife and threaten Leslie's eastern wing. It was to be a feint only, but a feint so menacing as to force the enemy to act by one course or another. The passage chosen was approximately where the Forth Bridge now spans the water from South Queensferry to North Queensferry, passing by the island rock of Inchgarvie, which was in possession of the Scots and which Deane had been bombarding from his ships for three days without effect.

The northern landing-place by this crossing is upon a bold peninsula, shaped very like the continent of Africa, a mile and a quarter long from south to north, and joined to the mainland of Fife at the north-west by a narrow isthmus only a quarter of a mile wide. From its surrounding shores the little peninsula swells up into the Ferry Hills, a rocky mass 240 feet high, topped by a cluster of tumbling summits. To the north-west these hills, like a little Gibraltar, dominate the low-lying isthmus and look across it to the stony village of Inverkeithing and to wave upon wave of the swelling hills of Fife. It is upon the fringes of this sea of hills, where it breaks upon the level isthmus in a fantastic surge, that the "essential agony" of Inverkeithing is to be endured.

On the edge of the isthmus, and to its left when looking from Ferry Hills, this surge of rock ends sharply in a wooded spur of Castland Hill, 300 feet high. In the centre, running obliquely down towards the isthmus, and successively diminishing in size, is a range of three bold eminences like knuckles on a giant hand. Rough, broken and clothed in gorse, they are known as The Whins, but their old name of The Selvedge suits more aptly the steep drop with which to the west they edge the valley between themselves and the spur of Castland Hill. In this valley between them lies the Dunfermline road by which the Scots will come, and as it mounts inland this road crosses the crest where Castland and The Selvedge meet.

On July 17th, while Deane's warships engaged the batteries of Inchgarvie and North Queensferry, Overton crossed from South Queensferry to the peninsula with four troops of Lydcot's horse, Daniel's regiment of foot and some further infantry details — about 1,600 in all. Landing perhaps in the northern or the eastern side of the peninsula, he captured its batteries by attack from the rear and also seized some store-ships in the bay. Having in this meritorious exploit lost only six men, he then hewed out rocky entrenchments across the steep north-western shoulder of the Ferry Hills, commanding the isthmus, immediately above what is now the sixteenth fairway of the golf-course.

As soon as news of Overton's landing was received at Charles's headquarters Leslie dispatched against him a mixed force of about 3,600, commanded either by Sir James Brown of Fordell or by Lieutenant-General James Holborn, the same who had relieved Blake at Taunton and whose present fidelity to Charles was held in doubt.[182] Some of the troops had had little military experience, but the expedition included also Sir Walter Scott and his hardy Border raiders, Augustin the freebooter, Colonel Colin Pittscottie and the regiments of Lord Balcarres and Lord Brechin.

Their orders, still in pursuit of strict defensive tactics, were merely to bar the inland road and block up the English within the peninsula.

Meanwhile, south of the Forth, Cromwell moved yet once more against the royalists' main body, hoping that Leslie would be moved by the threat to his rear, but Leslie was not to be tempted against such a small demonstration, and Cromwell was obliged to retire again. Every move that he made was being astutely foiled and it was only by the magnificent audacity of Lambert that the sound and calculating Fabianism of the Scots was to be overthrown, and that the English army was to be saved from being ignominiously outmanoeuvred.

----

[182] All the English accounts, including that of Lambert, who took him prisoner, are explicit that Brown commanded, whereas the Scots versions by Balfour and Maidment's *Private Hand* give Holborn, but Balfour is altogether unreliable.

It was resolved that Overton's little expedition into Fife should become an invasion in greater force. Upon the day after Overton's landing Lambert received orders to cross over to him with some 3,000 additional troops and assume command. Accordingly, at dawn on Saturday, July 19th, he assembled at South Queensferry his own regiments of horse and foot, Okey's dragoons, and the infantry of either West or Syler, and embarked them in a fleet of double shallops.

All that day and all through the next night the transportation continued. At four o'clock in the afternoon John, having ridden forward no doubt to the crown of Castland Hill with Scoutmaster Downing, saw, beneath the skyline of the distant Ochils, the Scottish expedition marching into Dunfermline, whose towered abbey crowned the intervening crest five miles away.

With his own forces only half-disembarked, it must have been with some relief that John observed that the Scots came no farther that sunny afternoon, but pitched camp at Dunfermline for the night. By eleven o'clock or thereabouts of the summer night John had disembarked all the infantry and his own cavalry regiment, but it occupied the further labour of the night to bring over Okey's dragoons, and before the last boatload was ashore on Sunday morning, July 20th, 1651, Downing brought word to Lambert that the Scots were at hand, and presently the general saw the blue banners of St. Andrew top the crest of Castland Hill and flow down into the valley leading to the isthmus. The English stood to arms in their entrenchments till Okey's men at length rode up. Then events moved swiftly.

As he looked from the northern escarpment of Ferry Hills across the isthmus, John saw to his right front the little walled port of Inverkeithing, the giant knuckles of The Selvedge running obliquely away from him immediately opposite, and across the valley to its left the high spur of Castland Hill — an uncouth, crumpled, formless landscape, with here and there a smooth patch of sloping corn-land, but clothed for the most part in a rough mantle of gorse starred with lingering blossom. He saw at once that if the Scots halted on the high crest where Castland joins the farthest knuckle of The Selvedge, which they call the Muckle Hill, theirs would be a fine strategic position, dangerous of assault from any side and commanding all roads inland, either by the valley, by Inverkeithing, or coastwise by Rosyth. It was therefore with satisfaction that he saw them come nearer, and perhaps, as Downing relates, he teased them with skirmishing parties to do so. At length, changing from column into line, they spread across the foothills opposite him. Just where they formed is a matter of conjecture, but presently he observed them to re-form and to wheel, as though either to march away or else to take the advantage of the higher ground behind that has already been described.[183]

John did not intend that they should succeed in either course. With a shrewd instinct, he at once sent forward Okey to attack the Scottish rear. So threatened, the Scots halted, turned about and formed up "in battalia" ready for action.

Thus, though their position, lofty and fenced about by broken, thorny ground, was sufficiently formidable of attack, Lambert's movement had denied them a much more

---

[183] The spur of Castland Hill answers better to the "steep mountain" of Lambert's dispatch, but if the Scots' move had been in this direction it would hardly have appeared to him that they might be "marching away."

Downing's account of how Lambert enticed the enemy nearer must, I think, be considered a different and less accurate version of the move that Okey was presently to make, as reported by Lambert himself.

advantageous one, and one which, guarded by the oblique bastion of The Selvedge, would have been far more hazardous to approach in the audacious assault to come. The position upon which they in fact now formed was upon the crumpled slopes of The Selvedge, with the musketeers of their central infantry covering the valley, and it may be assumed with considerable certainty, both because it was the custom of the day, and because Brown would have been criminally remiss not to have done so, that the lancers of the right wing were posted on the easy slopes of the valley itself.

Joined that morning by 500 Highlanders, the royalists now counted about 4,100 in their force. Lambert numbered about 4,600, and, in response to the Scots' movement, he also drew up in battle order. His left wing being upon "very ill ground," rocky and precipitous, he concentrated his greatest strength on the right. Here he had his own cavalry regiment, two troops of Okey's and two troops of Lydcot's, the whole wing being under the command of Okey. In the centre were his own infantry and Daniel's, and on the left wing were four troops of Okey's and two of Lydcot's, commanded by the latter. Behind broken ground in the rear was a reserve of the infantry regiments of West and Syler, under the command of Overton.

In these positions the two little armies stood facing each other for an hour and a half, John fully expecting that the Scots would attack, "being come so far to seek us." While he waited, however, he received a message from Cromwell saying that he had been obliged to fall back again upon Linlithgow and that the Scots had dispatched reinforcements to Brown and Holborn from Stirling.

The whole fate of Cromwell's campaign now hung upon Lambert's actions. Beyond the isthmus was a force nearly equal to his own, fresh from a night's sleep, and holding a powerful position. His own men, during thirty hours of continuous labour, had had "scarce a moment to eat or sleep," but in their high entrenchments they could confidently hope to resist attack. Yet he knew that if Brown and Holborn were substantially reinforced they would entirely frustrate the idea of a flanking invasion into Fife in force. Therefore he did not hesitate for a moment to discard the defensive and once more put all to the touch. Despite fatigue, his men were in high fettle, resolute and cheerful. In the simplest language he describes the intention to take that audacious risk. "It was resolved," he said, "we should climb the hill to them, which we accordingly did."

To the call of his trumpet and the tap of the drum, their rainbow colours floating in the mild July breeze of that Sabbath afternoon and the cry of "Providence" on their lips, his redcoats came down from their hill, squeezed through the isthmus, extended to the right and swept upwards to assault the enemy on their embattled hills above them. As the infantry bent their backs to the slope, the Scottish lancers in the valley charged down upon the six troops on Lydcot's wing and drove through their thin ranks by sheer impetus. For a moment the Ironsides were in imminent peril, but Lambert was ready. Himself leading them, he swung round Overton's infantry reserve, and, with a troop of horse led by Captain Bramston, struck the charging lancers in flank before they had space to draw rein and change front. As his pikes clashed against their shorter lances, his musketeers poured in their volleys. So vigorously did he strike that within fifteen minutes the royalist horse of that wing were routed.

Lambert turned again to the main attack. Two bullets rang upon his armour, and pierced it, to be found afterwards embedded in his clothing. But of that astonishing up-hill charge little else but a vision of the imagination is given us. We see only the shattering result. We see the Ironsides as a slow wave of steel breasting "the steep up-rising of the hill" with their packed ranks embarrassed but unbroken by the clustering thorns of the golden gorse. Poised above them and so balanced as to fall upon them as an avalanche, is an enemy nearly equal in numbers and lacking nothing in courage. Yet with magnificent discipline Lambert and his men maintain their upward surge, and immediately upon the clash of impact the inexorable strength of their welded unity shivers into splinters the simple courage of the Scots.

The royalists were instantaneously overwhelmed. Their battle-cry of "Scotland" died upon their stricken lips as the curlew wheeled overhead and the sea-gulls rose in alarm. Then, as at Dunbar, came the terrible cutting up, and, for such as could escape up the steep brae-side, the equally terrible pursuit. Over the lonely hills and away to Dunfermline the unrelenting swords rose and fell; Pinkerton Burn, they say to this day, ran deeply red and St. Margaret's Stone was splashed with blood. Somewhere near Pitreavie 500 Highlanders, mainly of the clan Maclean of Mull, in an epic last stand under their young chieftain, Sir Hector, died to a man with his name on their lips as Lambert's cavalry crashed into them in charge after charge.[184]

How much of half-heartedness or of fear or of treachery there may have been cannot be known, but Holborn fled early from the field. Relatively to the numbers engaged, Inverkeithing was an even more devastating victory than Dunbar, and far more decisive in its strategic results. Of the royalists' four thousand, no fewer than two thousand fell to the

---

[184] "Another for Hector!" was the cry with which "no less than eight gentlemen of the name of Maclean" rushed upon their death; and the heroic catchword has passed into a proverb. — DOUGLAS.

sword, and yet another 1,500 were taken prisoners, nearly all of them with wounds. Brown himself was wounded and taken, and shortly died. Maclean, Scott, Buchanan — all fell. Between forty and fifty colours were taken. Only 500 Scots escaped death or capture, and even of these Lambert observed tersely: "Indeed I am persuaded few of them escaped without a knock."

His own casualties were absurdly small, only eight or nine being killed and several wounded; nearly all these had been in Lambert's own cavalry, and he himself, his horse wounded, had been throughout in the heart of the battle.[185]

Strategically, Inverkeithing altered immediately the whole aspect of the campaign, and opened the way to that series of movements which was soon to establish once and for all the invincibility of Oliver Cromwell. The coming devastation of Worcester was its immediate fruits. For us, it had shown again Lambert's quick perception of the military issues, his instinct for their decisive settlement at once, his understanding of the employment of reserves, and his rare audacity. "The carriage of the major-general, as in all things so in this," wrote Cromwell to the Speaker, "is worthy your taking notice of."[186]

The next day Cromwell reinforced him with Lilburne's and Alured's regiments of horse and Ashfield's and Ingoldsby's infantry, making his total force now over 7,000. On July 24th

---

[185] By analogy again with Dunbar, where only 25 English as against 3,000 Scots were killed, there is no need at all to consider these figures, as Douglas has done, to be "flagrantly understated." They are confirmed in substance by the letter in E.638, 10.

[186] The chief authorities for the Battle of Inverkeithing are: Whitelocke, 499 (Lambert's Dispatch) and 500; Cromwell, clxxv, corrected by letter of July 22nd (E.786, 26); E.638, 2, 10 and 15; L.R.O., 35 and 36; Balfour's *Annales of Scotland*, iv, 313; Douglas, *Cromwell's Scotch Campaigns*, 274-287; Revd. William Stephen, *History of Inverkeithing and Rosyth*, 359-66.

the little island of Inchgarvie surrendered, and presently Cromwell came himself with his whole army over to Lambert's side to advance upon Perth itself. Thus he had again, as at Preston, interposed between the enemy and their sources of supply, and he now cut Leslie off completely from the royalist Highlands. A night or two later Lambert stayed with Cromwell at Brown's own house at Fordell.

Leslie would still have preferred to play Fabian. He had infinite patience; he had also 20,000 men against Oliver's 14,000, and might have wrought havoc with the English communications. But Charles and his cavaliers drove him to the southward path that Cromwell had laid temptingly open. Forgetful of 1648, they imagined that England would rise for their cause if they crossed the border. On July 31st Charles broke camp at Stirling and began his march upon England by the western road. Cromwell and Lambert watched them go with quiet satisfaction; it was the only way to bring them to decisive action, and with the precision of a master Cromwell laid his plans for their destruction. Thomas Harrison, freshly up from England with 3,000 new troops, had already been posted at Newcastle to keep watch and to threaten the invading left wing.

Tom Fairfax, ready once more to draw the sword at the threat of invasion, was raising his native Yorkshire, and farther south Fleetwood was collecting the Midlands contingents at Banbury. With complete equanimity Cromwell was prepared to see the Scots march nearly to London itself, knowing that the farther they were lured the more certain was their destruction, and knowing with a surer instinct than Charles's that scarce an Englishman would raise a finger to help the Stuart.

Having taken Perth on August 2nd, he left George Monck behind with 6,000 men to hold Scotland, flew back to Leith with the remainder of his army, and on August 5th sent Lambert forward with a flying column of 4,000 horsemen to co-operate with Harrison. Before setting out John wrote to Harrison, explaining his proposed method of cooperation: "I intend to keep as close in the rear as I can, yet something to the left hand, so as I may be in a capacity to correspond or join with you as occasion requires."[187] Thus the major-general had again to do the work of 1648, but his special purpose now was, in his own words, "to trouble the enemy in the rear" — to harass, to threaten and to impede their advance.

Then it had been a summer of drenching rain; now, however, it was one of pitiless sun, blazing down upon armour that scorched the touch, filling the ranks with the stench of sweating horses and men. Nevertheless, in the next ten days Lambert marched 200 miles. From Berwick he struck across to Penrith, only a day's march behind Charles. Passing through his native Craven, he kept in touch with Harrison by dispatch-rider, and on August 11th he wrote from Settle to the Council of State to relate how Charles was being greeted everywhere with sullen looks and how his own men were on the other hand receiving on all sides a "loving" welcome from the country people. He was feeling confident of success. On August 13th he joined hands with Harrison near Blackburn. Two days later, with a command of 6,000 regular troops and 3,000 militiamen from Cheshire and Staffordshire, he overtook Charles and confronted him south of the Mersey at Warrington Bridge.

He intended to destroy the bridge, but the royalist vanguard was upon him before he could do so. Finding the flat country south of Warrington Bridge so entangled with hedges that his cavalry were unable to operate, and being very weak in

---

[187] Tanner MSS., 54, 136.

infantry, he ordered a withdrawal, but engaged the enemy with his rear-guard, throwing them back and pursuing them a mile. He then took up position at Knutsford, hoping that there the enemy would be persuaded to give him battle. But the royalists, knowing Lambert "to be a man of courage and conduct, and his troops to be of the best," would not be drawn, and turned away, trusting to find support from royalist Wales.[188]

On August 22nd Charles's army, exhausted and dispirited by desertions, himself shunned by the English Presbyterians whose aid he was asking, arrived at Worcester and paused to rest. Only in Lancashire had he found some English help, and there Robert Lilburne, detached from Lambert's force, crushed with his single cavalry regiment, in a battle at Wigan on August 25th, the royalist levies raised by the Earl of Derby. On the previous day Cromwell joined forces with Lambert and Harrison at Warwick, moved presently to Evesham at the head of 30,000 men, and with a sure hand laid his plans for the enemy's destruction. Lambert was again to be a vital instrument.

Worcester lies on the east bank of the Severn, and a mile and a half below the city the Teme flows from the westward to join the major river. Cromwell planned that one division should cross the Severn below the city and that the whole army should then sweep northwards up both sides towards Worcester. But the nearest bridge by which the western division might cross the river, at Upton, some miles below Worcester, had been destroyed by the enemy, who had posted 300 men under Massey himself on the farther side.

---

[188] This minor incident has been much misrepresented by Royalist writers. Authorities: Tanner MSS., liv, 155; Whitelocke, 502; Clarendon, *Great Rebellion*, xiii, 60, 63; Tracts relating to Military Proceedings in Lancashire (Cheetham Soc.), 286-293. O.P.H., xix, 502; xx, 10, 14, 19; Cary, ii, 295.

It was the initiative of Lambert that found the solution. On August 28th Lambert with a party of horse and dragoons rode southwards to Upton, and found a single plank lying across the broken piers of the bridge. Across this plank, before the enemy had taken alarm, John sent eight dragoons, who, having clambered over, boldly threw themselves into the church under cover of a fire from the river bank. Amid this diversion Lambert's cavalry swam or waded the river, set fire to the church, and, after a brisk struggle in which Massey was severely wounded, drove the royalists into flight. The bridge was rapidly repaired, John himself putting his hand to the work. Thus was a passage provided for Fleetwood's cavalry, and that night 11,000 men crossed the river. Then, on a summons from Cromwell, Lambert rode to a critical council of war.[189]

The story of the Battle of Worcester is quickly told. On the morning of September 3rd, exactly a year after Dunbar, the Roundheads threw bridges of boats across both the Severn and the Teme and crossed to the assault at half-past two under a fiery sun and a steel-blue sky. To the western division first fell the main brunt of the battle. Again Lambert's horse was shot beneath him. As stiff a contest, said Cromwell, as ever he had seen. But with Oliver himself to help with four chosen regiments, the Scots were driven backwards from hedge to hedge, till at last they were forced into the ultimate walls of Worcester. Meanwhile, young Charles, watching the fight from the cathedral tower, saw that there was but one hope. Himself he led out his cavalry from Sudbury gate, with such infantry as he could muster, and charged the unengaged Roundhead division on the east bank. For three hours they fought, till Cromwell, hurrying back with reinforcements, at last overthrew him and drove him back into Worcester.

---

[189] E.787, 12; Whitelocke, 505. O.P.H., xx, 40.

Then there fell upon the street-penned regiments that terrible punishment by which the Ironsides turned tactical victory into utter destruction, as a conquering boxer hammers his stricken opponent till he drops. When the carnage of the streets was over, more than 10,000 who had scarce hoped for mercy were prisoners in Cromwell's hands; all the leaders — Leslie, the second Hamilton, Middleton, Massey, Lauderdale and Derby — were killed or taken. Only Charles himself and a few followers slipped away into the night, to begin those adventurous wanderings in strange disguises that led him at length to the safety of France, cherishing a repugnance towards Scotland and the Scot that abided long in the unsure habitation of his frivolous heart.

VI. "MY LORD LAMBERT"

Worcester, which had been the fruits of his victory at Inverkeithing, marks a turning point in John Lambert's life and leads him into a new road full of the promise of sublime heights, but ensnared with sudden twists and dizzy chasms. He was now to sheathe the sword, never to draw it again save for one brief skirmish eight years hence. The boy colonel of 1642 had become, after nine years of almost continuous fighting, the second soldier in the land, and he was still only thirty-two. Success had followed brilliant success. He had fought no fewer than twenty-four known actions, and in more than half of them had been in personal command. He had been twice wounded and four times unhorsed. In every action he had been at the red heart of the fight, for, in Robert Bridges' words, he was one of those brave gamesters of life

> whose joy danceth on peril's edge,
> for whom life hath no relish save in danger of
> death;
> who love sport for its hazards and of all their
> sports
> where hazard is at the highest look to find the
> best
> there on the field where hourly they may stake
> their all.

But this was not all. His meritorious defence of the Yorkshire clothing towns, his soldierly conduct at Marston Moor, his brilliant flank march in the Preston campaign, his quick eye and dominant part at Dunbar, his vital victory at

Inverkeithing, and finally his enterprise in the pursuit and battle of Worcester had marked him out as one with qualities that no other man had shown.

From the very outset of his career in arms — from Bradford to Appleby and Hamilton and Inverkeithing, no less than at Dunbar — he had manifested that particular characteristic of his of stepping out from a defensive position at the timely moment and striking a decisive blow. Moreover, his audacity and his perception of the moment and the place to strike were matched to an admirable patience when need be and a strategist's understanding of when to resist the desire to strike. Throughout the Scottish campaign he had been at Cromwell's right hand — in battle, in council, in reconnaissance and in pursuit — and to him the Lord General had entrusted every important task, for his keen intelligence rose high above the heads of the remarkable company of men who had really few other qualities than a compactness of soldierly efficiency never surpassed in history.

Lambert was now complete and accomplished, and he had risen to his young glory by the brilliance of his natural qualities matched with a manly virtue and an unfaltering fulfilment of each day's common task. By these and by his more human qualities he had won an extraordinary influence over the Roundhead soldiers. *"'Tis Lambert for my money, boys,"* was later to be the cry. To his charm of manner was added a cheerful humour and a ready generosity of heart and hand. He was no sour face, and, though himself one of the new "independents," was never bewitched by the abracadabra of any religious sect and extended his tolerance even to Roman Catholics. There was keen emulation to secure admission to his regiments, and he for his part more than once went out of his way to secure employment for those who were in need. His sword was unstained by any act of massacre or ruthlessness, and "the access and passage to remorse" were not in him stopped up.

It was in keeping with such a man that he should be particular in his dress. He followed Polonius's advice: his apparel costly as his purse could buy, but not expressed in fancy. He liked not gold and tinsel. Soon after Dunbar, when the rigours of a wet summer had played havoc with Lambert's wardrobe, Captain Walker wrote to Adam Baynes instructing him to send the major-general "two handsome sword-belts," "a good French hat of the best sort, and one of an ordinary sort with most fashionable black bands, for gold and silver pleaseth him not." Baynes was also to instruct Mr. Kendell to make "two pair of handsome walking boots, and one pair of summer riding boots, with two pair of Spanish leather shoes." "Tell him," added Walker, "to make them of better stuff than the last."[190]

But out of this fair frame there began after Worcester to take shape forms vaguely sinister. He had drunk deeply of the wine of success. He knew well how much of the merit of the Scotch campaign was due to him, and Parliament on September 9th had granted him lands in Scotland to the value of £1,000 a year, but when in November he was beginning to complain to Adam Baynes that he had "not been fairly dealt with," one may surmise that his grievances went farther than arrears of pay. He had already begun to nibble at the "insane root." Had the witches of Macbeth spoken to him in Scotland, and had Frances Lambert played the part of ambition's tragic queen? He was indeed to become greater yet, but we shall see how the impulses that were to make him so were to carry the seeds of their destruction — how his audacity began to grow into

---

[190] L.R.O., 36.

aggression, his pride into vanity and his dutiful soldiership into ambition.

For a little while, before the current of his life was to flow into strange new channels, Lambert returned once more to Scotland.

Having again exercised his persuasive gifts in settling the militia called up for Worcester, he crossed the Cheviots to further the settlement of Scotland according to Commonwealth ideas, being appointed by Parliament on October 23rd one of the eight Commissioners for that purpose. Stirling had now fallen and Monck had savagely plundered Dundee. Lambert rode back into Edinburgh with Richard Deane.

His first care was for the public order of the capital, and he won the highest report among the citizens for the establishment of an English magistracy which by its probity and evenhandedness outshone the lapsed administration of the Scots themselves. He took Dumbarton Castle, settled disputes, and further advanced his good name by enforcing seemly behaviour among his soldiers. He rode again into Fife to view his newly-granted lands, and thence, catching a breath of the "nimble and sweet air" of the Highlands, came to Dundee and so to Aberdeen, saluted with salvoes of artillery and escorted by a bodyguard of Highlanders. On December 29th, 1651, he published an ordinance for the regulation of Scottish currency.[191]

Lambert had not long been back in Scotland before honour came to him of a kind which he might believe to be his due. On January 30th, 1652, at the recommendation of the Council of State, Parliament appointed him Lord-Deputy of Ireland in succession to Ireton, who had died in November, shortly after

---

[191] C. J., vii, 20, 30; Whitelocke, 519, 520; Balfour, *Annales of Scotland*, iv, 343-4; Nicholl, 65-66.

reducing stubborn Limerick to final surrender. Accompanied part of the way by Monck, Lambert drove back south by coach at once in high fettle, for he was now to be a high officer of state. He made great preparations. On his way through Yorkshire he saw some of his old friends of the Fairfax days, and appointed them to his staff. Together they made up "a very proud train," and in London he began, says Lucy Hutchinson, "to put on the prince," laying out £5,000 "for his own particular equipage." His tone took on a louder note and his brows a higher lift.

Frances Lambert alike rose to the new tone. One day, so Lucy Hutchinson relates, Bridget Ireton, daughter of Cromwell and widow of the deceased general, was walking in St. James's Park; "the Lady Lambert, as proud as her husband, came by where she was, and as the present princess always hath precedency of the relict of the dead prince, so she put my Lady Ireton below; who, notwithstanding her piety and humility, was a little grieved at the affront."

Chance ordained that Charles Fleetwood, lieutenant-general of horse, should have observed the incident, and, going forward to condole with Bridget Ireton, was presently accepted as her husband — and as Cromwell's son-in-law.[192]

It was in accordance with the almost princely position they were now appointed to occupy that, like others of the Lords of the Commonwealth, the Lamberts should acquire a palace, and in May of this year they did so. Among the various royal properties that had fallen into the hands of Parliament at the death of Charles I had been Queen Mary's splendid mansion at Wimbledon, built by Sir Thomas Cecil in the year of the Armada. It had been bought from the State by Adam Baynes, and on May 17th, 1652, Baynes conveyed it to his commander

---

[192] Hutchinson, *Memoirs*, ii, 188-9.

Lambert for £16,822 17s. 8d. Wimbledon Hall, with which went the Manor of Wimbledon, was a sumptuous building in a "clean and neat situation" on the brow of the famous hill, approached from Putney Heath by a splendid avenue of elms three-quarters of a mile long, the line of which may still be traced. Built in the Hampton Court tradition of brick with quoins, cornices and mullions of bold ashlar, it lay about three sides of a quadrangle, and the gilded weathercocks that gleamed from its two low turrets were notable landmarks over all that country. Flanders gables and tall triple chimneys flanked and crowned its banqueting hall and its outbuildings.

Within, the house contained splendid galleries, a chapel with painted ceiling and marble floor, an organ room, a grotto of the kind so fashionable in great houses, its walls adorned with shells and mirrors and little polished rocks and wanting only the presence of a mermaid to complete the illusion of a marine arcadia. More unusual, there were also two bath-rooms. The house contained numerous pictures and mural paintings — "landscapes of battles, antics, heaven and hell and other curious works." For the greater part the walls within were panelled high in oak, most of which was painted green and adorned with golden stars.

But the most famous feature of Wimbledon Hall was its gardens. In front of the great quadrangle of the house the falling hill-side was stepped in two bold terraces, balustraded and buttressed with stone and breasted with sweeping ornamental stairways. The grounds covered 377 acres, stretching down the northern slope to the Thames near Putney and down the southern slope to the lake of Wimbledon Park. Henrietta Maria had made use of the gardens as nurseries for the cultivation of rare fruits and flowers, many of which had been sent over to her from France. There were over one thousand fruit-trees of every sort in cultivation, save the nectarine. There was an orangery for citrous fruits and pomegranates, there were many flowering shrubs, there were mazes, "wildernesses," and secluded alleys.

It was this fine mansion with its lovely grounds that no doubt inspired John Lambert, if he did not already possess them, with two passions that were to abide with him for the remainder of his life — art and gardening. Both were pursuits unusual in men of his time, and John's keen love of them marks him out from among all those hard-praying and plain-living men who so passionately pledged their hearts to a single purpose. Amongst these farmer-generals, these artisan-colonels and lawyer-politicians he stood out as a young man of good breeding and keen intellect, and to him the hurly-burly of public life required an aesthetic and intellectual relief for the accomplishment of full being. He found that relief in pictures and in flowers.

Interest in painting, almost unknown in England before Charles I's enlightened patronage, was now more than ever confined to the very few. To Lambert it made an immediate and lasting appeal. When Charles I's pictures were sold by order of Parliament, John bought a number of them and established a notable gallery at Wimbledon Hall. Nor was he a mere dilettante, but a labourer who knew the pangs of trial and failure. He retained Baptist Gaspars in his service, himself received instruction from him and became, it is said, a talented painter of flowers. Lucy Hutchinson was probably mistaken in saying that he "embroidered" flowers.

An interest in flowers was becoming to one whose traditional family emblem was the narcissus. At Wimbledon Lambert's gardens became famous and he himself an acknowledged expert. He had, says Roger Coke, "the finest tulips and gilliflowers that could be got for love or money," and in 1659 he was said to have introduced the Guernsey lily into England. He was, almost certainly, the true gardener who himself puts his hand to the spade. He was, besides, a keen practitioner in mathematics, and seems also to have been interested in music, which continued to flourish under the Commonwealth, and in 1656 resulted in the birth of English opera.[193]

Thus the young Lord-Deputy rose to a princely station in the infant Commonwealth, and he was henceforth, in like manner to a few other leading Cromwellians, to be known as Lord Lambert. In addition to Wimbledon Hall, he purchased Hatfield Chase, and he had, besides, his dower lands of Pontefract, his properties in Fife and Lauderdale, Yorkshire lands sequestrated from Marmaduke Langdale and his own family estates in Craven. He was a considerable landlord. In Scotland he had left Cornet John Baynes, a Commissary and later Receiver-General for that country, as his agent, but some of the properties were in very bad condition and Baynes had instructions to acquire new ones by purchase or exchange.

How much of this new-blown pride was the cause of his ensuing disappointment cannot be certain, but the Lamberts were to be frustrated of their princely hopes. For on May 19th, 1652, only two days after his purchase of Wimbledon Hall, Parliament, deeply suspicious of the new lords of the army, abolished the office of Lord-Lieutenant of Ireland, which was held by Cromwell, and the office of Lord-Deputy consequently lapsed with it. Deep was Lambert's vexation and he refused with disdain the lesser appointment that was presently offered

---

[193] Bartlett, *History and Antiquities of Wimbledon*, 1865; Brayley, *History of Surrey*, vol. iii; Hist. MSS. Commission, 7th R., 189; Walpole, *Anecdotes*, ed. Dallaway, ii, 362; *Notes and Queries*, 1st series, vii, 410 and 459; Hatton-Finch MSS., 29,569, fol. 212; Hutchinson, ii, 205W.

him of acting Commander-in-Chief in Ireland under Cromwell. Fleetwood took it instead.[194]

There were those who thought the thing was a plot by Cromwell: Mrs. Hutchinson thought that Cromwell, with his customary nepotism, coveted the appointment for his new son-in-law, Fleetwood; and Ludlow thought that by embittering Lambert against Parliament he could win his support for turning it out. But if John had any such suspicions he was perhaps reassured when he heard from Vane and Hazelrig that Cromwell had said to him:

"Not anything troubles me more than to see honest John Lambert so ungratefully treated."

Moreover, Cromwell, who was never covetous of this world's goods, out of the arrears of pay due to himself handsomely assigned to the disappointed Lord-Deputy a sum of £2,000.

No, it was not the Lord-General, but Parliament, this effete, suspicious and corrupt Parliament, that in their jealousy had cheated him, and against Parliament he marshalled the forces of his resentment. Whatever may have been Cromwell's part in the matter — and it is certain he did nothing to hinder Parliament's decision — the immediate result was that Lambert began to organise among the leading officers of the army a demand for the immediate dissolution of the Rump. In this agitation he had the active but fretful support of Major-General Harrison, that splendid and fearless soldier whose mad mysticism, however, was soon to bring them to a breach. Their demands were formulated in a petition on August 2nd, in which they called also for legal and religious reforms, provision for the poor and abolition of tithes, and the hand of Lambert can specially be seen in a demand for the fulfilment of

---

[194] C. J., vii, 142, 152.

promises made to royalists by articles of war, for the treachery to Hamilton, his prisoner of war, was still fresh in his mind.

Cromwell's reluctance to any precipitate action led to a murmured demand that Lambert or Fairfax should displace him, but Oliver was, nevertheless, wholly with John in his purpose. Both men saw that the Rump had fallen to the lowest levels of self-subservience. It was but the ghost of the great Long Parliament of 1640, and, on its shrunk shanks, had long since ceased to represent the nation. While among its members there were men of high principles, too many had thrust their hands deep into corruption, and nearly all were narrow-minded, jealous of their power and determined to perpetuate it as long as possible.

Amongst them we must notice two who are to be of special significance in Lambert's life — Vane and Hazelrig. Sir Henry Vane, the younger, was one of the striking members of the Long Parliament. So far as the House had one at all, he was its leader, but he had deeply incurred the odium of the Army in the quarrel of 1647. His strong-willed, turbulent, boyish face, with its ruddy cheeks, its brown hair, its forward-pressing chin and its obstinate mouth, gleams out from Walker's canvas with the vivid light of the incorruptible servant of lost causes. It is the face of a puzzled boy, indignant at the injustices of fortune and his fellows and resolute to defy them to the end. He was a great republican, but inelastic of intellect, unsusceptible to compromise, a political mystic. To him the cause was all, and the man nothing. To-day he was Lambert's adversary, but he was to die his friend and ally.

Sir Arthur Hazelrig was a very different firebrand. Equally pugnacious in his republicanism and equally dogmatic in his principles, he was a man of violent temper, of aggressive speech and provocative vanity — a man, says Ludlow, "of disobliging carriage," sour and morose of temper, liable to be transported with passion. He was said to have been brought up by Pym, and was one of the Five Members threatened by Charles I. In the first Civil War, before the Self-Denying Ordinance obliged his resignation, he had proved himself a redoubtable cavalryman in William Waller's army, and with his green standard at the head of his famous regiment of heavy cuirassiers had distinguished himself at Lansdowne, at Roundway Down and at Cheriton. Since then he had built a great estate and fortune by purchasing the confiscated lands of the diocese of Durham. He was Lambert's adversary almost to the very end.

Against the clique led by these two men, the Army was the only articulate section of a nation weary of politics and weary of war. But to the demands of Lambert's followers the Commons, seeking to perpetuate their seats, answered with evasion and procrastination, and Lambert and Harrison intensified their propaganda with prayers and preachings and circular letters, until at last Cromwell himself, his patience exhausted, marched down to the House with a squad of musketeers one memorable day in April, 1653, turned the members out of doors and with historic words ordered that the golden symbol of Parliamentary authority be seized and taken away. That evening a Cockney wit scrawled upon the outer doors of St. Stephen's: *This House to be let unfurnished.*

Lambert had no part in that forcible dissolution, but that afternoon accompanied Cromwell and Harrison when they strode in upon the Council of State and dismissed it likewise. Thus was Lambert revenged, and thus did the flame of revolution, in the manner that revolutions have, consume the hand that kindled it. King, Church, Lords — all had perished, and now the sere and shrunken form of the Commons themselves sank feebly into the furnace that they had fired, unmourned and unmonumented. In the Lord-General and his marshals was now all the power, to dispose as they might wish, and for a space the three nations were governed by a Council of State of which Lambert was President, with himself, Cromwell and Harrison as virtual dictators. Of the three, Cromwell alone had been bred in the pre-war Parliament tradition. To him the House of Commons was sacred, however unworthy its members might be of the divinity of the institution. Not so the two major-generals. Tom Harrison, so brave of heart and so simple of mind, saw salvation for a wicked generation only in the rule of military saints enforcing righteousness with blood. He was deep in the theological slough of the Fifth Monarchy men, who, inspired by a text from Holy Writ, believed that the millennium was about to begin.

Jack Lambert, however, had no patience just now with either kind of nonsense. On the one hand he was no extreme religionist, and on the other, unlike Cromwell and Vane and Hazelrig, he was a stranger to Parliamentary tradition; for he was a man

> Born in those younger years
> That shone with storms of spears
> And shook in the wind blown from a dead
> world's pyre.

His active brain saw all problems as matters of practical opportunism. To the swift the race, to the strong the fight. Had not saints and lawyers alike shown themselves creatures of cackling mischief, and had not the sword of the Ironsides overthrown them equally in Scotland and in England? Only by strong men could there be good administration — or better still one strong man.

Therefore, although in the Rump's declining hours he had urged the free election of a fresh Parliament, he now urged upon Cromwell the idea of government of the country by a small council of ten or twelve.[195] But for the present Oliver's Parliamentary tradition was too strong for "dear Johnny's" innovations. Nor did he altogether care for Harrison's Mosaic scheme of a council of seventy saints, a Sanhedrin of the new Jerusalem. But it seemed nearer the Parliamentary idea. Accordingly, after a careful scrutiny of lists, the Council of Officers, under Lambert's chairmanship, selected Mr. Praise-God Barebone and 139 fellow saints from all three nations and summoned them to Whitehall. They met on July 4th, 1653, and Cromwell addressed them in the thunders of Sinai. They declared themselves a Parliament, invited Lambert to become a member and appointed him to the Council of State. But Lambert's fears were justified, for Harrison's visionaries dominated their councils, and they began to re-model the three nations according to the tribal plan of Israel.

Out of health, and for the moment out of favour with Cromwell, John retired in August to Wimbledon, where the figs and peaches were ripening on the wall and where woodbine, rose and lavender and all the signal flowers of high summer shimmered in the hazy heat. There he watched and waited. It was the *annus mirabilis* of English naval arms, for, while these quarrels were going on at home in 1653, Blake and Monck and Deane had hammered the Dutch at the great battles of Portland and The Gabbard, and now to Lambert

---

[195] That Lambert at this particular moment proposed anything other than the council of twelve is not confirmed by documents, but it is extremely probable. See *Commonwealth and Protectorate*, ii, 272 *n*.

came news of the final overthrow of Tromp in the third great action of Scheveningen. Lambert's time of idleness was not long. Tired of Barebone's antics, Cromwell began to draw away from Harrison and came nearer to Lambert. In September the two were once more on terms of intimacy, and a scheme began to form itself in John's restless mind. With the influence of Ireton strong in him, he looked back to the old "Heads of the Proposals" and the "Agreement of the People" of 1647, seeing in their main principles of a written constitution, a limited monarchy, a controlled Parliament, religious toleration for all but Catholics, and equality for all in law, the only hope for stable and measured government, and to that ordered scheme he added an idea that seems to have been all his own. He would make Cromwell king.

Towards the end of November Harrison was at last dismissed from favour, and Lambert was expressly sent for. He assembled the principal officers of the Army, and put his plan to them from the chair, but Cromwell would not hear of being crowned, and John once more rode back to Wimbledon. Barebone itself, however, soon gave him an opportunity to bring matters to a head. It made a decision on the question of tithes that was opposed to Cromwell's wishes. Unknown to Cromwell, John assembled the moderate members of the Barebone on the Sabbath, December 11th, 1653, and having won the consent of the Speaker, planned on the morrow's regular sitting that they should take the godly party unawares and dissolve themselves. The next morning they were early in the Chamber and it was moved that

> the sitting of this Parliament any longer as now constituted will not be for the good of the Commonwealth.

Without allowing the question to be put, Speaker Rous left the

Chair and, followed by some fifty members, proceeded to Whitehall and put his resignation in the hands of the Lord-General.

There remained in the House some thirty or so of the godly party, but on Lambert's instructions Colonel Goffe and Lieutenant-Colonel White came in and bade them withdraw, and when they refused, brought in a file of soldiers. What, asked one of the colonels, were the members doing?

"Seeking the Lord," was the reply.

"Come out of this place then," answered the officer, "for to my knowledge the Lord has not been here these twelve years past."[196]

---

[196] Ludlow, 462-3, 472-5; Thurloe, i, 393, 589, 610, 637; C. J., vii, 281; E. 857. 1.

VII. DARLING OF THE ARMY

Harrison was dismissed, and it was Johnny's practical voice which now largely swayed the Lord-General. Indeed, there were those who said that his influence both with army and people was now greater than Cromwell's. He was the ruling spirit in the Council of State; he was the idol of the common soldier. Even royalists looked to him with expectation and approval, and throughout all these years he was distinguished for his generosity to former enemies. They remarked "that he had not his hand immediately in the last King's blood; that he is not severely of any opinion in religion inconsistent with monarchy"; moreover, he was "a gentleman born," "a man learned and well qualified, of courage, conduct, good nature, and discretion."[197]

But Johnny had no thought of being anything but loyal to Cromwell; on the contrary, though Cromwell had not long since referred to him as "bottomless Lambert," he was Oliver's staunchest friend. He it was who, when Presbyterians and Anabaptists alike were vilifying Cromwell, saw that in the person of this man was the one immediate hope of the practical good administration of the country, and that the political uncertainty must be ended by a written constitution. Of all the men who had so facilely pulled down the edifice of state, Lambert alone had any constructive plans for its repair. If Oliver would not have the name of king he should, nevertheless, have the power, for he would persuade him that in the crisis of the nation's affair it was his duty to shoulder the

---

[197] Clarendon MSS., ii, i, 153. Cal. Clar. S.P. 2, 206.

burdens of the throne. Therefore, immediately after the abdication of the Barebone he once more summoned the officers, and on December 13th put before them a document which he called "The Instrument of Government" and under that name destined to become one of the most memorable constitutional papers both of this country and of the United States.

Some of the officers protested that the plan tended to sacrificing all "to the lust and ambition of a single person" and began to declare their dissent. John, however, peremptorily cut short all criticism, telling them that the matter had been resolved and must not be disputed, and after a second meeting he dismissed the officers to their regiments. By December 15th he was able to persuade Cromwell to accept the title of Lord Protector.[198]

Thus it was that Lambert made Cromwell Protector, and immediately upon the next day the ceremony of installation was performed within the immemorial grey stones of Westminster Hall with all the panoply that could be devised for this impromptu act of state. To Lambert, as chief artificer of the grand design, was assigned the duty of installing the Protector. Leading the officers of the Army he carried before him a sword of state, and after a dissertation on the crisis in the affairs of the nation, he in the name of the Army and the three nations desired the Lord-General to accept the Protectorship. Then, the Instrument of Government having been read, and Cromwell having taken the oath prescribed in it, "Major-General Lambert, kneeling, presented him with a sword in the scabbard, representing the Civil Sword; which Cromwell accepting, put off his own, intimating thereby that he would no longer rule by the Military Sword."[199]

---

[198] Ludlow, 476-7; Thurloe, i, 362, 632, 754; Burton, i, 382.

Lambert's part in all these proceedings has without doubt been misconstrued in some chronicles, particularly by the admirers of Cromwell. Ambitious he was, autocratic he was, but a close examination shows no evidence, other than the contemporary venom which was spat at the public men of every party in those days, that he was actuated by any other motives than the establishment of efficient government. The government of the country clearly needed reform and he honestly tried to effect it. There was no place for himself in the Instrument of Government other than a seat on the Council, and he was reducing his position from that of a colleague of the Lord-General's to that of a virtual subject. Nor could he so mistake the masterful character of Cromwell as to suppose that in the new conditions himself would be suffered to usurp one jot of his authority. At a time when neither Cromwell nor any other man was able to produce a practical plan of constitutional navigation, it was Lambert's resourceful mind that, working on the experiments conducted by Ireton, devised a code that placed restraints upon unsteady pilots who threatened to bring up all standing by steering too close to the wind. The Instrument of Government gave to a bewildered people its first bearings back to the ways of sanity. However imperfect, the ship of state was at least provided with a chart.

The next three years were the heyday of Lambert's career. He exerted an influence and an authority second only to the Protector's. He was the brains of the Protectorate Council, as much above Oliver in the capacity for constructive thought as he had been below Ireton. He was recognised by many as the power behind the throne, seeming to some almost to be independent of the Protector and almost equal to him in power. "It lies in his power," wrote a royalist, "to raise Oliver

[199] Ludlow, 480.

higher or else to set up in his place." It was said that he would let him continue Protector but "would rule him as he pleased." "You might," said Cromwell himself later, "have given me a kick on the breech and turned me going."

These, however, were inaccuracies, and he was more in the position of the Protector's first minister. He was a member of the Council of State, a major-general and the darling of the Army, colonel of two regiments, and with Robert Blake joint Lord Warden of the Cinque Ports; presently he was also the military prefect of the North. The officers' ranks were filled by his nominations, and his popularity and influence in the Army were "four times that of Fleetwood." He had an income from all his offices of £6,500 a year, and lived at Wimbledon in the manner of a well-bred prince, not in gilded pomp, but with immense dignity. He was feasted in the City, and when Cromwell rode in state from Whitehall to open his Parliaments, first in 1654 and again in 1656, Lord Lambert rode in the same coach with him and carried the Sword of State. In 1656 it was again demanded by the Army, jealous lest the care of their interests should become submerged in civilian matters, that the Protector should relinquish the office of Commander-in-Chief and appoint Lambert instead; but Cromwell was too shrewd to give such independence to one so popular and so able.[200]

Indeed, it was a time, as the French Ambassador said, when the least soldier in the Army might expect one day to command England. In each man's knapsack was the sceptre of an empire. Cromwell himself had been their exemplar, and any man who so aspired might fight his way to that same pinnacle.

---

[200] Carte, Original Letters, ii, 89; *Narrative of the Late Parliament*, Harleian Misc. ed. Park, ii, 4521; Cal. Clarendon S.P., ii, 380; iii, 333, etc., and iii, 415-6; Whitelocke, 599.

Beneath its outward daily order the country was in a ferment, and Lambert knew the infant state to be encompassed on all sides with watching enemies. Royalists whispered and plotted in ruined manor-houses. The saints of the Fifth Monarchy shouted their gibberish in their weeping temples. Overton, Okey (now Lord of Ampthill) and Lawson the sailor were discovered in a plot and disgraced, and others followed. Republicans and communists lampooned the Protector in coarse scribblings and allegorical cartoons. Fanatic and lunatic alike fell into ecstasies; while Anna Trapnell fasted beneath Cromwell's windows in Whitehall in sentimental worship, Thomas Taney in a mad frenzy threw Bible, saddle, sword and pistol into the flames of his Lambeth bonfire.

It is small wonder that in such a world a man of John Lambert's upbringing should stand for a rule of order and firmness. "*Salus populi suprema lex*" was more than once his text, and in his eyes there was no health in a multitude of tongues unloosed. Therefore in both the Protectorate Parliaments he stoutly upheld the Instrument of Government and resisted the attempts of the Commons to increase their own powers or to minimise the Protector's.

"Having no rules to circumscribe Parliaments," he said in debate, "the power must be trusted in some person, and fittest in the supreme magistrate." And again: "A right understanding between His Highness and the Parliament is certainly the *salus populi*." During the first Parliament he spoke "several times and with great vigour" in an unsuccessful attempt to persuade the House that the office of Protector should be made hereditary and not elective. A letter-writer of the time said that he did so only to remove any suspicion that he was himself aspiring to the civil throne, and though this may have been only the common venom of the day, there grew up a widespread idea in men's minds in these years that he indeed dreamed of the diadem, not in displacement of Cromwell, for he was never guilty of that sort of sin, but in succession to him. He was, indeed, widely looked upon as Oliver's natural successor.

During these years John was without doubt on terms of personal friendship with the Protector, and their families were in intimate relations. Frances Lambert was on the best of terms with "Her Highness, the Protectress" and the Protector himself, who called her his "jewel," was her close friend and admirer, and even, the tongue of scandal said, "something else as well." On the other hand, Frances Lambert was at daggers drawn with Cromwell's favourite daughter, Betty Claypole, and the animosities between them "grew within one degree of the fishwives at Billingsgate." Cromwell was familiar with the children, too; one may suppose that the short drive over Putney Heath through Kingston to Hampton Court was one that John travelled often, there to hawk or to hunt the buck in the pleasant riverside pastures, to play bowls on the Palace lawns, or to listen to John Hingeston playing the organ. John was allowed even to pick the Protector's own Lifeguards. Cromwell more than once paid a visit to Lambert's Yorkshire home of Calton Hall, for during the years 1655-56 he signed the register of Kirby Malham Church three times as a witness to marriages.[201]

Politically, Lambert's views were usually in focus with the Protector's, save in the field of foreign affairs, wherein his opposition to Oliver's duplex policy adds something to Johnnie's reputation. Lambert disagreed with Cromwell strongly over the folly of the West Indian Expedition in 1654,

---

[201] *News from the New Exchange*, 1650; Noble, *Memoirs of the Cromwell Family*, 1789, ii, 369; Cal. Clarendon S. P., iii, 329, 239, 415. Kirby Malham Church Register.

forecasting accurately what would be its outcome, and he stood out for a course of friendship with Spain and war with France. For Spain was easily England's best customer, and the war proved to do great harm to the clothing industry, which was the first in importance and which had a close bond with Lambert as a West Riding man. Unlike Oliver, he did not look upon foreign policy as being dictated by religion, and in the later debates on the Baltic issue he said:

> I will not judge whether this be a Protestant war or no… The interest of England is, or ought to be, the great care in this business.[202]

When Lockhart went as ambassador to France, John sent his own Secretary, Swift, with him, and Swift, whom royalists seems to have considered "a most dangerous and subtle villain," evidently journeyed back and forth.[203] But otherwise there was little divergence. He had no regrets when the first Parliament, proving as difficult as the Barebone, was summarily dismissed by Cromwell after less than five months' life, and he heartily approved when in August, 1655, Cromwell instituted the reign of the major-generals as the only seeming alternative to insecurity and indiscipline, for, he said later, "the quarrel is now between light and darkness; not who shall rule, but whether we shall live, or be preserved, or no."[204]

It was but natural that the Lord Lambert should be appointed Major-General of the North, but he was too high in the State's councils to be spared from London, and he appointed Colonel Charles Howard and his old comrade Robert Lilburne as his deputies. By some he was considered to

---

[202] Clarke Papers, iii, App. B.; Burton, iii, 400.
[203] Cal. Clarendon S. P., iii, 416, 239.
[204] Burton, i, 319.

be the author of the hated system,[205] and from this period may be dated the growth of a body of animosity towards him. Nevertheless, though an autocrat in principle, he remained always tolerant and generous in habit, and not only the religious sects, but royalists and even Roman Catholics, also benefited from his tolerance; by many royalists he was looked upon as their best friend.

"I have laboured," he said later, "to oblige that party; to win them, as much as may be," but he had to add that he "found it impossible till time wear out the memory. They are as careful to breed up their children in the memory of the quarrel as can be."[206]

When the case of James Naylor, the blasphemous Quaker, who had served as quartermaster in his regiment of horse, came before the second Parliament, Lambert spoke actively in Naylor's defence, both for his own belief in liberty of conscience and for old soldiership's sake. "He was a man," Lambert told the House, "of a very unblameable life and conversation, a member of a very sweet society, of an independent Church."[207]

John was generous also in material things. To Robert Leslie, who, like himself, was a great lover of horse-flesh, he presented a rich coach and team of horses. To the watermen of Putney he gave a piece of river-side land to build a boathouse. He remitted the rents of distressed tenants and relieved the wants of necessitous soldiers.[208]

When Glencairn's rising took place in Scotland in '54, Lambert's regiment of horse went north to serve under

---

[205] By some modern writers this is too lightly accepted; there is no sort of proof, though there is a strong likelihood.
[206] Burton, i, 240.
[207] Ibid, i, 33, 218.
[208] Cal. Clarendon, iii, 195; Bartlett, *Hist, and Ants, of Wimbledon.*

Monck, and for the remainder of the years till '59 was stationed generally in Yorkshire. His lieut.-colonel, either now or later, was Jeremiah Camfield, and his major William Goodrick, who before long, however, began to be suspected of royalism and to be described as "a creature of the Court." Lambert's troop commanders included Capt. John Pockley, under whom John Hodgson served, and Captain Martin Lister, Frances Lambert's brother. Three of the Baynes family also held commissions, Adam lining his pockets at Westminster and John doing the like in Scotland.

Lambert's foot regiment was perhaps generally in London. Its lieut.-colonel, John Duckenfield, was an ardent supporter of Lambert, was constantly with him and remained staunch to him to the end. Among the gatherings of officers in London Lambert also had an ardent follower in Major Richard Creed, who was later to have a commission in Lambert's horse.[209]

---

[209] See, principally, numerous letters in L.R.O.

VIII. THE QUARREL

It was not till 1657 that the quarrel came. On February 23rd, Sir Christopher Pack, a wealthy wool merchant and one of the members for London, introduced a Bill, to be known as the Remonstrance, to revise the constitution, to re-establish the House of Lords, and to empower the Protector to assume the title and dignity of King. The plan had been devised by men of big vested interests with the help of the lawyers, and Lord Broghil, an Irish peer, ex-royalist and now close confidant of Cromwell, was one of its chief architects.

There was an immediate storm. For more than three years Lambert and the Army had been the main prop of the Cromwellian protectorate. Whenever Parliament had attacked that regimen it had been Lambert and the soldiers who had risen to defend it. But this strange reversal caused a like reversal in the Army. It was one thing to be King by gift of the Army and quite another to be so by gift of the civilians, and that which John had pressed upon Cromwell in 1653 he would in no wise favour now.

With the progress of events he had changed his views — as Cromwell had. He had, moreover, been put in an ill-temper by the rebuff that Parliament had dealt him and his followers in abolishing the major-generals against his strenuous protests. He now led a vigorous opposition to the Remonstrance, and he pointed out shrewdly that the crowning of an illegitimate king would cause very soon a reaction in favour of Charles Stuart, the "Common Enemy." Even Cromwell's own kinsmen in the Army, even Fleetwood and Disbrowe, were alarmed, and added their voices to Lambert's; and here for a moment we must look at these two others of Cromwell's captains whose destinies were to be closely linked with Lambert's in the swift *peripeties* of the next three years.

Charles Fleetwood, lieutenant-general and titular second-in-command of the Army, new lord of the great manor of Woodstock, was Cromwell's son-in-law by his marriage with the Protector's daughter Bridget, widow of Ireton. He had been a competent soldier, but in peace he was a man little to be admired — a man of pious duplicity, given to the hysteria of tears so common among these godly warriors, often referred to as "the weeping Anabaptist," and dubbed even by his father-in-law a "milk-sop." A man of feeble resolution, "of courage cold as a cucumber," he had no gifts of leadership, but lent himself readily to be pushed either by the passions of his wife or the designs of the Army officers.

Major-General John Disbrowe was of a very different build. A Cambridgeshire farmer, he had married Cromwell's sister and had been bred in Cromwell's own regiment of authentic Ironsides. There could therefore be small doubt of his prowess as a cavalryman, but he was a man devoid of gentler parts — an arrogant boor, a boastful swashbuckler, a barrack-room swaggerer. He was pig-headed, brusque of manner, violent of temper. Disbrowe was the real force behind Fleetwood.

These were the men — together with such as Adam Baynes, who had made a large fortune by profiteering in soldiers' "debentures,"[210] and the pretentious Colonel Sydenham — who were Lambert's chief associates in his campaign against conferring the crown upon Cromwell. One can hardly doubt that in the past three years of virtual dictatorship the flame of Lambert's own secret aspirations had waxed bright. He was

---

[210] The credit notes issued to soldiers whose pay was in arrear, often bought by officers cheaply in ready cash.

seated at the right hand of the Protector's throne and he felt no doubt that the reversion in it was rightly his, his as the chief instrument in its making and his as the Army's certain choice. He had without doubt been widely regarded as Cromwell's successor. Shortly before the Remonstrance, when the problem of the succession was troubling men's minds, he had said, if we may believe the French ambassador:

> The question is not whether Richard or John should succeed, but whether we shall go backwards or advance.

— whether, in others words, monarchy should be re-established or the republic be confirmed.[211] Such was his loyalty to Cromwell that thoughts of usurpation had no place in his mind, even had he supposed he possessed the power, but there was no disloyalty in dreaming that he might succeed him. As Colonel John Bridge said, every man in the nation had an equal right of succession on the death of the Protector.[212] It is too often forgotten that, as things stood then, Lambert was without doubt the obvious successor to Oliver, for, after him, there was no public man who loomed so large.

Moreover, the restraints on religious toleration which the Remonstrance included were against his settled notions, and, in a word, the whole Remonstrance, as compared with his own Instrument of Government, was reactionary legislation. As a child of the Army and as one who since 1653 had travelled far on the road of military dictatorship, he could see nothing but evil in the prospect of a return to civilian domination. And, in truth, it is small wonder that a practical and active man should

---

[211] Bordeaux to Mazarin, Feb. 5/15th, R. O. Transcripts.
[212] Lansdowne MSS., 821, fol. 89.

have little respect for Parliament after all the antic legislation and windy ecstasies that he had seen there in his own time.

There was no ground for Thurloe's fear that Lambert would attempt anything in the likeness of mutiny, and he held to a constitutional path. On February 26th he addressed a gathering of officers at Disbrowe's lodgings, urging them to unite in opposition to the Remonstrance, but to do so with moderation and patience, and the next evening, after the fast-day sermons had burnt their fires, he led a deputation of a hundred officers to wait upon Cromwell himself.

With Lt.-Colonel Mills as their spokesman, they told him, with that frankness of speech which he and they enjoyed between them, that the offer of the crown was not pleasing to the Army, was "a matter of scandal to the people of God," was hazardous to his own person and to the three nations. Cromwell answered them roundly and with equal frankness. Looking, it is said, directly at Lambert, he reminded them that they themselves had once offered him the crown and he had refused it. He had been their drudge long enough — calling and dismissing Parliaments, rooting out the ministry, appointing the major-generals, virtually, he said, at their behest. Now had come this Parliament which the Army's own impatience had demanded against his will, and they could blame no one if the House failed to be as compliant to the Army's wishes as they had confidently hoped.[213]

With a curt good night he dismissed them from that famous interview, and most of them slunk away abashed with their tails between their legs, but not so Lambert. When a deputation of the officers a few days later assured the Protector "of their satisfaction in his Highness," John remained unshaken in his

---

[213] Clarke Papers, iii, 92; Lansdowne MSS., 821; Burton, i, 381; Thurloe, vi, 93.

opposition. Throughout the March debates in the House he and Disbrowe and the plaintive Fleetwood maintained a violent opposition to the kingly title and the House of Lords. In spite of it all, however, the tide flowed against them, for there could now be no purgings or picketings of Parliament, no seizures of the mace. So at length the fateful proposals were passed, and on March 31st, under the new name of the "Humble Petition and Advice," they were submitted to his Highness in the Banqueting House of Whitehall.

From that august scene, the Lord Lambert, whose exalted office it was to bear the sword of state, was conspicuously an absentee. He had already broken with Cromwell, and, save once, he probably never again spoke to him as a friend. While young Montague performed his stately office, he watched and waited sullenly among the daffodils of Wimbledon. On April 3rd he had the satisfaction of learning that, in spite of Parliament, the influence of the Army had done its work. Cromwell rejected the Humble Petition. Then for five weeks, while Blake was making his victorious dash upon Santa Cruz, the leaders of the House laboured to persuade him to change his mind, and Lambert, rejoicing at Cromwell's decision, now studiously "stood at a distance," content that matters should take their course and satisfied as to the result.

Very soon, however, it became apparent that Cromwell was wavering, and there is no doubt that he felt the lure of the great prize. The leaders of the Commons plied him hard, and soon he told his friends that he would accept it. He dined with Fleetwood and Disbrowe and said to them that it was but a small thing and no harm could come of it, but they answered with set faces and averted eyes. It was time now for the officers to give a frank ultimatum. Lambert entertained the chief of them to a dinner in his own turn, and it was then, perhaps, that their minds were resolved. On May 6th, Disbrowe met Cromwell in St. James's Park and told his brother-in-law that if he took the crown he and Lambert and Fleetwood would resign from all their public offices. John himself was believed to have said to his face that if he accepted the crown he could not guarantee the loyalty of the Army. Pride (now lord of the royal manor of Nonesuch) also added his voice, organising a petition which was presented at the Bar of the House two days later.[214]

The voices of his old comrades in arms were too strong for Oliver, and on May 8th he once more refused the crown, but for Lambert there was to be small satisfaction in that refusal, for on the 25th of the same month Oliver came to terms with Parliament on the remainder of the Humble Petition, whereby, among its provisions for a House of Lords and other constitutional reforms, the Lord Protector was to have the right to nominate his successor. It was a monarchy in all but name, and John's hopes of succession were gone. He was angry with Cromwell, angry with the Commons, angry with the world. Was he to make way for such a simpleton as Richard Cromwell? He was a marked absentee from the royal ceremonial of Cromwell's second installation on June 26th and abstained from the meetings of the Council.

All this Lambert might have endured, but the final offence came when the Commons, against the opposition of himself, William Sydenham and John Baynes, resolved that all officers of State should take an oath of fidelity to the person of the Protector. Oaths, said John, were snares. There were men who

---

[214] Thurloe, vi, 219, 281; Ludlow, 588, 593; Clarke Papers, iii, 99; C. J., vii, 516; Bordeaux to Mazarin, May 14/24th. The exact date of Lambert's party is not known, but I have placed it as seems most probable.

would glibly swear to anything, but suppose an oath was of such a sort as to strain the conscience of those who had faithfully served the State? It was true that under the old Instrument, his own handiwork, members of the Council had been required to swear allegiance to the Commonwealth and the Protestant faith, but no oath of fealty to the Protector personally had been demanded of them, and on that rock Lambert struck.[215]

The first meeting of the Council under the new Constitution was summoned for July 3rd, and it was demanded of all members that they should now take the oath. Less than half did so on that day. One by one, however, they yielded, some not till months later. Even Sydenham threw his protestations to the winds. Lambert, however, was given no second chance. He had been particularly summoned to the Council, and his friends had urged him to submit, but "ambition dare not stoop." Cromwell's friends, on the other hand, had urged the Protector to grasp this opportunity of shutting out of doors one who stood too much in their way, though the sagacious Thurloe was opposed to such a course, believing that "a little time will give light in these things."

On July 11th, on the Protector's summons, John rode up from Wimbledon and attended upon him, and we may believe that Cromwell's words to his old comrade were spoken more in sorrow than in anger. Again reminding John that it was he who had first pressed the crown upon him, he said he was assured that Lambert's present refusal to take the oath "proceeded not on account of this new authority"; therefore, if he was dissatisfied with the present posture of affairs, he desired him to surrender his commission. To this Lambert replied coolly:

---

215 Burton, ii, 276, 286, 289, 295; Ludlow, 592; Thurloe, vi, 412.

"Having no suspicion that it would be demanded of me, I have not brought my commission with me; but if you will be pleased to send for it, I will deliver it."[216]

Accordingly five days later one of the clerks of the Council presented himself at the great mansion at Wimbledon, bearing the following letter, dated July 13th:

Sir, I have sent this bearer, Mr. William Jessop, to you for your commission as major-general, as also your other commissions, to whom I desire you to deliver them enclosed and sealed up in a paper.

Your loving friend,
Oliver, P.[217]

In spite of Lambert's ready compliance, it was a terrible blow to him. "My Lord Lambert," wrote Sir Francis Russell, "looks but sadly." The proud red uniform that he had worn for twelve years was laid aside, his regiments that had followed his standard to victory at Preston, at Dunbar, at Inverkeithing and at Worcester, and his post as commander of the finest cavalry on earth, were all taken from him, and, with that nepotism that characterised Cromwell, given to the Protector's relatives — the foot to Fleetwood, the horse to Lord Fauconberg, the cavalry command to Disbrowe; while the Council of State itself became likewise a Cromwellian family party. At thirty-seven John saw all his employments stripped from him by the man beside whom he had ridden so often into the face of death, the man with whom he had stood watching the Scottish hosts marching down from the height of Doon and compassed their destruction while he watched, the man to whose victories his quick brain and his unselfish sword had given so much, the

---

[216] Ludlow, 593; Thurloe, vi, 427.
[217] Historical MSS. Commission, 3rd Report: Clarke Papers, iii, 113.

man whom he had placed upon the unanointed throne of the three kingdoms. He may well have thought of Cromwell in the words that a royalist wrote of him to Monck:

"When his own turn be served, he cares not if his instruments are hanged; nay, he very often hangs them himself… Look at Lambert and several others of his creatures, how he hath served them."

No less hurtful must have been his realisation that, in the general opinion, his fall was unregretted. Few mourned him. Cromwell had brought Fleetwood and Disbrowe and the rest complacently to heel, but Lambert's stand upon a cause in which so many were professedly of his own mind won him small sympathy in that turbulent society. Though his following in the Army was large, it was a time when men bowed before the strong hand, and if Lambert had dared to outface Cromwell and had failed, then he must walk in the wilderness alone. To the strong still the fight. "Never was any man less pitied," wrote one; "he was all for himself; he hoped to be next Protector; and because the nominating of the successor was agreed of, therefore he was discontented."[218] Even the officers of Lambert's own regiments sent their protestations of fidelity to the Protector.

Cromwell's own feelings, like so much else of the man, remain still a mystery. In spite of their occasional differences — for both were strong-willed men and gusty — Oliver and John had during these years been the closest of friends. Royalists, looking for the seeds of discord, often supposed that Oliver was jealous of John, and a year before the Remonstrance it had been written that he "often goes about like one distracted, through jealousy and discontent with Lambert,"[219] but one doubts if this fits the character of the

---

[218] *The Grand Concernments of England Ensured*, 1659, 61.

man. He could, if he wished, have got rid of him as he had already got rid of Harrison and Ludlow and Harry Vane. The fact is that Cromwell never thought out a course of policy ahead (indeed it was Lambert who did the thinking), but acted as the circumstances of the moment dictated, and when he dismissed Lambert it may well be that, in these his irritable last years, he was not sorry to be freed of one so tameless and swift and proud.

Moved by ambition though he was, there is in the end something to be said for Lambert. Cromwell himself had shown him how to be a rebel, and no man was an apter pupil. He had been impulsive and inconsistent, but at least he did maintain the ensign of his courage. Alone of those who had so passionately sworn opposition he stood by that which he had declared to be his conviction. Alone of all the Council he refused subservience, and watched while the sons of Cromwell and the husbands of his daughters and his sisters were conducted to the seats that had been his or were raised to various other offices of State.

Nor were loss of place and power and pride his only misfortunes. For he lost besides an income of £2,200 a year. However, either for the sake of old days, or else because, as Ludlow says, he "did not think it safe to disgust him entirely" and deemed it expedient "to keep him from any desperate undertaking,'" Cromwell continued his major-general's pay of £365 a year.[220]

But no "desperate undertakings" were in John's mind. The wind was humming with plots against Cromwell's life, but he

---

[219] Cal. Clarendon S. P., iii, 416.
[220] Clarke Papers, iii, 114, 119; Harleian Miscellany, iii, 452. The pay for a colonel of foot was the same as that for a major-general; for a colonel of horse £474 10s., and for a member of the Council £1,000.

had no part in them, nor in one that Cromwell should be deposed and himself raised to his throne, and it was likewise in vain that the royalists looked to him to rise for the King. Instead he retired quietly to Wimbledon, where the roses were now in full bloom and the bees were busy among the lavender in the July haze. For a year or more his flowers and his pictures absorbed his attention. But in February of 1658, when advancing death was within but six months' march, Cromwell sought a reconciliation with his old friend.

At his invitation Lambert came once more to Whitehall and there Cromwell fell upon his neck, kissed him, called him "dear Johnny" and inquired tenderly after "his jewel," Frances, and all his children by name. The next day Frances Lambert called on Elizabeth Cromwell, "who immediately fell into a kind quarrel for her long absence, disclaimed policy and statecraft, but professed a motherly kindness to her and hers, which no change could ever alter." Four days later, however, Cromwell opened the wound afresh by depriving the Lamberts of the lodgings assigned to them in Whitehall and giving them to Fauconberg. Lambert was moved anew to wrath and his wife to tears, and to the end they remained hostile to the Protector.[221]

---

[221] Hutchinson, ii. 206; Clarendon S. P., iii, 329.

IX. THE CROMWELL TOUCH

Six months later, on September 3rd, 1658, Oliver Cromwell died, borne down with the weight of burdens beyond the strength of mortal shoulders. For a moment his world was struck with the dumb wonder that falls upon the mind when a great man dies, as though, in Bossuet's words, it were impossible to believe "that this mortal has died."[222] In that hushed moment the watching Lambert saw the sceptre that might have been his pass quietly and uncontested into the feeble hands of Richard Cromwell. But it required no great perspicacity to see that in that turbulent sea of opposing ideals and clashing ambitions so poor a pilot as Richard could not long hold the helm; for he was but a lazy country squire, unthrifty and insolvent, something of a boon companion, absorbed in pastoral and sporting pursuits and having neither training nor taste for public affairs.

It was not long before the wolves began snuffing at the heels of so easy a prey, and John saw the new Protector's own kinsmen, Fleetwood and Disbrowe, mantled with the same sin of which himself had been accused. It was at Fleetwood's residence, Wallingford House, on the site where the Admiralty now stands, that the Council of Officers was in the habit of meeting, and they at once began to scheme for a military dictatorship, determined to take advantage of Richard's weakness in order to make the Army independent of the civil power. For the Army, though content for the while to accept Richard as Protector, had no fancy for so pale a shadow of the

---

[222] Guizot, i, 6.

great Oliver as their commander-in-chief. "*We have seen,*" said Vane later, "*that he wears a sword at his side; but has he ever drawn it?*" They therefore waited upon Richard in deputation and demanded that Fleetwood should be appointed generalissimo. The gentle Richard surprised them by roundly refusing their demand, but the officers quietly retired, merely to gather impetus for a higher leap.

Lambert, no longer a member of the Army, stood at first aloof from these intrigues, quite satisfied to accept the new Protector, though many eyes turned once more to the handsome Yorkshireman for the execution of their hopes, and the royalists sought in vain to win him. This fidelity he acknowledged openly when Richard's Parliament met on January 27th, 1659, a Parliament elected freely and without dragoonings. Lambert was returned as member for Aldborough and for Pontefract, and for the latter he took his seat. There was at once a struggle over the recognition of the new Protector, and Lambert from the beginning took a prominent part. "We are all," he said, "for this honourable person that is now in the power." He was fully content to forget the past, and when others recounted their grievances he forbore from falling "into the same infirmity." "In this great matter (the constitution) every man should lay aside self, relations, and persons, and study to have a government so settled as may give strength, and a dependence upon the reformed interest and party of the nation."[223] Nevertheless, he warned the House repeatedly to limit the powers of the Protector, and he said to them:

> The best man is but a man at best. I have had great reason to
> know it. Therefore there ought to be a great deal of care even

---

[223] Burton, iii, 188.

of the best man… Whatever you say to him, let the people's liberties be on the backside of the bond.

Much more there was to the same purpose; for the same reasons he objected again to the House of Lords, as being merely a prop for the Chief Magistrate rather than a champion of the people, and he repeated his objection to monarchy. "Monarchy," he said bluntly, "is the worst government."[224]

John had no part in the councils of Wallingford House, where the senior officers, spurred on by Dr. John Owen, were praying and plotting for the domination of the sword. Nevertheless he still had hosts of friends in the Army — "an army," he told the House, "fit for God Almighty to do miracles withal" — and while the Wallingford House cabal was going on, the regimental officers — the colonels, majors and captains — who were his special friends and admirers, were meeting at the house of Robert Lilburne, and very soon this gathering was to prove of greater force than that of the generals.

In April, as the result of the vote of a House that rightly viewed these meetings with distrust, Richard sent express orders to the Army Council that they were to cease and that Fleetwood himself was to attend at Whitehall. The officers flatly disobeyed, and, with Fleetwood at their head, defiantly held a great parade at St. James's on April 21st. Fleetwood and Disbrowe demanded of him the immediate dissolution of Parliament, and Richard, shrinking from the bloodshed that would have followed a refusal, bowed to their strident cries and dissolved the House on April 21st, 1659. A fortnight later he had ceased to rule, the Protectorate was ended, and the Commonwealth restored.

---

[224] Burton, iii, 186.

The first onset of their passion spent, the leaders of the Army soon found themselves deeply embarrassed. All government had suddenly disappeared, and, with its pretended respect for the rule of law, the Army would not presume openly to reign in its own name. Disbrowe and Fleetwood had intended, not that Richard should be deprived of office, but that they themselves should govern the three nations in his name; but they found to their chagrin that they had raised a storm they could not control, and that presently Lambert was to ride on the crest of the wave in the waters that themselves had whipped into tumult.

For while the senior officers met next day at Wallingford House, the junior officers were doing likewise in the Chapel of St. James's, and there a momentous decision was made. John was advisedly absent, but at his instigation Robert Lilburne put forward the proposal that the Protectorate should end, the Commonwealth be restored, and that the Rump of the old Long Parliament — the very men whom Cromwell had turned out in 1653 — should be recalled to sit at Westminster. Prompted by Dr. Owen, the officers, who were ardent republicans and disliked a Protector as much as a King, readily agreed, and the next morning they presented their demands to Fleetwood and Disbrowe, urging as well that the Lord Lambert should be restored to his old commands in the Army. The two generals were furious, suspecting John's ambition to supplant them, but, knowing the great bulk of the Army to be behind the officers, they were powerless to refuse.[225]

At first John was restored only to the command of his old cavalry regiment, which had been given to Fauconberg, who had sided with Richard, and an immediate purge was made of other Cromwellian commanders likewise, not the least of

---

[225] Baker, 569; Whitelocke, 677.

whom was Colonel Richard Ingoldsby, who, though he had ridden under John in the Dunbar campaign, was now, with the zeal of the proselyte, his particular enemy, for he had begged Richard's permission to be personally responsible for Lambert, and he was at the last to be the agent of his downfall.

From this moment, however, Jack Lambert was at the head of the officers, and he found at once a hearty supporter in Harry Vane. The two men and their colleagues in Parliament and Army respectively met at Vane's house in Charing Cross and planned the return of the Rump, on certain terms that would protect the Army against any act of revenge for the arrogance of 1653. On May 6th the leaders of Army and Parliament visited old Speaker Lenthall at his house in Chancery Lane and John, acting as spokesman, invited him once more to take his place in the Chair of St. Stephen's and to send out writs to all the old "Rumpers" of 1653. The old man refused. He pleaded age and infirmity, but in truth he was thinking of the security of his Cromwellian pseudo-peerage. So they went forward without him, sending out messengers on all sides for the old members to reassemble the next day at St. Stephen's, extricating some from prison and rousing others from their beds.

Then on the morning of May 7th the authors of the plan proceeded to the House, and, protected by a guard provided by Lambert, waited for the old members to arrive. One by one there came in during the day from far and near all the queer shapes of that phantom republic — the upright and the servile, the saint and the knave, the hero and the sneak. Some ninety came in all, and at last old Lenthall came, too. Like an old dog jealous for his corner, he could not abide to see the old pack gathering in the familiar courts and be himself left out. Thus did the relics of the most famous of Parliaments once more reassemble, while the officers grouped outside swore to live and die with them.

From the beginning they really had no chance. The fervent haste of Vane and Hazelrig was itself witness to the undercurrent of unease, for beneath their republican zeal was a secret fear and in their faith in the cause was a deep anxiety for its destiny. For they feared not only the royalists, now in a fresh ferment of activity, but also the Army that had restored them, and they saw around them a people so indifferent to their actions and so contemptuous of their motives that only a few ironic jeers greeted this great and sudden constitutional change. It was by their own folly they were to be wrecked, for they failed to keep faith with their own saviours, and, standing upon a dignity that had no material foundation, irritated the Army leaders beyond endurance by little gratuitous indignities and by resistance to demands that had substantial justification and that common prudence should have persuaded them generously to grant. Of the coming quarrel Lambert was to be the storm-centre, for although he was restored to his place on the Council of State and although his infantry regiment was returned to him in addition to his cavalry, larger issues were to bring all to ruin.

The Rump had sat only a week when John, who was, of course, not a member of it, came before them at the head of a deputation of officers to present a petition, in which he asked the House for immediate fulfilment of the conditions on which in the conferences at Vane's house the Army had agreed to allow the Parliament to reassemble. One of these demands was for an act of oblivion for all anti-republican acts done under Cromwell, for John was far from blind to the danger that he himself was not the least of those who would be exposed to the jealousy, the revenge and the malice of those whom he had displaced after 1653 and whose principles of the sovereignty of the people he had so deeply offended before the rebuffs of fortune had made him in his own turn so protesting a republican.

Of these and the other demands of the petition the House promised satisfaction, but when at length the act of oblivion was passed, Lambert was still deeply dissatisfied, for it still left openings by which men who had received multiple salaries under the Protectorate might be brought to book. Meeting Ludlow and Hazelrig the next morning, he said:

"It signifies nothing and leaves us still at mercy."

"You are," replied Hazelrig, "only at the mercy of the Parliament, who are your good friends."

"I know not," John retorted, "why they should not be at our mercy as well as we at theirs."[226]

It was the first sign of a new breach. Lambert quarrelled violently with Hazelrig, whose pugnacious dogmatism seemed voluntarily to grasp every opportunity for creating new breaches in the weak political walls. Against his harsh voice Vane, Ludlow and Whitelocke raised their own as allies of Lambert, "knowing," in Ludlow's words, "how much it imported the very being of our cause to maintain a good correspondence between the Parliament and the Army." Harry Vane in particular was to be John's friend and ally to the end.

Less apparent, but none the less certain, was the secret undercurrent of royalism that swept afresh below the surface of the national life after Fleetwood's outrage of April. To the camps of the cavaliers had come their quondam enemies the Presbyterians, leaders of the old Parliamentary army such as the Earl of Stamford and Sir William Waller, and even Cromwellians such as Fauconberg and Broghil. Montague was

---

[226] Ludlow, 676, 677.

already holding the fleet in readiness for the return of Charles. The King's agents were everywhere active, and Charles himself, "The Common Enemy," stood upon the coast of France ready to cross for an expected rising.

On August 1st, Sir George Booth, who had so gallantly held Nantwich for Parliament in '44, but who had been one of the Presbyterians excluded from the House in Pride's Purge, took arms at Warrington. In a violent storm with torrents of summer rain, he summoned the squires and the tenantry of Cheshire to his standard. From Lancashire and from the marches of Wales more royalists came in to him, headed by the Earl of Derby and old Sir Thomas Middleton, who, defying his eighty years, rode in with brandished sword at the head of a troop of horsemen. They occupied Chester without resistance and their numbers rose to 4,500.

In this moment of crisis Parliament acted with all its old vigour, but the Council of State was assailed with doubts as to whom to trust with the command. They looked at once, not to Fleetwood, the commander-in-chief, but to Lambert, whom they recognised to be the most able and the most popular of the republic's soldiers, and while they deliberated came news which decided them. Some royalists came to Frances Lambert with magnificent offers if she would engage her husband for the King. But she told her husband at once, and John in turn reported to Vane, bringing in addition news from his own connections of a threatened rising in Craven. Here for the Council was proof enough of fidelity, and in spite of the enmity of Colonel Hutchinson, Lambert was appointed on August 5th forthwith to march against Booth.[227]

He left London the next day, and marched with great speed through Coventry and Shropshire. He had made his

---

[227] Ludlow, 691; Cal. S. P. Dom., 59-60, 72, 75.

dispositions carefully, had sent forward Creed (whom he had now secured as his own cavalry major in place of the covert royalist Goodrick) to watch and keep him informed of the enemy's movements, and had secured the promise of an Irish brigade from Ludlow. Having covered fifteen miles a day, he arrived at the head of 5,000 men in the familiar country of Cheshire. Here sixteen years before as a boy colonel, fighting beside the man who was now his adversary, he had first won the praise of Fairfax; here five years later as a rising young general, he had chased the fugitive horsemen of Hamilton; and here, later still, as the right hand of Cromwell, he had checked the advance of Charles Stuart.

To-day he found that Booth, disappointed in his hopes of a general royalist rising and left to play a lone part without plans, was plunged into indecision and desired a parley. Lambert refused him, and showing again all his old mastery of swift unhesitating action, faced his rebellious army at Winnington Bridge, near Northwich, on August 19th and overwhelmed it with scarcely a blow. Two days later Lambert recaptured Chester, and on the 24th Middleton surrendered to him in his castle of Chirk.[228]

The royalist cause, its standard untimely raised and its champions nervous and oppressed by the memory of ancient defeats, collapsed utterly. Lambert rode back southwards alone, but in triumph. He was in high fettle, for he had proved that in eight years' idleness his sword had not rusted and that the old mastery of touch dwelt still within his hand. He was rising now to the crest of the wave, and he felt the strong surge

---

[228] Booth escaped in the dress of a woman, riding pillion behind a man, but the suspicions of the innkeeper of the 'Red Lion' at Newport Pagnell, roused by an unmaidenly manner of dismounting, were confirmed by a tactless request for a razor and wash-ball, and he was arrested.

of the living waters beneath him. "He has so gained on the affections of the soldiery," wrote Charles's secretary, Sir Edward Nicholas, "that they begin already to cry him up as the only fit person to be their general."[229] Nevertheless, in spite of the tongues of scandal and suspicion, thoughts of personal aggrandisement seem to have been quite absent from him, and it was through the jealousies, the intrigues and the folly of others that he was presently to be drawn into the vortex of passionate enmities.

While John was yet away greeting old friends in the northern and the midland shires and travelling eastward as far as Norwich, Fleetwood requested the House that Lambert, as a reward for his services, should be restored to his rank of major-general. Again it was the pugnacious bigotry of Hazelrig, blind to the dictates of political prudence and pricked on by his animosity to Lambert, who led the denial of the demand and caused a stilted resolution that there was no need of more generals. As a solatium the House voted £1,000 to Lambert to buy himself a jewel, but the denial of a titular honour to the man chiefly responsible for restoring the Long Parliament was a needless rebuff to men who looked upon him as the champion of their cause.[230]

John himself, having, it is said, distributed his grant among his soldiers instead of buying a jewel, for his men had received from Parliament only sixpence each of the arrears due to them and were badly in need of shoes and stockings, took the matter coolly enough. The gossips of letter and diary who regarded him as the instigator of a deep design — too deep, indeed, to be credible — must be discounted. It is probable that, as his friend Baynes told a royalist spy, he thought of the

---

[229] Cal. S. P. Dom., 59-60, 234.
[230] Ludlow, 695; C. J., vii, 766.

establishment of "some moderate government," no doubt with himself well in the front. His good birth, his friendships and family links with northern royalists and the decency of his behaviour towards men of that party led their agents, and Lord Mordaunt in particular, to look to him as their chief hope, in spite of their recent rebuff. Their spies were in his very house, watching and courting his wife, his servants and his friends, and they only awaited his return to London to sound him personally.[231]

He returned on September 20th, to witness the outburst of a new storm. Two or three days afterwards Hazelrig received information that the officers of Lambert's brigade against Booth, provoked by Parliament's refusal of the request for his promotion, had met at Derby and prepared a petition to the House. The leaders in this matter were Colonel Zanchey, Colonel William Mitchell, Colonel Duckenfield and Major Creed, who had openly said that he knew no reason why Lambert should depend upon Parliament for any command. By these three the petition was prepared, and John was unaware of it and even of the fact that the meeting had taken place, and this fact, attested by Fleetwood, by Vane, by Lambert himself and notably by Colonel Mitchell in his letter to Monck's secretary, is important to remember in refutation of the indictments that were to be made against Lambert alike by his contemporaries and by historians.[232]

The petition reiterated the demands made in May as the Army's conditions for restoring the Long Parliament, upon which they felt that the House had not kept faith, and they also repeated the demand that Lambert should be restored to his

---

[231] Carte, ii, 204.
[232] Leyborne-Popham MSS., 122-3; Clarke Papers, iv, 58.

old rank, as well as asking for permanent appointments for Fleetwood, Disbrowe and Monck.[233]

Hazelrig learnt that the petition had been sent to Fleetwood in London with the request that it should be presented to the House, and he now demanded that Fleetwood should produce it at once. Fleetwood did so. The irreconcilables were enraged at what they considered an affront to their dignity, for the petition was in tones of insistence, and Hazelrig burst into one of his transports of passion. His fevered mind at once imagined the hand of Lambert. In secret session on September 23rd he "aggravated the heinousness of the offence," to use Ludlow's words, and demanded that Lambert, whom he declared to be the real author of the petition, should be impeached and committed to the Tower, and although the House would not endorse such folly, the harm was done. Their vote was a severe reprimand to all the petitioners.

It was a direct challenge, but for the moment the officers followed moderation. John himself, though present at their next meeting, stood aloof, a passive spectator of these scenes, disavowing the Derby petition, and even begging to be allowed to resign his commissions. A new and milder memorial was drawn up, perfectly reasonable in its terms, and on October 5th Disbrowe presented it at the Bar of the House with a speech of studied moderation. For several days the House debated it, with conflicting alternations of wise toleration and petulant asperity. Amidst it all Vane, who was thought to be aiming at the appointment of Lambert as Protector, stood forth as his champion, protesting that John was not responsible for the petition and that he deserved better treatment for his great services to the Commonwealth.[234] Then,

---

[233] "The Humble Petition and Proposals of the Officers under the Command of the Lord Lambert in the late Northern Expedition."

on October 12th, Okey informed the House that the officers'
petition had been printed and circulated throughout the Army,
together with a letter signed by nine officers, of whom
Lambert was one, asking for the support of every regiment in
testimony of the unanimity of their desires.

Hazelrig exploded. In a white heat of indignation the House,
jealously supposing that the canvass was an attempt to foment
the Army against them, cashiered the nine officers who had
signed the letter and terminated Fleetwood's personal
command of the Army, which was vested in a commission, and
before the House rose it ordered that the regiments of
Colonels Okey, Morley and Moss, on which Hazelrig deemed
he could rely, should guard the approaches to the House
throughout the night.

Though the House was sitting behind locked doors in secret
session, news of its decision reached Lambert and his brother
officers. He was incensed at the personal injustice. He had
been sent a warning letter which told him:

> Secure yourself, or to-morrow before this time your head will
> be in danger.

Hazelrig had openly stated his determination that he should
be arrested and shot without delay. Moreover, personal issues
apart, it was clear that the pugnacious vehemence of Hazelrig's
followers was an impossible obstruction to practical
government. What would the great Oliver have done in like
circumstances? With the precedents of his master before him
John resolved to act likewise, and, since his timid colleagues
wavered, to act alone.

---

[234] Carte, ii, 225; Guizot, i, 483.

Early the next morning he ordered both his horse and foot regiments to parade. Camfield, his lieutenant-colonel of horse, who had been appointed by Parliament the day before to command the regiment in his stead, protested, but was overborne by a more masterful will. Placing himself at their head, and with Duckenfield leading his foot, Lambert marched upon Westminster, gathering on the way some troops of cavalry and dragoons and some companies of Vane's new regiment.

As he marched he learnt that, though Okey's dragoons had refused duty, the regiments of Moss and Morley were guarding the approaches to St. Stephen's, but it was too late to turn back. As the early rising citizens were opening their shutters and setting up their stalls about Westminster Hall, wholly indifferent to a quarrel between two powers whom they had long ceased to esteem, Lambert's column emerged from Whitehall, with muskets loaded and matches alight. In every street by which members of Parliament might approach the House he set a detachment of musketeers and pikemen. He barricaded Millbank with carts. He cut off all communication with the City of London save only by the river. He sent Duckenfield with a strong guard to Palace Yard to arrest the Speaker. Then he strode forward in person to the opposing troops.

Morley met him, pistol in hand, and warned him he would fire if he advanced a step farther.

"Colonel," replied John, with studied restraint, "I will go another way, though, if I pleased, I could pass this way."

He turned off in another direction, but was met by Moss at the head of his troops. John advanced towards them, and called out:

"Would you suffer nine of your old officers, who have so often spent their blood for you and with you, to be disgraced and ruined with their families?"

"It were much better," replied Moss, "that nine families should be destroyed, than the civil authority of the nation trampled under foot."

Lambert maintained his stand, however, and addressed Moss's assembled soldiers. One by one, they began to go over to Lambert, while the remainder stood nervous and uneasy. Presently Lambert observed the mounted guard of Parliament under the command of Major Evelyn ride up to the Scotland Yard Gate. He strode over to them, alone and on foot. He ordered them to halt and commanded Evelyn to dismount. Evelyn looked behind, saw that several of his men wavered, heard his lieutenant advise him to submit, and obeyed. Major Creed then mounted his horse and took command of his troop, which then rode over in a body to Lambert.

At about this time Speaker Lenthall had driven up in his coach to Palace Yard, and had there been stopped by Duckenfield. Lenthall insisted on being allowed to pass, reminding the soldiers that, as Speaker of the sovereign Parliament, he was their senior general. But they jeered at the old man, asked was it he who had led them at Warrington Bridge and *"bade him get him home and take a cawdle of calves' eggs to comfort his learned coxcomb."* Lambert appeared, on whose head broke the furious waves of Lenthall's wrath, to which John replied by calling him an insolent fellow, taking away the mace, and ordering him to drive home.

It was by now towards midday; Lambert had scored a signal success, the City of London had refused Hazelrig's appeal for help, and there remained but the formal dissolution of the House. His passage no longer opposed, he proceeded within and attended a meeting of the Council of State. Disbrowe and Sydenham were there to support him, Hazel-rig, Scot and the dying Bradshaw indignantly to oppose, and after a tempestuous meeting the civilians were forced to submit. "The searching language of the sword puzzled their intellects." It was agreed that Parliament be deemed dissolved, and that the Council of Officers should undertake to maintain the public peace and should prepare for the summons of a new Parliament. The troops were ordered to return to their quarters, and Jack Lambert stood master of the situation, with the destiny of an empire in his hands.[235]

Though the ire of Milton was roused against Lambert, the citizens of London acclaimed with glee this expulsion of a worthless and overbearing soviet, for, if the Army had become an object of distaste, the Rump was one of contempt. The taverns and coffee-houses burst into songs of ridicule, one of which began:[236]

> Good morrow, my neighbours all. What news is this I heard
>   tell?
> As I passed through Westminster Hall, by the House that's
>   near to Hell,
> They told me John Lambert was there, with his bears, and
>   deeply did swear
> (As Cromwell had done before) those Vermin should sit there
>   no more.
> Sing Hi, Ho, Will Lenthall, who shall our General be?
> For the House to the Divel is sent all, and follow, gid faith,
>   mun ye.

---

[235] Baker, 576-9; Ludlow, 716-726; Carte, Original Papers, ii, 245-8, 265; Whitelocke, 683-5; Guizot, i, 216-227, 479, 483; C. T., vii, 785, 796; *Weekly Intelligencer*, Oct. 11/18th.

[236] "A Proper New Ballad on the Old Parliament." Hell, Purgatory and Heaven were three taverns adjoining Westminster Hall.

By the standards of the time it is difficult to condemn Lambert. He had been intolerably provoked. "Sir Arthur Hazelrig," he told Ludlow a few days later, "was so enraged against me that he would be satisfied with nothing but my blood." If it was his hand that had gone to the sword while others wavered it was because he, and not Fleetwood, was the real leader of the Army, and because he above all had been calumniated by the passions of overbearing bigots.

The allegations of his enemies were clearly false. He had, said Vane, "rather been made use of by the Wallingford House party than been in any manner the principal contriver of the late disorders."[237]

---

[237] Ludlow, 729, 730, 742-3.

X. ENTER GEORGE MONCK

One of the first steps of the Council of Officers was at last to restore Lambert to his old rank, and he was also naturally one of the Committee of Safety whom the Council of Officers appointed to undertake the government of the country. He was sedulously courted from many sides, and not least by the cavaliers, who urged him by letter and by suggestion to take up the King's cause openly. In the hope that he might thereby be bribed to declare for Charles, Lord Mordaunt had proposed that the Duke of York should marry Lambert's daughter, while Lord Hatton suggested that Charles himself should marry her.[238]

"No security," wrote Hatton to Hyde, "can serve him who can settle the King in his three thrones, but such a bond as the established law of the nation cannot violate or break: and that is, that the King should marry the Lord Lambert's daughter. The grounds of the motion are, the great ease and speed of settling the King's business this way rather than any other. The many difficulties and very hard conditions which, it is believed, are found in all other ways, will be cut off, it being in this case the lady's fate and interest that so it should be. And it is believed, no foreign aid will be so cheap, nor leave our master at so much liberty as this way. The race is a very good gentleman's family, and kings have condescended to gentlewomen and subjects. The lady is pretty, of an extraordinary sweetness of disposition, and very virtuously and ingenuously disposed; the father is a person, set aside his unhappy engagement, of very great parts, and very noble

---

[238] Leyborne-Popham MSS., 124; Cal. S. P. Dom., 1659-60, 246-7; Clarendon State Papers, iii, 592; see also Cal. S. P. Dom., 59-60, 235.

inclinations, and certainly more capable of being passed by than the rest."

If Lambert had followed a course of wisdom and moderation the country would have been behind him. But he had been taught in the wrong school. A study of his actions and his words must show that there is little substance in the notion that he sought the Protectorship for himself, and it is clear that after his quarrel with Oliver he gave up any such idea. The follies of these eighteen months were due, not to any such ambition, but to his impulsiveness, his rash judgment, the faults of his political education, and to the fact that he and his associates had no stated policy on which any portion of the nation could rally to them. The purpose of Parliament was in his mind merely to give the image of legality to the dictates of the Army. He could not see, it seems, that there must come a time when the Army itself, however content to accept such a regimen under the unchallenged command of Oliver Cromwell, must find itself faced, when there was no such dominating hand, with the searching test of alternative loyalties. For it was presently to be proved that a great part of the soldiers knew themselves to be also citizens.

Far north beyond the Cheviots one such man sat shrewdly watching and waiting. George Monck, commander of the army in Scotland, far removed from the vortex of these swirling events, looked upon them with the cool appraising eye of an aloof spectator, indifferent to the parrot-cries of either cause, but carefully calculating upon which side he should throw his great weight. For fat George Monck, though no blatant self-seeker, was also no purist. As in the field he had courage and technique, but little strategical ability, so in affairs he had small brains but a certain bovine cunning. He was a soldier of the old Dutch school, skilled in technique and thorough in detail, slow and wary, rarely moving until he had made sure of the ground ahead. Ever since Worcester he had been an able administrator over a restless people, and, a soldier among soldiers, unobsessed by religious bigotry, unconcerned with political polemics, coarse of manners, niggardly of speech, intolerant of indiscipline and inefficiency, but gifted with a sure knowledge of the human heart, he had won the unfaltering confidence of nearly his whole army and the respect of all parties in the Scottish nation. He was a camp-fire soldier, and the obedience he had won was founded on a simplicity of purpose and a diligent efficiency in daily administration.

In these giddy days of '59 Monck, though importuned by the royalist chaplains Gumble and Price, courted by royalist emissaries from London, and plagued by the indiscretions of his royalist wife, who had been his laundress and his mistress while in prison, had closely veiled his heart behind his mask of taciturnity — though once he had nearly betrayed himself. Although he had acquiesced in the restoration of the Rump in May, yet he had made ready to support Booth's rising, his purpose undeclared but his secret hopes revealed by the escape of a moment's indiscretion to his chaplain. Lambert's swift victory upset those hopes, threw him once more into indecision and prompted him even to offer his resignation to Parliament. He had miscalculated that affair of Cheshire, and nearly made a bad mistake. In future he was more careful.

At all times fully informed of the progress of events in London by his brother in law Clarges, an astute and subtle agent, he was now in frequent direct correspondence with Lambert and the other leaders of Parliament and Army, each of whom hoped for his support. Frankly, Monck was watching which way the cat would jump, and, on news that Fairfax was preparing to rise in Yorkshire, was ready to march and suppress him. It was not until Lambert's *coup* of October 13th that he began to take decisive steps.

If it was to be an affair of rival generals, then he would have his say with the others, and it was his aloofness from the central embroilment and his suspicion of its chief agents that determined him, after gingerly feeling his way, to declare ostensibly for the Parliament he had so lately been ready to betray, proclaiming that it was the duty of his office to support the civil government against the rule of the musket and the pike, though in his heart he was himself preparing to use those same weapons to effect the return of the Common Enemy who lay watching beyond the water.

To have revealed his real intentions would have spelt their ruin, for he knew well that against the royalist cause all the democratic elements — Hazelrig, Whitelocke, Vane, the Fifth Monarchists, and many Cromwellians likewise — would have sunk their differences and rallied immediately behind Lambert and Fleetwood. Scarce a man of his own regiments would have followed him, in spite of their devotion to "old George." He therefore embarked on a campaign of deliberate prevarication.

His first steps, on hearing the news of Parliament's ejection, were to secure the chief Lowland towns, stop the posts, assemble his officers and announce his intention of standing by the Parliament, though in August he had been ready enough to rebel against it. He then cashiered numerous officers whom the industry of Lambert had introduced into his regiments, and arrested Colonel Ralph Cobbett, the messenger whom the Council of Officers had sent to inform him of the news.

Lambert, meanwhile, had been attending meetings of the newly-formed Committee of Safety in London, endeavouring to untie the constitutional knot, when, on October 28th, he received by the post the following letter:[239]

Right Honourable,

Having notice that a part of the army under the Parliament's command have, contrary to their duty, put force upon them, I have therefore sent this messenger to your Lordship to entreat you to be an instrument of peace and good understanding between Parliament and army; for, if they shall continue this force, I am resolved, with the assistance of God, and that part of the army under my command, to stand by them, and assert their lawful authority. For, Sir, the nation of England will not endure any arbitrary power, neither will any true Englishman in the army; so that such a design will be ruinous and destructive; therefore I do earnestly entreat you, that we may not be a scorn to all the world, and a prey to our enemies, that the Parliament may be speedily restored to their freedom, which they enjoyed on the 11th of this inst. Which is all at present, from

Your Lordship's humble servant,
GEORGE MONCK.

The Committee was thrown into consternation, and Lambert offered immediately to take arms and march north against Monck. Though resolving to attempt conciliation first, the Committee accepted Lambert's offer, appointed him commander of all the forces in the north and ordered him, if conciliation should fail, to give battle to Monck forthwith. It was the worst possible step, for they were playing into Monck's hands, whereas a comradely invitation to join them in London would have had far different results.

Having replied to Monck, appealing to him "on the account of old friendship" to avoid a breach, John set out on November 3rd, leaving to the others the task of working out a new constitution. With his redcoats tramping to the tap of the drum, with the creak of saddlery, the flapping of many colours,

---

[239] Toland, *Monck's Letters* (1714), p. 14.

and the ring of sword-hilts upon armour, he began his last march, and no sign was given them that this proud army that had never been defeated in battle was to be bloodlessly defeated by its friends or that its leader was never to return save only as a hunted fugitive.

John made for Newcastle. At York, where his friend Lilburne was governor, he halted for a while to gather together the northern regiments, so that he had now an army of nearly 12,000 men. While he was at York there arrived three officers from Monck's army, on their way to London, ostensibly to treat with Wallingford House, but really intended by the astute Monck to waste time. John stopped them, with the intention of treating direct, but when he learnt that their first demand was the recall of the Long Parliament he bade them begone to London, but agreed with them that no hostile move should be made while the parties were in treaty.

At York John also met Thomas Morgan, the fiery little major-general who had so distinguished himself with the Cromwellian contingent under Turenne. At Lambert's request Morgan undertook to attempt conciliation with Monck, but as soon as he arrived in Scotland he forswore his promise and took a command under Monck instead.

Monck at first won small support among the fighting forces at large. The fleet and the army in Ireland alike conjured him not to break with his comrades; Newcastle and Carlisle, the two gates to England, refused to open to him; Overton, governor of the Hull arsenal, remained hostile to his advances; and Clarges, coming to him from London, told him he would no longer be trusted. Even the Roman Catholics were supporting Lambert, for under him they knew they would receive generous treatment, and the relations he had with Catholics at this time even led his enemies to accuse him of being a Papist himself.[240] For Lambert, child of the revolution, still held sway in the hearts of the Army at large, while among soldiers and civilians alike whose allegiance was in doubt his prowess served as a continual reminder of the respect due to the most brilliant of Cromwell's captains. "His reputation," wrote the French ambassador to Mazarin, "still maintains him in credit in the minds of the soldiers, and most honest persons in the army."

From York, hearing that Monck had advanced towards Berwick, John moved presently to Newcastle, and from thence sent out detachments along the border from Chilling-ham Castle to Carlisle. Monck conformed by moving to Coldstream, but he was not yet strong enough to give battle, and many of his men were deserting to Lambert. He therefore continued to dissemble, absolutely refusing all dealings with royalists and playing for the time which he knew to be on his side. "I do call God to witness," he had written to the Speaker, "that the asserting of a Commonwealth is the only intent of my heart."

Only Bulstrode Whitelocke seems to have fully understood his tactics and the deep purpose behind them. *"Fight Monck,"* he had said from the beginning, and again throughout these months of fencing he had urged that Lambert should bring him to battle without delay. But the Committee of Safety, in their hearts alarmed at their own audacity, and anxious to embitter the nation no further, sought the path of propitiation and were genuinely anxious to avoid any new effusion of blood. But he who puts on the mailed gauntlet should not change it for velvet until his enemies have been broken. Lambert's orders from the Committee had been "to beget an

---

[240] Carte, Original Papers, ii, 225; Kennet, 6, 7, 84.

understanding" and his obedience to those orders was to lead to the ruin of himself and the return of a worthless house.

For a time the Committee attempted to answer feint with feint. They cajoled and flattered Monck's commissioners and in high glee sent them back to Scotland with a draft treaty that would have spelt his ruin. Monck hedged and sent his commissioners back to London for "elucidations," while Lambert fidgeted at Newcastle, fretting at the unaccustomed inaction, and Whitelocke pressed yet again that he should attack. The Committee of Safety was newly angered on learning that, while his commissioners were in treaty, Monck had written direct to the Lord Mayor and to various others asking for their support. To Lambert and his colleagues this appeared a gross breach of faith, but when he complained to Monck, Old George replied with frivolous counter-complaints that Lambert was strengthening his forces and with more serious complaints that he was stopping letters. In this impasse it was decided to begin a second treaty at Newcastle, but early in December a sequence of events, together with the steady infiltration of a sure poison upon which Monck was relying, shattered Lambert's cause into irrecoverable loss.

For, while time was evaporating in the scales of fortune, the power of the purse began to turn their uneasy balance. Whereas Monck by good fortune had at his hand a hoard of £70,000, and the eager Scots, openly looking for the King's return, would gladly give him more, the Committee in London, powerless to raise money legally without the authority of the assembly they had chased out of doors, found their funds exhausted and their request to the City of London for a loan derisively refused. It was upon this turn of affairs that Monck from the beginning relied for the success of his duplicity, for he had said to one of his agents:

"My money will last until February, and if I do nothing but lie still, Lambert's army by their great wants must break of themselves."

Piece by piece Lambert's supports began through that want to fall away. Bitterly complaining against the nonpayment of his men, who in the grip of a hard winter were once again in sore straits for shoes and stockings, Lambert was forced to let them live at free quarters upon the population. Then he learnt that the garrison of Portsmouth had declared for Parliament and thrown open their gates to Hazelrig and Colonel Morley; that the army in Ireland had followed suit and seized Dublin Castle; that Lawson and the fleet had likewise changed course; that his old commander, Tom Fairfax, though racked by gout and stone, but with the old flame rekindled in his gaunt body, was preparing to rise against him in Yorkshire and was in secret treaty with Monck; that the apprentices of London were clamouring for "a free Parliament"; that the announcement by the Committee of Safety of a new Parliament to meet in January had failed to stem the rising tide of discontent among soldiers and civilians alike; that Whitelocke was, in despair, about to cross the Channel to bring back the King himself when Fleetwood stopped him, crying distractedly that he could not agree without Lambert's consent — and Lambert was 270 miles away.

Swiftly the *dégringolade* grew worse. Lambert sent Robert Lilburne back to York to watch Fairfax, but his own men, their money still unpaid and their conditions miserable in the deep snow that quilted the North, began to desert in numbers but with keen reluctance. Monck became more and more intractable, and just before Christmas John wrote to London to say that all prospects of a treaty with him had gone.

News soon came to him of the end. For several weeks a little group of Rumpers in London — the most worthless and most bigoted — had been meeting secretly under the chairmanship of Thomas Scot, watching their opportunity and encouraging Monck with the assurance of their support, and receiving in return the most earnest vows of his fidelity. Coming now into the open, they assembled at Lenthall's house, and issued an order for the troops in London to parade in Lincoln's Inn Fields on Christmas Eve, which the regiments, saluting Lenthall with cheers, meekly obeyed.

Thus deserted, Fleetwood and Disbrowe submitted at once, the latter flying to the shelter of Lambert's camp, the former lamenting that *"the Lord has blasted our councils and spit in our faces."* On the evening of December 26th forty irrepressible members of the Rump walked triumphantly by torchlight back to the chamber whence they had been twice ejected and resumed their chequered story.

For John the end was also near. On January 1st, 1660, Fairfax rode out into deep snow to raise the Yorkshire gentry and, his royalist sympathies scarcely disguised, marched on York. John turned about against him in Northumberland, and as he did so Monck crossed the ice at Coldstream on January 2nd, and followed in his rear, as Fairfax had asked. Daily Lambert's numbers fell away, many leaving him with tears in their eyes, and presently he heard that his Irish brigade under Colonel Kelsey had gone over to Fairfax. The end came when orders arrived from Westminster for his whole army to disperse to their various cantonments, and he did not attempt to disobey.[241]

With only a few horsemen to keep him company, he rode southward through the driving snow, and on the road he was

---

[241] Hist. MSS Report, v, 193-4; Fairfax Corr., iv, 163-8.

met by his wife's brother, Martin Lister, who told him that, with Robert Lilburne powerless to oppose, Fairfax had occupied York, where Lambert's regiment of horse was stationed. There came news also that Parliament had passed an Act of Indemnity for him and all his army, on making submission before January 9th, and he for the time bowed to the inevitable. On January 6th, 1660, his letter of submission was read in the House.

Monck, on reaching York, found Lambert's horse and foot regiments still there, and he immediately dismissed all the officers of both, save one or two. He awarded the cavalry regiment to Sir Hugh Bethel, who had lost an eye at Rowton Heath, had served under Lambert in '48 and '49 and had taken Scarborough. He also brought back, as lieutenant-colonel, the royalist William Goodrick, who afterwards became notorious for his persecutions of the nonconformists and republicans who had been his old comrades.[242]

So, with his hopes shattered, John struggled southward, anxious to confer with Harry Vane and to greet his wife, who was with child. Vane still looked to Lambert to save the republican cause and was ready that he should be martyred for it in a last desperate attempt. He had lately called on Frances, commended the piety of her resignation to her husband's unlucky star, and asked her if she had yet arrived at that state of grace wherein she could resign her lord to death for the Commonwealth; to which tears were her only answer.[243]

---

[242] Clarke Papers, iv, 253.
[243] Clarendon State Papers, iii, 635.

XI. THE LAST FLING

It was the end of Lambert's career, but by no means the end of his adventures, for though he had made a formal submission he remained a rebel at heart, and the events of the next few weeks were to show him ready to lead the most forlorn of hopes. For the re-establishment of the Rump had settled nothing. Though they complimented Monck, too blind to perceive that "he had the King in his belly," they were deeply suspicious that he might play the same game upon them as Cromwell and Lambert, and the dawn of a new fear awoke in their eyes as they saw the hand of the Common Enemy rising in the scarcely-veiled royalism of Fairfax and the open royalism of the London apprentices.

To their fears and suspicions John owed the relative indulgence that they showed him, but for the time Monck was nevertheless the lesser enemy, and the Rump ordered Lambert to confine himself to his family home of Calton Manor. But, disregarding the order, he went into hiding in London, in spite of repeated edicts.

Once more the eyes of the royalists, as distrustful of Monck as the Rumpers, were turned hopefully towards him, and it is to his credit that in this further adversity he still refused the easy way to worldly success and remained true to his republicanism. Soon, however, he was being pilloried on the stage by John Tatham, and lampoons began to flow from jeering scribblers who derided both him and Frances, saying that it was she who by her scheming aspirations had lured him to destruction's edge. His old foot regiment, their commander no longer with them, was in a mutinous condition for lack of pay, even assaulting their officers on parade.[244]

Meanwhile, Monck inexorably continued his march through the snows, at the head of 6,000 veterans filled with an unswerving fidelity to their "Old George," and showered as he passed through the country with petitions for "a free Parliament," to which he returned laconic and evasive answers, and he had no sooner done so than, having first chastised the City for demanding a free Parliament, he forswore all his vows of fidelity to the Rump, and under the threat of his muskets and his pikes forced them to readmit the Presbyterians and royalists of whom Pride had purged them in 1648.

To John Lambert and to Harry Vane this was the most treacherous betrayal of the cause for which they had all struggled, for the result of a new Parliament which Monck now ordered to be summoned must inevitably be the return of the Common Enemy. Both were labouring to avert that betrayal and both were therefore arrested. On March 5th John appeared before the Council of State and endeavoured to vindicate himself. He had already sent a petition to the House that he might have liberty to raise some men and take service in Sweden, but the request was not granted, and the Council now ordered him to give security to the extent of £20,000 to be of peaceable behaviour. That, said Lambert, was beyond his power to do. They therefore committed him to the Tower.[245]

He entered its old grey walls as the prisoner of his recent adversary, Colonel Morley, but he was not there long. Obliged by Monck to dissolve, the Long Parliament held its last sitting on March 16th, after twenty years of turbulence, of triumph

---

244 Whitelocke, 693; Clarendon State Papers, iii, 651, 661; Rugge, 48, 55-56; Nicholl, 275.
245 Ludlow, 582-3; Clarendon State Papers, iii, 695; C. J., vii, 857, 864.

and of shame, and the writs went out for a new assembly. The Lords were also to meet once more. The shadow of the throne began from the East to creep across the sea. The friends of republicanism, their eyes at last opened to the duplicity of Monck, were everywhere in despair. Those who had so recently been fiercest in their denunciation of Lambert, even Hazelrig himself, turned to him as the only man bold enough to lead a forlorn hope.

Plans were therefore made for his escape from the Tower. He made friends with Joan, the woman who made his bed and swept his room, and won the promise of her help, and he procured, it was said, a lady to knit him a ladder of silk.

At eight o'clock on the night of April 10th John, having made fast the rope to the window of his prison, slipped through the aperture, and slid down to the river-bank outside. There he found six men waiting for him, and he, accompanied by his Scottish servant, at once made away in a barge, which they had waiting. As he went out the loyal Joan slipped into his bed and donned his night-cap. So, when the warder made his rounds to lock the door at his usual hour, he found the bed-curtains drawn. He called out "Good night, my Lord," and heard in reply the noncommittal sound of one drowsy with sleep.

The good wench, however, made no attempt to escape herself. Coming the next morning to unlock the door, the warder saw her face and cried out:

"In the name of God, Joan, what makes you here? Where is my Lord Lambert?"

"He is gone," she replied, "but I cannot tell you whither."

Whereupon the warder carried her off to his officer, and she was committed to custody.[246]

---

[246] Rugge, 121; Nicholl, 280.

The next day Monck proclaimed Lambert a traitor, offered £100 for his capture and circulated all his officers. John, however, remained safe in the hiding of friends in London, and with the principal of them prepared plans for a rising. There was widespread discontent in the Army against the threatened return of the King, and John sent messengers far and wide among the regiments that Monck had astutely scattered, inviting them to rise and to join his standard at Daventry and at Edgehill. Then, accompanied by his Scottish servant, he left London in disguise. From the North, the Midlands and the West Country assurances of support came to him. Junior officers and private soldiers were leaving their regiments. York was nearly betrayed to him, at Nottingham a Monckish regiment was discomfited, and Ludlow was ready to raise the West.

But, in truth, the response was half-hearted. Numbers of Cromwell's old officers made to join him, and sent orders to their regiments to march, but Monck, having cautioned every man and every officer in measured terms, had disposed his troops very shrewdly, and many of Lambert's supporters were arrested on their way to his standard. Only a sharp success by an early blow could win for Lambert a substantial following, and when the moment came, against an unequal force, he shrank from striking it. Early on the morning of Easter Sunday, April 22nd, he was at Daventry at the head of six or seven troops of horse and one company of infantry — probably not more than 700 men all told. With him were Colonel Okey, so recently his active opponent, Captain Hazelrig, son of Sir Arthur, Colonel Axtell, Colonel Cobbett and his constant follower Richard Creed.

Warned of his intentions, Monck had dispatched Lambert's old enemy Colonel Ingoldsby to Northampton to watch for him. Learning of his presence, Ingoldsby, with all the zeal of the renegade, marched out from Northampton with a superior force, and the two forces met in the open fields outside Daventry, a little brook between them. For a while they faced each other at a stand, each unwilling to strike the first blow. A few shots were fired by Streeter's musketeers, and Lambert sent Hazelrig forward with one troop of horse, perhaps to parley, but Hazelrig, maybe by collusion, was taken an easy prisoner and his whole troop surrendered to Ingoldsby. Action was stayed, but Ingoldsby advanced close to his adversary. One of Lambert's officers begged his permission to charge, but John would not allow it, and, hoping to succeed by persuasion as he had done at St. Stephen's, desired a parley with Ingoldsby. His proposal was that Richard Cromwell should be restored to the Protectorship, but Ingoldsby would not listen.

Lambert still declined to fight, though one of his troopers discharged a pistol at Ingoldsby. More of his troops went over to the enemy, till presently there was only a little group standing round him talking to Ingoldsby. Ingoldsby then claimed Lambert as his prisoner. Creed and others begged Ingoldsby to do what he pleased with them, but to let Lambert escape. Ingoldsby resolutely refused, whereupon Lambert, mounted upon a fast Arab, turned sharply about and galloped for safety. Unfortunately, he rode straight into heavy plough, where Ingoldsby's stronger horse easily overtook him. He begged for an opportunity to escape, but Ingoldsby was inflexible. Creed and Cobbett were taken with him, but Okey and many others escaped.[247]

Two days later the trained bands of London held a great review in Hyde Park under their citizen colonels, drinking the

---

[247] Baker, 607-8; Kennett, 114-120; Whitelocke, 699; Clarendon State Papers, iii, 735; Ludlow, 873-877; Guizot, ii, 411, 415.

King's health on bended knees. In the midst of their loyal exercises a little cavalcade in red coats was seen approaching by the road from Edgware. It was Ingoldsby, with Lambert, Axtell and Creed, his prisoners, in a coach, and a mounted guard. Just before the Edgware road met the road to Oxford the cavalcade passed beneath the shadow of the Tyburn gallows, and a great shout went up from the citizen soldiers. Turning to Ingoldsby, Lambert remarked light-heartedly that the scene reminded him of the occasion when he and Cromwell had passed that very spot amid the applause of the people on their march to Scotland in 1650, and how Cromwell had prophetically warned him that the people would cheer just as much if he had been going to be hanged.[248]

So down the long lane, through the village of Holbourn, into the old City and back within the grey walls of the Tower. Still defiant, he made yet one more attempt at escape, Nicholl tells us, but was apprehended by the outer sentries and taken back in irons.[249] Twenty-three more years of life yet remained to him, and for all that weary while he was to remain to the end a prisoner. As the doors closed on him they closed, too, on the hopes of the republican party, for of all the great band that had led the New Model to glory and to dominion one was already in secret betraying their cause to the Common Enemy, and the remainder were in hiding or in flight. Vain he may have been, ambitious too, but Lambert alone, with a price on his head, had dared to risk all in one desperate throw for the cause he had served for nearly twenty years.

He did not tamely submit, like Fleetwood; he did not flee, like Disbrowe; he did not yield to the lure of the dukedom and

---

[248] Rugge, 126; Clarendon State Papers, iii, 735; Burnet, *Own Time*, ed. 1833, i 155.
[249] Nicholl, 283.

the Garter that might have been his instead of Monck's. He himself had not been the least to blame for the break-up of his cause, for he had been weak when he should have been strong, and when the moment came to put all to the touch, as in the great days, he had shown that he did not possess the ruthlessness of Cromwell or his masterful command over unruly men. Whitelocke had been right in October of '59 when he had urged instant battle. Now, the Army by Monck's astute deception dispersed throughout the length of the country and his own regiments from Scotland cozened into the belief that he sought only the restoration of the Parliament, Lambert passed, a victim of that betrayal, within the bars of a life-long imprisonment, a republican "without fear, without repentance, without hope."

It was upon the day after John's return to imprisonment that, Monck having got rid of the Parliament he had sworn to defend, there assembled at St. Stephen's the new "Convention" Parliament of Commons and reinstated Lords. It was but a few short weeks since Monck had sworn to Hazelrig: "Upon my soul I desire a Commonwealth," yet even while the elections for the Convention were in progress, he had secretly sent Sir John Grenville to see the King at Brussels. If it had been under a pretence of Parliamentary rule that Cromwell had resigned, it was equally under a Parliamentary pretence that Monck conspired for the return of one whom nearly every soldier in his army regarded as a tyrant and an enemy of the people.

In a burst of national enthusiasm, and without waiting to prescribe those terms which bitter experience should have taught them were so necessary, Parliament, having heard the messages that Grenville brought back from Charles, voted that "according to the ancient and fundamental laws of this kingdom, the government is, and ought to be, by King, Lords and Commons."

On May 26th, a young man whose thick lips, raven hair, sensuous face and lambent eyes presaged a return to ways and manners long dead, landed at Dover and kissed the Bible which the worthy Mayor handed to him, while the unseen spirit of comedy looked on and smiled in irony. In triumph he journeyed through Kent, and at Blackheath beheld a magnificent parade of 30,000 men, whom Monck had assembled to greet the "Common Enemy" they had so often forsworn and whom they had driven into desperate flight at Worcester.

It was the New Model's last "rendezvous." Betrayed by their commander and bereft of the old generals who had led them into battle, they faced the stranger King with resignation in their hearts. They were the very pick of Englishmen, and, fanatics if they were, they loved their country hardly less than their God, and, in the words of John Richard Green,[250] none of their victories was so glorious as that which they won over themselves. The "tapsters and such kinds of fellows," the cobblers, the draymen and the farmers who had dashed Rupert to ruin at Naseby, who had overwhelmed the flower of Scotland at Dunbar and Preston and Inverkeithing, and bloodily crushed the defenders of Drogheda, the men who had shown to France and Spain the magic of English infantry on the Dunes of Dunkirk, the men who for so long had held dominion over the people of three nations, quietly laid down their arms, and took themselves once more to their benches and their fields, often oppressed by revengeful masters and harried by the persecutions of such men as Goodrick, but distinguished everywhere by their soberness and their industry.

---

[250] From whom I borrow this scene.

Some one or two of their units remained to perpetuate their memory, and on the fields of Blenheim, of Waterloo and of Ypres there was to linger still something of those special soldierly virtues that dwelt in the teaching and the leadership of Cromwell and Lambert, Fairfax and Monck, Harrison and immortal Robert Blake.

Thus passed the New Model, the finest military force ever produced in these islands. But to their old major-general, now over forty and with his long brown curls turning to grey, no such comfortable citizenship was offered. Revenge was one of the first thoughts of the Convention, and although mercy and oblivion were extended to nearly all who in the past years had set their hands against the King's Majesty, Lambert and a score besides were wrongfully excepted from its provisions. Mrs. Monck is said to have clamoured for his death. Nevertheless, it was against the regicides who had sat in judgment upon Charles I in that bleak January of 1649 that their full hatred was turned, and Lambert had been no regicide.

He therefore escaped the blood bath of October, and remained still in prison when the news came to him of those dreadful days at Charing Cross when the hangman cut to pieces the quivering bodies of his friends, holding up their severed heads and plundered hearts reeking to the multitude. Of them all only Hugh Peters, the fiery gospeller, the swashbuckling soldier-priest of a conquering God, only Hugh Peters faltered for a moment as he climbed the ladder to the encarmined scaffold. The fearless Harrison ascended at last to the courts of his miraculous Monarchy, erect and defiant. Cooke the lawyer and even Thomas Scot, one not in life greatly to be admired, paid the penalty of their republicanism with no less fortitude than the soldiers who had ridden behind Lambert's standard.

There were those, indeed, who sought a like revenge upon Jack Lambert and Harry Vane, but Lambert's personal popularity helped to save him. His wife, his old soldiers, his friends in the other camps petitioned and spoke in his favour. Lambert himself also petitioned, declaring his acceptance of the new government and his resolve to spend the rest of his days in peace.[251]

Accordingly, his life was spared, but his great house at Wimbledon and everything in it, and the gardens on which he had spent such loving care, were taken from him and inventoried for the King, and Frances had even to ask for the return of some bedding and other articles of her own which had been wrongly confiscated. Some small satisfaction there may have been in that the King did not obtain all his pictures, for Baptist Gaspars, John's painting master, seems to have run away with some of them.

Nor did Henrietta Maria ever again occupy the house on its restoration to her by the King, for that sharp-tongued lady is said to have observed that "it smelt so strong of a rebel," and she accordingly disposed of it very profitably to the unpleasant George Digby, Earl of Bristol. Bitter to the Lamberts must have been the admonition that someone had scrawled on the walls of their great banqueting house:

"The way to ruin enemies is to divide their councils."[252]

---

[251] S. P. Dorn., 1660-1, 8, 175; *Old Parliamentary History*, xxii, 443, 472; L. R. O., 155; Lister's *Life of Clarendon*, ii, 117.
[252] S. P. Dom., 1660-1, 407, 411; 61-2, 118; Hist. MSS. Com. 7th Rep. 89; Bartlet, *History and Antiquities of Wimbledon* (1865), 43; Ludlow, iii, 46.

XII. BITTER BREAD

Though still a prisoner, John was again elected as member for Ripon in the "Cavalier" Parliament which in 1661 replaced the Convention. At the end of October, 1661, he was removed from the Tower and taken in the *Adventure* to a new captivity in Guernsey, while Vane was exiled to the Scillies.[253]

Others of his old friends fled overseas to be dogged by the assassins of the House of Stuart. Disbrowe went to Holland, Ludlow found sanctuary in the kindly democracy of the Swiss. Hewson died of starvation in Rouen, and Hazelrig had already succumbed in the Tower. Whalley fled to New England, hunted from place to place. Fleetwood sank into the timid obscurity suffered to one whom none could fear as an avenger of lost causes, for he had always been a man pushed rather than one gifted with the stuff of leadership. But for John there stretched ahead a desolate vista of prison, broken with illness and quarrels and petty oppression, till at last in the defencelessness of old age he was to find a lonely peace.

His confinement in Guernsey, where Sir Hugh Pollard was governor, was not intended to be rigorous, and on the petition of his wife she and three of their ten children were granted permission in February, 1662, to join him in captivity, but it is doubtful if they went. For by now the Cavalier Parliament had replaced the Presbyterian Convention and the revenge and malice of the old royalists looked angrily for blood. It was not enough that the corpses of Cromwell and Ireton and Bradshaw had been torn from their graves and hung in mutilated

---

[253] *Notes and Queries*, 3rd Series, iv, 89.

fragments from the Tyburn gallows; not enough that Blake and Deane and a dozen others had been roused from their sleep in Westminster Abbey and thrown into a nameless pit; not enough that in Scotland Argyll should have been brought to the block, or that in London Venner's trivial rising should have been quenched in blood. In response to Parliament's "merciless pertinacity" Charles reluctantly ordered that Lambert and Vane, though neither had been regicides, should be brought back from exile and tried for their lives.[254]

Accordingly, in April of 1662 John was taken from Guernsey back to the Tower, where he was allowed to see his wife and children in the presence of the keeper. On June 2nd he was arraigned in the Court of King's Bench for high treason in levying war against the King, while his old soldiers outside were praying for his life.

But, however revengeful had been the malice of the Cavalier Parliament, the King was bent on clemency, and Lambert won the favour of the court by his discreet and unaggressive bearing, so that when sentence had been pronounced the Lord Chief Justice announced that his Majesty was pleased to spare his life.[255] But Vane, proud Vane, defiant to the end, challenging the authority of a court that sat by warrant of a King, by his froward bearing forswore the hopes of mercy and engrossed the testament of his faith. On June 14th, proclaiming to the end the principles of liberty, though the drums beat and the trumpets blared to drown what he might say, and though the paper from which he read was snatched from his hands, he knelt calmly to the block and as his head

---

[254] S. P. Dom., 1661-2, 276, 329; C. J., viii, 287, 317, 342,368; *Notes and Queries*, 1st Series, vii, 459; Lister's *Life of Clarendon*, ii, 118.
[255] Ibid, 119; S. P. Dom., 1661-2, 350; State Trials, vi, 133, 136; The King's Intelligence, 9-16, June, 1662; Kennet, 704-5; Baker, 630.

was severed his boyish face remained unmoved in death, his eyes gleamed still with their visionary fire and his passionate lips gave no sign that his unconquerable spirit would speak no more to a people betrayed.

By only a hair's-breadth had Lambert escaped the same fate. Considered to be a condemned traitor, he was taken back again to the rocks of Guernsey, where the governor now was Lord Hatton, who had so lately advocated that the King should marry Lambert's daughter. He was stripped of all his possessions, not only those he had purchased at Wimbledon and Hatfield Chase and elsewhere, but also his ancestral estates of Craven, though these were granted to Lord Bellasis in trust for Frances, who was his kinswoman. From a position of wealth and grandeur John was reduced to one of poverty, and for the remainder of their lives together Frances had to provide for his charge in prison and to maintain herself and their ten children out of her small patrimony.

In Guernsey John was lodged in Castle Cornet, and at first was kept a close prisoner. In November orders were sent from the King that he was to be given such liberty as was consistent with security, but to these Hatton gave the harshest interpretation. Before long some of his daughters were allowed to visit him, but not his wife. Though ill with scurvy, he was kept for the greater part of the day locked up in his chamber, and the only exercise he was permitted was to walk upon a platform within the castle. Hatton, perhaps, did not forget that audacious escape from the Tower, and there were, moreover, frequent rumours among the persecuted Puritans at home of plots to rise once more under his leadership. His old servants at home were whispering foolishly.

No trace, however, could be found that John had anything to do with such incipient designs, though the closest watch was kept on his correspondence and his every movement. These rumours, however, did him great harm, and he became depressed and melancholy at the severity of his confinement. He complained also that the castle porter, John de la Marche, whose duty it was to accompany him wherever he went about the castle, was so odious a creature that he, and his children likewise, shrank from stirring outside their room rather than have him for a companion.[256]

One of his women, too, had a quarrel with a sentry, calling him a "saucy common soldier" when he rebuked her for throwing down some water and declaring that she served as good a master as he. "The King's service," the soldier replied, "is not so common," and even this trivial incident, overheard by the listening de la Marche, was reported home to the Secretary of State, lest it might be evidence of some new "plot." For two years this irksome condition of things continued, until, Mrs. Lambert having obtained an audience of Sir Henry Bennett, the Secretary of State, in March, 1664, orders were sent to Hatton that, in view of the dangerous state of his prisoner's health, he was to be allowed greater liberty.[257]

To one who had led a life so full of stirring activity, imprisonment must have been as mortifying as to the eagle caged. But in the last years he was blessed by the consolations of those gentler interests that his catholic mind had embraced. He was able to paint, he pursued mathematics, and it seems that he was allowed also to cultivate a garden. He seems to have become on better terms with Hatton before long, partly through the intercessions of Clarendon and of royalists whom he had befriended in the old days, and partly through a

---

[256] S. P. Dom., 1661-2, 555, 574; *Notes and Queries*, 1st Series, vii, 459; 3rd Series, iv, 89, 90.
[257] Ibid; S. P. Dom., 1663-4, 508, 514.

common interest they both found in gardening. John had in earlier days advised Hatton on the choice of plants, examined catalogues for him and supplied him with rare plants of his own cultivation not to be found even in the most famous gardens of France; and in return Hatton, when abroad, had obtained for him anemones, irises, tulips and other plants that he specially desired.[258]

Trouble of a more serious kind, however, arose in 1666, when the great fire devastated the habitations of London. Hatton received warning from a native of the island of a French design to seize Guernsey and to liberate Lambert. In London and in the Channel ports there was confirmation of the plot. Letters to John were intercepted, and his old butler, who kept a victualling shop in Charing Cross and acted as his postmaster, was reported to have said that his old master would soon be liberated and would be quickly in England to head a Puritan insurrection.

The leader of the design was Jean François de Briselance, Sieur de Vaucourt and commander of the little island of Chausey, off the Normandy coast. Prompt measures were taken in London, and on orders from the King, Vaucourt and the master of his ship, which was lying in port at Guernsey, were arrested and hanged. Orders were also sent that Lambert was once more to be kept a close prisoner and that if the French should attempt a landing he was immediately to be shot.[259]

It is doubtful if John himself had any part in this incipient plot. He continued in bad health, which his renewed confinement aggravated, and some eighteen months were to

---

[258] Hatton-Finch MSS., 29,569, fol. 212; Hatton Correspondence, i, 35, 38; Lister, *Life of Clarendon*, iii, 310.
[259] S. P. Dom., 1665-6, 480, 522; *Notes and Queries*, 3rd Series, iv, 90.

pass before he obtained any alleviation. He had already been relieved of the irritating presence of Hatton, who had been recalled as a result of complaints against him, and whose deputy, Colonel Jonathan Atkins, assumed his duties and reported home in '67 that his prisoner carried himself "with modesty and discretion."

That autumn Frances Lambert once more petitioned the King, begging that he might be allowed to take a little house on the island and that she and all her family might live with him. She was now very poor and had been obliged to sell her Coldhern estate in Earl's Court, which was purchased by Henry Muddiman, the journalist. She pleaded that she was not able to maintain her husband, herself and her ten children in separation, and that if the request were not granted she would starve.

To her small voice there were now added those of men who in happier times had been her adversaries, but who had not forgotten their personal friendships for the old major-general and his many acts of kindness to defeated royalists. Fauconberg, Bellasis and Sir Thomas Ingram made a like petition, but it seems to have been without avail, though in February of '68 permission was given for his daughter Frances to live with him, and for his daughter Mary to visit him during his ill-health.[260]

Mary, however, had already been the cause of trouble. Hatton had a son, and beneath the walls of Castle Cornet he and Mary met and fell in love. To have expected his father's consent to marriage with the daughter of a condemned traitor was a matter beyond hope (though he had thought differently a few short years ago), but Charles Hatton loved her enough to

---

[260] *Notes and Queries*, 3rd Series, iv, 91.

marry her without, and he did so in secret, to the fury of his father, who turned him out of doors without a penny.[261]

But the irksome days of Guernsey with their fierce winter winds and the odious presence of de la Marche were at last over and in September, 1670, John was transferred in the *Merlin* to Drake's Island in Plymouth Sound[262] — a closer and more desolate imprisonment, one would suppose, but nevertheless one where he seems at last to have found some measure of contentment. Here in due time he was allowed to have his wife and family with him, here he was able once more to cultivate a garden and here he continued his study of mathematics. About 1671 his second daughter married Capt. John Blackwell, who became governor of Massachusetts in '88. Occasionally he was allowed to receive visitors, and a picture of one such visit is given us by the Quaker Myles Halhead, an intimate little picture full of the flowing grace of Quaker speech and of Jack Lambert's frank and friendly way with men.

Halhead came to the island in 1673, with the purpose of charging him with permitting the persecution of the Quakers during the time of his power — a charge for which there were no grounds and of which the case of Naylor was a refutation. After relating how he landed on St. Nicholas Island with a friend from Plymouth and obtained permission from the lieutenant of the guard to see his prisoner, Halhead continues in this manner the story of their meeting.[263]

> When I came before him I said: "Friend, is thy name John Lambert?" And he said, "Yea."

---

[261] Ibid.

[262] S.P. Dom., 1670, 443, 445, 452, 453.

[263] Sufferings and Passages of Myles Halhead, 1690, extracted from *Notes and Queries*, 1st Series, vi, 103. I have altered the paragraphing.

Then said I unto him: "Friend, I pray thee hear what the servant of the Lord hath to say to thee."

"Friend, the Lord God made use of thee and others for the deliverance of His people; and when you cried to Him He delivered you in your distresses, as at Dunbar and other places, and gave you an opportunity into your hands to do good, and you promised what great things you would do for the Lord's people; but truly, John Lambert, you soon forgot your promises you made to the Lord in that day and time of your great distress, and turned the edge of your sword against the Lord's servants and hand-maids whom He sent forth to declare His eternal truth; and made laws, and consented to laws, and suffered and permitted laws to be made against the Lord's people."

Then John Lambert answered and said: "Friend, I would have you to know, that some of us never made nor consented to laws to persecute you nor any of your friends, for persecution we ever were against."

I answered and said: "John Lambert, it may be so; but the scripture of truth is fulfilled by the best of you; for although that thee and some others have not given your consent to make laws against the Lord's people, yet ye suffered and permitted it to be made and done by others; and when power and authority was in your hands, you might but have spoken the word and the servants and hand-maids of the Lord might have been delivered out of the devourer's hands; but none was found amongst you that would be seen to plead the cause of the innocent; so the Lord God of life was grieved with you, because you slighted the Lord and His servants, and began to set up your self-interest, and lay field to field, and house to house, and make your names great in the earth; then the Lord took away your power and authority, your manhood and your boldness, and caused you to flee before your enemies, and your hearts fainted for fear, and some ended their days in grief and sorrow, and some lie in holes and caves to this day; so the Lord God of Heaven and Earth will give a just reward to every one according to his works; so my dear Friend, prize the great love of God to thee, who hath not given thy life into the hands of the devourers, but hath given thee thy life for a prey, and time to prepare thyself, that thou mayest end thy days in peace… Glory and honour, and living eternal praises be given and returned to the Lord God and the Lamb for ever."

So when I had cleared myself, he desired me to sit down, and so I did; and he called for beer, and gave me to drink; and when he had done, he said to me:

"Friend, I do believe thou speakest to me in love, and so I take it." Then he asked me, If I was at Dunbar fight? I answered "No." Then he said to me, "How do you know what great danger we were in at that time?"

I answered: "A little time after the fight I came that way and laid me down on the side of the mountain for the space of two hours, and viewed the town of Dunbar and the ground about it, where the English army lay; how the great ocean sea was on the one hand of them, and the hills and mountains on the other hand, and the great Scotch army before and behind them: then I took it into a serious consideration the great danger the English were in, and thought within myself, how greatly Englishmen were engaged to the great Lord of life for their deliverance, to serve Him in truth and uprightness of heart all the days of their appointed time. Truly, John, I never saw thy face before that I knew thee, although I have been brought before many of our English commanders in the time of Oliver Cromwell."

Then John said: "I pray you what commanders did you know?"

"I knew Fleetwood, and have been before him when he was deputy in Ireland, and I knew General Disbrowe, and have often been before him; and I knew Colonel Fenwick, and have been before him when he was governor of Edinburgh and the town of Leith, in Scotland, and many more."

John Lambert said: "I knew the most of these men to be very moderate, and ever were against persecution."

And I said: "Indeed they were very moderate, and would not be much seen to persecute or be severe with the Lord's people: but truly, John, they could suffer and permit others to do it, and took little notice of the suffering of the people of God; so none were found to plead our cause, but the Lord God of life and love. Glory be given and returned to His name for evermore."

Then Lambert answered and said: "Altho' you and your friends suffered persecution, and some hardship in that time, your cause therein is never the worse for that."

I answered and said: "That was very true, but let me tell thee, John, in the plainness of my heart, that's no thanks to you, but glory to the Lord for ever."

So he, and his wife, and two of his daughters, and myself, and a friend of Plymouth, discoursed two hours or more in love and plainness of heart: for my heart was full of love to him, his wife, and children; and when I was free, I took my leave of them, and parted with them in love.

The scene suggests some measure of quiet content, despite the loneliness and the constant guards. John was fifty-three, and the fingers of age were stealing over him, and three years later a greater loneliness was to descend upon his spirit, for the wife he had loved so much, who had joyed at his triumphs, who had urged him on in his ambitions, who had defended his reputation and who through the last sad days had desired no other lot than to be by his side, was lost to him for ever. Frances Lambert was one of the most striking of the Commonwealth women — beautiful in her youth, courageous, intelligent, keenly interested in public affairs, high-spirited, but with it all meddlesome, quick-tempered, jealous, a little overbearing in her social relations.

She was constantly courted by those who wished to influence her husband, and it is certain that she was the mainspring of his ambition and chiefly responsible for quickening him towards those courses of high-handedness which brought him within grasp of a dictatorship, only to find that at the last he had no head for such giddy heights. One feels that he was often reluctant. She could not impart to him that masterfulness which was hers and by which alone he could have overcome a turbulent company of men. The simple truth is that Lambert lacked the ruthlessness of Cromwell and of Monck, now resplendent in his gartered dukedom and indifferent to the sufferings of those by whose aid he had risen from the impotence of captivity to the opportunity of glory.

So in loneliness the last years passed for the old major-general. Gardening and occasional correspondence with the outside world eased something of the monotony of the years. In 1677 he was visited by Charles II and the Duke of York while they were at Plymouth, and in '83 by Samuel Pepys. In '78 we find him exchanging mathematical problems with the Rev. Thomas Baker. We hear too that he had written to his son John, admonishing him for his extravagance, for the young man, accomplished in sports, an excellent scholar and a talented artist, had fallen a victim to the new gaiety and vice of Stuart society, and the old major-general did not hold with such ways. In '78, too, memories of his tolerance to Roman Catholics led Titus Oates to allege that he was implicated in the "Popish Plot," but by now his mind had begun to falter and his memory to fade.[264]

The last scene opens. The year 1684 began with the bitterest of winters. In London the Thames was frozen over so rigidly that booths and taverns were erected on its surface and bull-baitings waged. At Plymouth an east wind blew without rest

---

[264] *Notes and Queries*, 1st Series, vi, 183; 2nd Series, iii, 473; Baker, 690; Burnet, *Own Time*, ed. 1833, ii, 159.

and snow covered the ground for three months. The cattle starved and died, birds dropped frozen from the trees, and the fish fled southward from the icy waters. Old Jack Lambert, sixty-four now, a little tired in mind and body, "old and grey and full of sleep," but pursuing still the one service that returns perennially the love of him who labours well, came out to tend his garden. He was in his "night-gown." A boat crossed from the mainland and some visitors landed to call upon him. He hastened indoors to dress, that he might worthily receive them.

But the east wind had done its work. On March 28th, in the churchyard of St. Andrew's, Plymouth, he was buried beside his wife in the same earth as held the remains of his brother-in-arms, Robert Blake.[265]

---

[265] Leyborne-Popham MSS., 263; *Notes and Queries*, 1st Series, iv, 340.

AUTHORITIES FOR LAMBERT

The only lives of Lambert hitherto written, at the date of completion of this book, are the short outlines in the Dictionary of National Biography and in Morkill's and Whitaker's local histories.

The following are the main sources and authorities here relied upon, in addition to the general authorities and those quoted in the notes:

The Baynes MSS. (British Museum).

The Tanner MSS.

The Fairfax Correspondence.

The Lansdowne MSS.

The Leyborne-Popham MSS. (Historical MSS. Commission, 1899).

The Clarke Papers (Camden Society and Royal Historical Society).

Collection of Original Papers, Thomas Carte, 1739.

"Memorials of English Affairs," Bulstrode Whitelocke, ed. 1732.

"Memorials of the Civil War," Henry Cary, ed. 1842.

"Vindication of Sir William Waller," 1793.

"Letters of Roundhead Officers," Bannatyne Club, 1856.

"Annales of Scotland," Sir James Balfour, ed. Haig, 1824.

Diary, John Nicholl, Bannatyne Club, 1836.

Memoirs of Sir William Turner (1632-70), Bannatyne Club, 1829.

"Letters and Journals," Robert Baillie, Bannatyne Club, 1841.

"Cromwell's Scotch Campaigns," W. S. Douglas, 1899.

"Memoirs," Capt. John Hodgson, edn. of 1806, printed with

Slingsby's.

"Historical Collection of Private Papers of State," John Rushworth, 1721.

"Memoirs of James and William, Dukes of Hamilton," Gilbert
Burnet, 1677.

Calendar of the Clarendon State Papers (Macray), 1869.

"Memoirs," Edmund Ludlow, 1698-9.

"Chronicle of the Kings of England, etc.," Sir Richard Baker,
ed. Phillips, 1783.

"Register and Chronicle, etc.," White Kennet, 1728.

"The Great Lord Fairfax," Sir Clement Markham, 1870.
"Diary," Thomas Burton, ed. Rutt, 1828.

"Collection of State Papers," John Thurloe, ed. Birch, 1742.
"Mercurius Politicus Redivivus," Thomas Rugge, 1659-61
(British Museum Additional MSS.)

"Histoire du Protectorat de Richard Cromwell et du
Rétablissement des Stuarts," M. Guizot, 1856.

"Memoirs of the Life of Colonel Hutchinson," Lucy
Hutchinson, ed. Firth, 1885.

"The Last Years of the Protectorate," Sir Charles Firth, 1909.

"Life of Monck," T. Gumble, 1671.

"Life of Monck," T. Skinner, 1723.

"Mystery and Method of His Majesty's Happy Restoration," J.
Price, in Masere's "Select Tracts."

"The Parish of Kirby Malhamdale," J. W. Morkill, 1934.

"History and Antiquities of the Deanery of Craven," T. D.
Whitaker (ed. Morant), 1878.

GENERAL AUTHORITIES

For the period as a whole the following are the principal authorities that have been referred to, besides the special authorities quoted for the individual memoirs, and besides various modern histories and studies:

The Thomason Tracts.

"History of the Great Rebellion," Earl of Clarendon, ed. Macray, 1888.

Journals of the House of Commons.

Journals of the House of Lords.

Calendar of State Papers, Domestic.

"Collection of all Public Orders, Ordinances, etc.," E. Husband, 1646.

"Collection of Acts and Ordinances," H. Scobell, 1658.

Harleian Miscellany, ed. T. Park, 1808-13.

"Cromwell's Letters and Speeches," Carlyle, ed. Lomas, 1904.

"History of England," 1603-42, S. R. Gardiner, 1886.

"History of the Great Civil War," S. R. Gardiner, 1893.

"History of the Commonwealth and Protectorate," S. R. Gardiner, 1903.

"Constitutional Documents 1625-60," ed. S. R. Gardiner, 1906.

"Oliver Cromwell," John Buchan, 1934.

"Oliver Cromwell," Sir Charles Firth, 1900.

"The Early Stuarts, 1603-1660," Godfrey Davies, 1937.

Old Parliamentary History, 1751-62.

Somers Tracts, ed. Scott, 1809-15.

"Select Tracts Relating to the Civil War," ed. F. Maseres, 1815.

"Englische Geschichte," L. von Ranke, ed. Boase and Kitchen, 1875.

"Memoirs of Prince Rupert and the Cavaliers," E. Warburton,
  1849.
"Worthies of England," Thomas Fuller, 1662.
"Brief Lives of Eminent Men," John Aubrey, ed. A. Clark,
  1898.

ABBREVIATIONS

In addition to those that are otherwise apparent, the following abbreviations are used in the annotations:

C. J.: Journals of the House of Commons.

Cromwell: "Cromwell's Letters and Speeches."

C. S. P. Dom.: Calendar of State Papers, Domestic.

L. J.: Journals of the House of Lords.

L. R. O.: Letters of Roundhead Officers.

O. P. H.: Old Parliamentary History.

V. S. P.: Venetian State Papers.

Annotations prefaced by the letter "E," or indicated by "Th," refer to the Thomason Tracts in the British Museum.

CHRONOLOGY OF MAIN EVENTS, 1642-1660

1642

Jan. 4. Attempt upon the five members.

Jan. 10. Skippon appointed to command London trained bands. Charles leaves London.

Apr. 23. Charles refused admittance to Hull.

July 2. Fleet declares for Parliament.

July 4. Houses appoint Committee of Safety.

July 12. Essex appointed to command the Parliamentary army.

Aug. 22. The King sets up his standard at Nottingham.

Sep. 2. Ordinance for the closing of theatres.

Sep. 23. The first scuffle at Powick Bridge, Rupert scatters Fiennes.

Oct. 23. Battle of Edgehill.

Oct. 29. Charles enters Oxford.

Nov. 12. Rupert's attack on Brentford.

Nov. 13. The King's army checked at Turnham Green.

Dec. 1. Earl of Newcastle enters Yorkshire.

Dec. 6. Tadcaster; Northern Roundheads retire before Newcastle's approach.

1643

Jan. 19. Hopton and Bevil Grenville defeat Parliamentarians under Ruthven at Bradock Down, Cornwall.

Feb. 23. Queen lands at Bridlington from Holland.

Mar. 7. Rupert fails in first attempt on Bristol.

Mar. 19. Fight at Hopton Heath.

Mar. 24. Waller defeats Lord Herbert's Welsh at Highnam and secures Gloucestershire for Parliament.

Apr. 26. Reading falls to Essex.

May 13. Skirmish near Grantham. Cromwell's first important engagement.

May 16. Hopton and Grenville defeat Stamford at Battle of Stratton.

June 18. Chalgrove Field.

June 24. Death of Hampden.

June 30. Battle of Adwalton Moor; Royalists dominate the North.

July 5. Waller defeated at Lansdown by Hopton and Bevil Grenville.

July 13. Waller again defeated at Roundway Down.

July 26. Bristol surrenders to Rupert.

Aug. 10. Charles lays siege to Gloucester.

Sep. 2. Newcastle lays siege to Hull.

Sep. 5. Essex relieves Gloucester.

Sep. 20. First Battle of Newbury; death of Falkland.

Sep. 25. The Commons take the Covenant.

Oct. 11. Thomas Fairfax and Cromwell scatter royalists at Winceby.

Oct. 12. Newcastle abandons siege of Hull.

Oct. 15. The Lords take the Covenant.

Dec. 8. Death of Pym.

Dec. 13. Waller defeats Crawford at Alton, Hants.

Dec. 22. Charles summons royalist members of Parliament to meet at Oxford on January 22nd.

1644

Jan. 19. The Scots cross the Tweed.

Jan. 25. Thomas Fairfax defeats Byron at Nantwich.

Feb. 6. Rupert marches north from Oxford.

Feb. 16. Committee of Both Kingdoms instituted.

Mar. 21. Rupert defeats Meldrum before Newark.

Mar. 29. Waller defeats Forth and Hopton at Cheriton.

Apr. 11. Thomas Fairfax storms Selby.

Apr. 20. Newcastle besieged in York.

June 6. In Council of War at Stow-on-the-Wold, Essex decides to leave Waller and march west.

June 15. Maurice abandons siege of Lyme.

June 29. Waller's reverse at Cropredy Bridge.

July 1. Rupert relieves York.

July 2. Battle of Marston Moor.

July 8. Blake and Pye seize Taunton.

July 12. Charles sets out after Essex.

July 16. Surrender of York; the North lost to Charles.

Aug. 3. Essex at Lostwithiel.

Sep. 1. Montrose's victory at Tippermuir.

Sep. 2. Skippon surrenders at Castle Dore.

Sep. 13. Montrose sacks Aberdeen.

Oct. 19. Newcastle Town surrenders to Scots.

Oct. 21. Essex joins forces with Manchester and Waller at Basing.

Oct. 27. Second Battle of Newbury.

Nov. 24. Milton publishes "Areopagitica."

1645

Jan. 2. Prynne's "Truth Triumphing," for absolute suppression of sectaries.

Jan. 10. Execution of Laud.

Jan. 21. Thomas Fairfax appointed to command the New Model.

Feb. 2. Montrose crushes the Campbells at Inverlochy.

Feb. 15. New Model Ordinance passed.

Mar. 10. Charles adjourns the Oxford Parliament.

Apr. 3. (Second) Self-Denying Ordinance passed.

Apr. 30. The New Model begins its first march.

May 8. Royalist Council of War at Stow-on-the-Wold; Charles to march north.

May 9. Montrose defeats Urry at Auldearn.

May 11. End of second siege of Taunton.

May 22. First siege of Oxford begins.

May 31. Royalists sack Leicester.

June 14. Battle of Naseby.

June 28. Carlisle surrenders to Scots.

July 2. Montrose defeats Baillie at Alford.

July 3. End of third and last siege of Taunton.

July 10. Fairfax defeats Goring at Langport.

July 21. Pontefract surrenders to Lambert.

July 25. Scarborough Castle surrenders.

Aug. 15. Montrose defeats Covenanters at Kilsyth.

Sep. 11. Rupert surrenders Bristol and is disgraced.

Sep. 13. David Leslie overwhelms Montrose at Philiphaugh.

Sep. 24. Poyntz defeats Charles and Langdale at Rowton Heath.

Oct. 15. Digby defeated at Sherburn.

1646

May 5. Charles places himself under protection of the Scots.

June 24. Surrender of Oxford.

1647

Jan. 30. The Scots surrender Charles to the English.

Mar. 21-22. Meetings of officers at Saffron Walden — beginning of quarrel between Army and Parliament.

June 4. Cornet Joyce abducts the King.

June 12. Army marches towards London.

June 26. Withdrawal of the Eleven Members.

Aug. 6. Army enters London.

Oct. 28. The Debates at Putney. "The Agreement of the People" considered.

Nov. 11-14. The King escapes from Hampton Court to Carisbrooke Castle.

Dec. 26. The "Engagement."

1648

Mar. 23. Poyer seizes Pembroke — outbreak of Second Civil War.

June 1. Fairfax defeats Kentish royalists at Maidstone.

June 1. Morris surprises Pontefract Castle.

June 14. Fairfax lays siege to Colchester.

July 8. Scots invade England under Hamilton.

July 11. Pembroke capitulates to Cromwell.

Aug. 17. Battle of Preston.

Aug. 27. Colchester surrenders to Fairfax.

Oct. 29. Murder of Rainsborough.

Nov. 16. The Army's final overture to the King.

Nov. 20. "The Remonstrance of the Army" presented to the Commons.

Dec. 6. Pride's Purge.

Dec. 19-23. The King brought to Windsor.

1649

Jan. 11. Rupert puts to sea from Holland.

Jan. 20. Beginning of the King's trial.

Jan. 29. Rupert at Kinsale.

Jan. 30. Execution of Charles I.

Feb. 6. Abolition of House of Lords.

May 2. Dorislaus, English envoy, assassinated by royalists in Holland.

May 22. Blake blockades Rupert in Kinsale.

Aug. 15. Cromwell lands in Ireland.

Sep. 11. The storm of Drogheda.

Oct. 6. Milton's "Eikonoklastes."

Oct. 11. The storm of Wexford.

1650

Mar. 10. Blake blockades Rupert in the Tagus.

May 21. The Scots execute Montrose.

May 26. Cromwell leaves Ireland.

June 2. Charles II sails for Scotland.

June 26. Cromwell appointed Captain-General on resignation of Fairfax.

June 28. Cromwell marches for Scotland.

July 29. Engagement before Edinburgh.

Sep. 3. Battle of Dunbar.

Sep. 14. Blake destroys Portuguese treasure fleet from Brazil.

Oct. 12. Rupert puts out from Lisbon.

Nov. 2-5. Dispersal of Rupert's fleet.

Dec. 1. Lambert defeats Ker at Hamilton.

Dec. 24. Surrender of Edinburgh Castle.

Dec. 26. Spain recognises the Commonwealth.

1651

Jan. 1. Charles II crowned in Scotland.

Feb. 14. St. John and Strickland go to The Hague.

Apr. 15. Thomas Hobbes's "Leviathan."

May 23. The Scillies surrender to Blake.

July 20. Battle of Inverkeithing.

July 31. Charles begins dash for England.

Sep. 3. Battle of Worcester.

Oct. 27. Limerick surrenders to Ireton.

Dec. 12. Blake completes reduction of Jersey.

1652

May 19. Blake's action with Tromp off Dover. Beginning of Dutch war.

Sep. 4. Blake destroys Vendôme's fleet off Dunkirk.

Sep. 28. Blake defeats de With in Battle of Kentish Knock.

Nov. 30. Tromp defeats Blake off Dungeness.

1653

Feb. 18-20. Tromp defeated at the Battle of Portland.

Apr. 20. Cromwell forcibly dissolves the Rump.

June 2-3. Tromp defeated at the Battle of The Gabbard.

July 4. The Barebone Parliament meets.

July 31. Battle of Scheveningen; Tromp killed.

Dec. 12. The Barebone dissolves itself.

Dec. 16. Cromwell installed as Protector.

1654

Apr. 5. Peace with Holland.

Sep. 3. First Protectorate Parliament meets.

Oct. 8. Blake sails for Mediterranean.

Dec. 20-25. Penn and Venables sail for the West Indies.

1655

Jan. 22. First Protectorate Parliament dissolved.

Apr. 4. Blake's raid on Porto Farina.

May 17. Jamaica surrenders to Venables.

Aug. 9. The Major-Generals appointed.

1656

Mar. 28. Blake's last voyage — to blockade Cadiz.

Sep. 9. Stayner destroys Spanish treasure fleet off Cadiz.

Sep. 17. Second Protectorate Parliament meets.

Oct. 31. Naylor's case in Parliament.

1657

Feb. 23. Pack presents the "Remonstrance"; beginning of dispute over Crown.

Mar. 13. Treaty with France.

Apr. 20. Blake's victory at Santa Cruz.

June 26. Cromwell's second Installation.

Aug. 7. Death of Blake.

1658

June 4. Battle of The Dunes.

June 14. Surrender of Dunkirk.

Sep. 3. Death of Cromwell.

1659

Jan. 27. Third Protectorate Parliament (Richard's) meets.

Apr. 22. Parliament dissolved.

May 7. The Rump recalled by the Army.

Aug. 19. Lambert defeats Booth at Winnington Bridge.

Oct. 13. Lambert forces dissolution of the Rump.

Nov. 3. Lambert marches against Monck.

Dec. 26. The Rump reassembles.

1660

Feb. 3. Monck enters London.

Feb. 21. Return of excluded members of Long Parliament.

Apr. 22. Capture of Lambert.

Apr. 25. "Convention" Parliament meets.
May 26. Charles II lands at Dover.

A NOTE TO THE READER

If you have enjoyed this book enough to leave a review on **Amazon** and **Goodreads**, then we would be truly grateful.

The Estate of C. E. Lucas Phillips

Sapere Books is an exciting new publisher of brilliant fiction and popular history.

To find out more about our latest releases and our monthly bargain books visit our website: **saperebooks.com**